THE NEW TESTAMENT
in the Language of Today

The
NEW
TESTAMENT

IN THE LANGUAGE OF TODAY

By WILLIAM F. BECK

(B. A., B. D., M. S. T., Th. D.)

CONCORDIA PUBLISHING HOUSE
SAINT LOUIS, MISSOURI

Concordia Paperback Edition 1964
Eighth Printing 1967
Corrected and Slightly Revised

Concordia Publishing House, St. Louis, Missouri
Concordia Publishing House Ltd., London, E. C. 1
© 1963 Concordia Publishing House

Library of Congress Catalog Card No. 63-8909

MANUFACTURED IN THE UNITED STATES OF AMERICA

ϹΡΟΝ

This is the word for "cross" in Papyrus 75, our oldest manuscript of Luke. It is found in this special form at Luke 9:23; 14:27; 24:7.

If you spell out this Greek word, it is *stauron*. But the letters *au* are omitted and their omission is indicated by the line above the word. Then the *r,* which in Greek has the form of a *p,* is superimposed on the *t* so that we have a head suggesting a body on a cross.

"Cross" is the only word in the manuscript selected for such a special design. The Savior, crucified for us, is the reason why the New Testament was written —

and why it is here translated.

PREFACE

The preservation of our New Testament is a marvel of God's wisdom. It came through fire and sword.

In the persecution of A. D. 303 Emperor Diocletian ordered a systematic search that swept away the Biblical manuscripts from Asia Minor and Syria. The sacred writings were shoveled into carts and hauled to the market places to be burned. The goal was to wipe out Christianity. Later the Goths, Vandals, Moslems, and Mongols did their worst to destroy the Christian faith.

But Jesus had promised, "Heaven and earth will pass away, but what I say will not pass away" (Luke 21:33). How was it done? Not by keeping one original copy in an ark of the covenant which men could destroy but by sending out thousands of manuscripts all over the earth. We have almost 5,000 Greek manuscripts of the New Testament or parts of it plus many thousands of the Latin, Syriac, and other translations. Every manuscript and fragment is a flame of the Spirit's fire appearing in such an inextinguishable quantity everywhere in the world no organized hostility of men can ever put it out.

To match this vast evidence for the truth, God wants us to have a passion for it, to use all the best evidence from the manuscripts, dictionaries, and grammars as light on the text, and to search with burning hearts for its exact meaning.

In recent years two very important papyri, called P^{66} and P^{75}, both from about A. D. 200, have been published. These papyri now provide us with the finest evidence for the following readings:

Luke 22:19-20: "Jesus took bread, gave thanks, broke it, and gave it to them, saying, 'This is My body, which is given for you. Do this to remember Me.' He did the same with the cup when the supper was over, saying, 'This cup is the new covenant in My blood, poured out for you.' "

Every word in these and other fine manuscripts was carefully checked to make this an accurate New Testament.

And what is the language of the papyri? When Matthew, John, Paul, and the others wrote the New Testament, which language did they use?

Not the Hebrew of the Old Testament.

Not the classical Greek of Aristotle and Plato.

Not even the literary Greek of the first century.

But the *everyday Greek* of the people of Jesus' day.

The many papyri that were found are like a tape recording of what people said offguard, at their "coffee and doughnuts." This is the language of the New Testament.

If Jesus came into our home today, how would He talk? Just as we talk to one another. He would take the words out of our lives and put heaven's meaning into them.

This is the most winning way. We see it on Pentecost. Watch the people from many different countries, talking their own dialects, and see the sparkle in their eyes as they are stirred to say, "How does every one of us hear his own language he was born in . . . ? In our own languages we hear them tell about God's wonderful things" (Acts 2:8, 11). This is Paul's way — "I would rather say five words that can be understood, in order to teach others, than ten thousand words in a language nobody understands." (1 Cor. 14:19)

Today our language carries a world responsibility. It is written, spoken, broadcast, and understood on every continent. 250 million people use English as their primary language, and 600 million people understand it. It is spreading at an accelerating speed.

Radio and television are bringing the world together, and the closer the world lives the more it will talk our language.

God wants to use our language to talk to the world — before the end! He means to reach every man, woman, and child everywhere. We hold in our hands the doorknob to millions of hearts.

And so this New Testament is in the living language of today and tomorrow. It uses "you" and "don't" and "12 o'clock" and "hurry" and "worry." It says, "Jesus looked at him and loved him." (Mark 10:21)

Let's not feel ashamed of our language. The Father's only Son CAME DOWN to be our flesh, was counted among criminals and considered too shameful to be crucified in the holy city. He did this to take away our sins and give us His glory. And just as He became flesh like ours, so He talked to people in a language that was flesh of their flesh. Today He would talk a language that is direct and forceful — like the prophets; that is fresh and simple — like His telling the lame man, "Get up and walk."

In His Word the Spirit of the living God is talking to us, and His book is the book of life. His vital touch is on every page, in every word. And when we let God speak the living language of today, a reader can instantly get into the spirit of the words to the point where the printed book seems to vanish and he hears the truth fresh from the lips of his God. He reads on and on, delighted with the meaning that shines to light up his way.

When we personally ground everything we believe in His Word, we have God so near, we will not go wrong. We will sharply distinguish what God says from what men say and will know what is true and false, what is right and wrong.

We need a spiritual missile. This is it — the sword of the Word in its unveiled power. As we find in the atom a kind of pure power of God, so we get in His unencumbered Word a pure power that cleanses and creates life.

Let His full power work on you and grip you, and you will feel secure, ready to stand your ground alone, like Jesus answering every challenge with the invincible "It is written."

And so you get the kind of faith with which you can stand strong and free, ready to face anything, a faith that makes you want to tell everybody about it, a certainty that will enable you to say yes even when all the world says no.

Starting with God in His Word, we have a striking power. "Publicly and vigorously Apollos proved the Jews were wrong as he showed them from the Bible that Jesus is the promised Savior." (Acts 18:28)

That's the kind of man and woman God wants. That's what the church must have. That's what the world needs desperately.

NOTE. The New Testament quotes the Old Testament about 1.005 times. In this New Testament such words quoted from the Old Testament are in *italics* and numbered; see, for example, Matt. 1:23. The Old Testament sources are listed at the end of each book.

The chapter-and-verse numbering is the same as that of the King James Version. Whenever the beginning of a verse isn't clearly indicated by a punctuation mark, a little vertical line is used; see, for example, Matt. 1:25.

THE FIRST CENTURY

		High Priest / King / *Governor* / EMPEROR	
	NEW TESTAMENT BOOKS		
5 B. C. Jesus Is Born		Herod	37-4 B. C.
1 A. D. Paul Is Born		AUGUSTUS	31 B. C.-14 A. D.
		Archelaus	4 B. C.-6 A. D.
		Annas	6-15 A. D.
26 Jesus Begins Public Work		TIBERIUS	14-37
30 Jesus Dies, Rises, Ascends		**Caiaphas**	18-36
32 Paul Is Converted		*Pilate*	26-36
(Acts 9:1-30)		CALIGULA	37-41
		Herod Agrippa	41-44
47—48 Paul's First Journey		CLAUDIUS	41-54
(Acts 13:2—14:26)		**Ananias**	47-58
48 Antioch	Galatians		
49—51 Paul's Second Journey			
(Acts 15:36—18:11)			
50 Corinth	1 Thessalonians		
	2 Thessalonians		
52—56 Paul's Third Journey		*Felix*	52-58
(Acts 18:23—19:20)			
54—55 Ephesus	Philippians	NERO	54-68
	1 Corinthians		
	Philemon		
	Colossians		
	Ephesians		
55 Macedonia	2 Corinthians		
(Acts 19:21—20:1)			
56 Corinth	Romans		
50—60	Matthew		
59—61 Paul's First Imprison-		*Festus*	58-60
ment in Rome			
(Acts 28:15-31)			
60	Mark		
57—61	Luke		
61	Acts		
61	James		
61—62	1 Peter		
	2 Peter		
62 Macedonia	1 Timothy		
63 On the Way to Nicopolis	Titus		
64 Rome (Paul's Death)	2 Timothy		
60—70	Jude	GALBA	68-69
64—70	Hebrews	OTHO	69
66—70 Jewish War		VITELLIUS	69
70 Jerusalem Destroyed		VESPASIAN	69-79
		TITUS	79-81
90—100	1 John	DOMITIAN	81-96
	2 John		
	3 John		
	John	NERVA	96-98
	Revelation	TRAJAN	98-117

THE GOOD NEWS

as it was told by

MATTHEW

THIS IS A RECORD showing how Jesus Christ was a descendant **1**
of David and of Abraham.

Abraham was the father of Isaac, **2**
Isaac was the father of Jacob,
and Jacob was the father of Judah and his brothers.
Judah was the father of Perez and Zerah, **3**
and Tamar was their mother.
Perez was the father of Hezron,
Hezron was the father of Ram,
Ram was the father of Aminadab, **4**
Aminadab was the father of Nahshon,
Nahshon was the father of Salmon,
and Salmon was the father of Boaz, and Rahab was his mother. **5**
Boaz was the father of Obed, and Ruth was his mother.
Obed was the father of Jesse,
and Jesse was the father of King David. **6**
David was the father of Solomon,
and Uriah's wife was his mother.
Solomon was the father of Rehoboam, **7**
Rehoboam was the father of Abijah,
Abijah was the father of Asa,
Asa was the father of Jehoshaphat, **8**
Jehoshaphat was the father of Joram,
Joram was the father of Uzziah,
Uzziah was the father of Jotham, **9**
Jotham was the father of Ahaz,
Ahaz was the father of Hezekiah,
Hezekiah was the father of Manasseh, **10**
Manasseh was the father of Amon,
Amon was the father of Josiah,

and Josiah was the father of Jechoniah and his brothers
12 when the people were taken away to Babylon. After they had
been taken away to Babylon,

> Jechoniah was the father of Shealtiel,
>
> Shealtiel was the father of Zerubbabel,

13 Zerubbabel was the father of Abiud,

> Abiud was the father of Eliakim,
>
> Eliakim was the father of Azor,

14 Azor was the father of Zadok,

> Zadok was the father of Achim,
>
> Achim was the father of Eliud,

15 Eliud was the father of Eleazar,

> Eleazar was the father of Matthan,
>
> Matthan was the father of Jacob,

16 and Jacob was the father of Joseph, the husband of Mary;
she was the mother of Jesus, who is called Christ.

17 So there are, in all, fourteen generations from Abraham to
David, fourteen from David to the Babylonian Captivity, and
fourteen from the Babylonian Captivity to Christ.

An Angel Comes to Joseph

18 This is how Jesus Christ was born.

His mother Mary had promised Joseph to be his wife. But
before they lived together, it was found that she was going to
19 have a child — by the Holy Spirit. Joseph, her husband, was
a good man and didn't want to disgrace her. So he decided to
divorce her secretly.

20 After he thought about it, he in a dream saw the Lord's angel,
who said, "Joseph, son of David, don't be afraid to take your
wife Mary home with you; her Child is from the Holy Spirit.
21 She will have a Son, and you will call Him Jesus, because He
22 will save His people from their sins. All this happened so that
what the Lord said through the prophet would come true:
23 *The virgin will conceive and have a Son, and He will be called
Immanuel,"* [1] which means God-with-us.

24 When Joseph awoke, he did what the Lord's angel had or-
25 dered him to do. He took his wife home with him [l] but didn't
live with her as a husband till she had a Son. And he called
Him Jesus.

2   *Nazareth, summer, 5 B. C.*

The Wise Men

Jesus was born in Bethlehem in Judea when Herod was king. **2**
Then Wise Men came from the east to Jerusalem. "Where is **2**
the Child who was born King of the Jews?" they asked. "We
saw His star rise and have come to worship Him."

When King Herod heard about this, he became alarmed and **3**
all Jerusalem with him. He called together all of the people's **4**
ruling priests and men trained in the Bible and tried to find out
from them where the promised Savior was to be born.

"In Bethlehem, in Judea," they told him, "because the prophet **5**
has written: *And you, Bethlehem,* land of Judah, *are* not at all **6**
*the least among the leading towns of Judah, since from you will
come a leader who will be the Shepherd of My people Israel."* [2]

Then Herod secretly called the Wise Men and found out **7**
from them the exact time the star appeared. Then he sent them **8**
to Bethlehem. "Go and search carefully for the little Child," he
said. "And when you find Him, report to me, so that I too may
go and bow down before Him."

After hearing the king, they started out. And there was the **9**
star they had seen when it rose! It led them on till it came to
a stop over the place where the Child was. They were extremely **10**
happy to see the star. They went into the house and saw the **11**
little Child with His mother Mary. Kneeling, they worshiped
Him. Then they opened their treasure chests and offered Him
gifts: gold, incense,[3] *and myrrh.*

But God warned them in a dream not to go back to Herod. **12**
So they went home to their country by another road.

To Egypt!

After the Wise Men left, Joseph in a dream saw the Lord's **13**
angel, who said, "Get up, take the little Child and His mother,
and flee to Egypt. Stay there till I tell you. Herod is going
to search for the Child to kill Him."

Joseph got up at night, took the little Child and His mother, **14**
and went to Egypt. He stayed there till Herod died. In this way **15**
what the Lord said through the prophet was to come true: *I called
My Son from Egypt.*[4]

When Herod saw that the Wise Men had tricked him, he got **16**
very angry and sent men to kill all the boys in Bethlehem and

2:17 in all the country around it, up to two years old, according to the exact time he had found out from the Wise Men. Then what the prophet Jeremiah said came true:

18
> *A cry is heard in Rama!*
> *Weeping and bitter wailing:*
> *Rachel crying over her children,*
> *And refusing to be comforted*
> *Because they are gone.*[5]

19
20 But when Herod died, the Lord's angel appeared to Joseph in Egypt in a dream [1] and told him, "Get up, take the little Child and His mother, and go to the land of Israel. Those who tried to kill the little Child are dead."

21
22 Joseph got up, took the little Child and His mother, and came to the land of Israel. But when he heard, "Archelaus has succeeded his father Herod as king of Judea," he was afraid to go back there. And being warned in a dream, he went to Galilee.
23 He came and made his home in a town by the name of Nazareth. And so what the prophets said came true: Jesus was to be called a man from Nazareth.*

John Prepares the Way

3
2 The time came when John the Baptizer appeared in the wilderness of Judea and preached: "Repent — the kingdom of heaven
3 is near." He was the one of whom the prophet Isaiah said:

> *Someone will be calling in the wilderness,*
> *"Prepare the way for the Lord,*
> *Make the paths straight for Him."* [6]

4 John wore clothes of camel's hair and a leather belt around his waist. And he lived on grasshoppers and wild honey.

5
6 Then Jerusalem, all Judea, and the whole Jordan valley came out to him. As they confessed their sins, he baptized them in the Jordan River.

7
8 He also saw many Pharisees and Sadducees coming for baptism. "Brood of snakes, who warned you to run away from the punishment waiting for you?" he asked them. "Do the works
9 that show you have repented. Don't think you can tell yourselves, 'Abraham is our father.' I tell you, God can raise children for

---

* According to Is. 11:1 the Savior would be a Nezer, a sprout, growing from the roots of the tree of David.

Abraham from these stones. The ax is now ready to strike at the roots of the trees, and any tree that doesn't produce good fruit will be cut down and thrown into the fire. I baptize you [11] with water for a change of heart. But the One who is coming after me is mightier than I. I'm not good enough to carry away His shoes. He will baptize you with the Holy Spirit and fire. | He [12] has the winnowing shovel in His hand and will clean up His threshing floor. His wheat He'll gather into His barn, but the chaff He'll burn in a fire that can't be put out."

John Baptizes Jesus

Then Jesus came from Galilee to John at the Jordan to be [13] baptized by him. | John tried to stop Him. "I need to be bap- [14] tized by You," he said, "and You come to me?"

"Let Me have My way now," Jesus answered him. "That is [15] how we should accomplish every righteous purpose."

Then John gave in to Him. | As soon as Jesus was baptized, [16] He stepped out of the water, and now heaven was opened, and He saw God's Spirit coming down on Him as a dove. And a voice [17] from heaven said, "This is *My Son,* whom I love and *delight in.*" [7]

The Devil Tempts Jesus

Then the Spirit led Jesus into the wilderness to be tempted [4] by the devil. He didn't eat anything for forty days and then got [2] hungry.

The tempter came to Him. "If You're God's Son," he said [3] to Him, "tell these stones to become loaves of bread."

"It is written," Jesus answered, *"A man doesn't live on bread [4] alone but on every word that God speaks."* [8]

Then the devil took Him into the Holy City and had Him [5] stand on the edge of the temple. "If You're God's Son," he told [6] Him, "jump down. It is written: *He will order His angels to help you. They will carry you in their hands* and *never let you stub your foot against a stone."* [9]

"It is also written," Jesus answered him, *"Don't test the Lord [7] your God."* [10]

Then the devil took Him to a very high mountain and showed [8] Him all the kingdoms in the world and their glory. "All this [9] I'll give You," the devil told Him, "if You'll bow down and worship me."

Then Jesus answered him, "Go away, devil! It is written: Worship *the Lord your God, and serve Him* [11] only."

11   Then the devil left Him, and angels came and served Him.

At Home in Capernaum

12   When Jesus heard John had been put in prison, He went back
13   to Galilee. Leaving Nazareth, He went and made His home in
14   Capernaum by the lake, in the area of Zebulun and Naphtali. And
so what the prophet Isaiah said was to come true:

15   *Land of Zebulun and land of Naphtali,*
The way to the sea, across the Jordan,
Galilee of the Gentiles!
16   *The people sitting in the dark will see a great light.*
For those sitting in the land of the shadow of death a light
will rise.[12]

17   Then Jesus began to preach: "Repent — the kingdom of heaven is here!"

"Come with Me"

18   As He was walking along the shore of the Lake of Galilee, He saw two brothers, Simon, also called Peter, and his brother Andrew (who were fishermen), casting a net into the lake.
19   "Come, follow Me," Jesus told them, "and I will make you fishers
20   of men." Immediately they left their nets and followed Him.

21   He went on and saw two other brothers, James, Zebedee's son, and his brother John. They were in their boat with their
22   father Zebedee, mending their nets. He called them,[1] and immediately they left the boat and their father and followed Him.

Preaching in Galilee

23   Then He went around everywhere in Galilee, teaching in their synagogs, preaching the good news of the Kingdom, and healing every kind of disease and sickness among the people.
24   The news about Him spread all over Syria. And the people brought to Him all who were suffering from various diseases and were in great pain, those who were plagued by devils, the epilep-
25   tics, and the paralyzed, and He made them well. Large crowds followed Him from Galilee, the Ten-Towns, Jerusalem, Judea, and the other side of the Jordan.

Happy People

When Jesus saw the crowds, He went up the hill. And when 5
He sat down, His disciples came to Him. Then He began to ²
teach them:

"Happy are those who are *poor in spirit* ¹³ — ³
    they have the kingdom of heaven.

Happy are *those who mourn* — ⁴
    they will *be comforted.*¹⁴

Happy are *those who are gentle* — ⁵
    they *will own the land.*¹⁵

Happy are those who hunger and thirst to be righteous — ⁶
    they will be satisfied.

Happy are *those who are merciful* — ⁷
    *they will find mercy.*¹⁶

Happy are *those whose hearts are pure* ¹⁷ — ⁸
    they will see God.

Happy are those who make peace — ⁹
    they will be called God's sons.

Happy are those who are persecuted for doing right — ¹⁰
    they have the kingdom of heaven.

Happy are you when people insult you, persecute you, lie and ¹¹
    tell only evil about you on account of Me. Be happy and ¹²
    delighted because you have a great reward in heaven.
    That's how they persecuted the prophets who were before
    you."

A Salt and a Light

"You are the salt of the world. If salt loses its taste, how will ¹³
it be made salty again? It's no longer good for anything but to
be thrown out and trampled on by people.

"You are the light of the world. A town can't be hid when ¹⁴
it's built on a hill. And you don't light a lamp and put it under ¹⁵
the peck measure but on the lampstand, where it gives light to
everybody in the house. So let your light shine before people ¹⁶
that they may see the good you do and praise your Father in
heaven."

Jesus Keeps the Law

"Don't think that I came to set aside the Law or the prophets. ¹⁷
I didn't come to set them aside but to fulfill them. I tell you the ¹⁸
truth, till heaven and earth pass away, not an *i* or the dot of an *i* of

5:19 the Law will pass away till everything is done. Anyone, then, who sets aside one of the least of these commandments and teaches others to do the same will be called the least in the kingdom of heaven. But anyone who does and teaches what they

20 say will be called great in the kingdom of heaven. I tell you, unless your righteousness is much better than that of the Bible scholars and Pharisees, you will never get into the kingdom of heaven."

Don't Kill

21 "You have heard that long ago the people were told: *'Don't kill.*[18] Whoever kills must answer for it in court.'

22 "But I tell you, anyone who is angry with his brother must answer for it in court. Anyone who calls his brother an 'empty-head' must go before the highest court. Anyone who calls him a 'fool' must go into hellfire.

23 "So if you're bringing your gift to the altar and remember
24 there that your brother has something against you, leave your gift there before the altar and go. First make up with your brother, and then come and offer your gift.

25 "If someone wants to sue you, be quick to make up with him while you are still on the way with him, or your accuser will hand you over to the judge, and the judge to the officer, and you will
26 be put in prison. I tell you the truth, you will never get out until you pay the last cent."

Don't Lust

27 "You have heard it was said: *'Don't commit adultery.'* [19]

28 "But I tell you, anyone who looks at a woman to lust after her has already committed adultery with her in his heart.

29 "If your right eye causes you to sin, tear it out and throw it away. It is better for you to lose a part of your body than to
30 have all of it thrown into hell. And if your right hand causes you to sin, cut it off and throw it away. It is better for you to lose a part of your body than to have all of it go to hell.

31 "It was said: 'Anyone who divorces his wife *must give her*
32 *a divorce paper.'* [20] But I tell you, anyone who divorces his wife, except for her being sexually unfaithful, makes her a partner in adultery. And also the man who marries the divorced woman is living in adultery."

8   *Near Capernaum, early summer, 28*

Don't Swear

"Again, you have heard that long ago the people were told: *'Don't swear to a lie,'* [21] and: *'Give the Lord what you swear to give Him.'* [22]

"But I tell you, don't swear at all, not by *heaven* — it *is God's throne;* | or by *the earth* — it *is His footstool;* [23] or by Jerusalem — *it is the city of the great King.*[24] And don't swear by your head, because you can't make one hair white or black. Just say, 'Yes, yes; no, no.' Anything more comes from the evil one." [34] [35] [36] [37]

Love Your Enemies

. "You have heard it was said, *'An eye for an eye, and a tooth for a tooth.'* [25] [38]

"But I tell you, don't oppose an evil man. If anyone slaps you on your right cheek, turn the other cheek to him. If anyone wants to sue you for your shirt, let him have your coat too. If anyone makes you go one mile, go two miles with him. If anyone asks you for anything, give it to him, and when anyone wants to borrow from you, don't turn away. [39] [40] [41] [42]

"You have heard it was said, *'Love your neighbor,*[26] and hate your enemy.' [43]

"But I tell you, Love your enemies, and pray for those who persecute you. In this way you will show you are sons of your Father in heaven. He makes His sun rise on people whether they are bad or good and lets rain fall on them whether they do right or wrong. [44] [45]

"If you love those who love you, what's your reward? Don't tax collectors do that too? If you treat only your brothers kindly, are you doing anything extraordinary? Don't the people of the world do that too? *Be perfect* [27] as your Father in heaven is perfect." [46] [47] [48]

Don't Blow Your Horn

"Be careful not to do your good works before people to be seen by them. If you do, your Father in heaven will not reward you. So when you give to the poor, don't blow your horn, as hypocrites do in the synagogs and on the streets to be praised by people. I tell you, that's really all the reward they'll get. | When you give to the poor, don't let your left hand know what your right hand is doing, | that your giving may be secret. Then your Father, who sees what is secret, will reward you." [6] [2] [3] [4]

How to Pray

6:5 "When you pray, don't be like hypocrites, who like to stand praying in synagogs and on street corners in order to be seen
6 by people. I tell you, that's really all the reward they'll get. But when you pray, *go into your own room, shut your door, and pray* 28 to your Father, who is with you when you're alone, and your Father, who sees what is secret, will reward you.

7 "When you pray, don't say meaningless words, like pagans,
8 who think they'll be heard if they talk a lot. Don't be like them. Your Father knows what you need before you ask Him.

9 "This is how you should pray:

Our Father in heaven —
May Your name be kept holy,
10 Your kingdom come,
And Your will be done on earth as it is done in heaven.
11 Give us today our daily bread.
12 And forgive us our sins as we have forgiven those who sin against us.
13 And don't bring us into temptation,
But deliver us from evil.*

14 "If you forgive the sins of others, your Father in heaven will
15 forgive you. But if you don't forgive the sins of others, your Father will not forgive your sins."

Fasting

16 "When you fast, don't look sad like hypocrites. They disfigure their faces to show people they are fasting. I tell you, that's
17 really all the reward they'll get. But when you fast, anoint your
18 head, and wash your face so that nobody will see you fasting except your Father, who is with you when you're alone. And your Father, who sees what is secret, will reward you."

Treasures

19 "Don't store up for yourselves treasures on earth,
Where moth and rust destroy them
And thieves break in and steal.
20 "But store up for yourselves treasures in heaven,

* The doxology is found in later manuscripts: "You are the King who rules with power and glory forever. Amen."

Where no moth or rust destroys them
And no thieves break in and steal.

Where your treasure is, there your heart will be. 6:21

"The eye is the lamp of the body. If your eye is healthy, you 22
have light for your whole body. But if your eye is bad, your 23
whole body will be dark. How dark it is when the light in you
is dark!

"Nobody can serve two masters. Either he will hate the one 24
and love the other or be loyal to the one and despise the other.
You can't serve God and money."

Don't Worry!

"So I tell you, don't worry about what you'll eat or drink to 25
keep alive or what you'll wear on your bodies. Isn't life more
than food, and the body more than clothes?

"Look at the birds in the air. They don't sow or cut grain 26
or gather anything into barns; but your Father in heaven feeds
them. Aren't you worth more than they?

"Can any of you by worrying add anything to your life? 27

"And why worry about clothes? See how the flowers grow in 28
the field, and learn from them. They don't work and they don't
spin. Yet, I tell you, even Solomon in all his glory didn't dress 29
like one of these. If that's how God dresses the grass in the field, 30
which lives today and tomorrow is thrown into a stove, how much
more certainly will He put clothes on you — who trust Him so
little?

"Don't worry, then, and say, 'What are we going to eat?' or, 31
'What are we going to drink?' or, 'What are we going to
wear?' ¹ The people of the world run after all these things. Your 32
Father in heaven knows you need them all. First be eager to 33
have God as your King and His righteousness, and you'll get all
these other things too.

"So, don't worry about tomorrow. Tomorrow will take care 34
of itself. Each day has enough trouble of its own."

Criticize Yourself

"Don't judge, so that you will not be judged. The way you 7 1-2
judge others, you'll be judged, and the measure you measure with
will be used for you.

"Why do you look at the speck in your brother's eye and 3

7:4 don't notice the log in your own eye? Or how can you say to your brother, 'Let me take the speck out of your eye,' when you
5 have that log in your own eye? You hypocrite, first throw the log out of your own eye. Then you'll see clearly enough to take the speck out of your brother's eye."

Pearls to Pigs

6 "Don't give anything holy to the dogs or throw your pearls to the pigs, or they'll trample them under their feet and then turn and tear you to pieces."

Pray

7 "Ask, and it will be given to you. Search, and you will find.
8 Knock, and the door will be opened for you. Anyone who asks receives; anyone who searches finds; and anyone who knocks, the door will be opened for him.
9 "If your son asks you for bread, will any of you give him
10-11 a stone? Or if he asks for a fish, will you give him a snake? Now if you, bad as you are, know enough to give your children good gifts, how much more will your Father in heaven give good things to those who ask Him?"

The Golden Rule

12 "Do for others everything you want them to do for you. That is the Law and the prophets."

The Narrow Gate

13 "Go through the narrow gate. The gate is wide, and the way is broad that leads to destruction, and many are going that
14 way. But the gate is small, and the way is narrow, that leads to life, and only a few are finding it."

False Prophets

15 "Beware of false prophets. They come to you dressed like sheep, but in their hearts they're greedy wolves.
16 "You will know them by what they do. Can we pick grapes
17 from thornbushes or figs from thistles? No, every good tree bears
18 good fruit, and a bad tree bad fruit. A good tree cannot bear
19 bad fruit, or a bad tree good fruit. Any tree that doesn't bear
20 good fruit is cut down and thrown into the fire. So you will know them by what they do.

"Not everyone who calls Me Lord, Lord, will get into the
kingdom of heaven, only he who does what My Father in heaven
wants. Many will say to Me on that Day, 'Lord, Lord, didn't we [22]
prophesy in Your name,[29] drive out devils in Your name, and do
many miracles in Your name?' Then I will tell them frankly, [23]
'I never knew you. *Get away from Me, you who are so busy
doing wrong.'* "[30]

Build on a Rock

"Anyone who hears and does what I say is like a man who [24]
had the sense to build his house on a rock. The rain poured [25]
down, the torrents came, the winds blew, and they dashed against
that house. But it didn't go down, because its foundation was
on the rock.

"Everyone who hears what I say but doesn't do it is like [26]
a man who was so foolish he built his house on sand. The rains [27]
poured down, the torrents came, the winds blew, and they dashed
against that house. And it went down with a big crash."

When Jesus finished speaking, the crowds were amazed at [28]
His teaching. He taught them with authority and not like their [29]
Bible scholars.

He went down the hill, and large crowds followed Him. [8]

Jesus Heals a Leper

There was a leper, who went to Him and bowed down to the [2]
ground before Him. "Lord, if You want to," he said, "You can
make me clean."

Jesus stretched out His hand and touched him. "I want to," [3]
He said. "Be clean!" Immediately the leprosy left him, and he
was clean.

"Be careful not to tell anyone," Jesus said to him, "but go, [4]
let the priest examine [31] you, and offer the sacrifice Moses ordered,
to show them you're well."

A Believing Captain

He went to Capernaum. There a captain came to Him and [5]
begged Him: | "Lord, my slave is lying paralyzed at home. He's [6]
suffering terribly."

"I will go and make him well," Jesus said.

8   "Lord," the captain answered, "I'm not good enough for you to come under my roof. But just say a word, and my slave will
9 be made well. I'm only a man who has to obey others, but I have soldiers under me. I tell one of them, Go, and he goes. And another, Come, and he comes. And my slave, Do this, and he does it."

10   Surprised to hear this, Jesus said to the people who were following Him, "I tell you the truth, not even in Israel have
11 I found such faith. I also tell you, many will come *from the east and the west* [32] and will eat with Abraham, Isaac, and Jacob in
12 the kingdom of heaven, but those who were born to be the heirs of the kingdom will be thrown out into the dark. There they will cry and grind their teeth."

13   "Go," Jesus told the captain. "Let it be as you believed." And the slave was made well in that hour.

Peter's Mother-in-Law

14   Jesus went into Peter's home, and there He saw his mother-
15 in-law down in bed with a fever. He touched her hand, and the fever left her. She got up and waited on Him.

16   In the evening the people brought Him many who were plagued by devils. He drove out the spirits by talking to them,
17 and all who were sick He made well. In this way what the prophet Isaiah said was to come true, *He took away our sicknesses and carried our diseases.*[33]

18   When Jesus saw a crowd around Him, He gave orders to cross to the other side.

"I Will Follow You, but —"

19   A man trained in the Bible came to Him and said, "Teacher, I will follow You anywhere You go."

20   "Foxes have holes," Jesus told him, "and birds in the air have nests, but the Son of Man doesn't have a place to lay His head."

21   "Lord," another disciple said to Him, "first let me go and bury my father."

22   But Jesus told him, "Follow Me and let the dead bury their dead."

Wind and Water Obey Him

Jesus stepped into a boat, and His disciples went with 8:23
Him. Suddenly a big storm stirred the lake so that the waves 24
were covering the boat. But He was sleeping.

So they went and woke Him up. "Lord, save us!" they said. 25
"We're drowning!"

"Why are you afraid?" He asked them. "You trust Me so 26
little!" Then He got up and ordered the winds and the lake to
be quiet, and they became very calm.

The men were amazed and said, "What kind of man is He? 27
Even the winds and the lake obey Him!"

The Gadarenes

He went to the country of the Gadarenes on the other side 28
of the lake. There two men with devils in them came out of the
burial places and met Him. They were so savage nobody could
go along that road.

"Let us alone, Son of God!" they shouted. "Did You come 29
here to torture us before it is time?"

Far away a herd of many hogs was feeding. "If You mean to 30-31
drive us out," the devils were begging Jesus, "send us into that
herd of hogs."

"Go," He told them. They came out and went into the hogs. 32
Then the whole herd stampeded down the cliff into the lake and
died in the water.

Those who had taken care of the hogs ran away and went 33
into the town, where they told everything, especially about the
men plagued by devils. Then the whole town came out to meet 34
Jesus. When they saw Him, they begged Him to leave their
country.

He got into a boat and crossed over. 9

Jesus Forgives Sins

Jesus came to His own town. There people brought Him 1-2
a paralyzed man, lying on a bed.

When Jesus saw their faith, He said to the paralytic, "Courage,
son! Your sins are forgiven."

Then some of the Bible scholars said to themselves, "He's 3
blaspheming."

Jesus knew what they were thinking. "Why do you think 4
evil in your hearts?" He asked them. "Is it easier to say, 'Your 5

9:6 sins are forgiven,' or to say, 'Get up and walk'? I want you to know the Son of Man has power on earth to forgive sins." Then He said to the paralyzed man, "Get up, take your bed, and go home."

7-8 He got up and went home. When the crowd saw this, they were frightened, and they praised God for giving such power to men.

Matthew

9 When Jesus left that place, He saw a man by the name of Matthew sitting in the tax office. "Come with Me," He told him. He got up and went with Him.

10 As Jesus was lying down to eat at his home, many tax collec-
11 tors and sinners came and ate with Jesus and His disciples. When the Pharisees saw this, they asked His disciples, "Why does your Teacher eat with tax collectors and sinners?"

12 Jesus heard them and said, "Those who are healthy don't need
13 a doctor, but the sick. Go and learn what this means: *I like mercy and not* mere *sacrifice.*[34] I didn't come to call righteous people but sinners."

The Bridegroom

14 Then John's disciples came to Jesus. "We and the Pharisees fast," they said. "Why don't Your disciples fast?"

15 Jesus asked them, "Can the bridegroom's friends mourn while the bridegroom is with them? The time will come when the bridegroom will be taken away from them; then they'll fast.

16 "Nobody sews a piece of new cloth on an old garment. The patch will tear away some of the garment, and the hole will get
17 worse. Nobody pours new wine into old wineskins. If you do, the skins burst, the wine runs out, and the skins are ruined. No, you pour new wine into fresh skins; then both are preserved."

The Daughter of Jairus

18 While He was talking to the people, a leader came to Him and bowed down to the ground before Him. "My daughter just died," he said, "but come, lay Your hand on her, and she will live."

19 Jesus and His disciples got up and followed him.

20 Now there was a woman who had a flow of blood for twelve years. She came to Him from behind and touched the tassel of

His garment. "If I only touch His garment," she said to herself, "I'll get well."

Jesus turned and saw her. "Cheer up, daughter," He said, "your faith made you well." After that the woman was well. ²²

When Jesus came to the leader's home, He saw the flute players and the noisy crowd.¹ "Go away," He said. "The little girl isn't dead; she's sleeping." But they laughed at Him. ²³ ²⁴

When the crowd had been put outside, He went in and took her hand, and the little girl got up. ²⁵

The news about this spread all over that part of the country. ²⁶

Two Blind Men

When Jesus left that place, two blind men followed Him and called, "Have pity on us, Son of David." ²⁷

He went into a house, and there the blind men came to Him. "Do you believe I can do this?" Jesus asked them. ²⁸

"Yes, Lord," they told Him.

Then He touched their eyes and said, "As you believed, so it must be done to you!" Then they could see again. ²⁹ ³⁰

"See that nobody finds out about this!" He sternly ordered them. But they went out and spread the news about Him all over that part of the country. ³¹

A Dumb Man

As they were going out, a dumb man with a devil in him was brought to Him. But as soon as the devil was put out, the dumb man spoke. ³² ³³

The crowds were amazed and said, "We've never seen anything like this in Israel."

But the Pharisees declared, "The ruler of the devils helps Him drive out the devils." ³⁴

Pray for Workers

Then Jesus traveled through all the towns and villages, teaching in their synagogs, preaching the good news of the Kingdom, and healing every disease and sickness. ³⁵

As He saw the crowds, He felt sorry for them, because they were troubled and helpless *like sheep without a shepherd*.³⁵ Then He said to His disciples, "There's much grain to be harvested, but there are only a few workers. Ask the Owner of the crop to send out workers to bring in His grain." ³⁶ ³⁷ ³⁸

Matthew

Jesus Sends Out the Twelve

10 Jesus called His twelve disciples and gave them authority to drive out unclean spirits and heal every disease and sickness.

2 These are the names of the twelve apostles: first, Simon, called Peter, and his brother Andrew; James, Zebedee's son, and his 3 brother John; Philip and Bartholomew, Thomas and Matthew, the tax collector; James, the son of Alphaeus, and Thaddaeus; 4 Simon the Zealot, and Judas, the man from Kerioth, who betrayed Him.

5 Jesus sent these twelve out with the following instructions: "Don't go among the Gentiles or into any town of the Samaritans. 6-7 But go to the lost sheep of Israel. As you go, preach, 'The king- 8 dom of heaven is here.' Heal the sick, raise the dead, cleanse lepers, drive out devils. Give these things as you received them — without pay.

9 "Don't take any gold, silver, or copper money along in your 10 pockets, and no bag for the way. Don't take two tunics, or shoes, or a stick — a worker earns his keep.

11 "When you go into any town or village, look for a person 12 there who is deserving, and stay with him till you leave. When 13 you go into a home, greet it. If the home is deserving, let your peace come on it. But if it's unworthy, let your peace come back 14 to you. If anyone doesn't welcome you or listen to what you say, leave that house or town, and shake the dust off your feet. 15 I tell you the truth, on Judgment Day it will be easier for the land of Sodom and Gomorrah than for that town.

16 "You see, I'm sending you like sheep among wolves. So be 17 shrewd as snakes and innocent as doves. Be on your guard against men, because they'll hand you over to their courts and whip 18 you in their places of worship. On My account you'll be dragged before governors and kings to testify to them and to the nations. 19 But when they hand you over to the authorities, don't worry how you'll speak or what you'll say. When the time comes, you'll be 20 told what to say. It isn't you speaking but your Father's Spirit speaking through you.

21 "A brother will betray his brother to death, and a father his child. Children will *turn against* [36] their parents and kill them. 22 Everybody will hate you because of My name. But be faithful to 23 the end, and you will be saved. When they hunt you in one town, flee to another. Let Me assure you, before you have gone through all the towns of Israel, the Son of Man will come.

"A pupil isn't above his teacher, or a slave above his master. A pupil should be satisfied to share his teacher's lot and a slave to share his master's. If the master of the house was called Beelzebul, how much more certainly the members of his household! So, don't be afraid of them.

"All that's covered will be uncovered, and all that's hidden will be known. What I say to you in the dark, tell in the daylight; and what you hear whispered in your ear, preach from the housetops. Don't be afraid of those who kill the body and can't kill the soul, but fear Him who can destroy soul and body in hell. Aren't two sparrows sold for a cent? And not one of them will fall to the ground without your Father's permission. As for you, even the hairs on your head are all counted. So don't be afraid. You're worth more than many sparrows. ˡ Whoever will confess Me before other people, him will I confess before My Father in heaven. Whoever will deny Me before others, him will I deny before My Father in heaven.

"Don't think that I came to bring peace to the earth. I didn't come to bring peace but a sword. I came to set *a man against his* *father, a daughter against her mother, a daughter-in-law against her mother-in-law. A man's enemies will be those in his own* *home.* ³⁶ If you love father or mother more than Me, you're not worthy of Me; and if you love son or daughter more than Me, you're not worthy of Me. If you don't take your cross and follow Me, you're not worthy of Me. If you find your life, you'll lose it, but if you lose your life for Me, you'll find it.

"Anyone who welcomes you welcomes Me; and anyone who welcomes Me welcomes Him who sent Me. Anyone who wel- comes a prophet because he is a prophet will get a prophet's reward. Anyone who welcomes a righteous man because he is righteous will get a righteous man's reward. Anyone who will give one of these little ones just a cup of cold water because he is My disciple, I tell you, will certainly not lose his reward."

After Jesus finished giving His twelve disciples these instruc- tions, He went on from there to teach and preach in their towns.

About John

When John, who was in prison, heard about the works of Christ, he sent his disciples ˡ to ask Him, "Are You the One who is coming, or should we look for someone else?"

"Go," Jesus answered them, "tell John what you hear and

11:5 see: *The blind see,* the lame walk, lepers are made clean, the *deaf*
6 *hear,* the dead are raised, and *the poor hear the good news,*[37] and
happy is anyone who doesn't turn against Me."

7   When they were leaving, Jesus talked to the crowds
about John:

"What did you go out into the wilderness to see — a reed
8 shaken by the wind? What, then, did you go out to see — a man
dressed in soft robes? Those who wear soft robes you'll find in
the palaces of kings.

9   "What, then, did you go out for — to see a prophet? Let
10 Me assure you, he's even more than a prophet. This is the one of
whom it is written, *'I will send My messenger ahead of You to*
11 *prepare* Your *way before*[38] You.' I tell you the truth, there never
has appeared a woman's son greater than John the Baptizer. Yet
12 the least in the kingdom of heaven is greater than John. From the
time of John the Baptizer till now the kingdom of heaven has
been suffering violence, and violent men are trying to take it
13 by force. All the prophets and the Law prophesied up to the time
14 of John, but he (are you willing to accept it?) is the Elijah who
15 has to come. If you can hear, listen!

16   "How should I picture the people of this age? They're like
little children sitting in the marketplaces and calling to others:
17 'We played a tune on the flute for you, but you didn't dance.
18 We sang a funeral song, but you didn't beat your breasts.' | John
the Baptizer has come; he doesn't eat or drink, and people say,
19 'There's a devil in him!' The Son of Man has come; He eats and
drinks, and people say, 'Look at the glutton and drunkard, the
friend of tax collectors and sinners!' And yet what a wise person
does proves he's right."

Woe!

20   Then He began to denounce the cities where He had done
21 most of His miracles, because they had not repented: "Woe to
you, Chorazin! Woe to you, Bethsaida! If the miracles done in
you had been done in Tyre and Sidon, they would long ago have
22 repented in sackcloth and ashes. I tell you, on Judgment Day
23 it will be easier for Tyre and Sidon than for you. And you,
Capernaum, will you be *lifted up to heaven? You will go down*
to hell![39] If the miracles that have been done in you had been
24 done in Sodom, it would still be there today. I tell you, on
Judgment Day it will be easier for the country of Sodom than
for you."

"Come to Me!"

At that time Jesus said, "I praise You, Father, Lord of heaven 11:25
and earth, for hiding these things from wise and intelligent people
and uncovering them for little children. Yes, Father, I praise You 26
for wanting it to be that way.

"My Father put everything in My hands. Only the Father 27
knows the Son. And only the Son — and anyone to whom the
Son wants to reveal Him — knows the Father.

"Come to Me, all you who are working hard and carrying a 28
heavy load,
And I will give you rest.
Take My yoke on you and learn from Me — 29
I am gentle and humble-minded —
Then *you will find your rest.*[40]
My yoke is easy, 30
And My load is light."

Lord of the Sabbath

At that time Jesus walked through the grainfields on a Sabbath. 12
His disciples were hungry and began to pick the heads of grain
and eat them.

When the Pharisees saw this, they said to Him, "Look, Your 2
disciples are doing something they shouldn't do on a day of rest."

"Haven't you read what David did," Jesus asked them, "when 3
he and his men got hungry — how he went into God's house and 4
ate the *loaves laid before God,*[41] which he and his men had no
right to eat, but only the priests? Or haven't you read in the Law 5
that the priests in the temple work on a Sabbath as on other days
and yet do no wrong? I tell you, here is something greater than 6
the temple. If you knew what this means, *I like mercy and not* 7
mere *sacrifice,*[42] you would not have condemned the innocent.
The Son of Man is Lord of the Sabbath." 8

The Shriveled Hand

He went on to another place and went into their synagog, and 9
there was a man with a shriveled hand.

"Is it right to heal on a Sabbath?" they asked Him. They 10
wanted to accuse Him of something.

"If anyone of you has only one sheep," Jesus asked them, 11
"and it falls into a hole on a Sabbath, won't you take hold of it

and lift it out? Now, isn't a man much more valuable than a sheep?
12:12 It is right, then, to do good on a day of rest!"

13 Then He told the man, "Stretch out your hand." He stretched it out and it was made healthy again like the other hand.

14 But the Pharisees left and plotted against Him to kill Him.
15 Jesus knew about this, and so He left.

The Servant

15-16 Many followed Him, and He healed them all, ' but He ordered
17 them not to tell people who He was. In this way what the prophet Isaiah said was to come true:

18 *Here is My Servant whom I have chosen,*
Whom I love and delight in.
I will put My Spirit on Him,
And He will announce justice to the nations.
19 *He will not quarrel or shout.*
Nor will anyone hear His voice in the streets.
20 *He will not crush a bruised reed*
Or put out a smoking wick
Till He has made justice victorious.
21 *And His name will be the hope of the nations.*[43]

Power over the Devil

22 At that time some people brought to Jesus a man who had a devil and was blind and couldn't talk. Jesus healed him so that he could talk and see.

23 The people were all amazed. "Could this be the Son of
24 David?" they asked. When the Pharisees heard about it, they said, "He can drive out the devils only with the help of Beelzebul, who rules over the devils."

25 Knowing what they were thinking, Jesus said to them, "If one part of any kingdom fights another, it loses its people. And if one part of any town or home fights another, it will not stand.
26 If the devil drives out the devil, he's fighting against himself. How
27 then will his kingdom stand? Now if Beelzebul helps Me drive out the devils, who helps your sons drive them out? That's why
28 they'll be your judges. But if God's Spirit helps Me drive out
29 the devils, then God's kingdom has come to you. How can anyone go into a strong man's house and take away his goods without first tying the strong man up? After that he'll rob his house.

30 "Anyone who's not with Me is against Me, and anyone who

doesn't help Me gather scatters. So I tell you, any sin or slander will be forgiven, but slandering the Spirit will not be forgiven. Anyone who talks against the Son of Man will be forgiven, but ³² anyone who talks against the Holy Spirit will not be forgiven in this world or the next.

"Either the tree is good, and then its fruit is good. Or the ³³ tree is bad, and then its fruit is bad. You can tell a tree by its fruit. Brood of snakes, how can you who are so evil say anything ³⁴ good? What you say flows from your hearts. ¹ A good man pro- ³⁵ duces good things from the good stored in him, but an evil man produces evil from the evil stored in him. But I tell you, on ³⁶ Judgment Day people will have to give an account of every useless word they say. By your words you'll be acquitted, and by your ³⁷ words you'll be condemned."

The Sign of Jonah

Then some Bible scholars and Pharisees said, "Teacher, we ³⁸ want You to show us some wonderful proof."

"The wicked and unfaithful people of today are looking for ³⁹ a proof," He answered them, "but the only proof they'll get is the prophet Jonah. As *Jonah was in the belly of the big fish three* ⁴⁰ *days,*⁴⁴ so the Son of Man will be in the bosom of the earth three days. The men of Nineveh will rise up in the Judgment with these ⁴¹ people and condemn them, because they repented when Jonah preached; and here you see more than Jonah. The queen from ⁴² the south will rise up in the Judgment with these people and condemn them, because she came from the ends of the earth to hear Solomon's wisdom; and here you see more than Solomon.

"When an unclean spirit comes out of a man, he goes through ⁴³ dry places looking for a place to rest but doesn't find any. Then ⁴⁴ he says, 'I'll go back to the home I left.' He comes and finds it empty, swept, and decorated. Then he goes and takes home ⁴⁵ with him seven other spirits worse than himself, and they go in and live there. In the end that man is worse than he was before. That's what will happen to the wicked people of today."

The Mother and Brothers of Jesus

He was still talking to the people when His mother and ⁴⁶ brothers were standing outside wanting to talk to Him. "Your ⁴⁷ mother and Your brothers are standing outside," somebody told Him, "and want to talk to You."

48 "Who is My mother," He asked the man that told Him, "and
49 who are My brothers?" Pointing with His hand to His disciples,
50 He said, "These are My mother and My brothers. If you do what
My Father in heaven wants, you are My brother and sister and
mother."

The Sower

13 That same day Jesus left the house and sat down by the lake.
2 But so many people gathered around Him that He stepped into
3 a boat and sat there while all the people stood on the shore. Then
He told them many things in parables.
4 "A sower went out to sow," He said. ¹ "As he was sowing,
some seed fell along the road, and the birds came and ate it.
5 Some seed fell on rocky ground, where it didn't have much soil.
6 Because the soil wasn't deep, the seed came up quickly. ¹ When
the sun rose, it was scorched, and because it had not taken root,
7 it withered. Some seed fell on thorns, and the thorns grew up
8 and choked it. But some seed fell on good ground and produced
grain, some a hundred, some sixty, and some thirty times as much
9 as was sown. You have ears to hear; then listen."
10 The disciples came to Him. "Why are You talking to them in
parables?" they asked Him.
11 "You are given the privilege to know the secrets of the kingdom of heaven," He answered, "but it isn't given to the others.
12 If you have something, you'll be given more, and so you'll get
more and more. But if you don't have what you should have,
13 even what you have will be taken away from you. I talk to them
in parables because they see and yet don't see, and hear and
14 yet don't hear or understand. In them more and more Isaiah's
prophecy is coming true:
You will hear but never understand,
You will look but never see.
15 *These people have become dull at heart and hard of hearing*
And have shut their eyes
So that their eyes will never see, their ears never hear,
or their hearts understand,
*And they will never turn to Me and let Me heal them.*⁴⁵

16 "Happy are your eyes because they see and your ears because
17 they hear. Let Me assure you, many prophets and righteous
people longed to see what you see and didn't see it, to hear what
you hear and didn't hear it.

"Listen to what the parable of the sower means. When anyone hears the message of the Kingdom but doesn't understand it, the evil one comes and takes away what was sown in his heart. That is what was sown along the road. In another the seed falls [20] on rocky ground. He's one who welcomes the Word with joy as soon as he hears it, but it doesn't take root in him. He believes [21] for a while, but as soon as the Word brings him trouble or persecution, he falls away. In another the seed is sown among thorns. [22] He's one who hears the Word, but the worry of the world and the deceitful pleasure of riches choke the Word, and it can't produce anything. But in another the seed is sown on good ground. [23] He's one who continues to hear and understand the Word and so goes on producing good things, one a hundred, another sixty, and another thirty times as much as was sown."

Weeds in the Wheat

Jesus pictured it to them another way: "The kingdom of [24] heaven is like a man who sowed good seed in his field. But while [25] people were sleeping, his enemy came and sowed weeds among the wheat and went away. When the wheat came up and formed [26] kernels, then the weeds showed up too.

"The owner's slaves came to him and asked him, 'Master, [27] didn't you sow good seed in your field? Where did the weeds come from?'

" 'An enemy did that,' he told them.

" 'Do you want us to go and pull them out?' the slaves [28] asked him.

" 'No,' he said, 'if you pull out the weeds, you may pull up [29] the wheat with them. Let both grow together till the harvest. [30] When the grain is cut, I will tell the reapers, "Gather the weeds first, and tie them in bundles to be burned, but bring the wheat into my barn." ' "

A Mustard Seed and Yeast

He pictured it to them another way: "The kingdom of heaven [31] is like a mustard seed a man took and sowed in his field. It's the [32] smallest of all seeds, but when it has grown, it's the largest of the garden plants; it becomes a tree big enough for the *birds* to come and *nest in its branches*." [46]

He pictured it to them another way: "The kingdom of heaven [33] is like yeast a woman took and mixed into a bushel of flour till it was all fermented."

13:34   Jesus used parables to tell the crowds all these things.
35 He wouldn't tell them anything without a parable, ' so that what the prophet said would come true:

I will open My mouth to speak in parables,
*I will tell what has been hidden since the world was made.*⁴⁷

The Meaning of the Weeds in the Wheat

36   When Jesus had dismissed the people and gone into the house, His disciples came to Him and said, "Tell us what the parable of the weeds in the field means."

37   "The sower who sows the good seed," He answered, "is the
38 Son of Man. ' The field is the world. The good seed are the sons
39 of the kingdom. The weeds are the sons of the evil one. ' The enemy who sowed them is the devil. The harvest is the end of
40 the world. The reapers are the angels. ' As the weeds are gathered
41 and burned, so it will be at the end of the world. The Son of Man will send His angels, and they will take out of His kingdom
42 *those who do wrong and all who lead others to do wrong,* ⁴⁸ and will throw them into the fiery furnace, where they will cry and
43 grind their teeth. Then *the righteous will shine like* ⁴⁹ the sun in their Father's kingdom. If you have ears, listen!"

The Treasure, the Pearl, and the Fish

44   "The kingdom of heaven is like a treasure buried in a field. When a man found it, he buried it again and was so delighted with it he went and sold everything he had and bought that field.
45   "Here's another picture of the kingdom of heaven: A dealer
46 was looking for fine pearls. When he found a very expensive pearl, he went and sold everything he had and bought it.
47   "Again, the kingdom of heaven is like a net that was let down
48 into the lake, and it gathered all kinds of fish. When it was full they pulled it on the shore, sat down, and picked out the good fish and put them in containers but threw the bad ones away.
49 ' So it will be at the end of the world. The angels will go out and
50 separate the wicked from the righteous ' and throw them into the fiery furnace, where they will cry and grind their teeth.
51   "Did you understand all this?"

"Yes," they answered.
52   "And so every Bible student trained for the kingdom of

heaven," He told them, "is like the owner of a house who brings out of his storeroom new things and old."

When Jesus had finished these parables, He left that place. ^{13:53}

His Last Visit to Nazareth

He went to His home town and taught the people in their ⁵⁴ synagog in such a way they were amazed. "Where did He get this wisdom and the power to do these miracles?" they asked. "Isn't He the carpenter's son? Isn't His mother's name Mary, and ⁵⁵ aren't James, Joseph, Simon, and Judas His brothers? And aren't ⁵⁶ all His sisters here with us? Where did He get all this?" So they ⁵⁷ turned against Him.

"A prophet is without honor only in his home town and in his family," Jesus told them. Their unbelief kept Him from doing ⁵⁸ many great works there.

Herod Kills John

At that time Herod, the governor, heard the news about Jesus. ¹⁴ "This is John the Baptizer!" he told his servants. "He's risen ² from the dead, and that's why these powers are working in Him."

Herod had arrested John, bound him, and put him in prison ³ on account of Herodias, the wife of his brother Philip, because ⁴ John was telling him, "It isn't right for you to have her." Herod ⁵ wanted to kill him but was afraid of the people because they considered John a prophet.

When Herod's birthday was celebrated, the daughter of Hero- ⁶ dias danced before the guests. Herod was so delighted with her ⁷ he swore to give her anything she might ask for.

Urged on by her mother, she said, "Give me here on a platter ⁸ the head of John the Baptizer."

Then the king felt sorry. But he had sworn to do it, and there ⁹ were the guests — so he ordered it given to her. He sent and had ¹⁰ John's head cut off in prison. And his head was brought on ¹¹ a platter and given to the girl, who took it to her mother.

John's disciples came and took his body away and buried it. ¹² Then they went and told Jesus.

Jesus Feeds Five Thousand

When Jesus heard about John, He left in a boat and went ¹³ to a deserted place to be alone. The people heard of it and followed Him on foot from the towns. When Jesus stepped out of ¹⁴

the boat, He saw a big crowd. He felt sorry for them and healed their sick.

14:15   In the evening the disciples came to Him. "This is a deserted place," they said, "and it's late. Send the crowds away to the villages to buy themselves some food."

16   "They don't need to go away," Jesus answered them. "You give them something to eat."

17   "All we have here is five loaves and two fish," they told Him.

18   "Let Me have them," He said.

19   He ordered the people to sit down on the grass. Then taking the five loaves and the two fish and looking up to heaven, He blessed them. Breaking the loaves, He gave them to the dis-
20 ciples, and they gave them to the people. All of them ate and had a hearty meal. They picked up the pieces that were left — twelve baskets full.

21   Some five thousand men had eaten, not counting women and children.

Jesus Walks on Water

22   Jesus quickly made the disciples get into the boat and go
23 on ahead to the other side while He dismissed the people. After sending them away, He went up the hill to be alone and pray. When it got late, He was there alone.

24   The boat, now many hundred yards from the shore, was troubled by the waves because the wind was against them.

25   Toward morning He came to them, walking on the lake.
26 When the disciples saw Him walking on the lake, they were terrified. "It's a ghost," they said, and they cried out in terror.

27   Immediately He talked to them. "Have courage," He said. "It is I. Don't be afraid."

28   "Lord, if it's You," Peter answered Him, "order me to come to You on the water."

29   "Come," He said. So Peter got out of the boat, walked on
30 the water, and went toward Jesus. But when he saw the wind, he was frightened and started to sink. "Lord, save me!" he cried.

31   Quickly Jesus stretched out His hand and caught him. "How little you trust Me!" He said to him. "Why did you doubt?"

32-33   When they stepped into the boat, the wind stopped. And the men in the boat bowed down before Him and said, "You certainly are God's Son."

They crossed over and came to the shore at Gennesaret. The men of that place recognized Jesus and sent messengers all around that country, and the people brought Him all the sick ones, [1] and they begged Him just to let them touch the tassel of His garment. All who touched it were made well. .

Unclean Hands

Then some Pharisees and Bible scholars came to Him from **15** Jerusalem. "Why do Your disciples sin against the rules handed **2** down by our fathers?" they asked. "They don't wash their hands when they eat."

"Why do you sin against God's commandment for the sake of **3** your rules?" He asked them. "For example, God has said, *Honor* **4** *father and mother,*[50] and, *Anyone who curses father or mother must die.*[51] But you say, 'Whoever tells his father or mother, "I'm **5** giving God anything by which I might help you," doesn't have to honor his father.' For the sake of your rules you have set aside **6** what God has said. Hypocrites, Isaiah was right when he prophe- **7** sied about you: *These people honor Me with their lips, but their* **8** *hearts are far away from Me. They worship Me in vain because* **9** *they teach men's rules."* [52]

Then he called the people and told them: "Listen to Me **10** and understand this: What comes into his mouth doesn't make **11** a person unclean, but what goes out of his mouth makes him unclean."

Then the disciples came to Him. "Do you know the Pharisees **12** were offended when they heard You say that?" they asked Him.

"Any plant My Father in heaven didn't plant," He answered, **13** "will be torn out by the roots. Let them go; they are blind leaders. **14** When one blind man leads another, both will fall into a ditch."

"Tell us what You mean by this illustration," Peter said **15** to Him.

"Are you still as dull as the others?" He asked. "Don't you **16-17** know that everything that goes into the mouth goes into the stomach and so passes away? But what goes out of the mouth **18** comes from the heart, and that makes a person unclean. Yes, out **19** of the heart come evil thoughts, murders, adulteries, sexual sins, stealing, lies, slanders. These are the things that make a person unclean. But eating without washing your hands doesn't make **20** you unclean."

A Non-Jewish Woman

15:21   Leaving that place, Jesus went away to the neighborhood of Tyre and Sidon.

22   There was a Canaanite woman of that territory who came out and called, "Have pity on me, Lord, Son of David! A devil is making my daughter miserable."

23   But He didn't answer her a word. Then His disciples came to Him and urged Him, "Send her away. She's yelling after us."

24   "I was sent only to the lost sheep of Israel," He answered.

25   She came and bowed down before Him. "Lord, help me!" she said.

26   "It isn't good," He answered, "to take the children's bread and throw it to the puppies."

27   "You're right, Lord," she said, "but even the puppies eat some of the crumbs that drop from their masters' table."

28   Then Jesus answered her, "O woman, you have a great faith! Let it be done for you as you wish." At that moment her daughter was made well.

29   Jesus left that place and went along the shore of the Lake of Galilee. Then He went up a hill and sat there.

30   Many people came to Him, bringing the lame, blind, crippled, 31 deaf, and many others and laid them at His feet. He made them well, so that the people were surprised to find that the dumb talked, the cripples had sound limbs, the lame walked around, and the blind could see. And they praised the God of Israel.

Jesus Feeds Four Thousand

32   Jesus called His disciples. "I feel sorry for the people," He said. "They've been with Me three days now and have nothing to eat. I don't want to let them go without eating; they may get exhausted on the way."

33   "Where could we get enough bread in a wilderness to feed such a crowd?" His disciples asked Him.

34   "How many loaves do you have?" Jesus asked them.

"Seven," they said, "and a few small fish."

35-36   He ordered the people to sit down on the ground. Then He took the seven loaves and the fish, gave thanks, broke them, and gave them to the disciples, and they gave them to the people.

37   All of them ate and had enough. They picked up the pieces that

were left — seven baskets full. Four thousand men had eaten, not counting women and children.

Then He dismissed the people.

A Proof from Heaven

He stepped into the boat and came into the neighborhood of Magadan. 39

The Pharisees and Sadducees came and, to test Him, asked Him to show them some wonderful proof from heaven. 16

He answered them, "In the evening you say, 'The weather will be fine, because the sky is red.' And in the morning: 'There will be a storm today, because the sky is red and gloomy.' You know how to judge the appearance of the sky correctly but can't judge the signs of the times.* 2 3

"The wicked and unfaithful people of today demand a proof, and the only proof they'll get is that of Jonah." 4

Then He left them and went away.

The Yeast of the Pharisees

When the disciples started out for the other side, they forgot to take bread. 5

Jesus said to them, "Beware of the yeast of the Pharisees and Sadducees!" 6

As they were arguing about this, they mentioned, "We didn't take any bread." 7

Aware of what was going on, Jesus asked, "Why are you arguing about not having any bread? You have so little faith! Don't you understand yet, and don't you remember the five loaves for the five thousand and how many baskets full you picked up? Or the seven loaves for the four thousand and how many baskets full you picked up? Why don't you see I wasn't talking to you about bread? But beware of the yeast of the Pharisees and Sadducees!" 8 9 10 11

Then they understood He didn't warn them against the yeast in bread but against the teaching of the Pharisees and Sadducees. 12

"You Are the Son of God"

When Jesus came to the neighborhood of Philip's Caesarea, He asked His disciples, "Who do people say the Son of Man is?" 13

* Jesus' words in verses 2-3 are omitted in some of our oldest manuscripts.

"Some say John the Baptizer," they answered, "others Elijah, still others Jeremiah, or one of the prophets."

15 "Who do you say I am?" He asked them.

16 "You are the promised Savior," Simon Peter answered, "the Son of the living God!"

17 "Happy are you, Simon, son of John," Jesus answered him, "because no flesh and blood, but My Father in heaven has re-
18 vealed this to you. I tell you, you are Peter, and on this rock I will build My church, and the forces of hell will not over-
19 power it. I will give you the keys of the kingdom of heaven. Anything you bind on earth will be bound in heaven, and anything you free on earth will be freed in heaven."

20 Then He warned the disciples not to tell anyone that He was the promised Savior.

"I Will Die and Rise Again"

21 After this, Jesus Christ kept pointing out to His disciples He had to go to Jerusalem, suffer much from the elders, ruling priests, and Bible scholars, be killed, and then on the third day rise.

22 But Peter took Him aside and started to correct Him, "God be merciful to You, Lord! This must never happen to You!"

23 Turning, He said to Peter, "Get behind Me, devil! You're tempting Me to sin, because you're not thinking what God thinks but what men think."

Take the Cross

24 Then Jesus said to His disciples, "If you want to follow Me,
25 deny yourself, take up your cross, and come with Me. If you want to save your life, you will lose it. But if you will lose your
26 life for Me, you will find it. What good will it do you to win the whole world and lose your life? Or what would you give to buy
27 back your life? The Son of Man is going to come with His angels in His Father's glory, and then *He will give each one*
28 *according to what he has done.*[53] Let Me assure you, there are some standing here who will never taste death till they see the Son of Man coming to rule as King."

Jesus Shows His Glory

17 After five days Jesus took with Him Peter, James, and John, the brother of James, and led them up a high mountain to be alone with them.

He was changed before them, His face shone like the sun, and His clothes became as white as light. And there Moses and Elijah appeared to them and were talking with Him.

"Lord," Peter said to Jesus, "it's good for us to be here. If You wish, I'll put up three shelters here, one for You, one for Moses, and one for Elijah."

He was still speaking when a bright cloud suddenly overshadowed them, and a voice came out of the cloud: "This is *My Son* whom I love and *delight in. Listen to Him.*" 54

When the disciples heard this, they fell down with their faces on the ground; they were terrified. But Jesus came and touched them. "Get up," He said, "and don't be afraid." ' They looked up and saw no one but Jesus.

On their way down the mountain Jesus ordered them, "Don't tell anyone what you have seen till the Son of Man has risen from the dead."

So the disciples asked Him, "Why, then, do those who know the Bible say, 'First Elijah has to come'?"

"Elijah does come," He answered, "and *must put* everything *in order again.*[55] But I tell you Elijah has already come, and people didn't know him, but treated him as they pleased. In the same way they're going to make the Son of Man suffer."

Then the disciples understood He was talking about John the Baptizer.

The Epileptic Boy

When they came to the people, a man came to Jesus and knelt before Him. ' "Lord," he said, "have pity on my son. He's epileptic and very sick. Often he falls into fire or into water. ' I brought him to Your disciples, but they couldn't make him well."

"O you unbelieving and perverted people!" Jesus answered. "How long must I be with you? How long must I put up with you? Bring him here to Me."

Jesus talked sharply to the devil, and he came out of the boy, and after that the boy was well.

Afterwards, when Jesus was alone, the disciples came to Him. "Why couldn't we drive out the spirit?" they asked.

"You have so little faith," He told them. "I tell you the truth, if you have faith no bigger than a mustard seed, you will

33

say to this mountain, 'Move from here to there,' and it will move.
* Then you can do anything."

"I Will Die and Rise Again"

17:22   While they were getting together as a group in Galilee, Jesus told them, "The Son of Man is going to be betrayed into the hands
23 of men, ¹ and they will kill Him, but on the third day He will rise." Then they felt very sad.

A Coin in a Fish's Mouth

24   When they came to Capernaum, the collectors of the temple tax came to Peter. "Doesn't your Teacher pay the temple tax?" they asked.

25   "Certainly," he answered.

Peter went into the house, but before he could speak, Jesus asked him, "What do you think, Simon? From whom do the kings of the world collect toll or tax — from their children or from other people?"

26   "From other people," he answered.

27   "Then the children are free," Jesus told him. ¹ "But we don't want to give them a reason to think wrong of us. So go to the lake and throw in a hook. Take the first fish that comes up, open its mouth, and you will find a coin. Take that and give it to them for Me and you."

Who Is the Greatest?

18   At that time the disciples came to Jesus and asked, "Who is really the greatest in the kingdom of heaven?"

2   He called a little child and had him stand in front of them.
3   "I tell you the truth," He said to them, "if you don't change and become like little children, you will never get into the kingdom
4   of heaven. If you become humble like this little child, you are
5   the greatest in the kingdom of heaven. And if you welcome a child like this in My name, you welcome Me."

Do I Lead Others to Sin?

6   "If anyone leads into sin one of these little ones who believe in Me, it would be better for him to have a big millstone hung around his neck and be drowned in the lake where it's deep.

---

* Our two oldest manuscripts do not have v. 21: "This kind goes out only by prayer and fasting." See Mark 9:29.

¹ Woe to the world because it tempts people to sin! Temptations to
sin must come, but woe to that man who tempts others to sin!

"If your hand or your foot makes you sin, cut it off and ⁸
throw it away. It is better for you to go into life without one
hand or one foot than to have two hands or two feet and be
thrown into the everlasting fire. If your eye makes you sin, tear ⁹
it out and throw it away. It is better for you to go into life with
one eye than to have two eyes and be thrown into hellfire.

"Be careful not to despise one of these little ones. I tell you ¹⁰
their angels in heaven always see the face of My Father in
heaven.

*

"What do you think? If a man has a hundred sheep and one ¹²
of them gets lost, will he not leave the ninety-nine in the hills
and go and look for the sheep that's wandering away? And if ¹³
he finds it, I tell you he's certainly more delighted with it than
with the ninety-nine that didn't get lost. So your Father in ¹⁴
heaven doesn't want one of these little ones to be lost."

Tell Him His Fault

"If your brother sins against you, go, and when you're alone ¹⁵
with him, show him how he is wrong. If he listens to you, you
have won your brother. But if he won't listen, take one or two ¹⁶
with you so that *you have two or three witnesses for everything.*⁵⁶
¹ If he won't listen to them, tell it to the church. But if he won't ¹⁷
even listen to the church, treat him like a pagan and a tax collector. I tell you the truth: Whatever you don't forgive on earth ¹⁸
will not be forgiven in heaven, and whatever you forgive on earth
will be forgiven in heaven.

"Again I tell you: If two of you here on earth agree to ask ¹⁹
for anything, My Father in heaven will certainly do it for you.
Where two or three have come together to be with Me, there ²⁰
I am among them."

Forgive!

Then Peter came to Jesus and asked Him, "Lord, how often ²¹
do I have to forgive my brother who sins against me? Seven
times?"

"I tell you," Jesus answered him, "not seven times but sev- ²²
enty times seven times.

"That is why the kingdom of heaven is like a king who ²³

* Our two oldest manuscripts do not have v. 11: "The Son of man came
to save the lost." See Luke 19:10.

wanted to settle accounts with his slaves. When he began to do so, there was brought to him one who owed him ten thousand
25 talents.* But he couldn't pay it, and so the master ordered him, his wife, his children, and all he had to be sold to pay the debt.
26 Then the slave got down on his knees and, bowing low before him, begged: 'Be patient with me, and I'll pay you everything.'
27 "The master felt sorry for his slave, freed him, and canceled
28 his debt. But when that slave went away, he found one of his fellow slaves who owed him a hundred denarii.** He grabbed him and started to choke him. 'Pay what you owe,' he said.
29 "Then his fellow slave got down on his knees and begged him,
30 'Be patient with me, and I'll pay you.' But he refused and went and put him in prison till he would pay what he owed.
31 "When his fellow slaves saw what had happened, they felt very sad and went and told their master the whole story.
32 "Then his master sent for him. 'You wicked slave!' he said to him. 'I canceled all you owed me, because you begged me.
33 Shouldn't you also have treated your fellow slave as mercifully
34 as I treated you?' His master was so angry he handed him over to the torturers till he would pay all he owed him.
35 "That is what My Father in heaven will do to you if each of you will not heartily forgive his brother."

Husband and Wife

19 When Jesus finished saying this, He left Galilee and went to
2 the part of Judea on the other side of the Jordan. Large crowds followed Him, and He made them well there.
3 Some Pharisees, coming to Him to test Him, asked Him, "Is it right for a man to divorce his wife for any reason?"
4 "Haven't you read," He asked them, "He who created them
5 from the beginning *made them a male and a female?"* [57] And He added: *"That is why a man will leave his father and mother
6 and live with his wife, and the two will be one flesh.*[58] And so they are no more two but one flesh. Now, what God has joined together man must not separate."
7 "Why, then, did Moses order a man *to make out a divorce paper and divorce his wife?"* [59] they asked Him.
8 He answered them, "Because your minds are closed, Moses let you divorce your wives, but originally there was no such thing.

* One "talent" of silver weighed about as much as 1,500 silver dollars.
** One denarius was a day's pay.

I tell you, if anyone divorces his wife, except for adultery, and marries another, he's living in adultery."

"If a man has to have such grounds in dealing with his wife," the disciples told Him, "it's better not to marry." 10

"Not all can do this," He told them, "only those to whom it 11 has been given. Some can't marry because they were born 12 that way. Others, because they have been mutilated by men. And still others have decided to do without marriage for the kingdom of heaven. If anyone can do it, let him do it."

Jesus Loves Children

Then some people brought little children to Jesus to have 13 Him lay His hands on them and pray. But the disciples sternly told them not to do it.

"Let the little children come to Me," Jesus said, "and don't 14 keep them away. The kingdom of heaven belongs to such as these." He laid His hands on them and then went away. 15

The Rich Young Leader

There was one who came and asked Him, "Teacher, what 16 good thing should I do to get everlasting life?"

"Why do you ask Me about something good? Only One is 17 good. If you want to go into life, keep the commandments."

"Which commandments?" he asked Him. 18

Jesus said, *"Don't murder, don't commit adultery, don't steal, don't lie,* [1] *honor father and mother,*[60] *and love your neighbor like* 19 *yourself."* [61]

"I've kept all these," the young man told Him. "What else do 20 I need?"

"If you want to be perfect," Jesus told him, "go, sell what 21 you have, give the money to the poor, and you'll have a treasure in heaven. Then come and follow Me."

When the young man heard this, he went away sad, because 22 he was very rich.

"I tell you the truth," Jesus said to His disciples, "it is hard 23 for a rich man to get into the kingdom of heaven. Again I tell 24 you it's easier for a camel to go through a needle's eye than for a rich man to get into God's kingdom."

The disciples, hearing this, were dumfounded. "Who, then, 25 can be saved?" they asked.

"Men can't do this," Jesus said as He looked at them, "but *God can do anything.*" [62]

27 Then Peter spoke up: "Look! We gave up everything and followed You. So what will we get?"

28 "Let Me assure you," Jesus said to them, "in the new life, when the Son of Man sits on His throne of glory, you who followed Me will also sit on twelve thrones and rule the twelve 29 tribes of Israel. And everyone who gave up homes, brothers or sisters, father, mother, or children, or fields for Me will get 30 many times as much, and then everlasting life. But many who are first will be last, and many who are last will be first."

"The Last Will Be First"

20 "The kingdom of heaven is like the owner of a place who went out early in the morning to hire men to work in his vineyard. 2 He agreed with the workers to pay them a denarius a day and 3 sent them into his vineyard. About nine o'clock he went out and 4 saw others standing in the marketplace doing nothing. 'You go into the vineyard too,' he told them, 'and I'll pay you what's right.' So they went.

5 "He went out again about twelve o'clock and three o'clock 6 and did the same thing. About five o'clock he went out and found some others standing around. 'Why are you standing here all day long doing nothing?' he asked them.

7 " 'Nobody has hired us,' they answered him.

" 'You go into the vineyard too,' he told them.

8 "When evening came, the owner of the vineyard told his manager, 'Call the men and give them their pay. Start with the last and go on to the first.'

9 "Those who started working around five o'clock came, and 10 each got a denarius. When the first ones came, they expected to 11 get more, but each of them, too, got a denarius. They took it, 12 but they grumbled against the owner: 'These last men worked only one hour, and you've treated them exactly like us who have worked hard all day in the blazing sun.'

13 " 'Friend, I'm doing you no wrong,' he answered one of 14 them. 'You agreed with me on a denarius, didn't you? Take your money and go. I want to give this last man as much as 15 I give you. Don't I have the right to do as I please with what is mine? Or are you jealous because I'm generous?'

16 "In this way the last will be first and the first last."

The Cup of Suffering

When Jesus was going up to Jerusalem, He took the twelve 20:17
by themselves and said to them on the way: "Look, we're going 18
up to Jerusalem, and the Son of Man will be betrayed to the ruling
priests and Bible scholars, who will condemn Him to die and 19
hand Him over to the Gentiles to be mocked, scourged, and crucified, but on the third day He will rise."

Then the mother of Zebedee's sons came to Jesus with her 20
sons and bowed before Him to ask Him for something.

"What do you want?" He asked her. 21

She told Him, "Promise that one of my two sons will sit at
Your right and the other at Your left in Your kingdom."

"You don't know what you're asking," Jesus answered. "Can 22
you drink the cup I'm going to drink?"

"We can," they told Him.

"You'll drink My cup," He told them. "But sitting at My 23
right and left is something I can give only to those for whom My
Father prepared it."

When the other ten heard about it, they got angry with James 24
and John. Jesus called them and said, "You know the rulers of 25
the nations are lords over them, and their great men are tyrants
over them. But among you it's different. Anyone who wants to 26
become great among you must be your servant, and anyone 27
who wants to be first among you must be your slave, just as 28
the Son of Man did not come to be served but to serve and
give His life as a ransom for all people."

Two Blind Men

As they were leaving Jericho, a large crowd followed Him. 29
And there were two blind men sitting by the road. When they 30
heard, "Jesus is passing by," they called, "Lord, have pity on
us, Son of David!"

The crowd urged them to be quiet. But they called all the 31
louder, "Lord, have pity on us, Son of David!"

Jesus stopped and called them. "What do you want Me to 32
do for you?" He asked.

"Lord, we want to see," they told Him. 33

Jesus felt sorry for them and touched their eyes, and imme- 34
diately they could see. And they followed Him.

The King Comes to Jerusalem

21 When they came near Jerusalem and had reached Bethphage
2 and the Mount of Olives, Jesus sent two disciples. "Go into the
village ahead of you," He told them, "and without any trouble
you'll find a donkey tied up and a colt with her. Untie them and
3 bring them to Me. If anybody says anything to you, say, 'The
Lord needs them,' and immediately he will send them."

4 This happened so that what the prophet said would come true:

5 *Tell the daughter of Zion,*
"Look! Your King is coming to you,
Gentle, riding on a donkey and on a colt of a donkey." [63]

6-7 The disciples went and did as Jesus had directed them. They
brought the donkey and the colt and laid their garments on
8 them; and Jesus sat on them. Most of the people spread their
garments on the road. Others cut branches from the trees and
9 spread them on the road. The people who went ahead of Him
and followed Him were shouting:

"Our Savior, the Son of David!
Blessed is He who is coming in the Lord's name! [64]
Our Savior — in the highest heavens!"

10 When He came into Jerusalem, the whole city was excited,
asking, "Who is this?"

11 The crowds answered, "This is the Prophet Jesus from Nazareth in Galilee."

In the Temple

12 Jesus went into the temple and put out all who were selling
and buying in the temple and upset the tables of the money
13 changers and the chairs of those who sold pigeons. "It is written,"
He told them, *"My house should be called a house of prayer,* [65]
but you're making it *a den of robbers!"* [66]

14 Blind and lame persons came to Him in the temple, and He
made them well.

15 When the ruling priests and the Bible scholars saw the wonderful things He did, and the children shouting in the temple,
16 *"Our Savior,*[64] the Son of David!" they didn't like it at all. "Do
You hear what they're saying?" they asked Him.

"Yes," Jesus answered them. "Haven't you ever read, *You
have made children and babies at the breast praise You?"* [67]

17 He left them and went out of the city to Bethany and spent the
night there.

Nothing but Leaves

In the morning as He went back to the city, Jesus was hungry, and seeing a fig tree by the road, He went up to it and found nothing on it but leaves. "May no fruit ever grow on you again!" Jesus said to it. And immediately the fig tree dried up. 21:18 19

The disciples were surprised to see this. "How did the fig tree dry up so quickly?" they asked. 20

"I tell you the truth," Jesus answered them: "If you believe and don't doubt, you will not only do what I did to the fig tree, but if you will say to this mount,* 'Be lifted up and be thrown into the sea,' ** it will be done. Anything you ask for in prayer, believe, and you will get it." 21 22

From Heaven

When He came to the temple and was teaching, the ruling priests and the elders of the people came to Him. "By what authority are You doing these things?" they asked. "And who gave You the right to do them?" 23

Jesus answered them, "I will ask you a question. And if you answer Me, I'll tell you by what authority I'm doing these things. John's baptism — was it from heaven or from men?" 24 25

They argued among themselves, "If we say, 'From heaven,' He will ask us, 'Then why didn't you believe him?' But if we say, 'From men,' we're afraid of the people; they all think John is a prophet." So they answered Jesus, "We don't know." 26 27

Then Jesus also told them, "Neither will I tell you by what authority I'm doing these things."

Say and Do

"Now, what do you think of this? A man had two sons. He went to the first and said, 'Son, go and work in the vineyard today.' 28

" 'I won't,' he answered. Later he changed his mind and went. 29

"The father went to the other one and told him the same thing. He answered, 'I will, sir,' but didn't go. 30

"Which of the two did what the father wanted?" 31
They answered, "The first."
Jesus said to them, "I tell you the truth, tax collectors and

* The Mount of Olives.
** The Dead Sea, which can be seen from the Mount of Olives.

prostitutes are going into God's kingdom ahead of you. John came to you in a righteous way, but you didn't believe him; the tax collectors and prostitutes believed him. But even when you had seen that, you didn't change your minds and believe him."

God's Vineyard

33   "Listen to another story:

"A man who owned property *planted a vineyard. He put a wall around it, cut a winepress into the rock, and built a watchtower.*[68] Then he rented it out to workers and left home.

34   "When the grapes were getting ripe, he sent his slaves to the
35 workers to get his share of the grapes. The workers took his
36 slaves and beat one, killed another, and stoned a third. Then he sent other slaves, this time a larger number, and they treated these the same way.

37   "Finally he sent his son to them, saying, 'They will respect my son.'

38   "When the workers saw the son, they said to one another, 'This is the heir. Come, let's kill him and get his inheritance.'
39 So they took him, threw him out of the vineyard, and killed him.
40   "Now, when the owner of the vineyard comes, what will he do to those workers?"

41   He was told, "He will have those scoundrels die a miserable death and rent out the vineyard to other workers who will bring him the grapes when they're ripe."

42   Jesus asked them, "Haven't you ever read in your Bible, *The stone the builders rejected has become the cornerstone. The Lord*
43 *has done it, and we think it is wonderful?* [69] That is why I tell you, God's kingdom will be taken away from you and be given to
44 a people who will do its works. Anyone who falls on that Stone will be dashed in pieces, and if It falls on anyone, It will scatter him like dust."

45   When the ruling priests and Pharisees heard His stories, they
46 knew He was talking about them. They wanted to grab Him but were afraid because the people thought He was a prophet.

Come to the Wedding!

22   Again Jesus used stories in talking to them. He said:

2   "The kingdom of heaven is like a king who prepared a wed-
3 ding for his son. He sent his slaves to call those who had been
4 invited to the wedding, but they refused to come. Then he sent

other slaves and said to them, 'Tell the people who are invited, "Look here! I prepared my dinner. My bulls and fattened calves are killed, and everything is ready. Come to the wedding." '

"But they paid no attention and went away, one to his farm, another to his business, and the rest took his slaves, shamefully mistreated them, and murdered them. 22:5 6

"The king got angry. He sent his soldiers, and they killed those murderers and burned their city. 7

"Then he said to his slaves: 'The wedding is ready, but the people who were invited didn't deserve the honor. Now go where the roads leave the city, and call everybody you find there to the wedding.' Those slaves went out on the roads and brought in all the people they found, bad and good. And the wedding hall was filled with guests. 8 9 10

"When the king came in to look at the guests, he saw there a man without a wedding garment. 'Friend,' he asked him, 'how did you get in here without a wedding garment?' 11 12

"The man couldn't say a thing. Then the king told the servants, 'Tie him hand and foot, and throw him out into the dark. There he will cry and grind his teeth.' 13

"Many are invited, but few are chosen." 14

· *Taxes*

Then the Pharisees went and plotted to trap Him with a question. They sent their disciples with Herod's men to say to Him: "Teacher, we know You're honest and really teach God's way and don't care what others think, because You don't favor any special persons. Now tell us: What do You think? Is it right to pay a tax to Caesar or not?" 15 16 17

Seeing through their wicked way, Jesus asked, "Why do you test Me, you hypocrites? Show Me the coin with which the tax is paid." 18 19

They brought Him a denarius. "Whose head is this and whose inscription?" He asked them. 20

"Caesar's," they said.

"Give Caesar what is Caesar's," He told them, "and God what is God's." 21

They were surprised to hear this. Then they let Him alone and went away. 22

Matthew

The Dead Live

22:23 On that day some Sadducees, who say the dead don't rise,
24 came to Him with this question: "Teacher, Moses said, *If any-one dies childless, his brother should marry his widow and have*
25 *children for his brother.*[70] Now, there were seven brothers among us. The first married and died, and since he had no
26 children, he left his widow to his brother. The second brother did the same, and so did the third and the rest of the seven.
27-28 Last of all the woman died. Now, when they rise from the dead, which of the seven will be her husband? You know they all married her."

29 "You're wrong," Jesus answered them. "You don't know
30 your Bible or God's power. When the dead rise, men and women
31 don't marry but are like angels in heaven. About the dead
32 rising — didn't you read what God told you: *I am the God of Abraham, the God of Isaac, and the God of Jacob?*[71] He's not the God of the dead but of the living."

33 His teaching amazed the people who heard Him.

Love God and Your Neighbor

34 When the Pharisees heard He had silenced the Sadducees,
35 they got together. One of them, an expert in the Law, tested
36 Him by asking Him, "Teacher, which is the greatest command-ment in the Law?"

37 Jesus answered him, *"Love the Lord your God with all your*
38 *heart, with all your life, and with all your* [72] mind. This is the
39 greatest and most important commandment. The next is like it:
40 *Love your neighbor like yourself.*[61] All the Law and the prophets depend on these two commandments."

David's Son

41 While the Pharisees were still together, Jesus asked them,
42 "What do you think of the promised Savior? Whose Son is He?"

"David's," they answered Him.

43 He asked them, "Then how can David by the Spirit call Him Lord? He says,

44   *The Lord said to my Lord,*
    'Sit at My right
    Till I put Your enemies under Your feet.' [73]

45 Now, if David calls Him Lord, how can He be his Son?"

Nobody could answer Him, and after that nobody dared to ask Him another question.

Beware!

Then Jesus said to the crowd and to His disciples: **23**

"The Bible scholars and the Pharisees sit in Moses' seat. **2** Do everything they tell you, and follow it; but don't do what **3** they do, because they don't do what they say. They tie together **4** heavy loads that are hard to carry and lay them on the shoulders of others, but they won't raise a finger to move them.

"They do everything in order to be seen by others. They **5** make their phylacteries broad and the tassels of their garments long.* They like the places of honor at dinners and the front **6** seats in synagogs, to be greeted in the marketplaces and have **7** people call them rabbi. But don't you let them call you rabbi, **8** because you have only one Teacher, and you are all brothers. And don't call anyone on earth your father; you have only one **9** Father, and He is in heaven. Don't have others call you teachers; **10** you have only one Teacher, and that is Christ. The greatest **11** among you will be one who serves you. If you honor yourself, **12** you will be humbled, but if you humble yourself, you will be honored."

Woe!

"Woe to you Bible scholars and Pharisees, you hypocrites! **13** You lock people out of the kingdom of heaven. You won't come into it yourselves, and when others try to come in, you won't let them. ******

"Woe to you Bible scholars and Pharisees, you hypocrites! **15** You go around lake and land to convert a single person, and when he's converted, you make him twice as fit for hell as you are.

"Woe to you blind guides! You say, 'If anyone swears by **16** the temple, that's nothing. But if anyone swears by the gold in the temple, he must keep his oath.' Blind fools! Which is greater, **17**

* A phylactery was a small leather box fastened by a leather strap on the forehead or on the left arm. In the box were pieces of parchment on which were written the words of Ex. 13:1-10, 11-16; Deut. 6:4-9, 13-21. — An Israelite wore a tassel on each of the four corners of his outer garment. (Num. 15:38-40; Deut. 22:12)

** Our oldest manuscripts do not have v. 14: "Woe to you Bible scholars and Pharisees, you hypocrites! You swallow the widows' houses and then, to cover up, make long prayers. For this you'll be punished all the more." See Mark 12:40; Luke 20:47.

the gold or the temple that made the gold holy? Or again, 'If anyone swears by the altar, that's nothing. But if anyone swears by

19 the gift that's on it, he must keep his oath.' You blind men! Which is greater, the gift or the altar that makes the gift holy?

20 If you swear by the altar, you swear by it and by everything on it.

21 If you swear by the temple, you swear by it and by Him who

22 lives there. And if you swear by heaven, you swear by God's throne and by Him who is sitting on it.

23   "Woe to you Bible scholars and Pharisees, you hypocrites! You give a tenth of mint and dill and cummin but have neglected the more important things of the Law: to be just, merciful, and trustworthy. You should have done the one without neglecting

24 the other. Blind guides! You strain out the gnat but swallow the camel.

25   "Woe to you Bible scholars and Pharisees, you hypocrites! You clean the outside of a cup and of a dish, but inside they're

26 full of greed and uncontrolled lust. You blind Pharisee! First clean the inside of the cup and of the dish in order to make also

27 the outside of it clean. Woe to you Bible scholars and Pharisees, you hypocrites! You're like white-washed graves that look beautiful on the outside but inside are full of dead men's bones and

28 every kind of decay. So on the outside you look good to people, but inside you're full of hypocrisy and crime.

29   "Woe to you Bible scholars and Pharisees, you hypocrites! You build the tombs of the prophets and decorate the graves

30 of the righteous [1] and say, 'If we had lived at the time of our fathers, we wouldn't have helped them murder the prophets.'

31 And so you testify against yourselves that you are the sons of

32 those who murdered the prophets. Go on, finish what your fathers started!

33   "You snakes! Brood of vipers! How can you escape being

34 condemned to hell? That's why I'm sending you men to speak God's Word, men who are wise and know the Bible. Some of them you will kill and crucify. Others you will whip in your synagogs

35 and hunt from town to town, so that all the innocent blood poured on the ground will come on you, from the blood of righteous Abel to the blood of Zechariah, Barachiah's son, whom you mur-

36 dered between the holy place and the altar. I tell you, all this will certainly come on the people of today.

37   "Jerusalem, Jerusalem, you murder the prophets and stone those sent to you! How often I wanted to bring your children

together as a hen gathers her chicks under her wings, but you didn't want to! Now your *house will be left* to you *a deserted place.*[74] 23:38
I tell you, you will not see Me again till you say, '*Blessed is He* 39
who is coming in the Lord's name.' " [64]

Sorrow Ahead!

When Jesus walked out of the temple and was going away, 24
His disciples came to show Him the buildings of the temple.
" "You see all these things?" Jesus asked them. "I tell you the 2
truth: Not a stone will be left on another here but will be torn down."

When He was sitting on the Mount of Olives, His disciples 3
came to Him alone, saying, "Tell us, when will this be and how can we tell when You're coming back and the world will come to an end?"

"Be careful not to let anyone deceive you," Jesus answered 4
them. "Many will come using My name and saying, 'I am Christ' 5
and will deceive many.

"You will hear of wars and rumors of wars. See that you 6
don't get alarmed. It *must happen,*[75] but that's not the end yet.
Nation will fight against nation, and *kingdom against kingdom,*[76] 7
and there will be famines and earthquakes in different places. But 8
all these are only the first pains.*

"Then they will hand you over to those who will make you 9
suffer, and they will kill you, and all nations will hate you on account of My name. Then *many will fall away* [77] and betray 10
one another and hate one another. Many false prophets will arise 11
and lead many people astray. And because there will be more 12
and more wickedness, the love of most people will turn cold. But 13
endure to the end, and you will be saved.

"This good news of the Kingdom must be preached all over 14
the world so that all nations hear the truth, and then the end will come."

Jerusalem Will Be Detroyed

"When you see what the prophet Daniel told about, *the abom-* 15
ination laying waste the land and standing *in the holy place* [78] (anyone who reads this should understand it), then if you're in 16
Judea, flee to the hills. If you're on the roof, don't come down 17

* As in childbirth, sharper pains will follow before the Savior comes in glory.

to get the things in your house. If you're in the field, don't turn back to get your garment.

19   "Woe to the women who in those days are expecting babies
20 or nursing them. Pray that it may not be winter or a Sabbath
21 when you flee. It will be a time of great *misery such as hasn't been from the beginning* of the world *till now* [79] and never will be
22 again. And if that time had not been cut short, nobody would be
23 saved. But that time will be cut short for the sake of those whom He has chosen."

Jesus Is Coming

23   "If anyone tells you then, 'Look, here is Christ!' or, 'There
24 He is!' don't believe it, ¹ because false Christs and false *prophets* will *come and do* great *miracles and wonders* [80] to deceive if
25 possible even those whom God has chosen. You see, I've told
26 you this before it happens. So when you're told, 'There He is in the wilderness,' don't go out; or, 'Here He is in the inner rooms,'
27 don't believe it. The Son of Man will come like the lightning that
28 flashes from the east to the west. — Where the dead body is, there the vultures will gather.

29   "Right after the misery of that time *the sun will turn dark, the moon will stop shining, the stars will be falling from the sky,*
30 and *the powers of heaven* [81] will be shaken. Then the sign announcing the Son of Man will appear in the sky, and then *all the people on earth will mourn* [82] when they see *the Son of Man com-*
31 *ing on the clouds in the sky* [83] with power and great glory. And *with a loud trumpet call* [84] He will send out His angels, and they *will gather* His chosen ones *from the north, south, east, and west, from one end of the sky to the other.*[85]

32   "Learn this lesson from a fig tree: When its branch gets
33 tender and grows leaves, you know summer is near. So also when you see all these things, you know that He is near, at your door.

34   "I tell you the truth: These people will not pass away till all
35 this happens. Heaven and earth will pass away, but what I say will not pass away."

Be Ready!

36   "No one knows about that day or hour, not the angels in heaven, not even the Son, but only the Father.

37   "When the Son of Man comes, it will be like the time of
38 Noah. In the days before the flood, they were eating and drink-

ing, and men and women were marrying till the day *Noah went into the ark*. They learned nothing till *the flood came* [86] and swept them all away. That's how it will be when the Son of Man comes.

"Then there will be two men in the field — one will be taken and the other left. Two women will be grinding at a mill — one will be taken and the other left. [40][41]

"Watch, then, because you don't know which day your Lord is coming. You know if the owner of a house had known what time of the night the burglar was coming, he would have stayed awake and not let anyone break into his house. You, too, get ready, because the Son of Man is coming when you don't expect Him. [42][43][44]

"Now, who is the faithful and sensible slave whom the Master has put in charge of his servants to give them their food at the right time? Happy is that slave whom his master finds doing this when he comes. I tell you, he will certainly put him in charge of all his property. But if that slave is wicked and says to himself, 'My master is staying a long time,' [1] and starts to beat his fellow slaves and eats and drinks with the drunkards, the master of that slave will come one day when he's not expecting him and at a time he doesn't know and will cut him in pieces and put him with the hypocrites. There they will cry and grind their teeth." [45][46][47][48][49][50][51]

The Bridegroom Is Coming

"Then the kingdom of heaven will be like ten girls who took their lamps and went out to meet the bridegroom. Five of them were foolish, and five were wise. The foolish girls brought their lamps, but they took no extra oil. The wise took flasks of oil with their lamps. But the bridegroom delayed, and so they all dozed off to sleep. [25][2][3][4][5]

"At midnight there was a shout, 'Here's the bridegroom! Come out and meet him!' Then all those girls woke up and got their lamps ready. [6][7]

"But the foolish asked the wise, 'Give us some of your oil. Our lamps are going out.' [8]

"The wise girls answered, 'There will never be enough for us and for you. Better go to the dealers and buy some for your-selves.' [9]

"While they were away buying it, the bridegroom came, and [10] the girls who were ready went with him to the wedding, and the door was shut.

25:11 "Later the other girls also came and said, 'Lord, lord, open the door for us!'

12 " 'I tell you the truth,' he answered them, 'I don't know you.'

13 "Keep awake, then, because you don't know the day or the hour."

Three Kinds of Workers

14 "It's like a man going on a trip. He called his slaves and put

15 his money in their hands. He gave one man $10,000,* another $4,000, and another $2,000, each according to his ability. Then he left.

16 "The one who got $10,000 immediately went and put it

17 into business and made another $10,000. The one who had

18 $4,000 did the same and made another $4,000. But the one who got $2,000 went and dug a hole in the ground and hid his master's money.

19 "After a long time the master of those slaves came and had

20 them give an account. The one who got $10,000 came and brought another $10,000. 'Master,' he said, 'you let me have $10,000. See, I've made another $10,000.'

21 " 'Well done, good and faithful slave!' his master answered him. 'You proved you could be trusted with a little. I will put you in charge of something big. Come and be happy with your master.'

22 "The one who got $4,000 came and said, 'Master, you let me have $4,000. See, I've made another $4,000.'

23 " 'Well done, good and faithful slave!' his master answered him. 'You proved you could be trusted with a little. I will put you in charge of something big. Come and be happy with your master.'

24 "Then came also the one who got $2,000. 'Master,' he said, 'I found out you're a hard man. You get grain where you didn't

25 sow, and you gather where you didn't scatter. I was afraid, so I went and hid your $2,000 in the ground. There's your money!'

26 " 'You wicked and lazy slave!' his master answered him. 'You knew I get grain where I didn't sow and gather where

27 I didn't scatter? Then you should have invested my money with

* It is hard to estimate the real value of a "talent." It is here taken to be equal to $2,000.

the bankers, and when I came back, I could have gotten my money back with interest. Take the $2,000 away from him, and give it to the one who has $10,000. Whoever has anything will receive, and so he will have more and more. And from him who doesn't have what he should have, even what he has will be taken away. Throw this good-for-nothing slave out into the dark where there will be crying and grinding of teeth.' "

Jesus Will Judge the World

"When the Son of man *comes* in His glory *and all the* angels *with Him,*[87] then He will sit on His throne of glory. And all nations will be gathered before Him, and He will separate them from one another, as a shepherd separates the sheep from the goats, and He will have the sheep stand at His right but the goats at His left.

"Then the King will say to those at His right, 'Come, you whom My Father blessed, inherit the kingdom prepared for you from the time the world was made. I was hungry, and you gave Me something to eat; I was thirsty, and you gave Me a drink; I was a stranger, and you took Me into your homes; naked, and you gave Me something to wear; sick, and you looked after Me; in prison, and you visited Me.'

"Then the righteous will ask Him, 'Lord, when did we see You hungry and feed You, or thirsty and give You a drink? When did we see You a stranger and take You into our homes, or naked and give You something to wear? When did we see You sick or in prison and visit You?'

"And the King will answer them, 'Let Me assure you, anything you did for one of My brothers here, however humble, you did for Me.'

"Then He will say to those at His left, 'Go away from Me, you cursed ones, into the everlasting fire prepared for the devil and his angels. I was hungry, and you gave Me nothing to eat; thirsty, and you didn't give Me a drink; a stranger, and you didn't take Me into your homes; naked, and you didn't give Me anything to wear; sick and in prison, and you didn't look after Me.'

"Then they, too, will ask, 'Lord, when did we see You hungry or thirsty or a stranger or naked or sick or in prison and didn't help you?'

"Then He will answer them, 'I tell you the truth, anything you didn't do for one of these, however humble, you didn't do for Me.'

46 "Then *these* will go away *to everlasting* punishment, but the righteous *to everlasting life."* [88]

The Plot

26 When Jesus finished saying all this, He told His disciples,
2 "You know that in two days the Passover will be celebrated, and the Son of Man will be handed over to be crucified."

3 Then the ruling priests and the elders of the people met in
4 the palace of the high priest, whose name was Caiaphas. They
5 plotted by some trick to arrest Jesus and kill Him. But they said, "Not in the festival crowd, or there may be a riot among the people."

Mary Anoints Jesus

6 Jesus came to Bethany and went into the home of Simon
7 the leper. There a woman came to Him with an alabaster jar of expensive perfume, and she poured it on His head while He was lying at the table.

8 The disciples saw it and didn't like it. "Why should there be
9 such a waste?" they asked. "This could have been sold for a big sum and the money given to the poor."

10 Knowing what was going on, Jesus asked them, "Why do you
11 trouble the woman? She has done a beautiful thing to Me. The poor you always have with you, but you will not always have Me.
12 She poured this perfume on My body to prepare Me for My
13 burial. I tell you, wherever this good news is preached in the whole world, certainly what she has done will also be told in memory of her."

Judas Plans to Betray Jesus

14 Then one of the twelve, called Judas, the man from Kerioth,
15 went to the high priests. "What will you give me?" he asked. "I will betray Him to you."

16 They *weighed out thirty shekels* * *of silver* [89] for him. And from then on he was looking for a chance to betray Him.

* A silver shekel weighed as much as our half dollar.

The Passover

On the first of the Passover days of bread without yeast the 26:17
disciples came to Jesus. "Where do You want us to get things
ready for You to eat the Passover?" they asked.

"Go into the city," He said, "to a certain man and tell him: 18
'The Teacher says, "My time is near. I'm going to celebrate the
Passover with My disciples at your house." ' "

The disciples did as Jesus directed them and got the Passover 19
ready.

In the evening He lay down with the twelve for the supper. 20

"Is It I?"

While they were eating, He said: "I tell you the truth: One of 21
you is going to betray Me!"

Feeling deeply hurt, they asked Him one by one, "You 22
don't mean me, Lord?"

"One who is dipping into the bowl with Me will betray Me!" 23
He answered. "The Son of Man is going away as it is written 24
about Him, but woe to that man who betrays the Son of Man!
It would be better for that man if he had never been born."

"You don't mean me, Master?" asked Judas, who was going 25
to betray Him.

"I do!" He told him.

The Lord's Supper

While they were eating, Jesus took bread and blessed it. He 26
broke it and gave it to the disciples and said, "Take and eat.
This is My body."

Then He took a cup and gave thanks. He gave it to them, 27
saying, "Drink of it, all of you. This is My *blood of the cov-* 28
enant,[90] poured out for all to forgive their sins.

"I tell you, I will not drink again of this product of the vine 29
till that day when I drink it with you in a new way in My
Father's kingdom."

Then they sang a hymn.* 30

"You Will Deny Me"

They started out for the Mount of Olives. 30

Then Jesus said to them, "Tonight you will all turn against 31
Me. It is written: I will *strike down the Shepherd, and the sheep*

* Perhaps Psalms 115—118.

26:32 *of the flock will be scattered.*[91] But after I have risen, I will go ahead of you to Galilee."

33 "Even if they all turn against You," Peter answered Him, "I'll never turn against You."

34 "I tell you the truth," Jesus told him, "tonight, before the rooster crows, you will deny Me three times."

35 "Even if I have to die with You," Peter told Him, "I'll never deny You!" All the other disciples said the same thing.

Gethsemane

36 Then Jesus went with the disciples to a place called Gethsemane and told them, "Sit down here while I go over there and pray."

37 Taking Peter and Zebedee's two sons with Him, He started
38 to feel sad and troubled. Then He said to them, *"I am so full of sorrow* [92] I am almost dying. Stay here and keep awake with Me."

39 Going ahead a little, He bowed down with His face on the ground and prayed, "My Father, if it is possible, let this cup pass away from Me. But let it not be as I want it but as You want it."

40 Coming to the disciples, He finds them asleep. He says to
41 Peter, "So you couldn't keep awake with Me one hour! Stay awake and pray that you may not be tempted. The spirit is willing, but the flesh is weak."

42 Then He went away a second time and prayed, "My Father, if this cannot pass by without My drinking it, Your will be done."

43 He came again and found them asleep. They couldn't keep their eyes open.

44 Leaving them again, He went and prayed the same prayer
45 a third time. Then He came to the disciples. "Are you going to sleep on now and rest?" He asked them. "Now the time has come, and the Son of Man will be betrayed into the hands of
46 sinners. Get up, let us go. Here comes the man to betray Me!"

The Arrest

47 While He was still talking, there came Judas, one of the twelve, and with him a large crowd with swords and clubs, from
48 the ruling priests and elders of the people. The traitor had given them a signal. "The One I kiss," he said, "is the man. Grab Him."

Then Judas quickly stepped up to Jesus and said, "Greetings, Master!" and kissed Him.

"Friend, what are you here for?" Jesus asked him. 50

Then the others came forward, took hold of Jesus, and arrested Him. One of the men with Jesus reached for his sword 51 and drew it. He struck the high priest's slave and cut off his ear. Then Jesus told him, "Put your sword back in its place. 52 All who take the sword must die by the sword. Or do you think 53 I couldn't call on My Father to send right now more than seventy thousand angels to help Me? How, then, could the 54 Bible be true when it says this must happen?"

Then Jesus said to the crowd, "You came out to arrest Me 55 with swords and clubs as if I were a robber! Day after day I sat and taught in the temple, and you didn't arrest Me. But all this 56 has happened so that what the prophets have written would come true."

Then all the disciples left Him and ran away.

The First Trial Before the Jewish Court

Those who arrested Jesus took Him to Caiaphas, the high 57 priest, where the Bible scholars and the elders had been called together. Peter followed Him at a distance till he came to the 58 high priest's courtyard. Going inside, he sat with the attendants to see how this would end.

The ruling priests and the whole Jewish court tried to get 59 false testimony against Jesus in order to kill Him but didn't find 60 any, although many came forward to give false testimony. At last two men came forward, saying, "He said, 'I can tear down God's 61 temple and build it in three days.'"

The high priest got up and asked Him, "Don't You have any- 62 thing to say to this? What are these men testifying against You?"

But Jesus was silent. 63

Then the high priest said to Him, "Swear by the living God, and tell us, are You the promised Savior, the Son of God?"

"I am," Jesus answered him. "But I tell you, from now on 64 you will all see *the Son of Man sitting at the right hand* of power and *coming on the clouds of heaven.*" 93

Then the high priest tore his robes. "He has blasphemed!" 65 he declared. "Why do we need any more witnesses? You just heard the blasphemy. What's your verdict?" 66

"He must die!" they answered.

Then they spit in His face, struck Him with their fists, and
68 some slapped Him, ¹ saying, "Prophesy, You Christ, and tell us:
Who hit You?"

Peter Denies Jesus

69   Peter was sitting out in the courtyard. A maid came to him,
saying, "You, too, were with Jesus, the Galilean."

70   But he denied it in front of all of them: "I don't know what
you're talking about."

71   As he went out to the entrance, another maid saw him.
"He was with Jesus from Nazareth," she told those who were there.

72   Again Peter denied, and he swore, "I don't know the Man!"

73   After a little while the men who were standing there came
and told Peter, "Sure, you're one of them. Anyone can tell by
the way you talk."

74   Then he started to curse and swear, "I don't know the Man!"

75 Just then the rooster crowed, and Peter remembered Jesus saying,
"Before the rooster crows, you will deny Me three times." And
he went outside and cried bitterly.

The End of Judas

27   In the morning all the ruling priests and the elders of the
2 people decided to kill Jesus. They bound Him, led Him away,
and handed Him over to Pilate, the governor.

3   When Judas, who betrayed Him, saw that Jesus was condemned, he felt sorry and brought the thirty shekels of silver back
4 to the high priests and elders. "I have sinned," he said. "I have
betrayed innocent blood."

"What do we care about that?" they asked. "See to it
yourself."

5   Then he threw the money into the temple and left. He went
away and hanged himself.

6   The high priests took the money. "It isn't right to put this
7 into the temple treasury," they said; "it's blood money." So they
decided to buy with it the potter's field for the burial of strangers.

8 That's why that field has ever since been called the Field of Blood.

9 Then what the prophet Jeremiah said came true: *I took the thirty
shekels of silver, the price of Him on whom some* men of Israel
10 *set a price,* ¹ *and I gave them for the potter's field, as the Lord
directed me.*[94]

Before Pilate

Jesus stood before the governor. "Are You the King of the   27:11
Jews?" the governor asked Him.

"Yes," Jesus answered.

While the ruling priests and elders were accusing Him, He   12
said nothing. Then Pilate asked Him, "Don't You hear how many   13
accusations they are bringing against You?"

But Jesus didn't answer him in regard to anything that was   14
said, so that the governor was very much surprised.

Barabbas

Now, at every festival the governor used to free one prisoner   15
whom the crowd wanted. Just then there was a well-known prisoner   16
by the name of Barabbas. When the people had gathered, Pilate   17
asked them, "Whom do you want me to set free for you, Barabbas
or Jesus, who is called Christ?" He knew they had handed Jesus   18
over to him because they were jealous.

While he was sitting on the judge's seat, his wife sent someone   19
to tell him, "Let that righteous Man alone. I suffered much in
a dream last night on account of Him."

But the ruling priests and elders persuaded the people to ask   20
for Barabbas and kill Jesus.

"Which of the two," the governor asked them, "do you want   21
me to set free for you?"

They said, "Barabbas."

"Then what should I do with Jesus, who is called Christ?"   22
Pilate asked them.

"He must be crucified!" all of them said.

"Why, what wrong has He done?" he asked.   23

But they kept yelling all the louder, "He must be crucified!"

When he saw he wasn't getting anywhere, but a riot was break-   24
ing out instead, Pilate took water and washed his hands before
the crowd. "I am innocent of this One's blood," he said. "See
to it yourselves!"

And all the people answered, "His blood be on us and on   25
our children."

Then he freed Barabbas for them, but Jesus he scourged and   26
handed over to be crucified.

"Hail, King!"

27:27   Then the governor's soldiers took Jesus into the governor's palace and gathered the whole troop of soldiers around Him.
28-29 They took off His clothes and put a scarlet cloak on Him. They twisted some thorns into a crown, placed it on His head, and put a stick in His right hand. Then they knelt before Him and mocked
30   Him, saying, "Hail, King of the Jews!" They spit on Him, took the stick, and hit Him on the head.

"They Crucified Him"

31   After mocking Him, they took off the cloak and put His own clothes on Him. Then they took Him away to crucify Him.

32   Going out, they found a man from Cyrene by the name of Simon. They forced him to carry His cross.

33   They came to a place called Golgotha, which means Skull
34 Place. *They offered Him a drink* of wine, mixed with *gall*,[95] but
35 when He tasted it, He refused to drink it. They crucified Him. And *they divided His clothes among them by throwing lots*.[96]
36-37 Then they sat down there and kept watch over Him. They put above His head a notice stating why He was being punished.
38   It read: THIS IS JESUS, THE KING OF THE JEWS. | Then they crucified two robbers with Him, one at His right and the other at His left.

39-40   Those who passed by abused Him, *shaking their heads* [97] | and saying, "You tear down the temple and build it in three days — save Yourself, if You are God's Son, and come down from
41 the cross." The ruling priests, with the Bible scholars and elders, mocked Him in the same way, saying, "He saved others — but
42 He cannot save Himself. He's King of Israel — He should come
43 down from the cross now, and we'll believe Him. *He trusts God — God deliver Him now, seeing He delights in Him.*[98] He said,
44 'I am God's Son.' " In the same way also the robbers crucified with Him insulted Him.

Jesus Dies

45   At twelve o'clock darkness came over the whole country and
46 lasted until three in the afternoon. About three o'clock Jesus called out loud, *"Eli, Eli, lema, sabachthani?"* [99] which means, "My
47 God, My God, why did You forsake Me?" Hearing Him some
48 of those standing there said, "He's calling Elijah." And just then

one of the men ran, took a sponge, soaked it in *sour wine,* put it on a stick, and *gave Him a drink.*[95] The others' said, "Let's see if Elijah comes to save Him." 27:49

But Jesus called out loud again and gave up His spirit. Just then the curtain in the temple was torn in two from top to bottom, the earth was shaken, the rocks were split, the graves were opened, and many bodies of the holy people asleep in death were brought back to life; they came out of the graves and after He had risen went into the holy city, where many saw them. Now, when the captain and those watching Jesus with him saw the earthquake and the other things happening, they were terrified. "He certainly was the Son of God," they said. 50-51 52 53 54

There were many women watching *from a distance.*[100] They had followed Jesus from Galilee to help Him. Among them were Mary from Magdala and Mary, the mother of James and Joseph, and the mother of Zebedee's sons. 55 56

Jesus Is Buried

In the evening there came a rich man from Arimathea by the name of Joseph, who had also become a disciple of Jesus. He went to Pilate and asked for Jesus' body. Then Pilate ordered it given to him. 57 58

Joseph took the body, wrapped it in some clean linen cloth, and laid it in his own unused grave that he had cut in the rock. After rolling a big stone against the door of the grave, he went away. Mary from Magdala and the other Mary were there, sitting opposite the grave. 59 60 61

The Guard

The next day — the Saturday after the day of preparation — the ruling priests and Pharisees met with Pilate. "Sir," they said, "we remember how that deceiver said while He was still alive, 'On the third day I will rise.' Now, order the grave to be made secure till the third day, or His disciples may come and steal Him and tell the people, 'He rose from the dead.' Then the last deception will be worse than the first." 62 63 64

"Take a guard," Pilate told them; "go and make it as secure as you know how." 65

So they went and secured the grave by sealing the stone and setting the guard. 66

Jesus Rises

28 After the Sabbath, as the first day of the week was dawning, Mary from Magdala and the other Mary went to look at the grave.

2 There was a great earthquake. The Lord's angel came down **3** from heaven, went and rolled the stone away and sat on it. He was **4** as bright as lightning, and his clothes were as white as snow. The guards were so afraid of him they shook and became like dead men.

5 "Don't be afraid," the angel said to the women. "I know **6** you're looking for Jesus, who was crucified. He is not here. He has risen as He said. Come, see the place where He was lying. **7** And go quickly, tell His disciples, 'He has risen from the dead. You know, He is going ahead of you to Galilee. There you will see Him.' Now, I have told you."

8 They hurried away from the grave with fear and great joy and ran to tell His disciples.

9 And there — Jesus met them and said, "Good morning!" They went up to Him, took hold of His feet, and worshiped Him. **10** Then Jesus said to them, "Don't be afraid. Go, tell My brothers to go to Galilee, and there they will see Me."

The Guards

11 While the women were on their way, some of the guards went into the city and told the high priests everything that happened. **12** These met with the elders and agreed on a plan. They gave **13** the soldiers a large sum of money ¹ and told them, "Say, 'His dis- **14** ciples came at night and stole Him while we were sleeping.' And if this comes to a hearing before the governor, we'll persuade him and see that you have nothing to worry about."

15 They took the money and did as they were told. And that story has been spread among the Jews to this day.

"Go!"

16 The eleven disciples went to the mountain in Galilee where **17** Jesus had told them to go. When they saw Him, they worshiped Him, but some doubted.

18 Coming nearer, Jesus spoke to them. "I have been given all **19** power in heaven and on earth," He said. "Go and make disciples of all people: Baptize them into the name of the Father, the Son, **20** and the Holy Spirit, ¹ and teach them to do everything I have commanded you. And remember, I am with you always till the end of the world."

OLD TESTAMENT REFERENCES

1. Is. 7:14; 8:8, 10
2. Micah 5:2, 4; 2 Sam. 5:2
3. Is. 60:6; Ps. 72:10, 15
4. Hos. 11:1
5. Jer. 31:15
6. Is. 40:3
7. Ps. 2:7; Is. 42:1
8. Deut. 8:3
9. Ps. 91:11-12
10. Deut. 6:16
11. Deut. 6:13
12. Is. 9:1-2
13. Is. 57:15
14. Is. 61:2
15. Ps. 37:11
16. 2 Sam. 22:26; Ps. 18:25
17. Ps. 24:4; 51:10; 73:1
18. Ex. 20:13; Deut. 5:17
19. Ex. 20:14; Deut. 5:18
20. Deut. 24:1
21. Lev. 19:12
22. Num. 30:2; Deut. 23:21; Ps. 50:14
23. Is. 66:1
24. Ps. 48:2
25. Ex. 21:24; Lev. 24:20; Deut. 19:21
26. Lev. 19:18
27. Deut. 18:13
28. 2 Kings 4:33; Is. 26:20
29. Jer. 14:14; 27:15
30. Ps. 6:8
31. Lev. 13:7, 49
32. Mal. 1:11
33. Is. 53:4
34. Hos. 6:6
35. Num. 27:17; 1 Kings 22:17; Ezek. 34:5
36. Micah 7:6
37. Is. 29:18; 35:5; 61:1
38. Ex. 23:20
39. Is. 14:13, 15
40. Jer. 6:16
41. Lev. 24:5-8; 1 Sam. 21:6
42. Hos. 6:6
43. Is. 41:8-9; 42:1-4; Hab. 1:4
44. Jonah 1:17
45. Is. 6:9-10
46. Ps. 104:12; Ezek. 17:23; 31:6
47. Ps. 78:2
48. Zeph. 1:3; Job 12:16
49. Dan. 12:3
50. Ex. 20:12; Deut. 5:16
51. Ex. 21:17; Lev. 20:9
52. Is. 29:13
53. Ps. 62:12; Prov. 24:12
54. Ps. 2:7; Is. 42:1; Deut. 18:15
55. Mal. 4:5-6
56. Deut. 19:15
57. Gen. 1:27; 5:2
58. Gen. 2:24
59. Deut. 24:1
60. Ex. 20:12-16; Deut. 5:16-20
61. Lev. 19:18
62. Gen. 18:14; Job 42:2; Zech. 8:6
63. Is. 62:11; Zech. 9:9
64. Ps. 118:25-26
65. Is. 56:7
66. Jer. 7:11
67. Ps. 8:2
68. Is. 5:1-2
69. Ps. 118:22-23
70. Gen. 38:8; Deut. 25:5-6
71. Ex. 3:6
72. Deut. 6:5
73. Ps. 110:1
74. Jer. 12:7; 22:5
75. Dan. 2:28
76. Is. 19:2; 2 Chron. 15:6
77. Dan. 11:41
78. Dan. 9:27; 11:31; 12:11
79. Dan. 12:1
80. Deut. 13:1
81. Is. 13:10; 34:4
82. Zech. 12:10, 12
83. Dan. 7:13
84. Is. 27:13
85. Deut. 30:4; Zech. 2:6
86. Gen. 7:6-7
87. Zech. 14:5
88. Dan. 12:2
89. Zech. 11:12
90. Ex. 24:8; Jer. 31:32; Zech. 9:11
91. Zech. 13:7
92. Ps. 42:5; 43:5
93. Ps. 110:1; Dan. 7:13
94. Zech. 11:12-13; Jer. 32:6-9
95. Ps. 69:21
96. Ps. 22:18
97. Ps. 109:25
98. Ps. 22:8
99. Ps. 22:1
100. Ps. 38:11

THE GOOD NEWS

as it was told by

MARK

1 BEGINNING THE GOOD NEWS about Jesus Christ, God's Son:

2   It is written in the prophet Isaiah:

I will send My messenger ahead of You to prepare the way [1]
for You.

3   *Someone will be calling in the wilderness:*
"Prepare the way for the Lord,
Make the paths straight for Him." [2]

4   So John the Baptizer came into the wilderness, preaching that
5 people repent and be baptized to have their sins forgiven. All
Judea and all the people of Jerusalem were coming out to him.
As they confessed their sins, he baptized them in the Jordan River.

6   John was dressed in camel's hair with a leather belt around
his waist. And he lived on grasshoppers and wild honey.

7   He preached: "The One who is mightier than I is coming after
me. I'm not good enough to bend down and untie His shoe
8 straps. I have baptized you with water. He will baptize you with
the Holy Spirit."

John Baptizes Jesus

9   It was in those days that Jesus came from Nazareth in Galilee
10 and was baptized by John in the Jordan. Just as He stepped out
of the water, He saw heaven torn open and the Spirit coming
11 down as a dove on Him. And a voice from heaven said, "You
are *My Son,* whom I love. *I am delighted* [3] with You."

The Devil Tempts Jesus

12-13   Then the Spirit drove Him out into the wilderness, and He
was in the wilderness for forty days while the devil tempted Him.
He was there with the wild animals. And the angels served Him.

"Come with Me"

After John had been put in prison, Jesus went to Galilee and   1:14
preached God's good news: "The time has come, and God's king-   15
dom is here. Repent, and believe the good news."

As He was walking along the Lake of Galilee, He saw Simon   16
and Simon's brother Andrew (who were fishermen) casting a net
into the lake. "Come, follow Me," Jesus told them, "and I will   17
make you fishers of men." Immediately they left their nets and   18
went with Him.

Going on a little farther, He saw James, Zebedee's son, and his   19
brother John in their boat mending the nets. Then He called them,   20
and they left their father Zebedee with the hired men in the boat
and followed Him.

Jesus Drives Out a Devil

Then they went to Capernaum. The next Sabbath Jesus went   21
into the synagog and began to teach. His teaching amazed the   22
people because He taught them as one who had authority and not
like the Bible scholars.

There was in their synagog just then a man with an unclean   23
spirit. And he screamed, "Leave us alone, Jesus from Nazareth!   24
You've come to destroy us! I know who You are — God's Holy
One."

Jesus talked sharply to him: "Be quiet, and come out of him."   25
The unclean spirit threw the man into convulsions and with a   26
loud shriek came out of him.

They were all so amazed they argued with one another: "What   27
is this? A new teaching! With authority! He gives orders to the
unclean spirits, and they obey Him!"

The news about Him quickly spread everywhere in all the   28
surrounding country of Galilee.

Peter's Mother-in-Law

Right after leaving the synagog, they went into the home of   29
Simon and Andrew. James and John went with them. ¹ Simon's   30
mother-in-law was down in bed with a fever, and so the first thing
they did was to tell Him about her. He went to her, took her hand,   31
and helped her get up. The fever left her, and she waited on them.

In the evening when the sun had gone down, the people   32
brought to Him all the sick and those plagued by devils. The   33

whole town had gathered at His door. He healed many who were suffering from various sicknesses and drove out many devils and wouldn't let the devils talk, because they knew Him.

Preaching in Galilee

35   In the morning, long before daylight, Jesus got up and went
36 out to a lonely place, and there He prayed. Simon and those who
37 were with him searched for Jesus. When they found Him, they told Him, "Everybody's looking for You."

38   "Let us go somewhere else," He told them, "to the small towns that are near, so that I may preach there too. That's why I've come."

39   He went and preached in their synagogs everywhere in Galilee and drove out the devils.

Jesus Heals a Leper

40   A leper came to Him and begged Him on his knees, "If You want to, You can make me clean."

41   Jesus felt sorry for him, stretched out His hand, and touched
42 him. "I want to," He said. "Be clean!" [1] Immediately the leprosy left him, and he was made clean.

43-44   Jesus sent him away with a stern warning: "Be careful not to say anything to anyone, but go, *let the priest examine* [4] you, and for your cleansing offer the sacrifices Moses ordered, to show them you're well."

45   But when he had left, he talked so much and spread the news till Jesus could no longer openly go into a town. He stayed out in lonely places, and still the people kept coming to Him from everywhere.

Jesus Forgives Sins

2   Some days later Jesus came again to Capernaum, and people
2 heard, "He's home." So many gathered that there was no room even in front of the door. He was speaking the Word to them.

3   Then some people came and brought Him a paralyzed man,
4 carried by four men. But when they couldn't bring him to Jesus on account of the crowd, they opened up the roof over the place where Jesus was. Through the opening they had dug they let down the bed on which the paralytic was lying.

Seeing their faith, Jesus said to the paralytic, "Son, your sins are forgiven."

There were some Bible scholars sitting there, and they questioned within themselves: "Why does He say this? He's blaspheming. Who but God alone can forgive sins?"

Immediately Jesus knew in His spirit what they were thinking. "Why do you have these thoughts in your hearts?" He asked them. "Is it easier to say to this paralyzed man, 'Your sins are forgiven,' or to say, 'Get up, take your bed, and walk'? I want you to know the Son of Man has power on earth to forgive sins" — then He said to the paralyzed man, "I tell you, get up, take your bed, and go home."

The man got up, immediately took his bed, and walked out before all of them, so that all were amazed and praised God. "Never have we seen anything like this," they said.

Matthew

Again Jesus went out along the lake. All the people were coming to Him, and He taught them.

As He passed by, He saw Levi, the son of Alphaeus, sitting in the tax office. "Come with Me," He told him. He got up and went with Him.

As Jesus was lying down to eat at his home, many tax collectors and sinners were eating with Jesus and His disciples, because there were many who followed Him. When the Bible scholars, who were Pharisees, saw Him eating with sinners and tax collectors, they asked His disciples, "Why does He eat with tax collectors and sinners?"

Jesus heard them and answered them: "Those who are healthy don't need a doctor, but the sick. I didn't come to call righteous people but sinners."

The Bridegroom

John's disciples and the Pharisees, who were fasting, came to Jesus. "John's disciples and the disciples of the Pharisees fast," they told Him. "Why don't Your disciples fast?"

Jesus asked them, "Can the bridegroom's friends fast while the bridegroom is with them? As long as they have the bridegroom with them, they can't fast. The time will come when the bridegroom will be taken away from them, and on that day they'll fast.

"Nobody sews a piece of new cloth on an old garment. If you do, the new patch will tear away some of the old cloth, and the
22 hole will get worse. Nobody pours new wine into old wineskins. If you do, the wine will burst the skins, and the wine and the skins will be lost. Yes, new wine has to be poured into fresh skins."

Lord of the Sabbath

23 Jesus was going through the grainfields on a Sabbath. As the disciples walked along, they were picking the heads of grain.

24 The Pharisees asked Him, "Look, why are they doing something they shouldn't do on a day of rest?"

25 "Haven't you ever read what David did," Jesus asked them,
26 "when he and his men were in need and got hungry — how he went into God's house when Abiathar was high priest, and he ate the *loaves laid before God*,[5] which only the priests had the right to eat? And he gave his men some too."

27 Then He added, "The Sabbath was made for man, not man
28 for the Sabbath. The Son of Man is Lord also of the Sabbath."

The Shriveled Hand

3 He went again into a synagog, and there was a man with
2 a shriveled hand. Some men were watching Jesus to see if He would heal him on a Sabbath; they wanted to accuse Him of something.

3 "Get up," He told the man with the shriveled hand, "and
4 come forward." Then He asked them, "Is it right on a day of rest to do good or to do evil, to save a life or to kill?"

5 But they were silent. Looking around at them, He felt angry as well as sorry because their minds were closed. Then He told the man, "Stretch out your hand." He stretched it out, and his hand was made healthy again.

6 But the Pharisees left and immediately started plotting with Herod's men how to kill Him.

Many Are Healed

7 Jesus went away with His disciples to the lake. A big crowd
8 from Galilee followed Him; and also from Judea, Jerusalem, Idumea, the other side of the Jordan, and the neighborhood of Tyre and Sidon there were many people who heard about everything He was doing and came to Him. To keep the crowd from
9

crushing Him He told His disciples to have a small boat ready for
Him. He healed many so that all who had diseases rushed up 3:10
to Him in order to touch Him. Whenever the unclean spirits saw 11
Him, they would fall down before Him and yell, "You're God's
Son!" But He strictly ordered them not to tell who He was. 12

Twelve Apostles

He went up the hill and called those whom He wanted, and 13
they came to Him. He appointed twelve to be with Him and be 14
sent out by Him to preach ¹ and have power to drive out devils. 15

He appointed the twelve and gave Simon the name Peter; 16
James, Zebedee's son, and John, the brother of James — He also 17
gave these the name Boanerges, which means "thunderbolts";
¹ Andrew, Philip, Bartholomew, Matthew, and Thomas; James, the 18
son of Alphaeus, and Thaddaeus; Simon the Zealot; ¹ and Judas, 19
the man from Kerioth, who betrayed Him.

Power over the Devil

Then Jesus came home. Again such a crowd gathered that 19-20
Jesus and those with Him couldn't eat. When His family heard 21
about it, they went to take charge of Him, because they were saying, "He's out of His mind!"

The men trained in the Bible who had come down from Jeru- 22
salem said, "Beelzebul is in Him," and, "The ruler of the devils
helps Him drive out the devils."

He called them to Him and pictured it to them in this way: 23
"How can the devil drive out the devil? If one part of a kingdom 24
fights another, that kingdom can't stand. And if one part of 25
a home fights against the other, it can never stand. And so if the 26
devil rebels and fights against himself, he can't stand, but his
end has come.

"Nobody can go into a strong man's house and take away his 27
goods without first tying up the strong man. After that he will
rob his house.

"I tell you the truth: Anything that people do will be forgiven, 28
their sins and their slanders, though they slander ever so much.
But anyone who slanders the Holy Spirit will never be forgiven. 29
Yes, he is guilty of an everlasting sin." ¹ He said this because they 30
had said, "The Spirit in Him is unclean."

The Mother and Brothers of Jesus

3:31 His mother and His brothers came. They stood outside and
32 sent someone to Him to ask Him to come out. The crowd sitting around Jesus told Him, "Your mother and Your brothers are outside looking for You."

33-34 "Who are My mother and My brothers?" He asked them. Then looking around at those who sat in a circle around Him, He said,
35 "Here are My mother and My brothers. If you do what God wants, you are My brother and sister and mother."

The Sower

4 Again Jesus began to teach by the lake. The crowd that gathered around Him was so very big that He stepped into a boat and sat in it on the lake, while all the people were on the shore,
2 facing the lake. Then He used parables to teach them many things.
3, 2, 3 "Listen!" He said as He taught them. "A sower went out to
4 sow. As he was sowing, some seed fell along the road, and the
5 birds came and ate it. Some seed fell on rocky ground, where it didn't have much soil. Because the soil wasn't deep, the seed
6 came up quickly. When the sun rose, it was scorched, and because
7 it had not taken root, it withered. Some seed fell among thorns.
8 The thorns grew up and choked it, and it produced no grain. ¹ But some seed fell on good ground. It came up, grew, and produced grain, thirty, sixty, and a hundred times as much as was sown."
9 He added, "You have ears to hear; then listen."
10 When He was alone, the twelve and the others around Him asked Him about the parables.
11 "You are given the privilege of knowing the secret of God's kingdom," He answered them, "but to those on the outside every-
12 thing comes in parables ¹ *that they may see and yet not see, hear and yet not understand, and so may never turn to Me and let Me forgive them.*⁶
13 "You don't understand this parable," He said to them. "Then how will you understand any parables?
14-15 "The sower sows the Word. And these are the ones along the road where the Word is sown: as soon as they hear it, the devil
16 comes and takes away the Word that was sown into them. It is the same with those in whom the seed falls on rocky ground.
17 As soon as they hear the Word, they welcome it with joy, ¹ but it doesn't take root in them. They believe for a while. But when the Word brings them trouble or persecution, they immediately

fall away. ' In others the seed falls among thorns. They hear the
Word, ' but the worries of the world, the deceitful pleasure of
riches, and the desires for other things come in and choke the
Word, and it can't produce anything. The ones in whom the seed
falls on good ground are those who continue to hear the Word,
welcome it, and go on producing good things, thirty, sixty, and
a hundred times as much as was sown.

"Do you get out a lamp," He asked them, "to put it under
a bucket or under a bed? Shouldn't it be put on a lampstand?
Something is secret only to be told, and hidden only to come to
light. If you have ears to hear, listen!

23

"Be careful what you hear!" He told them. "The measure you
measure with will be used for you. Yes, you will get even more.
' If you have something, you will be given more. But if you don't
have what you should have, even what you have will be taken
away from you."

Growing by Itself

"God's kingdom," He said, "is like this: A man will sow seed
on the ground. He will sleep through the night and get up for
the day, and the seed will come up and grow, he doesn't know how.
The ground by itself produces grain, first the green blade, then
the head, then the full wheat in the head. When the grain is
ready, he *swings the sickle, because it is time to cut the grain.*" [7]

The Mustard Seed

"What should we say God's kingdom is like," He asked, "or
how should we picture it? It's like a mustard seed, which when
sown on the ground is the smallest of all the seeds on earth. But
when it's sown, it comes up and becomes the largest of all the
garden plants. It grows such large branches that *the birds in
the air* can *make nests in its shade.*" [8]

He used many parables like these to speak the Word as they
were able to hear it. He wouldn't speak to them without a parable. But when He was alone with His disciples, He would
explain everything to them.

Wind and Water Obey Him

In the evening of that day Jesus said to His disciples, "Let us
cross over to the other side."

Leaving the crowd behind, they took Jesus, just as He was, with them in the boat. There were other boats with Him.

37
38 Then a violent storm came up, and the waves dashed into the boat so that it was filling up fast. Meanwhile, in the back of the boat, He was sleeping on the cushion.

They woke Him up. "Teacher, we're drowning," they told Him. "Don't You care?"

39 He got up and ordered the wind to stop. "Hush!" He said to the lake. "Be still!" And the wind quieted down, and it became very calm.

40 "Why are you such cowards?" He asked them. "Haven't you learned to trust yet?"

41 Struck with awe, they asked one another, "Who is He? Even the wind and the lake obey Him."

The Gerasenes

5 They went to the country of the Gerasenes on the other side
2 of the lake. Just as He stepped out of the boat, a man with an
3 unclean spirit came out of the burial places and met Him. He lived in these burial places. Nobody could bind him any more, not even
4 with a chain. He had often been bound with chains on hands and feet, but he had torn the handcuffs and ground to pieces the chains
5 on his feet, and nobody was strong enough to control him. Always, day and night, he was shrieking in the burial places and in the hills and bruising himself with stones.

6 When he saw Jesus at a distance, he ran, bowed down before
7 Him, ' and yelled at the top of his voice, "Let me alone, Jesus, Son of the most high God! I tell You by God, don't torture me." Jesus had told him, "You unclean spirit, get out of the man."

9 "What is your name?" Jesus asked him.

"My name is Six Thousand," he told Him, "because we are
10 many." They begged Him earnestly not to send them out of
11 the country. There was a large herd of hogs feeding on the hill-
12 side. "Send us to the hogs," they begged Him; "we want to go into them."

13 He let them do this. The unclean spirits came out and went into the hogs, and the herd, about two thousand hogs, stampeded down the cliff into the lake and was drowned.

14 Those who had taken care of them ran away and told about it in the town and in the country, and the people came to see what
15 had happened. They came to Jesus ' and looked at the man who

had been plagued by a legion of devils, but now was sitting there dressed and in his right mind; and they were frightened. Those 5:16 who had seen it told them what had happened to the man plagued by devils and about the hogs. Then the people begged Jesus to 17 leave their country.

As He was stepping into the boat, the man in whom the devils 18 had been begged Jesus to let him go with Him. But Jesus didn't 19 let him. "Go home to your people," He told him, "and tell them how much the Lord has done for you and how merciful He has been to you."

So the man left and began to tell publicly in the Ten Towns 20 how much Jesus had done for him. And all were amazed.

The Daughter of Jairus

When Jesus had again crossed over in the boat to the other 21 side of the lake, a big crowd gathered around Him by the lake.

A synagog leader by the name of Jairus came, and when he 22 saw Jesus, he knelt at His feet and earnestly pleaded with Him: ¹ "My little daughter is dying. Come and lay your hands on her 23 so she will get well and live."

He went with him. A big crowd followed Him and pressed 24 Him on all sides. There was a woman who had a flow of blood 25 for twelve years. She had suffered much under many doctors and 26 had spent all she had. And she had not been helped at all but had actually gotten worse. Since she heard about Jesus, she came 27 from behind in the crowd and touched His garment. "If I touch 28 His clothes," she said, "I'll get well." Immediately her blood 29 stopped flowing, and she felt in her body her trouble was gone and she was well.

At that moment Jesus felt power had gone from Him. Turning 30 around in the crowd, He asked, "Who touched My clothes?"

"You see how the crowd is pressing you on all sides," His 31 disciples said to Him, "and You ask, 'Who touched Me?'"

But He was looking around to see her who had done this. The 32-33 woman, trembling with fear because she knew what had been done to her, came, bowed down before Him, and told Him the whole truth.

"Daughter," He told her, "your faith made you well. Go in 34 peace, be healthy and rid of your trouble."

While He was still talking, some men came from the home 35

of the synagog leader. "Your daughter died," they said. "Why trouble the Teacher any more?"

5:36   Paying no attention to what they said, Jesus told the synagog leader, "Don't be afraid! Only believe!"

37   He let only Peter, James, and John, the brother of James, go
38   with Him. So they came to the home of the synagog leader. ¹ There
39   He saw the noisy crowd, crying and wailing aloud. "Why do you make a noise and cry?" He asked them when He came into the house. "The child isn't dead; she's sleeping."

40   They laughed at Him. But He put them all outside, took the child's father and mother and those who were with Him, and
41   went in where the child was. He took the child's hand and said to her, "Talitha,* koom!" which means, "Little girl, I tell you, wake up!"

42   Immediately the girl got up and walked around. She was twelve years old. Then the others were utterly amazed.

43   He gave them strict orders not to let anyone know about this. And He told them to give her something to eat.

His Last Visit to Nazareth

6   Leaving that place, Jesus went to His home town, and His
2   disciples went with Him. When the Sabbath came, He taught in the synagog. Many who heard Him were amazed. "Where did He get this?" they asked. "What is this wisdom given to Him?"
3   and "Such miracles His hands are doing! Isn't He the carpenter, Mary's son, and a brother of James, Joseph, Judas, and Simon? And aren't His sisters here with us?" So they turned against Him.

4   But Jesus told them, "A prophet is without honor only in
5   his home town, among his relatives, and in his family." He couldn't do any miracle there except lay His hands on a few sick people
6   and make them well. Their unbelief amazed Him.

Then He went around in the villages and taught.

Jesus Sends Out the Twelve

7   Jesus called the twelve and sent them out by twos, giving
8   them authority over the unclean spirits. He gave them these instructions: "Don't take anything with you on the way except a stick — no bread, no bag, and no copper money in your pocket.
9   ¹ But have sandals strapped on your feet. And don't wear two tunics.

* Talitha originally meant "lamb."

"Wherever you go into a home," He told them, "stay there till you leave the place. If the people of any place don't welcome you or listen to you, leave that place, and shake the dust off the soles of your feet as a warning to them."

They left and preached that people should repent. They also drove out many devils and poured oil on many who were sick and made them well.

Herod Kills John

King Herod heard about Jesus, because His name was now well known. "John the Baptizer has risen from the dead," he said, "and that's why these powers are working in Him." Others said, "He is Elijah." Still others, "He is a prophet like one of the other prophets." But when Herod heard about it, he said, "John, whose head I cut off, has risen!"

Herod had sent men who arrested John, bound him, and put him in prison, because Herod had married Herodias, the wife of his brother Philip. "It isn't right for you to have your brother's wife," John had told Herod.

Herodias had a grudge against John and wanted to kill him, but she couldn't do it. Herod was afraid of John because he knew John was a good and holy man. So he protected him. When he listened to John, he was very much disturbed, and yet he liked to hear him.

An opportunity came on Herod's birthday, when he gave a dinner for his noblemen, the tribunes, and the leading men of Galilee. His daughter, that is, the daughter of Herodias, came in and danced, and Herod and his guests were delighted with her. "Ask me for anything you want," the king told the girl, "and I'll give it to you." And he solemnly swore to her: *"I'll give you anything you ask, up to half of my kingdom."* [9]

She went out and asked her mother, "What should I ask for?"

"The head of John the Baptizer," her mother told her.

She hurried right back to the king. "I want you to give me right now," she demanded, "on a platter the head of John the Baptizer."

The king felt very sorry. But he had sworn to do it, and there were the guests — so he didn't want to refuse her. The king quickly sent a guard and ordered him to bring John's head. He went and cut off John's head in prison. Then he brought the head on a platter and gave it to the girl, and the girl gave it to her mother.

When John's disciples heard about it, they came and took his body and laid it in a grave.

Jesus Feeds Five Thousand

30 The apostles gathered around Jesus and reported to Him
31 everything they had done and taught. "Now you come away to some deserted place," He told them, "where you can be alone, and rest a little." So many were coming and going there wasn't even time to eat.

32 So they went away in the boat to a deserted place to be alone.
33 But many saw them leave and recognized them. And they ran
34 there from all the towns and got there ahead of them. When Jesus stepped out of the boat, He saw a big crowd and felt sorry for them because they were *like sheep without a shepherd*.[10] He began to teach them many things.

35 When it was quite late, His disciples came to Him. "This is
36 a deserted place," they said, "and it's late. Send them away to the farms and villages around us to buy themselves something to eat."

37 "You give them something to eat," Jesus answered them.

"Should we go and buy bread for two hundred denarii," they asked Him, "and give it to them to eat?"

38 "How many loaves do you have?" He asked them. "Go and see."

They found out and said, "Five, and two fish."

39 He ordered them all to sit down in groups on the green grass.
40 They sat down in groups of hundreds and fifties.

41 Taking the five loaves and the two fish and looking up to heaven, He blessed them. He broke the loaves and gave them to the disciples to give to the people. He also gave pieces of the
42 two fish to everybody. All of them ate and had a hearty meal.
43 They picked up pieces of bread and of the fish — twelve baskets
44 full. There were five thousand men who had eaten the bread.

Jesus Walks on Water

45 He quickly made His disciples get into the boat and cross over to Bethsaida ahead of Him; meanwhile He would send the people
46 away. After saying good-by to them, He went up the hill to pray.
47 When it got late, the boat was in the middle of the lake, and He was alone on the land.

Jesus saw they were in great trouble as they rowed, because the wind was against them. Toward morning He came to them, walking on the lake. He wanted to pass by them. ⁴⁹ They saw Him walking on the lake, and thinking He was a ghost, they cried out, because they had all seen Him and were terrified. ⁵⁰

Immediately He talked to them. "Have courage!" He said. "It is I. Don't be afraid." He came into the boat with them, ⁵¹ and the wind died down. The disciples were completely dumfounded. They hadn't understood about the loaves. Their minds ⁵² were dull.

They crossed over and came to the shore at Gennesaret and ⁵³ anchored there.

As soon as they stepped out of the boat, the people recognized ⁵⁴ Him. They ran all over that part of the country and started to ⁵⁵ carry the sick on their beds to any place where they heard He was. And wherever He came — to villages, towns, or farms — ⁵⁶ they would lay down the sick in the public places and beg Him just to let them touch the tassel of His garment. And all who touched it were made well.

Unclean Hands

The Pharisees and some Bible scholars who had come from ⁷ Jerusalem gathered around Jesus. They saw some of His disciples ² eat with unclean hands, that is, without washing them. (Now the ³ Pharisees, like all other Jews, don't eat without washing their hands up to the wrist — to keep the rules handed down by their fathers. Coming from the marketplace, they don't eat without first ⁴ washing; and there are many other rules they've learned to keep — baptizing cups, pitchers, copper pans, and couches.)

"Why don't Your disciples live according to the rules handed ⁵ down by our fathers?" the Pharisees and the Bible scholars were asking Him. "They eat with unclean hands!"

He told them, "Isaiah was right when he prophesied about you ⁶ hypocrites as it is written: *These people honor Me with their lips, but their hearts are far away from Me. They worship Me in vain* ⁷ *because they teach men's rules.*[11] You give up God's command- ⁸ ment and keep men's rules." He added: "You have a fine way of ⁹ setting aside God's commandment in order to keep your rules! For example, Moses said, *Honor your father and your mother,* ¹⁰ and, *Anyone who curses father or mother must die.*[12] But you ¹¹

say, 'If anyone says to his father or mother, "Anything by which
7:12 I might help you is Korban" ' " (that is, a gift to God), "then
you don't let him do anything for his father or his mother any-
13 more. In this way, by the rules you have taught you set aside
what God has said. And you're doing many things like that."

14 Then He called the people again and said to them, "Listen
15 to Me, all of you, and understand this: Nothing that comes from
the outside into a person can make him unclean, but what comes
* out of a person makes him unclean."

17 When He had left the people and gone home, His disciples
asked Him about the illustration.

18 "Are you just as dull as the rest?" He asked them. "Don't you
know that nothing coming from the outside into a person can make
19 him unclean, because it doesn't go into his heart but into his
stomach and so passes away?" (Here Jesus made all foods clean.)
20 He added: "What comes out of a person makes him unclean.
21 Yes, from within, out of men's hearts, come evil thoughts, sexual
22 sins, stealing, murders, adulteries, greed, wickedness, cheating,
23 lust, a jealous eye, slander, pride, foolishness. All these evils come
from within and make a person unclean."

A Non-Jewish Woman

24 Leaving that place, Jesus went away to the neighborhood of
Tyre. He went into a house and didn't want anyone to know it
but couldn't keep it secret.

25 There was a woman in whose little daughter there was an
unclean spirit. As soon as she heard about Him, she came and
26 bowed down at His feet. The woman wasn't Jewish but was born
a Phoenician in Syria. She was asking Him to drive the devil
out of her daughter.

27 "First let the children eat all they want," He answered her.
"It isn't good to take the children's bread and throw it to the
puppies."

28 "You're right, Lord," she answered Him, "but even the
puppies under the table eat some of the children's crumbs."

29 "Because you said this, go!" Jesus told her. "The devil has
gone out of your daughter."

30 The woman went home and found the little child lying on
the bed and the devil gone.

* Our two oldest manuscripts do not have v. 16: "If you have ears to
hear, listen!" See 4:23.

A Deaf and Dumb Man

Jesus again left the country of Tyre and went through Sidon 7:31
and the country of the Ten Towns to the Lake of Galilee.

Some people brought Him a man who was deaf and tongue- 32
tied, and they urged Jesus to lay His hand on him. Taking him 33
away from the crowd to be alone with him, He put His fingers
into the man's ears. He spit and touched his tongue ¹ and looked 34
up to heaven and sighed. Then He said to him, "Ephphatha!"
which means, "Open!" His ears were opened, his tongue was 35
set free to speak, and he talked naturally.

Jesus ordered the people not to tell anyone. But the more He 36
forbade them, the more widely they spread the news. They were 37
dumfounded. "He has done everything well," they said. "He even
makes the deaf hear and the dumb speak."

Jesus Feeds Four Thousand

At that time there were again many people who had nothing 8
to eat. So He called the disciples. ¹ "I feel sorry for the people," 2
He said to them. "They've been with Me three days now and have
nothing to eat. If I let them go home without eating, they will 3
get exhausted on the road. Some of them have come a long way."

"Where could anyone get enough bread here in the wilderness 4
to feed these?" His disciples asked Him.

"How many loaves do you have?" Jesus asked them. 5

"Seven," they answered.

He ordered the people to sit down on the ground. Then He 6
took the seven loaves, gave thanks, broke them, and gave them
to His disciples to hand out, and they handed them to the people.
¹ They also had a few small fish. He blessed them and asked that 7
these, too, be handed out. ¹ They ate and had a hearty meal. And 8
they picked up the pieces that were left — seven baskets. There 9
were about four thousand.

Then He dismissed the people.

A Proof from Heaven

Then Jesus and His disciples got into the boat and came 10
into the neighborhood of Dalmanutha.

The Pharisees came and started to argue with Him. To test 11
Him, they asked Him for some wonderful proof from heaven.

With a deep sigh from His spirit He asked, "Why do the 12

people of today want a proof? Surely, I tell you, these people will get no proof!"

8:13   Then He left them.

The Yeast of the Pharisees

13   He got into the boat again and started to cross to the other
14   side. They forgot to take bread and had only one loaf with them in the boat.

15   Then Jesus definitely warned them: "Beware of the yeast of the Pharisees and of Herod!"

16   Arguing about this with one another, they mentioned that they had no bread.

17   Aware of what was going on, Jesus asked, "Why are you arguing about not having any bread? Don't you know or under-
18   stand yet? Are your minds closed? I *You have eyes — don't you*
19   *see? You have ears — don't you hear?* 13 I And don't you remember? When I broke the five loaves for the five thousand, how many baskets full of pieces did you pick up?"

  "Twelve," they told Him.

20   "And the seven loaves for the four thousand — how many baskets full of pieces did you pick up?"

  "Seven," they answered Him.

21   "Don't you understand yet?" He asked them.

A Blind Man

22   So they came to Bethsaida. There people brought a blind
23   man to Jesus and begged Him to touch him. He took the blind man's hand and led him out of the village. Then He spit on his eyes and laid His hands on him. "Can you see anything?" He asked him.

24   He looked up. "I see the people," he said. "They look to me like trees walking around."

25   When Jesus again laid His hands on his eyes, he saw dis-
26   tinctly; sight came back, and he saw everything clearly. Jesus sent him home, saying, "But don't go into the village."

"You Are the Promised Savior"

27   Then Jesus and His disciples went to the villages around Philip's Caesarea. On the way He asked His disciples, "Who do people say I am?"

28   "John the Baptizer," they answered Him. "Others say Elijah, and still others, one of the prophets."

"But who do you say I am?" He asked them.

"You are the promised Savior!" Peter answered Him.

He warned them not to tell anyone about Him. 30

"I Will Die and Rise Again"

Then He was teaching them: "The Son of Man has to suffer 31
much, be rejected by the elders, the ruling priests, and the Bible
scholars, be killed, and then rise on the third day." He was 32
speaking quite frankly.

But Peter took Him aside and started to correct Him. | Turning, 33
He looked at His disciples and corrected Peter. "Get behind Me,
devil!" He said. "You're not thinking what God thinks but what
men think."

Take the Cross

He called the people as well as His disciples. "If you want 34
to follow Me," He told them, "deny yourself, take up your cross,
and come with Me. If you want to save your life, you will lose it. 35
But if you will lose your life for Me and for the good news, you
will save it. What good does it do you to win the whole world 36
and lose your life? Or what would you give to buy back your life? 37
If among the unfaithful and sinful people of today you're ashamed 38
of Me and what I say, then the Son of Man will be ashamed of
you when He comes with the holy angels in His Father's glory.

"Let Me assure you," He told them, "there are some standing 9
here who will never taste death till they see God has come to
rule with power."

Jesus Shows His Glory

After five days Jesus took Peter, James, and John with Him 2
and led them up a high mountain to be alone with them.

He was changed before them, and His clothes became dazzling 3
white — nobody on earth could bleach them so white. Elijah and 4
Moses appeared to them and were talking with Jesus.

"Master," Peter said to Jesus, "it's good for us to be here. 5
Let's put up three shelters, one for You, one for Moses, and one
for Elijah." He didn't know what he was saying; they were so 6
terrified.

A cloud came and overshadowed them, and a voice came 7
out of the cloud: "This is *My Son* whom I love. *Listen to Him*." 14

79

Suddenly, as they looked around, they no longer saw anyone but Jesus with them.

9   On their way down the mountain Jesus ordered them not to tell anyone what they had seen, till the Son of Man had risen
10 from the dead. They kept in mind what He said and argued with
11 one another, asking, "What is this rising from the dead?" So they asked Him, "Why do those who know the Bible say, 'First Elijah has to come'?"

12 "First *Elijah* does come," He told them, "and *puts* everything *in order again.*[15] And what is written about the Son of Man? That
13 He must suffer much and be treated shamefully. Yes, I tell you, Elijah has come, and people treated him as they pleased, as it is written about him."

The Epileptic Boy

14 When they got back to the other disciples, they saw a big crowd around them and some Bible scholars arguing with them.
15 Then the whole crowd was amazed to see Jesus, and they ran and welcomed Him.

16 "What is this argument about?" He asked them.

17 "Teacher," someone in the crowd answered, "I brought You
18 my son. There's a speechless spirit in him. Wherever the spirit takes hold of him, it throws him down; he foams at the mouth and grinds his teeth and gets rigid. I asked Your disciples to drive out the spirit, but they couldn't do it."

19 "O you unbelieving people!" Jesus answered. "How long must I be with you? How long must I put up with you? Bring him to Me."

20 They brought the boy to Him. As soon as the spirit saw Jesus, it threw the boy into convulsions. He fell on the ground and rolled around and foamed at the mouth.

21 Jesus asked his father, "How long has he been like this?"

22 "Since he was a child," he said. "It often threw him into fire or into water to kill him. Oh, if You can do anything, have pity on us and help us."

23 "You say, 'If You can'!" Jesus answered him. "Anything can be done if you believe."

24 Immediately the child's father cried out, "I do believe; help me with my unbelief."

When Jesus saw a crowd quickly gather around Him, He talked sharply to the unclean spirit: "You deaf and dumb spirit, I order you, 'Come out of him, and don't go into him again.' "

It screamed and wrenched him violently and came out. The 26 boy became like a corpse, so that everybody said, "He's dead."

Jesus took his hand, helped him get up, and he stood up. 27

When He went into a house and His disciples were alone with 28 Him, they asked Him, "Why couldn't we drive out the spirit?"

"This kind can be driven out only by prayer," He told them. 29

"I Will Die and Rise Again"

Leaving that place, they started to go on byways through 30 Galilee. Jesus didn't want anybody to know about it, ' because 31 He was teaching His disciples and telling them: "The Son of Man is going to be betrayed into the hands of men, and they will kill Him, but on the third day after He's killed He will rise."

They didn't understand what He said and were afraid to 32 ask Him.

Who Is the Greatest?

They went to Capernaum. When He came home, He asked 33 the disciples, "What were you discussing on the way?" They were 34 silent because they had on the way discussed who was the greatest.

He sat down and called the twelve. ' "If anyone wants to 35 be first," He told them, "he will have to be last of all and serve everybody." He took a little child, had him stand in 36 front of them, put His arms around him, and said to them, "If you 37 welcome a child like this in My name, you welcome Me. And if you welcome Me, you welcome not only Me but Him who sent Me."

"He Is for Us"

"Teacher," John said to Jesus, "we saw a man drive out devils 38 in Your name, and we tried to stop him because he hasn't been with us."

"Don't try to stop him," Jesus said. "Anyone who does a 39 miracle in My name cannot turn around and speak evil of Me. Anyone who isn't against us is for us. I tell you, anyone who gives 40-41 you a cup of water to drink because you belong to Christ will certainly not lose his reward."

Do I Lead Others to Sin?

9:42   "If anyone leads into sin one of these little ones who believe in Me, it would be better for him to have a big millstone hung around his neck and be thrown into the lake.

43   "If your hand makes you sin, cut it off. It is better for you to go into life crippled than to have two hands and go to hell, where
* 45 the fire can't be put out. If your foot makes you sin, cut it off. It is better for you to go into life with only one foot than to have
* 47 two feet and be thrown into hell. If your eye makes you sin, throw it away. It is better for you to go into God's kingdom with one
48 eye than to have two eyes and be thrown into hell, where *the worm that consumes them doesn't die and the fire isn't put out.*[16]

49-50   "Everyone has to be salted with fire. | Salt is good. But if salt loses its taste, how will you make it taste salty again? Keep salt within you, and so live in peace with one another."

Husband and Wife

10   Jesus left that place and went into the country of Judea and on the other side of the Jordan, and again the crowds gathered around Him. And again He taught them as He used to do.

2   Some Pharisees came to Him. "Is it right for a man to divorce his wife?" they asked Him in order to test Him.

3   "What did Moses order you to do?" He asked them.

4   "Moses let a man *make out a divorce paper and divorce his wife,*"[17] they said.

5   "He wrote this law for you on account of your closed minds,"
6 Jesus told them. "But when God made the world, He in the
7 beginning *made them a male and a female.*[18] *That's why a man*
8 *will leave his father and mother* | *and the two will be one flesh.*[19]
9 And so they are no more two but one flesh. | Now, what God has joined together man must not separate."

10-11   In the house the disciples also asked Him about this. "If anyone divorces his wife," He answered them, "and marries another,
12 he's living in adultery with her. And if a wife divorces her husband and marries another man, she's living in adultery."

Jesus Loves Children

13   Some people brought babies to Jesus to have Him touch them, but the disciples sternly told them not to do it.

---

* Our two oldest manuscripts do not have vv. 44 and 46: *"Where their worm doesn't die and the fire isn't put out."* See v. 48.

But when Jesus saw this, He didn't like it at all. "Let the little children come to Me," He told them. "Don't keep them away. God's kingdom belongs to such as these. [1] I tell you the truth, if you don't receive God's kingdom like a little child, you will not get into it." [15]

He took them in His arms, laid His hands on them, and blessed them. [16]

The Rich Young Leader

As Jesus was coming out to the road, a man came running to Him and knelt before Him. "Good Teacher," he asked Him, "what should I do to get everlasting life?" [17]

"Why do you call Me good?" Jesus asked him. "Nobody is good except One — God. You know the commandments: *Don't murder, don't commit adultery, don't steal, don't lie,* don't rob, *honor your father and mother.*" [20] [18] [19]

"Teacher," he told Him, "I've kept all these since I was a child." [20]

Jesus looked at him and loved him. "You lack one thing," Jesus told him. "Go, sell everything you have, and give the money to the poor, and you'll have a treasure in heaven. Then come and follow Me." [21]

When he heard that, he looked gloomy and went away sad, because he was very rich. Jesus looked around and said to His disciples, "How hard it is for rich people to get into God's kingdom!" [22] [23]

The disciples were surprised that He said that. But Jesus said to them again, "Children, how hard it is to get into God's kingdom! It's easier for a camel to go through a needle's eye than for a rich man to get into God's kingdom." [24] [25]

They were more amazed than ever. "Who can be saved?" they asked one another. [26]

"Men can't do this," Jesus said as He looked at them. "But God can, because *God can do anything.*" [21] [27]

Then Peter spoke up: "Look! We gave up everything and followed You." [28]

"Let Me assure you," Jesus said, "everyone who gave up his home, brothers or sisters, mother, father, or children, or fields for Me and for the good news, will certainly get a hundred times as much here in this life: houses, brothers and sisters, mothers [29] [30]

10:31 and children and fields, with persecutions, and in the coming world everlasting life. But many who are first will be last, and the last first."

The Cup of Suffering

32 As they were on their way up to Jerusalem, Jesus walked ahead of them. They were amazed, and the others who were following Him were afraid. So once again He took the twelve with Him and told them what was going to happen to Him: 33 "Look, we're going up to Jerusalem, and the Son of Man will be betrayed to the ruling priests and the Bible scholars, who will 34 condemn Him to die and hand Him over to the Gentiles. They'll mock Him and spit on Him, scourge Him and kill Him. But on the third day He will rise."

35 James and John, the sons of Zebedee, came to Him. "Teacher," they said to Him, "we want You to do for us what we ask."

36 "What do you want Me to do for you?" He asked them.

37 "Let one of us sit at Your right," they told Him, "and the other at Your left in Your glory."

38 "You don't know what you're asking," Jesus answered them. "Can you drink the cup I'm drinking or be baptized with the baptism with which I'm being baptized?"

39 "We can," they told Him.

"You'll drink the cup I'm drinking," Jesus told them, "and be baptized with the baptism with which I'm being baptized. 40 But sitting at My right or left is something I can give only to those for whom it is prepared."

41 When the other ten heard about it, they got angry with James 42 and John. Then Jesus called them and told them, "You know that those who are considered rulers of the nations are lords over 43 them, and their great men are tyrants over them. But among you it's different. Anyone who wants to become great among you 44 will have to serve you, and anyone who wants to be first among 45 you will have to be everybody's slave. Why, even the Son of Man didn't come to be served but to serve and give His life as a ransom for all people."

Blind Bartimaeus

46 Then they came to Jericho. As Jesus and His disciples and many people were leaving Jericho, Bartimaeus, the son of 47 Timaeus, a blind beggar, was sitting by the road. When he

heard it was Jesus from Nazareth, he began to call, "Son of David, Jesus, have pity on me!"

Many were urging him to be quiet. But he called all the 10:48 louder, "Son of David, have pity on me!"

Jesus stopped and said, "Call him!" They called the blind 49 man and told him, "Cheer up! Get up! He's calling you." He 50 laid aside his garment, jumped up, and went to Jesus.

"What do you want Me to do for you?" Jesus asked him. 51 "Master, I want to see again," the blind man told Him.

"Go," Jesus told him; "your faith has made you well." 52 Immediately he could see, and he followed Him on the road.

The King Comes to Jerusalem

When they were getting near Jerusalem and came to Beth- 11 phage and Bethany, at the Mount of Olives, Jesus sent two of His disciples. "Go into the village ahead of you," He told them, "and 2 just as you go into it, you'll find a young donkey tied up that nobody ever sat on. Untie it and bring it to Me. ¹ And if any- 3 body asks you, 'Why are you doing that?' say, 'The Lord needs it and will promptly send it back here.'"

They went and found the colt tied to the gate, outside in the 4 street, and they started to untie it.

"What are you doing, untying the colt?" some of the men 5 standing there asked them. They answered them just as Jesus 6 had told them, and the men let them go.

So they brought the colt to Jesus, put their garments on it, 7 and He sat on it. Many spread their garments on the road, and 8 others spread leafy branches that they cut in the fields. Those 9 who went ahead and those who followed Him were shouting:

> "Our Savior!
> Blessed is He who is coming in the Lord's name! ²² 10
> Blessed is the coming kingdom of our father David!
> Our Savior — in the highest heavens!"

He came into Jerusalem and into the temple and looked 11 around at everything. Since it was late now, He went with the twelve out to Bethany.

Nothing but Leaves

The next day when they left Bethany, Jesus was hungry. 12 In the distance He saw a fig tree with leaves, and He went to see 13 if He could find anything on it. When He came to it, He found nothing but leaves, because it wasn't the season for figs. Then He said to the tree, and His disciples heard Him: "May nobody ever eat fruit from you again!"

He Cleanses the Temple Again

15 When they came to Jerusalem, He went into the temple and proceeded to drive out those who were selling and buying in the temple, and He upset the tables of the money changers and the 16 chairs of those who sold pigeons. He would not let anyone carry a vessel across the temple grounds.

17 Then He taught: "Isn't it written, *My house should be called a house of prayer for all the nations?* 23 But you made it *a den of robbers.*" 24

18 When the ruling priests and Bible scholars heard Him, they tried to find a way to kill Him. They were afraid of Him, because He amazed all the people by His teaching.

19 When evening came, He would leave the city.

The Fig Tree Is Withered

20 When they walked by early in the morning, they saw the fig 21 tree withered from the roots up. Peter, remembering, said to Him, "Master, look! The fig tree You cursed is dried up."

22-23 "Believe in God!" Jesus answered them. "I tell you the truth: If you will say to this mount,* 'Be lifted up and be thrown into the sea,' * and have no doubt in your mind but believe 24 what you say will be done, it will be done for you. That's why I tell you, anything you ask for in prayer, believe that you re- 25 ceived it, and you will have it. When you stand and pray, if you have anything against anyone, forgive him, so that your ** Father in heaven will forgive you your sins."

From Heaven

27 They came again to Jerusalem. As He was walking in the temple, the ruling priests, the Bible scholars, and the elders came 28 to Him. "By what authority are You doing these things?" they asked Him. "Or who gave You the right to do them?"

29 Jesus answered them, "I will ask you a question. You answer Me, and then I'll tell you by what authority I'm doing these

---

* By this mount He means the Mount of Olives. By the sea He means the Dead Sea, which can be seen from the Mount of Olives.

** Our two oldest manuscripts do not have v. 26: "But if you don't forgive, your Father in heaven will not forgive your sins." See Matt. 6:14-15.

things. John's baptism — was it from heaven or from men? Answer Me."

They argued among themselves, "If we say, 'From heaven,' 31 He will ask, 'Then why didn't you believe him?' But should we say, 'From men'?" They were afraid of the people. Everybody 32 thought John certainly was a prophet. So they answered Jesus, 33 "We don't know."

Then Jesus told them, "Neither will I tell you by what authority I'm doing these things."

God's Vineyard

Then He used stories in talking to them: **12**

"A man *planted a vineyard. He put a wall around it, cut a vat into the rock, and built a watchtower.*[25] Then he rented it out to workers and left home.

"At the right time he sent a slave to the workers to get from 2 them a share of the products of the vineyard. But they took him, 3 beat him, and sent him back empty-handed. He sent another 4 slave to them. They hit him on the head and treated him shamefully. He sent another, and that one they killed. Then many 5 others. Some of these they beat, and others they killed.

"He had one more, a son, whom he loved. Finally he sent him 6 to them saying, 'They will respect my son.'

"But those workers said to one another, 'This is the heir. 7 Come, let's kill him, and then we'll get the inheritance.' They 8 took him, killed him, and threw him out of the vineyard.

"What will the owner of the vineyard do? He will come and 9 kill the workers and give the vineyard to others. Haven't you 10 read this in your Bible, *The stone the builders rejected has become the cornerstone. The Lord has done it, and we think it is* 11 *wonderful"?*[26]

They wanted to grab Him, because they knew His story was 12 aimed at them, but they were afraid of the crowd. So they let Him alone and went away.

Taxes

They sent some Pharisees and some of Herod's men to Him 13 in order to trap Him with a question. When they came to Him, 14 they said, "Teacher, we know You're honest and don't care what others think, because You don't favor any special persons but

You really teach God's way. Is it right to pay a tax to Caesar or not? Should we pay it or not?"

12:15   Seeing through their hypocritical way, Jesus asked them, "Why do you test Me? Bring Me a denarius; I want to see it."

16   They brought it. "Whose head is this and whose inscription?" He asked them.

"Caesar's," they told Him.

17   "Give Caesar what is Caesar's," Jesus told them, "and God what is God's." He amazed them.

The Dead Live

18   The Sadducees, who say the dead don't rise, came to Him with
19   this question: "Teacher, Moses wrote for us, *If anyone dies and leaves* a wife but *no child, his brother should marry his widow*
20   *and have children for his brother.*[27] Now, there were seven
21   brothers. The first took a wife, died, and left no children. | The second married her, died, and left no children. So did the third.
22 | None of the seven left any children. Last of all the woman died
23   too. | When the dead rise, whose wife will she be? You know, the seven had her as wife."

24   Jesus asked them, "Aren't you wrong because you don't know
25   your Bible or God's power? When they rise from the dead, men
26   and women don't marry but are like angels in heaven. About the dead rising, didn't you read in the book of Moses, in the story of the bush, how God told him, *I am the God of Abraham, the*
27   *God of Isaac, and the God of Jacob?* [28] He's not the God of the dead but of the living. You're badly mistaken!"

Love God and Your Neighbor

28   One of the men trained in the Bible came to Him. Hearing the others argue with Him and seeing how well Jesus answered them, he asked Him, "Which is the most important of all the commandments?"

29   Jesus answered, "The most important is: *Listen, Israel, the*
30   *Lord our God alone is Lord. Then love the Lord your God with all your heart, with all your life,* with all your mind, *and with all your*
31   *strength.*[29] The next is: *Love your neighbor like yourself.*[30] No other commandment is greater than these."

32   "Right, Teacher!" the Bible scholar said to Him. "You told the
33   truth: *He is the only One, and there is no other beside Him,* | and *loving Him with all your heart,* with all your understanding, *and*

with all your strength,[31] and *loving your neighbor like yourself* [30]
is more than all the *burnt offerings and sacrifices."* [32]

When Jesus saw how sensibly he answered, He told him, 12:34
"You're not far from God's kingdom."

Nobody dared to ask Him another question.

David's Son

While Jesus was teaching in the temple, He asked, "How can 35
the Bible scholars say the promised Savior is David's Son?
David himself by the Holy Spirit said, 36

> *The Lord said to my Lord,*
> *'Sit at My right*
> *Till I put your enemies under Your feet.'* [33]

David himself calls Him Lord. Then how can He be his Son?" 37

Beware!

The big crowd liked to hear Him. As He taught, He said, 37-38
"Beware of the Bible scholars, who like to go around in long
robes, be greeted in the marketplaces, sit in the front seats in 39
synagogs, and have the places of honor at dinners. They swallow 40
the houses of widows, and then, to cover up, make long prayers.
They will be punished all the more."

A Cent

As Jesus sat facing the contribution boxes, He was watching 41
how people put money into them. Many rich people put in
much. A poor widow came and dropped in two small coins, 42
worth about a cent.

He called His disciples. "I tell you," He said to them, "this 43
poor widow certainly put in more than all the others who put in
money. All the others took some of what they had left over 44
and dropped it in, but she put in what she needed herself, all
she had — all she had to live on."

Sorrow Ahead!

As He was going out of the temple, one of His disciples said 13
to Him, "Teacher, look at those wonderful stones and buildings!"

"You see these large buildings?" Jesus asked him. "Not 2
a stone will be left on another here but will be torn down."

When He was sitting on the Mount of Olives, facing the 3
temple, Peter, James, John, and Andrew asked Him privately:

"Tell us, when will this be, and how can we tell when all this is going to happen?"

5 "Be careful not to let anyone deceive you," Jesus told them.
6 "Many will come using My name and saying, 'I am He,' and will deceive many.

7 "When you hear of wars and rumors of wars, don't get
8 alarmed. *It must happen,*[34] but that's not the end yet. *Nation will fight against nation, and kingdom against kingdom.*[35] There will be earthquakes in different places, and famines. These are only the first pains.*

9 "Be on your guard! Men will hand you over to their courts and whip you in their synagogs. You will be brought before gov-
10 ernors and kings for My sake to tell them the truth. The good
11 news must be preached to all nations before the end comes. When they are taking you away to hand you over to the authorities, don't worry beforehand what you will say. But say whatever is given you to say when the time comes; you see, it isn't you speaking but the Holy Spirit.

12 "A brother will betray his brother to death, and a father his child. *Children will rebel against their parents* [36] and kill them.
13 Everybody will hate you because of My name. But endure to the end, and you'll be saved."

Jerusalem Will Be Destroyed

14 "When you see *the abomination laying waste the land* [37] and standing where it should not be (anyone who reads this should
15 understand it), then if you're in Judea, flee to the hills. If you're on the roof, don't come down and go into your house to get
16 anything. If you're in the field, don't turn back to get your garment.

17 "Woe to the women who in those days are expecting babies
18-19 or nursing them. Pray that it won't happen in winter. *It will be a time of misery such as never has been from the beginning* of the
20 world that God made *until now* [38] and never will be. And if the Lord had not cut short that time, nobody would be saved. But to help those whom He has chosen, God has cut short the time."

Jesus Is Coming

21 "If anyone tells you then, 'Look, here is Christ!' or, 'There
22 He is!' don't believe it. False Christs and false *prophets* will

* As in childbirth, sharper pains will follow before the Savior comes in glory.

come and do miracles and wonders [39] to deceive if possible those whom God has chosen. Be on your guard. You see, I've told you everything before it happens.

"Now, after the misery of that time *the sun will turn dark,* *the moon will stop shining, and the stars will be falling from the* *sky.* And *the powers of heaven* [40] *will be shaken.* Then people will see *the Son of Man coming in the clouds* [41] with great power and glory. And then He will send the angels and *gather* His chosen ones *from the north, south, east, and west, and from one* *end of the world to the other.*[42]

"Learn this lesson from a fig tree: When its branch gets tender and grows leaves, you know summer is near. So also when you see those things happen, you know He is near, at your door.

"I tell you the truth: These people will not pass away till all this happens. Heaven and earth will pass away, but what I say will not pass away."

Be Ready!

"No one knows about that day or hour, not the angels in heaven, not the Son, only the Father. Be careful and watch, because you don't know when it will happen. It's like a man who went on a trip. As he left home, he put his slaves in charge, assigned work to every one, and ordered the doorkeeper to watch. Watch, then, because you don't know when the master of the house is coming, whether in the evening, at midnight, at the time when the rooster crows, or early in the morning. Make sure he doesn't come suddenly and find you asleep. What I tell you, I tell everyone: 'Watch!' "

The Plot

It was two days before the festival of the Passover and of **14** bread without yeast. The ruling priests and the Bible scholars were looking for some treacherous way to arrest Jesus and kill Him. They said, "Not in the festival crowd, or there will be **2** a riot among the people."

Mary Anoints Jesus

While Jesus was in Bethany in the home of Simon the leper **3** and was lying at the table, a woman came with an alabaster jar of perfume, real nard and very expensive. She broke the jar and poured the perfume on His head.

Some who were there felt annoyed and said to one another,
5 "Why was the perfume wasted like this? This perfume could
have been sold for more than three hundred denarii and the
money given to the poor." And they were grumbling at her.

6 "Let her alone," Jesus said. "Why should you trouble her?
7 She has done a beautiful thing to Me. The poor you always
have with you, and you can help them whenever you want to,
8 but you will not always have Me. She has done what she could.
She came ahead of time to pour the perfume on My body to
9 prepare it for burial. I tell you, wherever the good news is
preached in the whole world, certainly what she has done will also
be told in memory of her."

Judas Plans to Betray Jesus

10 Judas, the man from Kerioth, one of the twelve, went to the
11 high priests to betray Jesus to them. They were delighted to hear
it and promised to give him money. So he was looking for
a chance to betray Him.

The Passover

12 On the first of the Passover days of bread without yeast, when
it was customary to kill the Passover lamb, the disciples asked
Jesus, "Where do You want us to go and get things ready for
You to eat the Passover?"

13 He sent two of His disciples and told them: "Go into the city,
14 and you will meet a man carrying a jar of water. Follow him, and
when he goes into a house, tell the owner: 'The Teacher asks,
"Where is My room in which I can eat the Passover with My
15 disciples?" ' Then he will show you a large room upstairs, furnished and ready. Get the things ready for us there."

16 The disciples left, went into the city, and found everything
17 as He had told them. And so they got the Passover ready.

In the evening He came there with the twelve.

"Is It I?"

18 While they were still lying down and eating, Jesus said, "I tell
you the truth: One of you is going to betray Me, one who is
eating with Me!" [43]

19 They felt hurt and asked Him one after another, "You don't
mean me?"

20 "One of the twelve," He told them, "one who is dipping into

the bowl with Me. The Son of Man is going away as it is written about Him, but woe to that man who betrays the Son of Man! It would be better for that man if he had never been born."

14:21

The Lord's Supper

While they were eating, Jesus took bread and blessed it. He [22] broke it and gave it to them and said, "Take it. This is My body."

Then He took a cup, gave thanks, and gave it to them. And [23] they all drank of it. He told them, "This is My *blood of the* [24] *covenant*,[44] poured out for all.

"Surely, I tell you, I will not drink again of the product of [25] the vine until that day when I drink it in a new way in God's kingdom."

Then they sang a hymn.* [26]

"You Will Deny Me"

They started out for the Mount of Olives. [26]

Then Jesus told them, "You will all turn against Me, because [27] it is written: I will *strike down the Shepherd, and the sheep will be scattered.*[45] But after I have risen, I will go ahead of you [28] to Galilee."

"Even if they all turn against You," Peter answered Him, [29] "I will not."

"I tell you the truth," Jesus told him, "tonight, before the [30] rooster crows twice, you will deny Me three times."

But he kept insisting all the more, "If I have to die with You, [31] I'll never deny You." All the others said the same thing.

Gethsemane

They came to a place called Gethsemane, and He said to His [32] disciples, "Sit down here while I pray."

He took Peter, James, and John with Him, and He started [33] to feel terror and grief. *"I am so full of sorrow,"* [46] He told [34] them, "I am almost dying. Stay here and keep awake."

Going ahead a little, He bowed down to the ground and [35] prayed that if it were possible He might not have to suffer what was ahead of Him. "My Father," He said, "You can do anything. [36] Take this cup away from Me. But let it not be as I want it but as You want it."

He came and found them asleep. "Simon, are you sleeping?" [37]

* Perhaps Psalms 115—118.

93

14:38 He asked Peter. "So you couldn't keep awake one hour! ¹ Stay awake and pray that you may not be tempted. The spirit is willing, but the flesh is weak."

39-40 He went away again and prayed the same as before. He came again and found them asleep — they couldn't keep their eyes open and didn't know what to say to Him.

41 He came back a third time. "Are you going to sleep on now and rest?" He asked them. "It's enough. The time has come. Now the Son of Man will be betrayed into the hands of sinners.

42 ¹ Get up, let us go. Here comes the man to betray Me!"

The Arrest

43 Just then, while Jesus was still talking, Judas, one of the twelve, came with a crowd of men with swords and clubs from

44 the ruling priests, the Bible scholars, and the elders. The traitor had given them a signal. "The One I kiss is the Man," he said. "Grab Him, take Him away, and don't let Him escape."

45 When he came there, he quickly stepped up to Jesus and said, "Master!" and kissed Him.

46-47 Then the men took hold of Jesus and arrested Him. One of those who were standing near Him drew his sword, struck the high priest's slave, and cut off his ear.

48 "Did you come out to arrest Me," Jesus asked them, "with

49 swords and clubs as if I were a robber? Day after day I was with you as I taught in the temple, and you didn't arrest Me. But what the Bible says has to come true."

50-51 Then all the disciples left Him and ran away. One young man who also was following Him had nothing on but a linen cloth.

52. They tried to grab him, ¹ but he left the linen cloth and ran away naked.

The First Trial Before the Jewish Court

53 The men took Jesus to the high priest, and all the ruling priests,

54 elders, and Bible scholars were coming together. Peter followed Him at a distance and even went into the high priest's courtyard. And he was sitting with the attendants, warming himself at the fire.

55 The ruling priests and the whole Jewish court tried to get some testimony against Jesus in order to kill Him but couldn't find any.

56 While many gave false testimony against Him, their statements didn't agree.

57 Then some got up and gave this false testimony against Him:

"We heard Him say, 'I will tear down this temple, made by human hands, and in three days build another not made by human hands.'" But even on this point their statements didn't agree. 59

Then the high priest stepped forward. "Don't You have anything to say to this?" he asked Jesus. "What are these men testifying against You?" 60

But He was silent and didn't answer. 61

Again the high priest asked Him, "Are You the promised Savior, the Son of the Blessed?"

"I am," Jesus said. "And you will all see *the Son of Man sitting at the right hand* of power and *coming in the clouds of heaven.*" [47] 62

Then the high priest tore his clothes, saying, "Why do we need any more witnesses? You've heard the blasphemy. What do you think?" 63 64

Then all condemned Him, saying He must die. Some of them started to spit at Him. They covered His face, hit Him with their fists, and told Him, "Prophesy!" The attendants also slapped Him when they took charge of Him. 65

Peter Denies Jesus

While Peter was down in the courtyard, one of the high priest's maids came and saw Peter warming himself. "You, too, were with the Man from Nazareth — this Jesus," she said, looking at him. 66 67

But he denied it: "I don't know Him, and I don't know what you're talking about." 68

He went out to the entrance. Then a rooster crowed.

The maid saw him. "He's one of them," she also told those who were standing around. Again he denied. 69 70

After a little while those who stood near him also told Peter, "Sure, you're one o them because you're a Galilean!"

Then he started to curse and swear: "I don't know this Man you're talking abou ." Just then a rooster crowed a second time, and Peter remembe ed Jesus telling him: "Before the rooster crows twice, you will den Me three times." And he started to cry. 71 72

Before Pilate

As soon as it vas morning, the ruling priests, the elders, and the Bible scholar , that is, the wh le Jewish court, came to a decision. They t und Jesus, took Him away, and handed Him over to Pilate. 15

15:2 Pilate asked Him, "Are You the King of the Jews?"
"Yes," Jesus answered him.
3 The ruling priests were accusing Him of many things.
4 "Don't You have anything to say to this?" Pilate asked Him
again. "See how many accusations they're bringing against You!"
5 But Jesus didn't answer him any more, so that Pilate was
surprised.

Barabbas

6 Now, at every festival Pilate used to free a prisoner whom the
7 people asked for. There was a man by the name of Barabbas.
He was in prison with the rebels who in their revolt had com-
8 mitted a murder. And the crowd came up and asked Pilate to do
9 for them as he had done before. Pilate answered them by asking,
10 "Do you want me to free the King of the Jews for you?" He knew
the ruling priests had handed Jesus over to him because they
were jealous.
11 The ruling priests stirred up the people to get him to free
Barabbas for them instead.
12 "Now, what should I do with Him you call the King of the
Jews?" Pilate again asked them.
13 Then they yelled, "Crucify Him!"
14 "Why, what wrong has He done?" Pilate asked them.
But they yelled all the louder, "Crucify Him!"
15 Then Pilate, wanting to satisfy the people, freed Barabbas for
them, but Jesus he scourged and handed over to be crucified.
16 The soldiers took Him into the courtyard of the governor's
17 palace and called together the whole troop of soldiers. They put
a purple cloak on Him, twisted some thorns into a crown and
18 placed it on His head, and started to greet Him: "Hail, King of
19 the Jews!" They hit Him on the head with a stick, spit on Him,
knelt, and worshiped Him.

"They Crucified Him"

20 After mocking Him, the soldiers took off the purple cloak and
put His own clothes on Him. Then they took Him out to crucify
21 Him. A certain Simon from Cyrene, the father of Alexander and
Rufus, was on his way in from the country, and as he was going
to pass by, they forced him to carry the cross of Jesus.
22 They took Him to the Golgotha place, which means Skull
23 Place. They tried to give Him wine mixed with myrrh, but He

didn't take it. ᵗ They crucified Him. And *they divided His clothes among them by throwing lots for them* [48] to see what each one should get. It was nine in the morning when they crucified Him. There was a notice stating why Jesus was being punished; it read: THE KING OF THE JEWS. With Him they crucified two robbers, one at His right hand and the other at His left.

25
26
27
*

Those who passed by were abusing Him, *shaking their heads* [49] and saying, "Ha! You tear down the temple and build it in three days — come down from the cross, and save Yourself!" In the same way the ruling priests and the Bible scholars made fun of Him among themselves and said, "He saved others — He can't save Himself. The promised Savior, the King of Israel, should now come down from the cross. He should let us see that, and we'll believe Him." Those crucified with Him also were insulting Him.

29
30-31
32

Jesus Dies

When twelve o'clock came, darkness came over the whole country and lasted till three in the afternoon. At three o'clock Jesus called out aloud, *"Eloi, Eloi, lama sabachthani?"* [50] which means, "My God, My God, why did You forsake Me?"

33
34

Hearing Him, some of those standing near said, "Listen! He's calling Elijah." Someone ran, soaked a sponge in *sour wine,* put it on a stick, and *gave Him a drink.*[51] "Let's see," he said, "if Elijah comes to take Him down."

35
36

Then Jesus called out loud and died. And the curtain in the temple was torn in two from top to bottom.

37-38

When the captain who stood facing Jesus saw how He gave up His spirit, he said, "This Man certainly was the Son of God!"

39

There were women watching *from a distance.*[52] Among them were Mary from Magdala and Mary, the mother of James the Less and of Joseph, and Salome. While He was in Galilee, they had followed Him and helped Him. There were also many other women who had come up to Jerusalem with Him.

40
41

Jesus Is Buried

In the evening, since it was the day of preparation, that is, Friday, ᵗ Joseph from Arimathea, an important member of the Jewish court who also was waiting for God's kingdom, dared to go to Pilate and ask for Jesus' body.

42
43

* Our oldest manuscripts do not have v. 28: "And what the Bible said came true, *He will be counted among criminals.*" See Luke 22:37.

Pilate was surprised He was already dead. He called the
45 captain and asked him, "Has He died already?" When the captain told him, Pilate let Joseph have the body.

46 Joseph bought some linen, took the body down, wrapped it in the linen, and laid it in a grave that had been cut in the rock, and rolled a stone against the door of the grave.

47 Mary from Magdala and Mary the mother of Joses watched where He was laid.

Jesus Rises

16 On Saturday evening Mary from Magdala, Mary the mother of James, and Salome bought spices to go and anoint Jesus.

2 On Sunday they were coming to the grave very early when the
3 sun was up. "Who is going to roll away the stone for us from
4 the door of the grave?" they asked one another; ¹ it was very large. But when they looked up, they saw the stone had been rolled
5 back. As they went into the grave, they saw a young man, dressed in a white robe, sitting at the right. And they were amazed.

6 "Don't be amazed," he told them. "You're looking for Jesus from Nazareth, who was crucified. He has risen. He is not here.
7 See the place where He was laid. ¹ But go and tell His disciples and Peter, 'He is going ahead of you to Galilee. There you will see Him, as He told you.' "

8 They went out and hurried away from the grave, because they were trembling and bewildered. They were so frightened they didn't tell anybody anything.

The Living Savior *

9 After Jesus rose early on Sunday, He showed Himself first to Mary from Magdala, out of whom He had driven seven devils.
10 She went and told the news to those who had been with Him and
11 were now mourning and crying. When they heard He was alive and had been seen by her, they didn't believe it.

12 Later He appeared in a different form to two of them as they
13 were walking into the country. They went back and told the
14 others, but these didn't believe them either. Still later He showed Himself to the eleven while they were lying at the table, and He scolded them because their minds were closed and they didn't believe those who had seen Him after He had risen.

* The two oldest and best manuscripts do not have Mark 16:9-20 but end Mark's Gospel with verse 8.

Then He told them, "Go everywhere in the world and preach [16:15]
the good news to the whole world. He who believes and is bap- [16]
tized will be saved, but he who doesn't believe will be damned.

"The believers will have these proofs: In My name they will [17]
drive out devils. They will speak new languages. ' They will pick [18]
up snakes. If they drink any deadly poison, it will not hurt them.
They will lay their hands on the sick, and these will get well."

After talking with them, the Lord was *taken up to heaven and* [19]
sat down at the right of God.[53]

They went out and preached everywhere, and the Lord worked [20]
with them and confirmed the Word by the wonderful proofs that
went with it.

OLD TESTAMENT REFERENCES

1. Mal. 3:1
2. Is. 40:3
3. Ps. 2:7; Is. 42:1
4. Lev. 13:7, 49
5. Lev. 24:5-8;
   1 Sam. 21:6
6. Is. 6:9-10
7. Joel 3:13
8. Ps. 104:12; Ezek.
   17:23; 31:6; Dan.
   4:12, 21
9. Esther 5:3; 7:2
10. Num. 27:17;
    1 Kings 22:17;
    Ezek. 34:5
11. Is. 29:13
12. Ex. 20:12; Deut.
    5:16; Ex. 21:17;
    Lev. 20:9
13. Jer. 5:21;
    Ezek. 12:2
14. Ps. 2:7;
    Deut. 18:15
15. Mal. 4:5-6

16. Is. 66:24
17. Deut. 24:1
18. Gen. 1:27; 5:2
19. Gen. 2:24
20. Ex. 20:12-16;
    Deut. 5:16-20
21. Gen. 18:14; Job
    42:2; Zech. 8:6
22. Ps. 118:25-26
23. Is. 56:7
24. Jer. 7:11
25. Is. 5:1-2
26. Ps. 118:22-23
27. Gen. 38:8;
    Deut. 25:5-6
28. Ex. 3:6
29. Deut. 6:4-5
30. Lev. 19:18
31. Deut. 4:35; 6:4-5
32. 1 Sam. 15:22
33. Ps. 110:1
34. Dan. 2:28
35. 2 Chron. 15:6;
    Is. 19:2

36. Micah 7:6
37. Dan. 9:27; 11:31;
    12:11
38. Dan. 12:1
39. Deut. 13:1
40. Is. 13:10; 34:4
41. Dan. 7:13
42. Deut. 30:4;
    Zech. 2:6
43. Ps. 41:9
44. Ex. 24:8; Jer.
    31:32; Zech. 9:11
45. Zech. 13:7
46. Ps. 42:5; 43:5
47. Ps. 110:1;
    Dan. 7:13
48. Ps. 22:18
49. Ps. 109:25
50. Ps. 22:1
51. Ps. 69:21
52. Ps. 38:11
53. 2 Kings 2:11;
    Ps. 110:1

THE GOOD NEWS

as it was told by

LUKE

1 MANY HAVE UNDERTAKEN to plan and write a story of what has
2 been done among us, just as we heard it from those who from
3 the first became eyewitnesses and servants of the Word. For this
reason I, too, decided to check everything carefully from the
beginning and to write it down in the proper order for you, excel-
4 lent Theophilus, so that you will be sure what you have heard
is true.

An Angel Comes to Zacharias

5   When Herod was king in the country of the Jews, there was
a priest by the name of Zacharias. He belonged to the division
of priests named after Abijah. His wife was a descendant of
6 Aaron, and her name was Elizabeth. Both were righteous before
God as they lived blamelessly according to all the rules and
regulations of the Lord.

7   But they had no children, because Elizabeth was barren and
both were old.

8   Once Zacharias was on duty with his division and serving as
9 priest before God. According to the custom of the priests he was
10 chosen by lot to go into the Lord's temple to burn incense. All
the people were praying outside while he was burning incense.

11   Then he saw the Lord's angel standing at the right side of the
12 altar of incense. Zacharias was startled to see him and was
terrified.

13   *"Don't be afraid,* Zacharias," the angel told him. *"Your
prayer has been heard.*[1] *You and your wife* Elizabeth *will have*
14 *a son, and you must call him*[2] John. He will be your joy and
delight, and many will be glad he was born.

15   "He will be a great man before the Lord. *He will drink no
wine or liquor.*[3] He will be filled with the Holy Spirit even before

100   *Judea, October, 6 B.C.*

he is born. And he will bring many in Israel back to the Lord their God. He will go ahead of Him with the spirit and power 17 of *Elijah, to move fathers to love their children,*[4] and the disobedient to think as righteous men — and so to get a people thoroughly prepared for the Lord."

"How can I be sure of this?" Zacharias asked the angel. "I'm 18 an old man, and my wife is old."

"I am Gabriel!" the angel answered him. "I stand before God 19 and was sent to speak to you and tell you this good news. And 20 now, you will be silent and not able to talk till the day this happens, because you didn't believe what I said. But it will come true at the right time."

Meanwhile the people were waiting for Zacharias and were 21 surprised he was staying so long in the holy place. When he did 22 come out, he couldn't speak to them. Then they realized he had seen a vision in the holy place. He kept motioning to them and wasn't able to talk.

When the days of his service were over, he went home. After 23-24 this, his wife Elizabeth conceived and for five months she didn't show herself in public. "The Lord did this for me," she said. 25 "I was feeling ashamed among people, but He was kind and helped me, and I don't have to feel ashamed any more."

The Angel Comes to Mary

Five months later God sent the angel Gabriel to a town in 26 Galilee called Nazareth, to a virgin engaged to a man by the name 27 of Joseph, a descendant of David. The virgin's name was Mary.

Coming into her home, the angel said, "Greetings, you blessed 28 one. The Lord is with you."

Startled by what he said, she tried to figure out what such 29 a greeting might mean.

"Don't be afraid, Mary," the angel told her. "God is good 30 to you. *You see, you will conceive and have a son, and you will 31 call Him*[5] Jesus. He will be great and will be called *the Son of 32 the most high God. And the Lord will give Him *the throne of 33 His ancestor David. He will be King over* the people of Jacob *forever, and His kingdom will never end."*[6]

"How can this be?" Mary asked the angel. "I'm not living 34 with a husband."

"The Holy Spirit will come over you," the angel answered her, 35 "and a power of the most high God will overshadow you. And for

1:36 that reason the Child will be called holy and God's Son. Now there is also Elizabeth, your relative. She is old, but she, too, conceived. People call her childless, but she's now in her sixth
37 month. *There's nothing that God will not be able to do."* [7]
38 "I am the Lord's servant," Mary answered. "Let it happen to me as you said."

Then the angel left her.

Mary Visits Elizabeth

39 Then Mary hurried away to the hill country to a town of Judah.
40 There she went into the home of Zacharias and greeted Elizabeth.
41 When Elizabeth heard Mary's greeting, the baby leaped in
42 her womb. Then Elizabeth was filled with the Holy Spirit, [1] and she shouted, "Blessed are you among women, and blessed is the
43 Child in your womb. But how does this happen to me that the
44 mother of my Lord comes to me? The moment I heard your
45 greeting, the baby leaped with delight in my womb. And you are happy for believing that the Lord will do what He promised you."
46 Mary said:

"My soul is praising *the Lord,*
47 And my spirit *delights in God, my Savior,*[8]
48 Because *He has looked kindly at His humble servant.*[9]
Yes, from now on the people in all the ages will call me blessed.
49 He has done great things to me —
He who is mighty
And *whose name is holy* [10]
50 And *who is always merciful to those who fear Him.*[11]

51 "Mighty are the deeds He has done *with His arm.*
He has scattered [12] those who feel and think so proudly.
52 *He has pushed strong rulers down* from their thrones
And *lifted up lowly people.*[13]
53 *Those who were hungry He has filled with good things,*[14]
And the rich He has sent away empty-handed.

54 *"He has come to help His servant Israel,*[15]
Because He wants to *remember His mercy* [16]
55 (as *He promised our fathers*),
*The mercy He has for Abraham
and his descendants forever."* [17]

Mary stayed with Elizabeth about three months and then went
back home.

John Is Born

The time came for Elizabeth to give birth, and she had a baby ⁵⁷
boy. Her neighbors and relatives heard how the Lord had been ⁵⁸
unusually kind to her, and they were happy with her.

On the eighth day they came to circumcise the baby. They ⁵⁹
were going to call him Zacharias because that was his father's
name. But his mother spoke up. "No!" she said. "He's going to ⁶⁰
be called John."

"But there's nobody among your relatives who has that name," ⁶¹
they told her.

Then they motioned to his father to see what name he might ⁶²
want him to have. He asked for a writing tablet and wrote, "His ⁶³
name is John." They were all surprised.

Just then he got his speech back and could talk again. He ⁶⁴
began to speak, praising God.

All who lived around them were overawed. And all over the ⁶⁵
hills of Judea people kept talking about all these things. All who ⁶⁶
heard of them kept them in mind. "What is this child going
to be?" they asked. It was clear — the Lord's hand was with him.

His father Zacharias was filled with the Holy Spirit, and he ⁶⁷
prophesied:

"*Praise the Lord, the God of Israel,*[18] ⁶⁸
Because He has visited *His people*
 And prepared *a ransom for them.*[19]
He has *given* a descendant of His servant *David* ⁶⁹
 To be our *victorious Savior,*[20]
As He said long ago through His holy prophets ⁷⁰
That *He would save* us *from* our *enemies,* ⁷¹
 From the power of all *who hate* [21] us.
He wanted to be *merciful to our fathers* [22] ⁷²
And *keep in mind His* holy *covenant,*
 The oath He swore to our father *Abraham* ⁷³
To rescue us from our *enemies* [23] ⁷⁴
And let us serve Him without fear
 In holiness and righteousness before Him all our life. ⁷⁵

"And you, child, will be called a prophet of the most high God. You will go *ahead of the Lord to prepare the ways for Him,*[24]

77 To tell His people they can be saved
  by the forgiveness of their sins,

78 Because our God is merciful
  And will let a heavenly Sun rise among us,

79 *To shine on those who sit in the dark
  and in the shadow of death.*[25]
And to guide our feet into *the way of peace.*" [26]

80 The child John grew and became strong in spirit. He lived in the wilderness till he appeared publicly before Israel.

Jesus Is Born

2 In those days Emperor Augustus ordered a census taken of
2 the whole world. This was the first census, and it was taken while
3 Quirinius was ruling Syria. Everybody went to register, each to his own town.

4 Joseph also went up from the town of Nazareth in Galilee to David's town, called Bethlehem, in Judea, because he was one
5 of the descendants of David, [1] to register with Mary, his bride, who was going to have a child.

6 And while they were there, the time came for her to have
7 her child. She had her first Son, and she wrapped Him up and laid Him in a manger because there was no room for them in the inn.

The Shepherds

8 There were shepherds not far away, living in the field and taking turns watching their flock during the night.

9 Then the Lord's angel stood by them, and the Lord's glory
10 shone around them. They were terrified. [1] "Don't be afraid," the angel said to them. "I have good news for you. A great joy will
11 come to all the people: The Savior, who is Christ the Lord, was
12 born for you today in David's town. And this is how you will know Him: you will find a Baby all wrapped up and lying in a manger."

13 Suddenly there was with the angel a large crowd of the angels
14 of heaven, who were praising God and saying: "Glory to God in the highest heavens, and on earth peace among people who have His good will!"

15 When the angels had left them and gone to heaven, the shep-

herds said to one another, "The Lord has told us what has happened. Let's go to Bethlehem and see it."

They hurried over there and searched until they found Mary 2:16
and Joseph, and the Baby lying in the manger. When they had 17
seen Him, they told others what they had been told about this
Child. And everybody was surprised to hear the story the shep- 18
herds told.

But Mary treasured all these things in her heart and kept 19
thinking about them.

The shepherds went back, glorifying and praising God for 20
everything they had heard and seen. It was just as they had
been told.

In the Temple

On the eighth day the time came to circumcise the Child, and 21
He was called Jesus, the name the angel gave Him before He
was conceived.

· When *the time came* for them *to be purified* [27] according to 22
the Law of Moses, Joseph and Mary took Jesus up to Jerusalem
to give Him to the Lord (as it is written in the Law of the Lord, 23
Every firstborn boy should be called *the Lord's holy one* [28]) and to 24
offer a sacrifice according to the Law of the Lord, *a pair of turtle-
doves or two young pigeons.*[29]

Now, there was in Jerusalem a man by the name of Simeon. 25
He was a good man, fearing God and waiting for the One who
would comfort Israel. The Holy Spirit was on him. ¹ The Holy 26
Spirit had told him that before he would die he would see the
Savior sent by the Lord.

Moved by the Spirit, he went into the temple. When the 27
parents brought in the Child Jesus to do for Him what was customary according to the Law, Simeon took Him in his arms, 28
praised God, and said:

"Lord, now You are letting Your servant go in peace as You 29
    promised,

Because my eyes have *seen Your salvation* [30] 30

That You prepared for all people to see, 31

A light to shine on the Gentiles, 32

And the *glory of* Your people *Israel.*" [31]

His father and mother were surprised such things were said 33
about Him. Then Simeon blessed them and said to His mother 34
Mary, "Here is what this Child is appointed for: Many in Israel

2:35 will fall and rise again because of Him; and He'll be a sign that many will talk against, to show what they're thinking in their hearts. And pain, like a sword, will go through your own soul too."

36 Anna, a prophetess, was also there. She was a daughter of Phanuel, of the tribe of Asher. She was now very old. When she was a girl, she had married a man and lived with him seven years.

37 ¹ After that she was a widow till she was eighty-four. She never left the temple but worshiped day and night, fasting and praying.

38 She, too, came forward just then, thanked God, and talked about the Child to all who were looking for Jerusalem to be set free.

39 When Joseph and Mary had done everything the Law of the Lord told them to do, they went back to Galilee to their town of Nazareth.

The Boy Jesus

40 The little Child grew big and strong and full of wisdom, and God's love was with Him.

41 Every year His parents would go to Jerusalem to celebrate
42 the Passover. And so when He was twelve, they went up for the festival as usual.

43 When the festival days were over and they started for home, the boy Jesus stayed behind in Jerusalem. But His parents didn't
44 know about it. They thought He was with the others who were traveling with them. After traveling a day, they started to look
45 for Him among their relatives and friends. When they didn't find Him, they went back to Jerusalem, looking for Him.

46 Two days later they found Him in the temple, sitting among
47 the teachers, listening to them and asking them questions. His understanding and His answers surprised all who heard Him.

48 His parents were amazed to see Him there. "Son, why did You do this to us?" His mother asked Him. "See how anxiously Your father and I have been looking for You!"

49 "Why were you looking for Me?" He asked them. "Didn't
50 you know I must be in My Father's house?" But they didn't understand what He told them.

51 Then He went back with them to Nazareth. And He obeyed them.

52 His mother kept all these things in her heart. ¹ And Jesus grew wiser and taller and *won the approval of God and of people.*³²

John Prepares the Way

In the fifteenth year of the rule of Emperor Tiberius, Pontius **3**
Pilate was governor of Judea, Herod ruled Galilee, his brother
Philip ruled Iturea and Trachonitis, Lysanias ruled Abilene, ' and **2**
Annas and Caiaphas were the high priests. Then God spoke to
John, the son of Zacharias, in the wilderness. He went into the **3**
whole Jordan valley and preached: "Repent and be baptized to
have your sins forgiven." This was what the prophet Isaiah had **4**
said in his book:

> Someone will be calling in the wilderness:
> "Prepare the way for the Lord,
> Make the paths straight for Him.
> Every ravine must be filled, **5**
> And every mountain and hill must be cut down.
> The crooked must be made straight
> And the rough roads smooth.
> All people must see how God saves them." ³³ **6**

So he would say to the crowds who were coming out to be bap- **7**
tized by him, "Brood of snakes, who warned you to run away
from the punishment waiting for you? Do the works that show **8**
you have repented. And don't start telling yourselves, 'Abraham
is our father.' I tell you, God can raise children for Abraham
from these stones. The ax is now ready to strike at the roots **9**
of the trees, and any tree that doesn't produce good fruit will be
cut down and thrown into the fire."

"What should we do?" the crowds asked him. **10**

"If you have two garments," he answered them, "share them **11**
with him who has none, and if you have food, do the same."

Some tax collectors also came to be baptized. "Teacher," **12**
they asked him, "what should we do?"

"Don't collect more money than you're ordered to collect," he **13**
told them.

Some soldiers also asked him, "And what should we do?" **14**

"Don't use threats or blackmail to get money from anyone,"
he told them, "but be satisfied with your pay."

The people were expecting something and all were wonder- **15**
ing if John was perhaps the promised Savior. John answered them **16**
all: "I baptize you with water. But the One who is mightier than
I is coming. I'm not good enough to untie His shoe straps. He
will baptize you with the Holy Spirit and fire. He has the win- **17**

nowing shovel in His hand to clean up His threshing floor and gather the wheat into His barn, but the chaff He'll burn in a fire that can't be put out."

3:18 And so with many other challenging words he was telling the people the good news.

In Prison

19 When John was showing Herod, the governor, how wrong he was in regard to his brother's wife Herodias and all the other 20 wicked things Herod did, | he, on top of everything, locked John up in prison.

John Baptizes Jesus

21 When all the people were being baptized, Jesus was bap- 22 tized too. While He was praying, heaven opened, and the Holy Spirit came down on Him in the bodily form of a dove. And a voice from heaven said, "You are *My Son,* whom I love. *I am delighted* 34 with You."

23 Jesus was about thirty years old when He began His work.

The Son of Man

24 Jesus was a son, as people thought, of Joseph, of Heli, of 25 Matthat, of Levi, of Melchi, of.Jannai, of Joseph, | of Mattathias, 26 of Amos, of Nahum, of Esli, of Naggai, | of Maath, of Mattathias, 27 of Semein, of Josech, of Joda, | of Joanan, of Rhesa, of Zerub- 28 babel, of Shealtiel, of Neri, | of Melchi, of Addi, of Cosam, of El- 29 madam, of Er, | of Jesus, of Eliezer, of Jorim, of Matthat, of Levi, 30-31 | of Simeon, of Judas, of Joseph, of Jonam, of Eliakim, | of Melea, 32 of Menna, of Mattatha, of Nathan, of David, | of Jesse, of Obed, 33 of Boaz, of Salmon, of Nahshon, | of Amminadab, of Ram, of 34 Admin, of Arni, of Hezron, of Perez, of Judah, | of Jacob, of Isaac, 35 of Abraham, of Terah, of Nahor, | of Serug, of Reu, of Peleg, of 36 Eber, of Shelah, | of Cainan, of Arphaxad, of Shem, of Noah, of 37 Lamech, | of Methuselah, of Enoch, of Jared, of Mahalaleel, 38 of Cainan, | of Enos, of Seth, of Adam, of God.

The Devil Tempts Jesus

4 1-2 Jesus, full of the Holy Spirit, left the Jordan. For forty days 1-2 | the Spirit led Him in the wilderness | while the devil tempted Him.

He ate nothing during those days, and when they were over, He got hungry.

The devil said to Him, "If You're God's Son, tell this stone 4:3 to become a loaf of bread."

"It is written," Jesus answered him, *"A man doesn't live on* 4 *bread alone."* [35]

The devil took Him up and in a moment showed Him all the 5 kingdoms of the world. "I'll give You all this power and glory," 6 the devil told Him, "because it was given to me and I give it to anyone I please. So, if You'll worship me, all this will be Yours." 7

"It is written," Jesus answered him, "Worship *the Lord, your* 8 *God, and serve Him* [36] *only."*

The devil took Him into Jerusalem and had Him stand on 9 the edge of the temple. "If You're God's Son," he told Him, "jump down from here. It is written, *He will order His angels to* 10 *watch carefully over you. They will carry you in their hands* and 11 *never let you stub your foot against a stone."* [37]

"It is written," Jesus answered him, *"Don't test the Lord* 12 *your God."* [38]

When the devil had finished every way of tempting Him, he left 13 Him till the right time would come.

Nazareth Rejects Jesus

With the power of the Spirit Jesus went back to Galilee. The 14 news about Him spread all over the surrounding country. He 15 taught in their synagogs, and everybody praised Him.

Then Jesus came to Nazareth, where He had been raised. On 16 the Sabbath He went into the synagog as He used to do. He got up to read [1] and was given the scroll of the prophet Isaiah. Unroll- 17 ing the scroll, He found the place where it says:

The Spirit of the Lord is on Me because — 18
He anointed Me
   To tell the poor the good news.
He sent Me
   To announce to prisoners, "You are free,"
      to the blind, "You will see again,"
   To free those who are broken down,
   To announce a season when the Lord welcomes people.[39] 19

He rolled up the scroll, gave it back to the attendant, and sat 20 down. Everybody in the synagog was watching Him closely [1] as He said, "Today, while you're listening, what is written here has come true."

22   All spoke well of Him and were surprised to hear the beautiful words flowing from His lips. "Isn't this Joseph's son?" they were asking.

23   He answered them: "You will undoubtedly quote to Me the proverb 'Doctor, heal yourself!' and say, 'We've heard about everything You did in Capernaum. Do the same here in Your 24 home town.' I tell you," He added, "it is true no prophet is accepted in his home town.

25   "Let Me tell you this truth: There were many widows in Israel in the days of Elijah, when it didn't rain for three years and six 26 months and there was a big famine all over the country. But Elijah wasn't sent to anyone except *a widow at Zarephath in the* 27 *territory of Sidon*.[40] And there were lepers in Israel at the time of the prophet Elisha. But no one except *Naaman* from Syria *was made clean.*" [41]

28   As they were listening, all in the synagog became furious. 29 They got up, pushed Him out of the town, and took Him to a brow of the hill on which their town was built, to hurl Him down the 30 cliff. But He walked right through them and went away.

Jesus Drives Out a Devil

31   He went down to Capernaum, a town in Galilee, and was 32 teaching people on a Sabbath. His teaching amazed them because He spoke with authority.

33   In the synagog there was a man with a spirit of an unclean 34 devil. He screamed out loud, [1] "Oh, leave us alone, Jesus from Nazareth! You've come to destroy us! I know who You are — God's Holy One."

35   Jesus talked sharply to him: "Be quiet, and come out of him." The devil hurled him into the crowd, then came out of him without doing him any harm.

36   They were all amazed and said to one another, "What kind of speaking is this? With authority and power He gives orders to the unclean spirits, and out they go."

37   So the news about Him spread to every place in the surrounding country.

Peter's Mother-in-Law

Leaving the synagog, Jesus went to Simon's home. Simon's 4:38
mother-in-law was sick with a high fever, and they asked Him
to help her. He went to her and, bending over her, ordered the 39
fever to leave, and it left. She got up immediately and waited on
them.

When the sun was going down, all who had sick ones suffer- 40
ing from various diseases brought them to Him. He laid His
hands on each of them and made them well. The devils went 41
out of many, screaming, "You're God's Son." He talked sharply
to them and wouldn't let them go on talking, because they knew
He was the promised Savior.

In the morning He went out to a lonely place. The crowds 42
were looking for Him. When they came to Him, they tried to
keep Him from leaving them. But He said to them, "I have 43
to tell the good news of God's kingdom also in other towns.
That's what I was sent to do."

Then He kept on preaching in the synagogs of the country 44
of the Jews.

Fishers of Men

One day Jesus was standing by the Lake of Galilee, and the 5
people were crowding Him as they were listening to God's Word.
¹ He saw two boats on the shore of the lake. The fishermen had 2
stepped out of them and were washing their nets. So Jesus got 3
into one of the boats (it belonged to Simon) and asked him to
go out a little way from the shore. Then He sat down and taught
the people from the boat.

When He had stopped speaking, He told Simon, "Take the 4
boat out where the water is deep, and let down your nets for
a catch."

"Master," Simon answered, "we've worked hard all night and 5
caught nothing. But if You say so, I'll let down the nets."

When the men had done this, they caught a very large number 6
of fish, and their nets started to tear. So they waved to their 7
partners in the other boat to come and help them. They came,
and now they filled both boats so that they started to sink.

When Simon Peter saw this, he fell down at Jesus' knees. 8
"Leave me, Lord," he said. "I'm a sinful man." ¹ He and all who 9
were with him were amazed to see the fish they had caught, and 10

so were James and John, Zebedee's sons, who were Simon's partners.

"Don't be afraid," Jesus told Simon. "From now on you're going to catch men."

5:11 So when they had brought the boats to the shore, they left everything and followed Him.

Jesus Heals a Leper

12 One day Jesus was in a town where there was a man who had leprosy all over his body. When he saw Jesus, he bowed down to the ground. "Lord," he begged Him, "if You want to, You can make me clean."

13 Jesus stretched out His hand and touched him. "I want to," He said. "Be clean!" Immediately the leprosy left him.

14 "Don't tell anyone," Jesus ordered him, "but go, *let the priest examine* [42] you, and for your cleansing offer the sacrifice Moses ordered, to show them you're well."

15 But the news about Jesus spread all the more, and big crowds
16 were gathering to hear Him and have their diseases healed. And He would go away to lonely places and pray.

Jesus Forgives Sins

17 One day as He was teaching, Pharisees and Bible teachers were sitting there. They had come from every village in Galilee and Judea and from Jerusalem. And Jesus had the Lord's power to heal.

18 Then some men brought a paralyzed man on a bed and tried
19 to take him in and lay him in front of Jesus. But when they couldn't find a way to get him in on account of the crowd, they went up on the roof and through the tiles let him and the bed down among the people, right in front of Jesus.

20 When Jesus saw their faith, He said, "Man, your sins are
21 forgiven." Then the Bible scholars and the Pharisees began to argue, saying, "Who is this fellow, talking such blasphemies? Who but God alone can forgive sins?"

22 Jesus knew what they were thinking. "Why do you have such
23 thoughts in your hearts?" He asked them. "Is it easier to say,
24 'Your sins are forgiven,' or to say, 'Get up and walk'? I want you to know the Son of Man has power on earth to forgive sins" — then He said to the paralyzed man, "I tell you, get up, take your bed, and go home."

Immediately the man got up in front of them, took the bed he had been lying on, and went home, praising God.

All were amazed and praised God. Fearfully they declared, ²⁶ "You wouldn't believe what we've seen today!"

Matthew

After that He went out and saw a tax collector by the name ²⁷ of Levi sitting in the tax office. "Come with Me," He told him. He got up, left everything, and went with Him. ²⁸

Then Levi gave a big dinner for Him at his home, and there ²⁹ was a big crowd of tax collectors and others who were eating with them.

The Pharisees and their Bible scholars complained to His ³⁰ disciples: "Why do you eat and drink with tax collectors and sinners?"

"Those who are healthy don't need a doctor," Jesus answered ³¹ them, "but the sick. I didn't come to call righteous people, but ³² sinners to repent."

The Bridegroom

"John's disciples as well as the disciples of the Pharisees often ³³ fast and say prayers," they said to Him. "Why do Yours eat and drink?"

Jesus asked them, "Can you make the bridegroom's friends ³⁴ fast while the bridegroom is with them? The time will come when ³⁵ the bridegroom will be taken away from them, and in those days they will fast."

He pictured it to them in this way: "Nobody tears a piece of ³⁶ cloth from a new garment and sews it on an old garment. If you do, you'll tear the new cloth, and the patch from the new won't match the old. Nobody pours new wine into old wineskins. ³⁷ If you do, the new wine will burst the skins and run out, and the skins will be ruined. New wine has to be poured into fresh ³⁸ skins.

"Nobody who has drunk old wine wants the new. 'The old ³⁹ tastes good,' he says."

Lord of the Sabbath

While Jesus was walking through grainfields on a Sabbath, **6** His disciples were picking the heads of grain, rubbing them in their hands, and eating them.

113

Some of the Pharisees asked, "Why are you doing something you shouldn't do on a day of rest?"

3   "Haven't you read what David did," Jesus asked them, "when
4 he and his men were hungry — how he went into God's house and took the *loaves laid before God*,[43] and ate them and gave
5 his men some? Only the priests had the right to eat them." Then He added, "The Son of Man is Lord of the Sabbath."

The Shriveled Hand

6   On another Sabbath Jesus went into a synagog and taught.
7 And there was a man whose right hand was shriveled. But the Bible scholars and the Pharisees were watching Jesus to see if He would heal him on a Sabbath. They wanted to find something to accuse Him of.

8   But He knew what they were thinking; so He said to the man with the shriveled hand, "Get up and come forward." The man
9 got up and stood there. Then Jesus said to them, "I ask you, is it right on a Sabbath to do good or to do evil, to save a life or
10 to kill?" After looking around at all of them, He told the man, "Stretch out your hand." He did, and his hand was made healthy again.

11   They were furious and began to discuss with one another what they could do to Jesus.

Twelve Apostles

12   In those days Jesus went out to the hill to pray, and He prayed to God all night.

13   When it was day, He called His disciples. He chose twelve
14 of them and called them apostles: Simon, whom He also gave the name Peter, and his brother Andrew; James and John, Philip
15 and Bartholomew, Matthew and Thomas; James, the son of
16 Alphaeus; Simon, called Zealot; Judas, the son of James; and Judas, the man from Kerioth, who became a traitor.

Many Are Healed

17   He went down with them and stood on a level place with a big crowd of His disciples and very many people from the whole country of the Jews, from Jerusalem, and from the seacoast of Tyre and Sidon. They had come to hear Him and have their
18 diseases healed. And those who were plagued by unclean spirits

were made well. All the people were trying to touch Him, because
power came from Him and made them all well.

Happy and Unhappy

Jesus looked at His disciples and said: [20]

"Happy are you who are poor —
you have God's kingdom.

Happy are you who are hungry now — [21]
you will be satisfied.

Happy are you who are crying now —
you will laugh.

Happy are you when people hate you, exclude you from their com- [22]
pany, insult you, reject your name as evil because you believe
in the Son of Man. On that day be glad and dance with delight, [23]
because you have a great reward in heaven. You see, that's
how their fathers treated the prophets. But — [24]

Woe to you who are rich —
you've had your comfort.

Woe to you who are well fed now — [25]
you will be hungry.

Woe to you who are laughing now —
you will mourn and cry aloud.

Woe to you when everybody speaks well of you — [26]
that is how their fathers treated the false prophets."

Love Your Enemies

"But I tell you who are listening, love your enemies, be kind [27]
to those who hate you, ǀ bless those who curse you, and pray for [28]
those who insult you. If anyone hits you on your cheek, offer [29]
him the other cheek. If anyone takes your coat, don't stop him
from taking your shirt. If anyone asks you for anything, give it to [30]
him. And if anyone takes what is yours, don't insist on getting
it back.

"Treat others just as you want them to treat you. [31]

"If you love those who love you, how should anyone be [32]
especially pleased with you? Even sinners love those who love
them. If you help those who help you, how should anyone be [33]
especially pleased with you? Sinners do that too. ǀ If you lend [34]
anything to those from whom you expect to get something, how

115

should anyone be especially pleased with you? Sinners also lend
6:35 to sinners to get back what they lend. No, love your enemies,
help them, and lend to them without expecting to get anything
back. Then you will have a great reward and will be the sons
of the most high God, since He is kind to people who don't thank
36 Him and are wicked. Be merciful as your Father is merciful."

Criticize Yourself

37   "Don't judge, and you will not be judged. Don't condemn,
and you will not be condemned. Forgive, and you will be forgiven.
38 ˡ Give, and it will be given you. A good measure, pressed together, shaken down, and running over, will be put into your lap.
You see, the measure you use will be used for you."

39   He pictured it to them in this way: "Can a blind man lead
40 another blind man? Won't they both fall into a ditch? ˡ A pupil is
not above his teacher. But anyone who is well trained will be
like his teacher.

41   "And why do you look at the speck in your brother's eye and
42 don't notice the log in your own eye? How can you say to your
brother, 'Brother, let me take the speck out of your eye,' as long
as you don't see the log in your own eye? You hypocrite, first
throw the log out of your own eye. Then you'll see clearly enough
to take the speck out of your brother's eye."

Hear and Do!

43   "A good tree doesn't bear bad fruit, or a bad tree good fruit.
44 ˡ Every tree is known by its fruit. You don't pick figs from thorn-
45 bushes, or grapes from brambles. A good man produces good
things from the good stored in his heart, and an evil man produces
evil from his evil stored there. What you say flows from your
heart.

46   "Why do you call Me Lord, Lord, but don't do what I tell you?
47   "I will show you what kind of man anyone is who comes
48 to Me and hears and does what I say. He's like a man who built a
house. He dug deep and laid the foundation on a rock. When
there was a flood, the torrent dashed against that house. But it
49 couldn't move it, because it was built right. Anyone who hears
what I say but doesn't do it is like a man who built a house on the
ground without a foundation. When the torrent dashed against
it, that house immediately collapsed and went down with a big
crash."

A Believing Captain

When Jesus had finished all He had to say to the people who heard Him, He went to Capernaum. There a certain captain's slave was sick. He was dear to him and now he was dying. The captain heard about Jesus and sent some Jewish elders to ask Him to come and save his slave's life. They came to Jesus and earnestly pleaded with Him, "He deserves to have You do this for him, because he loves our people and built the synagog for us."

So Jesus went with them. He wasn't far from the house when the captain sent friends to tell Him, "Lord, don't bother. I'm not good enough for You to come under my roof. And so I didn't think I was fit to come to You either. But just say a word, and my slave will be made well. I'm only a man who has to obey others, but I have soldiers under me. I tell one, Go, and he goes. And another, Come, and he comes. And my slave, Do this, and he does it."

Surprised to hear him say this, Jesus turned to the crowd following Him. "I tell you," He said, "not even in Israel have I found such faith."

When the men who had been sent went back to the house, they found the slave well again.

Jesus Raises a Widow's Son

Soon after this, Jesus went to a town called Nain, and His disciples and a large crowd went with Him. As He came near the gate of the town, a dead man was carried out. He was his mother's only son, and she was a widow. A big crowd from the town was with her.

When the Lord saw her, He felt sorry for her. "Don't cry," He told her.

He went up to the open coffin and touched it, and the men who were carrying it stood still. "Young man," He said, "I tell you, wake up." The dead man sat up and started to talk. And Jesus *gave him to his mother.*[44]

They were all overawed and praised God. "A great prophet has risen among us," they said, and, "God has come to help His people." This story about Jesus spread all over the country of the Jews and in all the surrounding territory.

John Sends Two Disciples

John's disciples told him about all these things. Then John called two of his disciples and sent them to ask the Lord, "Are

You the One who is coming, or should we look for someone else?"

7:20   The men came to Jesus and said, "John the Baptizer sent us to ask You, 'Are You the One who is coming, or should we look for someone else?' "

21   Just then He had healed many people of their diseases, ailments, and evil spirits and had given sight to many who were blind.

22   "Go," Jesus answered, "tell John what you've seen and heard: *The blind see,* the lame walk, lepers are made clean, the *deaf hear,* the dead are raised, and *the poor hear the good news* 45 —

23 and happy is anyone who doesn't turn against Me."

About John

24   When John's messengers had left, Jesus talked to the crowds about John:

"What did you go out into the wilderness to see — a reed shaken by the wind? What, then, did you go out to see — a man

25 dressed in soft robes? Those who wear fine clothes and live in luxury you'll find in the palaces of kings.

26   "What, then, did you go out to see — a prophet? Let Me

27 assure you, far more than a prophet. This is the one of whom it is written, '*I will send My messenger ahead of You to prepare*

28 *Your way before* 46 *You.*' I tell you, no woman's son is greater than John, and yet the least in God's kingdom is greater than he.

29   "By letting John baptize them, all the people who heard him,

30 even the tax collectors, admitted that God was right. But the Pharisees and the learned men of the Law, by not letting John baptize them, rejected what God had planned for them.

31   "How should I picture the people of this age? What are they

32 like? They're like little children sitting in the marketplace and calling to one another, 'We played a tune on the flute for you, but you didn't dance. We sang a funeral song, but you didn't

33 weep.' John the Baptizer has come; he doesn't eat bread or

34 drink wine, and you say, 'There's a devil in him!' The Son of Man has come; He eats and drinks, and you say, 'Look at the glutton and drunkard, the friend of tax collectors and sinners!'

35 And yet wisdom is shown to be right by all her children."

"She Loved Much"

36   One of the Pharisees invited Jesus to eat with him. He went into the Pharisee's home and lay down for the meal.

In the town there was a sinful woman. When she found out He was eating at the Pharisee's home, she brought a flask of perfume ¹ and stood behind Him at His feet. She was weeping and started to wet His feet with her tears. Then with the hair of her head she dried His feet, kissed them, and poured perfume on them.

The Pharisee who had invited Jesus saw this and said to himself, "If He were a prophet, He would know who is touching Him and what kind of woman she is. She's a sinner."

"Simon," Jesus answered him, "I have something to tell you."

"Say it, Teacher," he said.

"Two men owed a moneylender some money: One owed him five hundred denarii, and the other fifty. When they couldn't pay it back, he was kind enough to cancel the debt for both of them. Now, which of them will love him more?"

"I suppose," Simon answered, "the one who had the bigger debt canceled."

"You're right," Jesus told him. Then, turning to the woman, He said to Simon, "You see this woman? I came into your home, and you gave Me no water for My feet, but she wet My feet with her tears and dried them with her hair. You gave Me no kiss, but ever since I came in, she hasn't stopped kissing My feet. You poured no oil on My head, but she poured perfume on My feet. That's why I tell you her sins are forgiven, many as they are. You see, she has loved much. Of course, he to whom little is forgiven loves only a little."

Then He said to her, "Your sins are forgiven." His fellow guests began to ask among themselves, "Who is This that He should even forgive sins?"

Jesus said to the woman, "Your faith saved you. Go in peace!"

Through Galilee

After this Jesus traveled from one town and village to another, preaching and telling the good news of God's kingdom. The twelve were with Him. ¹ Also some women who had been healed of evil spirits and diseases: Mary, also called the woman from Magdala (seven devils had gone out of her); Johanna, the wife of Herod's manager Chusa; Susanna; and many other women. They supported Jesus and His disciples with their property.

The Sower

8:4   When a big crowd was gathering and people were coming to Him from every town, He told them a parable:

5   "A sower went out to sow his seed. As he was sowing, some seed fell along the road and was trampled on, and the birds in 6 the air ate it. ¹ Some fell on a rock. It came up and withered 7 because it had no moisture. Some seed fell among thorns, and 8 the thorns grew up with it and choked it. But some seed fell on good ground, and it came up and produced a hundred times as much as was sown."

When He had said this, He called out, "You have ears to hear. Then listen!"

9-10   His disciples asked Him what this parable meant. "You are given the privilege to know the secrets of God's kingdom," He answered, "but to the others they come in parables that *they may see and yet not see, and hear and yet not understand*.⁴⁷

11-12   "This is what the parable means: The seed is God's Word. The people along the road are those who hear it. Then the devil comes and takes the Word out of their hearts to keep them from 13 believing and being saved. ¹ In others it falls on a rock. As soon as they hear it, they welcome the Word with joy, but it doesn't take root in them. They believe for a while, but when they're 14 tempted, they desert. In others the seed falls among thorns. They hear the Word, but as they go along, worries, riches, and pleasures of life choke them, and they don't produce anything 15 good. ¹ But in others the seed falls on good ground. They are the ones who hear the Word and keep it in a good and honest heart and go on faithfully producing good things.

16   "Nobody lights a lamp and hides it under a jar or puts it under a bed. No, you put it on a lampstand so that those who 17 come in will see the light. Everything hidden will be uncovered, and every secret will be known and come to the light.

18   "Be careful, then, how you listen! If you have something, you'll be given more. But if you don't have what you should have, even what you think you have will be taken away from you."

The Mother and Brothers of Jesus

19   His mother and His brothers came to Him but couldn't get 20 near Him on account of the crowd. Jesus was told, "Your mother and Your brothers are standing outside and want to see You."

"My mother and My brothers are these," He .answered them, "who hear and do what God says."

Wind and Water Obey Him

One day He and His disciples stepped into a boat. "Let us 22 cross over to the other side of the lake," He said to them. They 23 started out. And as they were sailing along, He fell asleep.

A violent storm hit the lake, the boat was filling with water, and they were in danger. So they went to Him and woke 24 Him up. "Master, Master!" they called, "we're drowning."

He got up and ordered the winds and the waves to stop. They stopped and it became calm. ' "Where is your trust?" He 25 asked them.

Frightened and amazed, they asked one another, "Who is He? He orders even the winds and the water, and they obey Him!"

The Gerasenes

They landed in the country of the Gerasenes, which is op- 26 posite Galilee. When He stepped out on the shore, a man from 27 the town who had devils in him met Him. He had worn no clothes for a long time. He wouldn't stay in a house but in the burial places. When he saw Jesus, he screamed and bowed 28 down before Him. "Let me alone, Jesus, Son of the most high God," he shouted. "I beg You, don't torture me." ' Jesus had 29 been ordering the unclean spirit to come out of the man. For a long time it had a firm hold on him. He had been bound with chains on hands and feet and had been kept under guard, but he would tear the chains and be driven by the devil into lonely places.

"What is your name?" Jesus asked him. 30

"Six thousand," he answered, because many devils had gone into him. They begged Him not to order them to go into the 31 bottomless pit.

There was a herd of many hogs feeding on the hillside. So 32 they begged Him to let them go into these. He let them. ' The 33 devils came out of the man and went into the hogs, and the herd stampeded down the cliff into the lake and was drowned.

But when those who had taken care of the hogs saw what 34 had happened, they ran away and told about it in the town and in the country. The people went out to see what had happened. 35 They came to Jesus and found the man from whom the devils

had gone out, now sitting dressed and in his right mind at Jesus'
8:36 feet; and they were frightened. Those who had seen it told
them how the man plagued by devils had been made well.

37   Then all the people of the surrounding country of the
Gerasenes asked Jesus to leave them, because terror had gripped
them.

38   He got into a boat and started back. ¹ Now, the man from
whom the devils had gone out begged Jesus to let him be with
39 Him. But He sent him away and told him, ¹ "Go home and tell
how much God has done for you." So the man left and
preached all over the town how much Jesus had done for him.

The Daughter of Jairus

40   When Jesus came back, the people welcomed Him, because
they were all expecting Him.

41   A synagog leader by the name of Jairus came and, kneeling
42 at Jesus' feet, begged Him to come to his home, ¹ because his only
daughter, about twelve years old, was dying. As he went, the
crowd almost crushed Him.

43   There was a woman who had a flow of blood for twelve
44 years. Nobody could cure her. ¹ She came to Him from behind
45 and touched the tassel of His garment, and immediately her
blood stopped flowing.

"Who touched Me?" Jesus asked.

When everybody denied having touched Him, Peter said,
"Master, the people are crowding You and pressing against
You."

46   "Somebody did touch Me," Jesus said. "I noticed that
power went from Me."

47   When the woman saw she was discovered, she came trembling,
bowed down before Him, and in front of all the people told why
she touched Him and how she was made well immediately.

48   "Daughter," He told her, "your faith made you well. Go in
peace!"

49   While He was still speaking, someone came from the synagog
leader. "Your daughter is dead," he said. "Don't trouble the
Teacher any more."

50   Hearing this, Jesus told him, "Don't be afraid! Only believe,
and she'll get well."

51   Coming into the house, He let only Peter, John, James, and
52 the child's father and mother go in with him. Everybody was

crying and beating the breast, mourning her. "Don't cry," He said. "She isn't dead; she's sleeping."

They laughed at Him, because they knew she had died. He 8:53-54 took her hand and called, "Girl, wake up!" Her spirit returned, 55 and she got up immediately. Jesus ordered that she be given something to eat. And her parents were amazed. But He or- 56 dered them not to tell anyone what had happened.

Jesus Sends Out the Twelve

Jesus called the twelve together and gave them power and 9 authority over all devils and to heal diseases. He sent them to 2 preach God's kingdom and heal the sick.

"Don't take anything with you on the way," He told them, 3 "no stick or bag or bread or money. Don't take two tunics. When you go into a home, stay there, and from there go out. 4 If people don't welcome you, leave that town, and shake the 5 dust off your feet as a warning to them."

They left and went from village to village, telling the good 6 news everywhere and healing the sick.

Has John Come Back?

Herod, the governor, heard about everything Jesus was 7 doing and didn't know what to make of it, because some people said, "John has risen from the dead"; others, "Elijah has ap- 8 peared"; still others, "One of the old prophets has risen."

"I cut off John's head," Herod said. "Now who is this 9 about whom I hear such things?" And he wanted to see Jesus.

Jesus Feeds Five Thousand

The apostles came back and told Jesus all they had done. 10 He took them away with Him near a town called Bethsaida in order to be alone. But the crowds found out about it and fol- 11 lowed Him. He welcomed them, talked to them about God's kingdom, and healed those who needed healing.

Toward the end of the day the twelve came to Him and told 12 Him, "Send the crowd away to the villages and farms around us to get shelter and find food. We're here in a deserted place."

"You give them something to eat," He told them. 13

"All we have is five loaves and two fish," they answered, "unless perhaps we go and buy food for all these people." There were about five thousand men. 14

9:15 Then He told His disciples, "Have them sit down in groups of about fifty." They did this and got them all seated.

16 He took the five loaves and the two fish, looked up to heaven, blessed them and broke them, and gave them to the
17 disciples to give to the people. All of them ate and had a hearty meal. And they picked up the pieces that were left — twelve baskets full.

"You Are the Promised Savior"

18 Once when He was praying and only His disciples were with Him, He asked them, "Who do people say I am?"

19 "John the Baptizer," they answered Him; "others say Elijah, and still others that one of the old prophets has come back to life."

20 "And you," He asked them, "who do you say I am?"

"The Savior whom God has sent," Peter answered.

21 But He gave them strict orders not to tell anyone about this.

Take the Cross

22 "The Son of Man has to suffer much," He said, "be rejected by the elders, ruling priests, and Bible scholars, be killed, and then rise on the third day."

23 And He told all of them, "If you want to follow Me, deny yourself, take up your cross every day, and come with Me.
24 ¹ If you want to save your life, you will lose it. But if you will
25 lose your life for Me, you will save it. What good does it do you
26 to win the whole world and destroy or lose yourself? If you're ashamed of Me and what I say, then the Son of Man will be ashamed of you when He comes in His glory and the glory of the Father and the holy angels.

27 "Let me assure you, there are some standing here who will never taste death till they see God's kingdom."

Jesus Shows His Glory

28 About a week after He said this, Jesus took Peter, James,
29 and John with Him and went up the mountain to pray. While He was praying, His face changed and looked different, and His
30 clothes got dazzling white. And there were two men talking with
31 Him; they were Moses and Elijah. They appeared in glory and were talking about His leaving this world, which was to happen at Jerusalem.

But Peter and the men with him had been overcome by sleep. Waking up, they saw His glory and the two men standing with Him. When these were leaving Him, Peter said to Jesus, "Master, it's good for us to be here. Let's put up three shelters, one for You, one for Moses, and one for Elijah." He didn't know what he was saying. 33

While he was saying this, a cloud came and overshadowed them. They were frightened as they went into the cloud. ¹ Then a voice came out of the cloud: "This is *My Son whom I have chosen. Listen to Him.*" ⁴⁸ ¹ When the voice had spoken, they saw Jesus was alone. 34 35 36

They kept silent and in those days told nobody anything of what they had seen.

The Epileptic Boy

The next day, when they had come down from the mountain, He met a large crowd. Then a man in the crowd called, "Teacher, I beg You, look at my son, he is my only child. ¹ A spirit takes hold of him, and suddenly he shrieks. It throws him into convulsions, and he foams at the mouth. It will hardly stop mistreating him. I asked Your disciples to drive out the spirit, but they couldn't do it." 37 38 39 40

"O you unbelieving and perverted people!" Jesus answered. "How long must I be with you and put up with you! Bring your son here." 41

While the boy was coming, the devil dashed him on the ground and threw him into convulsions. 42

Jesus talked sharply to the unclean spirit, made the boy well, and gave him back to his father. All were amazed to see God's wonderful power. 43

"I Will Die and Rise Again"

While everybody thought how wonderful everything was that Jesus was doing, He said to His disciples, "Listen carefully to what I say. The Son of Man is going to be betrayed into the hands of men." 43 44

But they didn't know what He meant. It was hidden from them so that they didn't understand it. And they were afraid to ask Him about it. 45

Who Is the Greatest?

9:46   A discussion got started among them as to which of them
47 was the greatest. But Jesus knew what they were thinking. He
48 took a little child, had him stand by Him, and said to them,
"If you welcome this little child in My name, you welcome Me.
And if you welcome Me, you welcome Him who sent Me. You
see, if anyone is the least of all of you, he is great."

"He Is for Us"

49   "Master," John said, "we saw a man driving out devils in
Your name, and we tried to stop him, because he's not one
of us."

50   "Don't stop him," Jesus told him; "anyone who is not against
you is for you."

To Jerusalem

51   As the time was coming nearer for Him to be taken up to
52 heaven, He showed He was determined to go to Jerusalem. He
sent messengers ahead of Him. They went and stopped in a vil-
53 lage of the Samaritans to arrange a place for Him to stay. But
the people didn't welcome Him, because He was going to
54 Jerusalem. When His disciples James and John saw this, they
asked, "Lord, do You want us to order *fire to come down from
heaven and burn* [49] them up?"

55-56   But He turned and sternly corrected them. So they went on
to another village.

"I Will Follow, but —"

57   As they were walking along the road, a man said to Him,
"I will follow You anywhere You go."

58   "Foxes have holes," Jesus told him, "and birds in the air
have nests, but the Son of Man doesn't have a place to lay His
head."

59   He told another man, "Follow Me."

"Lord, first let me go and bury my father," he asked.

60   But Jesus told him, "Let the dead bury their dead. But you
go and tell about God's kingdom."

61   "I will follow You, Lord," said another, "but first let me
say good-by to my people at home."

62   "Anyone who lays his hand on a plow," Jesus answered
him, "and keeps looking back isn't fit for God's kingdom."

Seventy-Two Missionaries

After this the Lord appointed seventy-two others and sent **10** them out by twos to go ahead of Him to every town and place where He intended to go.

"There's much grain to be cut, but there are only a few **2** workers," He told them. "Ask the Owner of the crop to send out workers to bring in His grain. Go! I'm sending you like **3** lambs among wolves. Don't carry a purse, a bag, or shoes, and **4** don't stop to greet anyone on the way. When you go into a house, **5** say first, 'May there be peace in this house.' If a man of peace **6** lives there, your peace will rest on him; but if not, it will come back to you. Stay in that house and eat and drink whatever they **7** have, since a worker earns his pay. Don't move from one house to another. When you go into any town and the people wel- **8** come you, eat what they serve you. Heal the sick that are there, **9** and tell the people, 'God's kingdom has come close to you!'

"But if you go into a town and they don't welcome you, go **10** out on its streets and say, 'The dust of your town has clung to **11** our feet — we're wiping it off in protest against you! But realize this: God's kingdom has come near you!' I tell you, on that Day **12** it will be easier for Sodom than for that town.

"Woe to you, Chorazin! Woe to you, Bethsaida! If the **13** miracles done in you had been done in Tyre and Sidon, they would long ago have repented, sitting in sackcloth and ashes. In the **14** Judgment it will be easier for Tyre and Sidon than for you. ¹ And you, Capernaum, will you be *lifted up to heaven? You will* **15** *go down to hell.*⁵⁰

"Anyone who hears you hears Me, and anyone who rejects **16** you rejects Me. But anyone who rejects Me rejects Him who sent Me."

The seventy-two came back delighted. "Lord," they said, **17** "even the devils do what we tell them in Your name."

"I watched the devil fall from heaven like lightning," He told **18** them. "You know, I've given you the power to *step on snakes* ⁵¹ **19** and scorpions and to trample on all the enemy's power, and nothing will hurt you. Only don't be glad that the spirits obey **20** you but that your names are written in heaven."

In that hour the Holy Spirit filled Jesus with joy. "I praise **21** You, Father, Lord of heaven and earth," He said, "for hiding these things from wise and intelligent people and revealing them to little children. Yes, Father, I praise You for wanting it to be that way.

10:22   "My Father has put everything in My hands. Only the Father knows the Son. And only the Son — and anyone to whom the Son wants to reveal Him — knows the Father."

23   Turning to His disciples, He said to them alone, "Happy are
24   the eyes that see what you see. I tell you, many prophets and kings longed to see what you see but didn't see it, and hear what you hear but didn't hear it."

The Good Samaritan

25   Then an expert in the Law came forward to test Jesus. "Teacher," he asked, "what do I do to get everlasting life?"

26   "What is written in the Law?" Jesus asked him. "What do you read there?"

27   *"Love the Lord your God with all your heart,"* he answered, *"and with all your life and with all your strength* [52] and with all your mind, and *your neighbor like yourself."* [53]

28   "You're right," Jesus told him. *"Do that and you will live."* [54]

29   But he wanted to justify himself. So he asked Jesus, "And who is my neighbor?"

30   Jesus went into the matter and said:

"A man going from Jerusalem down to Jericho fell into the hands of robbers. They stripped him, struck him blow after blow, and went away leaving him half dead.

31   "Just at that time a priest happened to go along that road,
32   but when he saw him, he passed by on the other side. So did also a Levite who came to the place: he looked at him and passed by on the other side.

33   "Then a Samaritan, as he was traveling, came near him, and when he saw him, he felt sorry for him. He went to him and
34   bandaged his wounds, pouring on oil and wine. Then he put him on his own animal, brought him to an inn, and took care
35   of him. The next day he took out two denarii and gave them to the innkeeper. 'Take care of him,' he said, 'and anything else you spend on him I'll repay you when I come back.'

36   "Which of those three, do you think, was a neighbor to the man who had fallen into the hands of the robbers?"

37   "The one who was kind enough to help him," he said.

"Go and do as he did," Jesus told him.

Mary Listens to Jesus

As they were walking along, Jesus came to a village where a woman by the name of Martha welcomed Him to her home. ¹ She had a sister by the name of Mary. She sat down at Jesus' feet and listened to what He said. 10:38

39

But Martha was worried about all she had to do for them. So she came and asked, "Lord, don't You care that my sister has left me and I have to do the work alone? Now tell her to help me." 40

"Martha, Martha," the Lord answered her, "you worry and fuss about a lot of things. But there's only one thing you need. Mary has made the right choice, and it must not be taken away from her." 41

42

The Lord's Prayer

Once Jesus was praying in a certain place. When He stopped, one of His disciples asked Him, "Lord, teach us to pray as John taught his disciples." **11**

He told them, "When you pray, say: 2

'Father, may Your name be kept holy,

Your kingdom come,

Your will be done on earth as it is in heaven. 3

Give us every day our daily bread.

Forgive us our sins, as we, too, forgive everyone who sins 4

against us.

And don't bring us into temptation.' "

Pray!

"Suppose one of you has a friend," Jesus said to His disciples, 5 "and you go to him at midnight and ask him, 'Friend, lend me three loaves. A friend of mine on a trip has dropped in on me, 6 and I have nothing to serve him.' Will he answer from within, 7 'Don't bother me. The door is already locked, and my children are with me in bed. I can't get up and give you anything'? ¹ I tell 8 you, although he won't get up and give you anything even though he's your friend, yet because you persist, he'll get up and give you anything you need.

"So I tell you: Ask and it will be given to you. Search and 9 you will find. Knock and the door will be opened for you. Anyone who asks receives; anyone who searches finds; and 10 anyone who knocks, the door will be opened for him.

Judea, October to December, 29   129
Near Capernaum, summer, 28

"If your son asks you, his father, for a fish, will any of you
12 give him a snake instead of a fish? Or if he asks for an egg,
13 will you give him a scorpion? Now if you, bad as you are, know
enough to give your children good gifts, how much more will your
Father in heaven give the Holy Spirit to those who ask Him?"

Power over the Devil

14 He was driving out a devil who was speechless. When the
devil had gone out, the speechless man spoke.

15 The people were amazed. But some of them said, "He drives
out the devils with the help of Beelzebul, who rules over the
16 devils." Others, meaning to test Him, demanded that He show
them some wonderful proof from heaven.

17 Knowing what they were thinking, He said to them, "If one
part of any kingdom fights against another part, it loses its people,
18 and one house falls on another. If the devil fights against himself,
how can his kingdom stand? I say this because you say Beelzebul
19 helps Me drive out the devils. But if Beelzebul helps Me drive
out the devils, who helps your sons drive them out? That's why
20 they'll be your judges. But if God's finger helps Me drive out the
devils, then God's kingdom has come to you.

21 "When a strong man, completely armed, guards his palace,
22 his property is not disturbed. But when someone stronger than
he attacks him and defeats him, he'll take away his whole armor,
in which he trusted, and divide the plunder.

23 "Anyone who is not with Me is against Me, and anyone who
doesn't help Me gather scatters.

24 "When an unclean spirit comes out of a man, he goes through
dry places looking for rest but doesn't find any. Then he says,
25 'I'll go back to the home I left.' He comes and finds it swept
26 and decorated. Then he goes and takes home with him seven
other spirits worse than himself, and they go in and live there.
In the end that man is worse than he was before."

Hear Him!

27 When Jesus said this, a woman in the crowd called loud to
Him, "Happy is the mother who bore You and nursed You."

28 "Yes," He said, "but happy are those who listen to God's
Word and keep it."

29 As the people were crowding around Him, He said, "These
people of our time are wicked. They're looking for a proof,
30 but the only proof they'll get is Jonah. As Jonah became a proof

to the people of Nineveh, so the Son of Man will be a proof to these people. The queen of the south will rise up in the Judgment with the men of today and condemn them, because she came from the ends of the earth to hear Solomon's wisdom; and here you see more than Solomon. The men of Nineveh will rise up in the Judgment with the people of today and condemn them, because they repented when Jonah preached; and here you see more than Jonah."

Your Light

"You don't light a lamp and put it in a cellar or under the peck measure but on the lampstand so that those who come in will see it shine.

"Your eye is the lamp of your body. When your eye is healthy, you have light for your whole body. But when your eye is bad, your body is dark! Then see to it that the light in you isn't dark. Now if you have light for your whole body and no part of it is dark, it will all have light just as when a lamp shines brightly on you."

Warnings.

Jesus had been speaking, when a Pharisee invited Him to eat at his home. So He went in and lay down to eat. ¹ But the Pharisee was surprised to see He didn't wash before the meal.

The Lord said to him, "You Pharisees keep cleaning the outside of the cup and of the dish, but inside you're full of greed and wickedness. You fools, didn't He who made the outside make the inside too? Just give your heart in helping the poor, and you'll find everything clean.

"But woe to you Pharisees! You give a tenth of mint, rue, and every vegetable, and you fail to be just and to love God. You should have done these without neglecting the others.

"And woe to you Pharisees! You like to have the seats of honor in the synagogs and to be greeted in the marketplaces. Woe to you! You're like the unmarked graves people walk over without knowing what they are."

"Teacher," one of the men of the Law said to Him, "when You say that, You insult us too."

"Woe also to you experts in the Law!" He said. "You load people with burdens they can hardly carry, but not with one finger will you touch these burdens yourselves. Woe to you!

You build monuments for the prophets your fathers murdered.
11:48 So you are witnesses and approve of what your fathers did.
49 They murdered them, and you just build something. ¹ That's why
God's wisdom has said: I will send them prophets and apostles,
50 and they will murder or persecute some of them ¹ so that the
people of today may be punished for the blood of all the
51 prophets poured out since the world was made, from the blood
of Abel to the blood of Zachariah, who was killed between the
altar and the temple. Yes, I tell you, the people of today will
be punished for it.

52 "Woe to you experts in the Law! You've taken away the
key to knowledge. You didn't go in yourselves and kept out those
who tried to go in."

53 When Jesus went outside, the Bible scholars and the Pharisees
fiercely opposed Him and cross-examined Him about many things,
54 watching Him closely to trap Him in something He might say.

Don't Be Afraid of Men

12 When so many thousands of people came together that they
trampled on one another, Jesus began to speak first to His disciples: "Beware of the yeast of the Pharisees — I mean, their
2 hypocrisy. Everything that's covered will be uncovered, and
3 every secret will be known. Everything you said in the dark will
be heard in the light, and what you whispered in the ear in the
4 inner rooms will be announced from the roofs. But I tell you,
My friends, don't be afraid of those who kill the body and then
5 can't do any more. ¹ I will point out the One you must fear. Fear
Him who after killing you has the power to throw you into hell.
Yes, I tell you, fear Him!

6 "Aren't five sparrows sold for two cents? And God doesn't
7 forget any one of them. Why, even the hairs on your heads are all
counted! Don't be afraid — you're worth more than many spar-
8 rows! I tell you, whoever will confess Me before other people,
9 him the Son of Man will confess before God's angels. Anyone
who denies Me before other people will be denied before God's
10 angels. Anyone who will speak against the Son of Man will be
forgiven. But he who slanders the Holy Spirit will not be forgiven.

11 "When they bring you before synagogs, rulers, and authorities,
don't worry how you will defend yourselves or what you will say.
12 When that time comes, the Holy Spirit will teach you what to say."

Don't Be Greedy

"Teacher," someone in the crowd said to Him, "tell my 12:13
brother to give me my share of the property our father left us."

"Man," He asked him, "who appointed Me to be your judge 14
or to divide your property?

"Be careful," He told the people. "Guard against every kind 15
of greed. Even if you have more than enough, your property
doesn't give you life."

Then He told them a story: 16

"A rich man had good crops on his land. 'What am I going 17
to do?' he said to himself. 'I have no place to store my crops.'
Finally he said, 'This is what I'll do: I'll tear down my barns and 18
build bigger ones and store all my grain and goods in them. Then 19
I'll say to myself, You have a lot of good things stored up for
many years. Take life easy, eat, drink, and enjoy yourself.'

"But God said to him, 'You fool, tonight you die. And what 20
you've prepared — who will get it?' That's how it is when you 21
store up goods for yourself and aren't rich in God.

"That is why I tell you," He said to His disciples: "Don't 22
worry about what you'll eat to keep alive or what you'll wear on
your bodies. Life is more than food, and the body more than 23
clothes. Look at the crows. They don't sow or cut grain, they 24
have no storeroom or barn; and yet God feeds them. You're
worth much more than birds. And can any of you by worrying 25
add anything to your life? If you can't do even the smallest 26
thing, why worry about the rest? See how the flowers grow. 27
They don't work or spin. Yet I tell you, even Solomon in all his
glory didn't dress like one of them. If that's how God dresses 28
the grass, which lives in the field today and tomorrow is thrown
into a stove, how much more certainly will He put clothes on
you — who trust Him so little? So don't just think of what 29
you'll eat or drink, and don't worry. The people in the world run 30
after all these things, but your Father knows you need them.
Only be eager to have Him as your King, and you'll get these 31
things too. Don't be afraid, little flock. Your Father has decided 32
to give you the kingdom.

"Sell what you have and give the money to the poor. Make 33
yourselves purses that don't wear out and a treasure that will
never be used up — in heaven, where no thief gets near it and
no moth destroys it. Where your treasure is, there your heart 34
will be."

Be Ready

^{12:35} "Be ready for action with belts fastened and lamps burning,
³⁶ like men waiting for their master when he comes back from a wedding, so they can open the door for him the moment he comes
³⁷ and knocks. Happy are those slaves whom the master finds watching when he comes. I tell you he'll certainly fasten his belt,
³⁸ have them lie down for a meal, and come and serve them. Even if he comes in the middle of the night or toward morning and finds them that way, happy are they.

³⁹ "You know if the owner of a house had known just when the burglar was coming, he would not have let anyone break
⁴⁰ into his house. You, too, get ready, because the Son of Man is coming when you don't expect Him."

⁴¹ "Lord," Peter asked, "by this illustration do you mean to warn us — or everybody else too?"

⁴² The Lord asked, "Who do you suppose is the manager that can be trusted and has good sense whom the master will put in charge of his servants to give them their share of food at the
⁴³ right time? Happy is that slave whom his master will find doing
⁴⁴ just this when he comes. I tell you he certainly will make him
⁴⁵ manager of all his property. But if that slave says to himself, 'My master isn't coming back for some time,' and starts to beat the other slaves, men and women, and eats, drinks, and gets
⁴⁶ drunk, the master of that slave will come one day when he's not expecting him and at a time he doesn't know and will cut him in pieces and put him with the unfaithful.

⁴⁷ "That slave who knew what his master wanted and didn't
⁴⁸ prepare himself or do what he wanted will get many blows. But he who didn't know and did things for which he deserved to be beaten will get few blows. If you were given much, much will be expected of you, and if much was entrusted to you, all the more will be demanded of you."

Sorrow Ahead

⁴⁹ "I have come to bring fire on earth, and how glad I would
⁵⁰ be if it were already started! I must be baptized with a baptism, and how I am troubled till it is done!

⁵¹ "Do you think I came to bring peace on earth? No, I tell
⁵² you — to bring division. From now on five in one family will
⁵³ be divided, three against two and two against three. A father will be against a son and *a son against a father,* a mother against

a daughter and *a daughter against her mother,* a mother-in-law against her daughter-in-law and *a daughter-in-law against her mother-in-law."* [55]

This Is Your Opportunity

"When you see a cloud coming up in the west," Jesus said to the people, "you immediately say, 'There's going to be a heavy rain,' and so it rains. And when you see a wind blowing from the south, you say, 'It's going to be hot,' and so it is. You hypocrites! You can tell what the appearance of the earth and of the sky means. How is it that you can't interpret this present time? Why don't you yourselves decide what is right? [12:54] [55] [56] [57]

"When you go with your opponent to be tried before a ruler, do your best to settle with him on the way, or he may drag you before the judge, and the judge will hand you over to the officer, and the officer will put you in prison. I tell you, you will never get out till you pay the last cent." [58] [59]

Repent

At that time some men were there to tell Him about the Galileans whose blood Pilate had mixed with their sacrifices. Jesus asked them, "Do you think, because this happened to them, those Galileans must have been worse sinners than all the other Galileans? I tell you, no. And if you don't repent, you will all perish as they did. Or those eighteen the tower at Siloam fell on and killed — do you think they must have been worse transgressors than all the other people living in Jerusalem? I tell you, no. And if you don't repent, you will all perish as they did." [13] [2] [3] [4] [5]

Another Year

He told them this story: [6]

"A man had a fig tree growing in his vineyard. He came looking for fruit on it but didn't find any. So he said to the man who worked the vineyard, 'Look here! For the last three years I've come looking for figs on this fig tree and haven't found any. Cut it down. Why should it waste the ground?' [7]

" 'Master,' he answered him, 'let it stand one more year, and I'll dig around it and fertilize it; it may have figs next year. If not, cut it down.' " [8] [9]

Sick for Eighteen Years

13:10-11   Jesus was teaching in one of the synagogs on a Sabbath, and there was a woman whom a spirit had crippled for eighteen years.
12 She was bent over and couldn't stand up straight. When Jesus saw her, He called her and said, "Woman, you're rid of your
13 trouble." He laid His hands on her, and immediately she stood up straight and praised God.
14   But the synagog leader was annoyed with Jesus for healing on a Sabbath. "There are six days to do your work," he told the people. "Come on those days and get healed, but not on the day of rest."
15   "You hypocrites!" the Lord answered him. "Doesn't every one of you on a Saturday untie his ox or donkey from the manger
16 and take it out to water? And this woman, a daughter of Abraham, whom the devil has bound these eighteen years, shouldn't she on the day of rest be freed from what bound her?"
17   As He said this, all His enemies had to feel ashamed, but all the common people were happy over the wonderful things He was doing.

Mustard Seed and Yeast

18   "What is God's kingdom like," He asked, "and what will
19 I compare it with? It's like a mustard seed a man took and planted in his garden. It grew to be a tree, and the *birds in the air nested in its branches*.[56]
20   "With what should I compare God's kingdom?" He asked
21 again. "It's like yeast a woman mixed into a bushel of flour till it was all fermented."

The Narrow Door

22   Then Jesus went and taught in one town and village after another on His way to Jerusalem.
23   Someone asked Him, "Lord, are only a few people saved?"
24   "Struggle to get in through the narrow door," He told them.
25 "I tell you, many will try to get in and not succeed. After the Owner of the house gets up and closes the door, you'll be standing outside and knocking at the door. 'Lord, open up for us!' you'll say. But He'll answer you, 'I don't know where you're
26 from.' Then you'll say, 'We ate and drank with You, and You
27 taught in our streets.' But He'll tell you, 'I don't know where you're from. *Get away from Me, all you who do wrong.*'[57]

Then you will cry and grind your teeth when you see Abraham, Isaac, Jacob, and all the prophets in God's kingdom but yourselves thrown out. People will come *from the east and the west,*[58] the north and the south, and will eat in God's kingdom. You see, some who are last will be first, and some who are first will be last." 29 30

Jesus Warns Jerusalem

Just then some Pharisees came and told Him, "Leave and get away from here; Herod wants to kill you." 31

"Go," He answered them, "and tell that fox, 'Listen, today and tomorrow I will drive out devils and do healings, and on the third day I will finish.' But I must be on My way today, tomorrow, and the next day, because a prophet just can't be killed outside Jerusalem. 32 33

"Jerusalem, Jerusalem, you murder the prophets and stone those sent to you! How often I wanted to gather your children the way a hen gathers her chicks under her wings, but you didn't want to! Look, now your *house is left* [59] to you. I tell you, you will not see Me till you say, *'Blessed is He who is coming in the Lord's name.' ''* [60] 34 35

Dinner Is Ready!

Once on a Saturday Jesus went to the home of a leader of the Pharisees to eat a meal, and they were watching Him carefully. 14

In front of Him was a man who had dropsy. This led Jesus to ask the experts in the Law and the Pharisees, "Is it right to heal on a day of rest or not?" But they didn't say anything. 2-3

So Jesus took hold of the man, made him well, and sent him away. "If your son or your ox falls into a well," He asked them, "won't anyone of you pull him out immediately on a Sabbath?" They couldn't answer this. 4 5 6

He noticed how the guests were trying to get the places of honor, and so He used the scene to teach them: "When anyone invites you to a wedding, don't take the place of honor. He may have invited somebody more important than you. And he who invited you and him will come and tell you, 'Give this man your place,' and then you'll feel ashamed when you have to take the lowest place. No, when you're invited, go and take the lowest place, so that when your host comes he'll tell you, 'Friend, move up higher.' Then all your fellow guests will see how you're 7 8 9 10

14:11 honored. If you honor yourself, you'll be humbled, but if you humble yourself, you'll be honored."

12   Then He told the man who had invited Him, "When you give a dinner or a supper, don't invite your friends, your brothers, your relatives, or rich neighbors. Otherwise they'll invite you

13 too and pay you back. No, when you give a banquet, invite the

14 poor, crippled, lame, and blind. Then you'll be happy because they can't pay you back. You'll be paid back when the righteous rise from the dead."

15   When one of those eating with Him heard this, he said to Jesus, "Happy is he who will eat bread in God's kingdom."

16   Jesus said to him:

17   "A man once gave a big dinner and invited many. ¹When it was time for the dinner, he sent his slave to tell those who were invited, 'Come, it's ready now!'

18   "Then they all alike began to excuse themselves. 'I bought a field,' the first told him, 'and I've got to go out and see it.

19 Please excuse me.' ¹Another said, 'I bought five teams of oxen,

20 and I'm on my way to try them out. Please excuse me.' ¹And another said, 'I just got married, and that's why I can't come.'

21   "The slave went back and reported this to his master. Then the master of the house got angry. 'Go out quickly into the streets and alleys of the city,' he told his slave, 'and bring in here the poor, crippled, blind, and lame.'

22   "And the slave said, 'Master, it's done as you ordered, and there's still room.'

23   "Then the master told the slave, 'Go out to the roads and stone fences, and make them come in! I want my house to be

24 full. I tell you, none of those men who were invited will taste my dinner.' "

Leave Everything

25-26   Large crowds were going with Jesus. Turning to them, He said, "If you come to Me and don't hate your father, mother, wife, children, brothers, and sisters and even your own life, you can't

27 be My disciple. Whoever doesn't carry his cross and follow Me can't be My disciple.

28   "If anyone of you wants to build a tower, won't you first sit down and figure out what it costs, to see if you have enough to

29 finish it? Otherwise, when you've laid a foundation but can't

finish the building, all who watch you will make fun of you
and say, 'This fellow started to build but couldn't finish it.' 14:30

"Or suppose a king is going into battle against another king. 31
Won't he first sit down and consider if with ten thousand men
he can oppose the other coming against him with twenty thousand? If he can't, then, while the other is still far away, he sends 32
ambassadors to ask for terms of peace. Just so, anyone of you 33
who doesn't say good-by to everything he has can't be My
disciple.

"Now, salt is good. But if the salt loses its taste, how will it 34
be made salty again? It is no good for the ground or for the 35
manure pile. People throw it away.

"If you have ears to hear, listen!"

Lost — a Sheep

All the tax collectors and sinners were coming to Jesus to 15
hear Him. But the Pharisees and the Bible scholars grumbled 2
and said, "This man welcomes sinners and eats with them."

So He told them this story: 3

"If anyone of you has a hundred sheep and loses one of 4
them, don't you leave the ninety-nine in the wilderness and go
after the lost one till you find it? When you find it, you lay it on 5
your shoulders and are glad. You go home and call your friends 6
and neighbors together and say to them, 'Be happy with me.
I found my lost sheep!' So, I tell you, there will be more joy 7
in heaven over one sinner who repents than over ninety-nine
good people who don't need to repent."

Lost — a Coin

"Or suppose a woman has ten coins and loses one. Won't 8
she light a lamp and sweep the house and look for it carefully
till she finds it? When she finds it, she calls her women friends 9
and neighbors together and says, 'Be happy with me. I found
the coin I lost.' So, I tell you, God's angels will be happy over 10
one sinner who repents."

Lost — a Son

Then Jesus said: "A man had two sons. The younger of them 11-12
said to his father, 'Father, give me my share of the property.'
So he divided his property between them.

"A few days later the younger son cashed in all he had, 13

left home for a distant country, and there squandered his prop-
15:14 erty by wild living. When he had spent it all, a bad famine came
15 over that country, and he started to be in need. So he went and
hired himself out to a citizen of that country, who sent him to
16 his fields to feed hogs. And he would have been glad to fill up
on the pods the hogs were eating. And nobody would give him
anything.

17 "Then he came to his senses and said, 'How many of my
father's hired men have more food than they can eat, and here
18 I'm starving to death. I'll start out and go to my father and tell
19 him, "Father, I've sinned against heaven and against you. I don't
deserve to be called your son anymore. Make me one of your
hired men." '

20 "So he started out and went to his father. While he was still
far away, his father saw him and felt sorry for him. He ran and
21 put his arms around him and kissed him. 'Father,' the son told
him, 'I've sinned against heaven and against you. I don't deserve
to be called your son anymore. Make me one of your hired
men.'

22 " 'Quick,' the father told his slaves, 'bring out a robe — the
best — and put it on him, put a ring on his finger and shoes on
23 his feet. And bring the fattened calf, kill it, and let's eat and
24 celebrate. This son of mine was dead and is alive. He was lost
and is found.' And they started to celebrate.

25 "Now, his older son was out in the field. As he was coming in, he got near the house — he heard music and dancing!
26 Calling one of the servants, he asked, 'What's going on here?'

27 " 'Your brother's home,' he was told, 'and your father has
killed the fattened calf because he got him back safe and sound.'

28 "Then he got angry and wouldn't go in. So his father came
29 out and begged him. But he answered his father, 'All these
years I've been working like a slave for you and have never disobeyed your order, and you never gave me even a little goat to
30 celebrate with my friends. But as soon as this son of yours came
back, who devoured your property with prostitutes, you killed the
fattened calf for him.'

31 " 'Son,' the father said to him, 'you're always with me, and
32 everything I have is yours. But we had to celebrate and be glad.
This brother of yours was dead and is alive. He was lost and is
found.' "

The Dishonest Manager

Then Jesus said to His disciples: **16**

"There was a rich man whose manager was accused of squandering the man's property. He called the manager. 'What's **2** this I hear about you?' he asked him. 'Give an account of your management, because you can't manage my property any longer.'

" 'What'll I do?' the manager said to himself. 'My master is **3** taking my job away from me. I'm not strong enough to dig; I'm ashamed to beg. I know what I'll do so that when I've lost my **4** job people will welcome me into their homes.'

"So he called everyone who owed his master anything. 'How **5** much do you owe my master?' he asked the first.

" 'Eight hundred gallons of oil,' he answered. **6**

" 'Take your note,' he said, 'sit down quick and write "four hundred." '

"Then he asked another, 'How much do you owe?' **7**

" 'A thousand bushels of wheat,' he answered.

" 'Take your note,' he told him, 'and write "eight hundred." '

"And the master praised the dishonest manager for acting so **8** shrewdly.

"In dealing with their own kind of people the men of this world are shrewder than those who are in the light.

"And I tell you, with the money that's often used in wrong **9** ways win friends for yourselves so that when it's gone you'll be welcomed into the everlasting homes. If you can be trusted **10** with very little, you can be trusted with much. And if you're dishonest with very little, you're dishonest with much. If you **11** couldn't be trusted with wicked money, who will trust you with that which is really good? And if you couldn't be trusted with **12** someone else's things, who will give you your own?

"No servant can be the slave of two masters. Either he will **13** hate the one and love the other, or he'll be loyal to the one and despise the other. You can't serve God and money."

The money-loving Pharisees heard all this and turned up their **14** noses at Him. Then He said to them, "You try to make people **15** think you're good, but God knows your hearts. What people consider great is detested by God.

"The Law and the prophets were until John. Since then the **16** good news of God's kingdom is told, and everybody tries to force his way into it. It is easier for heaven and earth to disappear **17** than for the Law to drop one dot of an *i*.

"Anyone who divorces his wife and marries another is living in adultery. And the man who marries a woman divorced from her husband is living in adultery."

The Rich Man and Lazarus

19 "There was a rich man who used to dress in purple and fine
20 linen and live in luxury every day. A beggar by the name of
21 Lazarus was laid at his gate. He was covered with sores ¹ and longed to satisfy his hunger with anything that might fall from the rich man's table. And the dogs would even come and lick his sores.

22 "One day the beggar died, and the angels carried him to Abraham's bosom. The rich man also died and was buried.
23 Being tormented in hell, he looked up, and though far away, he
24 saw Abraham, and Lazarus at his bosom. 'Father Abraham,' he called, 'have pity on me and send Lazarus to dip the tip of his finger in water and cool off my tongue, because I'm suffering in this fire.'

25 "But Abraham said, 'Remember, son, you had your good things in your life, while Lazarus had his misery. Now he is
26 comforted here, while you're suffering. In all these things there's a wide chasm fixed between us and you, so that those who might want to cross from here over to you can't do it, nor do any from there come over to us.'

27 " 'Then I ask you, father,' he said, 'send him to my father's
28 home — ¹ I have five brothers — to warn them not to get into this place of torture.'

29 " 'They have Moses and the prophets,' Abraham said. 'They should listen to them.'

30 " 'No, Father Abraham,' he said, 'but if someone comes to them from the dead, they'll repent.'

31 " 'If they don't listen to Moses and the prophets,' he answered him, 'they won't be convinced even if somebody rose from the dead.' "

When Others Sin

17 "Temptations to sin are sure to come," Jesus told His dis-
2 ciples, "but woe to him through whom they come. It would be better for him to have a big millstone hung around his neck and to be thrown into the lake than to lead one of these little ones
3 into sin. Watch yourselves.

"If your brother sins, correct him; and if he's sorry, forgive him. Even if he sins against you seven times in one day and seven times comes back to you and says, 'I'm sorry,' forgive him." 17:4

Faith and Duty

Then the apostles said to the Lord, "Give us more faith." 5

"If you have a faith like a mustard seed," the Lord said, 6 "you could say to this mulberry tree, 'Be pulled up by the roots, and be planted in the lake,' and it would obey you.

"If your slave is plowing or watching sheep and comes in 7 from the field, will any of you say to him, 'Come quickly and eat'? Or won't you rather tell him, 'Prepare something for me 8 to eat, fasten your belt, and serve me while I eat and drink, and afterwards you eat and drink'? You won't thank the slave for 9 doing what he was ordered to do, will you? So you, too, when 10 you've done all you were ordered to do, say, 'We are slaves who claim no credit. We've only done our duty.' "

Only One Thanks God

On His way to Jerusalem, Jesus traveled along the border 11 between Samaria and Galilee. As He came to a village, ten 12 lepers came toward Him. They stopped at a distance ¹ and called 13 out, "Jesus, Master, have pity on us!"

When He saw them, He told them, "Go and *let the priests* 14 *examine* ⁴² you."

And here's what happened: As they went, they were cleansed of their leprosy. One of them, seeing he was healed, turned back 15 and loudly praised God. He bowed to the ground at Jesus' feet 16 and thanked Him. And he was a Samaritan.

"Weren't there ten cleansed?" Jesus asked. "But the nine — 17 where are they? Weren't there any who came back to give God 18 glory except this foreigner?"

And He told him, "Get up and go! Your faith made you 19 well."

Where Is God's Kingdom?

"When will God's kingdom come?" the Pharisees asked Jesus. 20

"People can't see the coming of God's kingdom," He answered them. "They will not say, 'Look, here it is!' or, 'There it is!' 21 You see, God's kingdom is now among you."

Jesus Is Coming

17:22   "The time will come," He told the disciples, "when you will long to see one of the days of the Son of Man and will not see it.

23   People will say, 'Look, there He is!' or, 'Here He is!' Don't go off and run after them.

24   "The Son of Man will be like the lightning that flashes and
25 lights up the sky from one end to the other. But first He must suffer much and be rejected by these people.

26   "When the Son of Man comes, it will be like the time of
27 Noah: They were eating and drinking, and men and women were marrying till the day *Noah went into the ark,* and *the flood came* [61] and destroyed them all.

28   "Or like the time of Lot: They were eating and drinking,
29 buying and selling, planting and building. But the day Lot left Sodom, *fire and sulfur rained from heaven and destroyed* [62]
30 them all. That is how it will be on the day the Son of Man is revealed.

31   "On that day, if you're on the roof and have your goods in the house, don't go down to get them. If you're in the field,
32-33 don't *turn back.* Remember *Lot's wife!* [63] If you try to save your life, you'll lose it, but if you'll lose it, you'll save it.

34   "I tell you, that night there will be two men in one bed.
35 One will be taken and the other left. Two women will be grinding
* together. One will be taken and the other left."

37   They asked Him, "Where, Lord?"

    "Where there's a dead body," He told them, "there the vultures will gather."

God Hears

18   Jesus told them a story to show that they should always pray and not get tired of it:

2   "In a town there was a judge who didn't fear God or care
3 what people thought. In that town there was also a widow who kept coming to him and saying, 'Get me justice and defend me against my enemy!'

4   "For a while he refused to do anything, but then he said to himself, 'Even though I don't fear God or care what people
5 think, yet because this widow keeps bothering me, I'll have to see that she gets justice, or she'll keep coming till she wears me out.' "

---

* Our three oldest manuscripts, including Papyrus 75, do not have v. 36: "Two will be in a field. One will be taken and the other left." See Matt. 24:40.

The Lord added, "Listen to what the unjust judge says. And won't God get justice for His chosen ones who cry to Him day and night? Is He slow to help them? I tell you, He will quickly 8 get justice for them. But when the Son of Man comes, will He find faith on earth?"

The Pharisee and the Tax Collector

Jesus told this story to some who were sure they were right- 9 eous and so looked down on everybody else:

"Two men went up to the temple to pray. One was a Pharisee 10 and the other a tax collector. The Pharisee stood and prayed 11 by himself: 'God, I thank You I'm not like the other people: robbers, wrongdoers, adulterers, or even like that tax collector. I fast twice a week and give a tenth of all my income.' 12

"But the tax collector, standing a distance away, wouldn't 13 even look up to heaven but was beating his breast and saying, 'God, forgive me, a sinner!'

"I tell you, this man, and not the other, went home righteous. 14 Everyone who honors himself will be humbled; but if you humble yourself, you will be honored."

Jesus Loves Children

Some people brought babies to Jesus to have Him touch them. 15 When the disciples saw them, they sternly told them not to do it.

But Jesus called the children to Him and said, "Let the little 16 children come to Me, and don't keep them away. God's kingdom belongs to such as these. I tell you the truth, if you don't receive 17 God's kingdom like a little child, you will not get into it."

The Rich Young Leader

An official asked Him, "Good Teacher, what do I do to get 18 everlasting life?"

"Why do you call Me good?" Jesus asked him. "Nobody is 19 good except One — God. You know the commandments: *Don't* 20 *commit adultery, don't murder, don't steal, don't lie, honor your father and mother.*" [64]

"I've kept all these since I was a child," he said. 21

When Jesus heard this, He told him, "You still lack one 22 thing: Sell everything you have, distribute the money among the poor, and you'll have a treasure in heaven. Then come and follow Me."

When he heard this, he got very sad, because he was very rich. 23

18:24 Jesus watched him and said, "How hard it is for rich people to
25 get into God's kingdom! It's easier for a camel to go through
a needle's eye than for a rich man to get into God's kingdom."

26 Those who heard Him asked, "Who can be saved?"

27 "What men can't do God can do," He answered.

28 Then Peter said, "Look, we've left our things and followed You."

29 "Let Me assure you," He answered them, "everyone who gave
up his home or wife, brothers, parents, or children for God's
30 kingdom ¹ will certainly get a hundred times as much in this life,
and in the coming world everlasting life."

The Shadow of the Cross

31 He took the twelve aside and said to them: "Look, we're
going up to Jerusalem, and everything the prophets wrote for
32 the Son of Man will be done: He'll be handed over to the
33 non-Jews. They'll mock and insult Him, spit on Him, ¹ scourge
and kill Him. And on the third day He will rise."

34 But they understood none of this. It was a mystery to them,
and they didn't know what He meant.

A Blind Man

35 As He came near Jericho, there was a blind man sitting by
36 the road, begging. Hearing a crowd go by, he tried to find out
what it was all about.

37 "Jesus from Nazareth is passing by," they told him.

38-39 He called, "Jesus, Son of David, have pity on me!" Those
who went ahead were urging him to be quiet. But he called all
the louder, "Son of David, have pity on me!"

40 Jesus stopped and ordered the man brought to Him. When
41 he came near, Jesus asked him, ¹ "What do you want Me to do
for you?"

"Lord, I want to see," he said.

42 "See!" Jesus told him. "Your faith has made you well."
43 Immediately he could see, and he followed Jesus, praising God.
And all the people praised God for what they had seen.

Zacchaeus

19 1-2 He went into Jericho and was passing through it. Here there
was a man by the name of Zacchaeus. He was an overseer of tax
3 collectors and was rich. He was trying to see what kind of
person Jesus was, but, being a small man, he couldn't see Him

on account of the crowd. So he ran ahead and climbed up a fig-mulberry tree to see Him, because Jesus was coming that way.

When Jesus came to the place, He looked up. "Zacchaeus, ⁵ hurry down," He told him. "Today I must stay at your home."

He hurried down and was happy to welcome Him. But all ⁶⁻⁷ who saw them started to grumble: "He went to be the guest of a sinful man."

Zacchaeus stood there and said to the Lord, "Look, Lord, ⁸ half of my property I'm giving to the poor, and if I've cheated anybody, I'm paying him back four times as much."

"Today salvation has come to this home," Jesus told him, ⁹ "since he, too, is a son of Abraham. The Son of Man came to ¹⁰ *look for* and save *the lost*." ⁶⁵

Use God's Gifts

While they were listening to this, Jesus went on to tell them ¹¹ a story, because He was near Jerusalem and they thought God's kingdom was to appear immediately.

"A nobleman," He said, "went to a distant country to be ¹² made a king and then come back. He called ten of his slaves, gave ¹³ them a thousand denarii,* and told them, 'Trade with these till I come.'

"But the men of his own country hated him and sent repre- ¹⁴ sentatives after him to say, 'We don't want this man to be our king.'

"But he was made king. When he came back, he said, 'Call ¹⁵ those slaves whom I gave the money. I want to see what each one has made by his trading.'

"The first came and said, 'Master, your hundred denarii have ¹⁶ made a thousand more denarii.'

" 'Well done, my good slave!' he told him. 'You proved you ¹⁷ could be trusted in a very small matter. Take charge of ten cities.'

"The second came and said, 'Your hundred denarii, master, ¹⁸ made five hundred denarii.'

" 'You be in charge of five cities,' he told this one. ¹⁹

"Then the one who was different came and said, 'Master, ²⁰ here are your hundred denarii. I put them away in a cloth and kept them there. I was afraid of you. You're a hard man. You ²¹ take what you didn't deposit, and you get grain you didn't sow.'

* One denarius was a day's pay.

" 'I'll judge you by what you say, you wicked slave!' he told him. 'You knew I'm a hard man, taking what I didn't deposit
23 and getting grain I didn't sow? Why didn't you put my money in the bank? Then, when I came back, I could have collected
24 it with interest.' So he told his men, 'Take his hundred denarii away and give them to the man who has a thousand.'
25 " 'Master,' they answered him, 'he has a thousand denarii.'
26 " 'I tell you, everyone who has something will be given more, and anyone who doesn't have what he should have, even what
27 he has will be taken away. But those enemies of mine who didn't want me to be their king — bring them here and kill them in front of me.' "

28 After Jesus had said this, He continued on His way up to Jerusalem.

The King Is Coming

29 When He came near Bethphage and Bethany at the Mount
30 of Olives, as it was called, He sent two of His disciples. "Go into the village ahead of you," He said, "and as you go in, you'll find a colt tied up that nobody ever sat on. Untie it and bring it
31 to Me. And if anybody asks you, 'Why are you untying it?' say, 'The Lord needs it.' "

32 The men whom He sent went and found it as He had told
33 them. While they were untying the colt, its owners asked them, "Why are you untying the colt?"

34 "The Lord needs it," they said.

35 So they brought it to Jesus, put their garments on the colt,
36 and set Jesus on it. As He was riding along, people spread their
37 garments on the road. And as He was coming near the place where the road goes down the Mount of Olives, the whole crowd of the disciples began to praise God joyfully and loudly for all
38 the miracles they had seen. They said,

"Blessed is the King who is coming in the Lord's name! 66
In heaven peace, and glory in the highest heavens."

39 Some of the Pharisees in the crowd said to Him, "Teacher, urge Your disciples to be quiet."

40 "I tell you," He answered them, "if these are quiet, the stones will cry out."

41 When He came near and saw the city, He wept loud over it
42 ǀ and said, "If today you only knew — yes, you — the way to
43 peace! But now it's hidden so that you can't see it. The time

will come for you when your enemies will put up ramparts against you and surround you and press against you from every side. They'll *dash* you and *your children* to the *ground* [67] and not leave one stone on another in you, because you didn't know the time your help came to you."

He Cleanses the Temple

Jesus went into the temple and proceeded to drive out the men who were selling things there. He said to them, "It is written, *My house·should be a house of prayer,*[68] but you have made it *a den of robbers.*" [69]

Every day He was teaching in the temple. The ruling priests, the Bible scholars, and the leaders of the people were trying to kill Him, but they couldn't find a way to do it, because the people were all eager to hear Him.

From Heaven

One day, as He was teaching the people in the temple and telling them the good news, the ruling priests, Bible scholars, and elders came to Him. "Tell us," they asked Him, "by what authority are You doing these things? Or who gives You the right to do them?"

Jesus answered them, "I will ask you a question. Tell Me, John's baptism — was it from heaven or from men?"

They argued among themselves, "If we say, 'From heaven,' He will ask, 'Why didn't you believe him?' But if we say, 'From men,' all the people will stone us. They're convinced John was a prophet." So they answered they didn't know where it was from.

Then Jesus told them, "Neither will I tell you by what authority I'm doing these things."

God's Vineyard

Then He told the people this story:

"A man *planted a vineyard,*[70] rented it out to workers, and left to be gone a long time.

"At the right time he sent a slave to the workers to get from them a share of the products of the vineyard. But the workers beat him and sent him back empty-handed. He sent another slave; they beat him, too, treated him shamefully, and sent him back empty-handed. Then he sent a third; they wounded him and threw him out.

"Then the owner of the vineyard said, 'What should I do? I'll send my son whom I love. Maybe they'll respect him.'

14   "When the workers saw him, they talked it over among themselves, saying, 'This is the heir. Let's kill him and get the in-
15   heritance.' So they threw him out of the vineyard and killed him.
16   "Now, what will the owner of the vineyard do to them? He will come and kill those workers and give the vineyard to others."

"That must never happen!" said those who heard Him.

17   Jesus looked at them and asked, "What does this mean in your Bible: *The stone the builders rejected has become the cor-*
18   *nerstone?* 71 Everyone who falls on that Stone will be dashed in pieces, and if that Stone falls on anyone, it will scatter him like dust."

19   The Bible scholars and the ruling priests wanted to grab Him then and there, because they knew He had aimed this story at them, but they were afraid of the people.

Taxes

20   They watched for an opportunity and sent spies to act holy in order to catch Him in what He would say. They wanted to
21   hand Him over to the governor's control and authority. They had a question for Him. "Teacher," they said, "we know You're right in what You say and teach, and You don't favor any special
22   persons but really teach God's way. Is it right for us to pay a tax to Caesar or not?"

23-24   Seeing through their tricky way, He told them, "Show Me a denarius. Whose head is on it and whose inscription?"

"Caesar's," they answered.

25   "Well, then, give Caesar what is Caesar's," He told them, "and God what is God's."

26   So they couldn't catch Him before the people in anything He said. His answer surprised them so much they didn't say anything.

The Dead Live

27   Some of the Sadducees, who say the dead don't rise, came
28   to Him with this question: "Teacher, Moses wrote for us, *If any* married *man dies and has no children, his brother should marry*
29   *the widow and have children for his brother.*72 Now, there were
30   seven brothers. The first married and died childless. ¹ Then the
31   second brother ¹ married the widow, and so did the third. In the

same way all seven died and left no children. Finally the woman
died too. Now, when they rise from the dead, whose wife will 33
she be? You know, the seven had her as wife."

"In this world men and women marry," Jesus told them; 34
"but those who are considered worthy to rise from the dead and 35
live in the other world don't marry. Nor can they die anymore, 36
because they're like the angels. They're God's children and share
in the resurrection.

"That the dead rise, Moses showed in the story about the 37
bush when he called the Lord *the God of Abraham, the God of
Isaac, and the God of Jacob.*[73] He's not the God of the dead but 38
of the living. All who are with Him are alive."

"Teacher," some Bible scholars told Him, "You have told 39
the truth." Nobody dared to ask Him another question. 40

David's Son

"How can people say the promised Savior is David's Son?" 41
He asked them. "David himself says in the book of Psalms, 42

The Lord said to my Lord,
'Sit at My right 43
Till I make Your enemies Your footstool.' [74]

So David calls Him Lord. Then how can He be his Son?" 44

Beware!

While all the people were listening, He said to the disciples: 45
"Beware of the Bible scholars. They like to go around in long 46
robes and love to be greeted in the marketplaces, to sit in the
front seats in the synagogs, and to have the places of honor at
dinners. They swallow the widows' houses and then, to cover 47
up, make long prayers. They'll be punished all the more."

A Cent

Looking up, He saw rich people dropping their gifts into the 21
contribution boxes. And He saw a poor widow drop in two small 2
coins. He said, "I tell you, this poor widow certainly put in more 3
than all the others. All the others took some of what they had 4
left over and dropped it in among the gifts. But she put in what
she needed for herself, all she had to live on."

Sorrow Ahead!

Some were saying about the temple, "It is beautifully con- 5
structed with fine stones and gifts."

"About these things that you see," He said, "the time will come when not a stone will be left on another here but will be torn down."

7   "Teacher," they asked Him, "when will this be, and how can we tell when this will happen?"

8   "Be careful not to let anyone deceive you," Jesus said. "Many will come using My name and saying, 'I am He!' and, 'The time has come.' Don't follow them.

9   "When you hear of wars and revolutions, don't get alarmed. These things *must happen* [75] first, but the end won't come right away."

10   Then He told them, *"Nation will fight against nation, and*
11   *kingdom against kingdom.*[76] There will be great earthquakes and famines and plagues in different places, terrible sights and great signs coming from heaven.

12   "Before all these things happen, men will arrest you and persecute you, hand you over to church councils, and put you in prisons. They'll bring you before kings and governors on account
13-14 of My name. It will be your chance to tell them the truth. So make up your minds not to worry beforehand how you'll defend
15   yourselves. I'll give you such speech and wisdom none of your enemies will be able to oppose it or talk against it.

16   "Even parents, brothers, relatives, and friends will betray you
17   and kill some of you, and everybody will hate you because of
18-19 My name. But not a hair on your head will be lost. Endure patiently, and you'll win your lives."

Jerusalem Will Be Destroyed

20   "When you see Jerusalem surrounded by an army, then know
21   the time has come for her to be destroyed. Then if you're in Judea, flee to the hills. If you're in Jerusalem, leave it. If you're
22   in the country, don't go into the city. Those will be *days of vengeance* [77] when everything must happen as it is written.

23   "Woe to the women who in those days are expecting babies or nursing them. There will be great distress in this country, and God
24   will punish this nation. The sword will cut them down, they'll be taken away as prisoners among all nations, and *the Gentiles will trample on Jerusalem* [78] till the time for the Gentiles has passed."

Jesus Is Coming

"There will be signs in the sun, the moon, and the stars, and 21:25 on the earth *nations* will be in distress, not knowing which way to turn from *the roaring and tossing of the sea.*[79] People will faint 26 as they fearfully wait for what will happen to the world. *The powers of the heavens* [80] will be shaken.

"Then they will see *the Son of Man coming in a cloud* [81] 27 with power and great glory.

"When these things begin to happen, stand ready and look 28 forward cheerfully because you will soon be set free."

Then He pictured it this way: "Look at a fig tree, or any of 29 the trees. As soon as leaves grow on it, you see and know without 30 being told that summer is near. So also when you see those 31 things happen, you know God's kingdom is near.

"I tell you the truth: These people will not pass away till 32 everything happens. Heaven and earth will pass away, but what 33 I say will not pass away.

"Be careful never to get your hearts burdened with drunken- 34 ness and its nausea and with worries about this life, or that day will take you by surprise like *a trap.* It will surprise all people 35 wherever they *live on the earth.*[82] But always watch and pray to 36 be considered worthy to escape all these things that are going to happen and to stand before the Son of Man."

During the day He would teach in the temple, but at night He 37 would go out to the Mount of Olives, as it was called, and stay there for the night. All the people used to get up early to go to 38 Him in the temple and hear Him.

The Plot

The festival of bread without yeast, called the Passover, was **22** near. Then the ruling priests and the Bible scholars were looking 2 for a way to kill Him. They were afraid of the people.

The devil went into Judas, called the man from Kerioth, one 3 of the twelve. He went to the high priests and the captains of 4 the temple and discussed with them how he might betray Jesus to them. They were delighted and agreed to give him some 5 money. He promised to do it and so was looking for a chance 6 to betray Him when He was away from the crowd.

The Passover

22:7 Then came the day of the festival of bread without yeast,
8 when the Passover lamb had to be killed. Jesus sent Peter and John, saying, "Go, get the Passover ready for us to eat."

9 "Where do You want us to get it ready?" they asked Him.

10 "Go into the city," He told them, "and you'll meet a man
11 carrying a jar of water. Follow him into the house he enters, and tell the owner of the house: 'The Teacher asks you, "Where is the room in which I can eat the Passover with My disciples?" '
12 ¹ He will show you a large furnished room upstairs. Get things ready there."

13 They went and found it as He had told them, and they got the Passover ready.

14 When the hour had come, He and the apostles lay down
15 for the meal. "I have very much longed to eat this Passover with
16 you before I suffer," He said to them. "I tell you, I will not eat it again till it comes true in God's kingdom." Then He was
17 handed a cup, and He gave thanks. "Take this," He said, "and share it."

The Lord's Supper

18 "I tell you, from now on I will not drink of the product of the vine till God's kingdom comes."

19 Jesus took bread, gave thanks, broke it, and gave it to them, saying, "This is My body, which is given for you. Do this to remember Me."

20 He did the same with the cup - when the supper was over, saying, "This cup is *the* new *covenant* in My *blood*,[83] poured out for you."

"Is It I?"

21 "Look, the hand of him who is betraying Me is with Me on
22 the table. The Son of Man is going as it is decreed, but woe to that man who is betraying Him."

23 They started to discuss with one another which of them was going to do this.

"Who Is the Greatest?"

24 Then the disciples started to quarrel among themselves as to which of them was considered the greatest.

25 "The kings of the nations lord it over them," He told them,
26 "and their rulers call themselves benefactors. With you it's dif-

ferent. The greatest among you should become like the youngest, and one who leads should be like one who serves. Who is greater, the one who lies down to eat or the one who serves? Isn't it the one who lies down to eat? But I am among you as one who serves.

"You have stood by Me in the troubles that have tested Me. 28 As My Father has appointed Me to be King, so I appoint you 29 I to eat and drink at My table in My kingdom and to sit on 30 thrones and rule the twelve tribes of Israel."

You Will Be Tested

"Simon, Simon," said the Lord, "you know the devil has 31 begged to have all of you to sift you like wheat. But I prayed 32 for you, Simon, that your faith will not die. And when you come back, strengthen your fellow disciples."

"Lord," he told Him, "I'm ready to go to prison and to die 33 with You."

"I tell you, Peter," He said, "the rooster will not crow tonight 34 till you deny three times that you know Me."

Then He asked them, "When I sent you out without purse, 35 bag, or shoes, you didn't lack anything, did you?"

"Not a thing!" they answered.

"But now," He told them, "if you have a purse, take it, and 36 also a bag. And if you don't have a sword, sell your garment and buy one. It is written, *He will be counted among criminals,*[84] 37 and I tell you, that must happen to Me. Whatever is written about Me must happen!"

"Lord, look, here are two swords!" they said. 38

"Enough of that!" He told them.

Gethsemane

Jesus went out and as usual came to the Mount of Olives. 39 The disciples went with Him. When He came to the place, He 40 told them, "Pray that you may not be tempted."

He withdrew from them about as far as you'd throw a stone, 41 knelt, and prayed, I "Father, if You wish, take this cup away 42 from Me; but let it not be as I want it but as You want it."

An angel from heaven appeared to Him, and gave Him 43 strength. And as He began to struggle inwardly, He prayed more 44 earnestly, and His sweat became like thick drops of blood falling on the ground.*

22:45 After praying, He got up, went to the disciples, and found 46 them sleeping because they were feeling sad. "Why are you sleeping?" He asked them. "Get up and pray that you may not be tempted."

The Arrest

47 While He was still talking, the crowd came. The one called Judas, one of the twelve, was leading them, and he came close to Jesus to kiss Him.

48 "Judas," Jesus asked him, "are you betraying the Son of Man with a kiss?"

49 The men around Jesus, seeing what was going to happen, 50 asked, "Lord, should we strike with our swords?" And one of them struck the high priest's slave and cut off his right ear.

51 But Jesus said, "Let them do it. No more of this!" And, touching the ear, He healed him.

52 Then Jesus said to the ruling priests, captains of the temple, and elders who had come for Him, "You came out for Me with 53 swords and clubs as if I were a robber! Day after day I was with you in the temple, and you laid no hands on Me. But this is your time when darkness rules."

54 They arrested Him, led Him away, and took Him to the high priest's palace.

Peter Denies Jesus

54 Peter followed at a distance.

55 The men had lit a fire in the middle of the courtyard, and as 56 they sat together, Peter sat among them. A maid saw him sitting in the light of the fire, and looking straight at him, she said, "He, too, was with Him."

57 But he denied and said, "I don't know Him, woman."

58 A little later someone else looked at him and said, "You're one of them."

"Man, I'm not!" Peter said.

59 About an hour later another insisted: "Certainly he was with Him. Why, he's a Galilean!"

60 "Man, I don't know what you're talking about," Peter said. Just then, while he was still speaking, a rooster crowed.

---

* Papyrus 75 and other old manuscripts omit verses 43-44.

Then the Lord turned and looked at Peter, and Peter remembered the Lord telling him, "Before the rooster crows today, you will deny Me three times." So he went outside and cried bitterly. ⁶²

The Jewish Court Condemns Jesus

The men who were holding Him were making fun of Him as ⁶³ they struck Him. They covered His face and kept asking Him: ⁶⁴ "Prophesy! Who hit You?" And so they went on insulting Him ⁶⁵ in many other ways.

In the morning all the elders of the people, ruling priests, ⁶⁶ and Bible scholars had a meeting. They brought Jesus before their court and asked, ¦ "Are You the promised Savior? Tell us." ⁶⁷

"If I tell you, you won't believe Me," He said to them. ¦ "And ⁶⁸ if I ask you a question, you won't answer. But from now on *the* ⁶⁹ *Son of Man* ⁸⁵ will be *sitting at the right of God's* ⁸⁶ *power.*"

"Are You, then, the Son of God?" all of them asked. ⁷⁰

He answered them, "As you say: I am He."

"Why do we need any more testimony?" they asked. "We've ⁷¹ heard Him say it ourselves."

Then the whole crowd of them got up and took Him to Pilate. 23

Before Pilate

Then they started to accuse Him: "We found that He makes ² our people disloyal, keeps them from paying taxes to the emperor, and says He is Christ, a king."

Pilate asked Him, "Are You the King of the Jews?" ³

"Yes," He answered him.

Pilate told the ruling priests and the crowd, "I don't find ⁴ this Man guilty of anything."

Before Herod

The priests and the crowd kept urging him: "He stirs up the ⁵ people by teaching all over the country of the Jews, beginning in Galilee and coming here."

When Pilate heard that, he asked, "Is the Man from Galilee?" ⁶ And when he found out Jesus came from the country governed ⁷ by Herod, he sent Him to Herod, who also was in Jerusalem at that time.

Herod was very glad to see Jesus. For a long time he wanted ⁸ to see Him because he was hearing about Him, and he was expecting to see Jesus do some miracle. He asked Him a lot of ⁹ questions, but Jesus didn't answer him. The ruling priests and ¹⁰

157

the Bible scholars were standing there and accusing Him vehemently.

23:11 So Herod and his soldiers treated Him with contempt and made fun of Him. They put a splendid garment on Him and
12 then sent Him back to Pilate. On that day Herod and Pilate became friends. Before this they had been enemies.

13 Then Pilate called the ruling priests, the other leaders, and
14 the people together. "You brought me this Man as one who turns the people against the government," he told them. "And now look, I've examined this Man before you and found Him inno-
15 cent of the things you accuse Him of. And Herod did, too, because he sent Him back to us. You see, He hasn't done any-
16 thing to deserve death. So I'm going to teach Him a lesson and
* let Him go."

Barabbas

18 Then the whole crowd yelled: "Away with Him. Free Barab-
19 bas for us." He had been put in prison for a revolt that had taken place in the city and for murder.

20 But Pilate wanted to let Jesus go, so he called to them again.

21 But they kept yelling: "Crucify, crucify Him!"

22 And Pilate spoke to them a third time: "Why, what wrong has He done? I haven't found anything in Him that deserves death. So I will teach Him a lesson and let Him go."

23 But they kept pressing him with loud shouts, demanding He
24 be crucified, and their shouts were overpowering Pilate. Then
25 Pilate decided what they demanded should be done: he let them have Barabbas, who had been put in prison for revolt and murder, but whom they were asking for, and he handed Jesus over to them to do what they wanted.

On the Way

26 As they led Jesus away, they took hold of Simon, a man from Cyrene, who was coming in from the country, and they laid the cross on him, to carry it behind Jesus.

27 A large crowd of the people followed Him. The women in the crowd were beating their breasts and weeping over Him.
28 Turning to them, Jesus said, "Daughters of Jerusalem, don't cry

* Our oldest papyrus, P75, and our oldest parchment, Codex Vaticanus, do not have v. 17: "At every festival he had to set someone free for them." See Matt. 27:15; Mark 15:6; John 18:39.

over Me, but cry over yourselves and your children, │ because the
time is coming when people will say: .

'Happy are —
> The women who couldn't have children,
> The wombs that didn't bear,
> And the breasts that didn't nurse.'

Then people will say —   30
> *To the mountains: 'Fall on us!'*
> *And to the hills: 'Cover us!'* [87]

If this is done to the green tree, what will be done to a dry one?"   31
Two others, who were criminals, were also taken away to be   32
killed with Him.

"They Crucified Him"

When they came to the place called Skull, they crucified Him   33
there with the criminals, one at His right and the other at His
left.

Then Jesus said, "Father, forgive them; they don't know what   34
they are doing." *

They divided His clothes among them by throwing lots [88] *for
them.*

The people stood there *watching*. The rulers were *sneering*,[89]   35
"He saved others. He should save Himself if He's the Savior
whom God has chosen." The soldiers also made fun of Him by   36
going up to Him and *offering Him sour wine*.[90] "If You're the   37
King of the Jews," they said, "save Yourself."

There was a notice placed above Him: THIS IS THE KING OF   38
THE JEWS.

A Robber Turns to Jesus

One of the crucified criminals was mocking Him, "Aren't You   39
the promised Savior? Save Yourself and us!"

But the other warned him. "Aren't you afraid of God?" he   40
asked him. "You're condemned just as He is. │ Our punishment   41
is just. We're getting what we deserve for what we've done.
But this One has done nothing wrong."

Then he said, "Jesus, remember me when You come to Your   42
kingdom."

* Papyrus 75 and some other old manuscripts omit this first word
from the cross.

"I tell you the truth," Jesus said to him, "today you will be with Me in Paradise."

Jesus Dies

44 It was about twelve o'clock when darkness came over the
45, 44 whole country, because the sun stopped shining, and the darkness
45 lasted till three in the afternoon. The curtain in the temple was torn in two.

46 Then Jesus called out loud, "Father, *into Your hands I entrust My spirit.*" [91] After He said this, He died.

47 When the captain saw what had happened, he praised God
48 and said, "This Man certainly was righteous." When all the people who had come there to see this saw what happened, they
49 beat their breasts and turned back. All *His friends were standing at a distance,*[92] also the women who had followed Him from Galilee and now were watching these things.

Jesus Is Buried

50 There was a man by the name of Joseph, a member of the
51 Jewish court, a good and righteous man ǀ who had not voted for their plan and action. He was from Arimathea, a Jewish town, and was looking forward to God's kingdom.

52-53 He went to Pilate and asked for Jesus' body. He took it down, wrapped it in some linen, and laid it in a grave cut in
54 the rock, in which no one had yet been laid. It was the day of preparation, and the day of rest was just starting.

55 The women who had come with Him from Galilee, following
56 close behind, saw the grave and how His body was laid. Then they went back and prepared spices and perfumes. But on Saturday they rested according to the commandment.

Jesus Rises

24 Very early on Sunday morning the women came to the grave
2 bringing the spices they had prepared. They found the stone rolled
3 back from the grave, ǀ but when they went in, they didn't find the
4 body of the Lord Jesus. While they were troubled about this, suddenly two men stood beside them in clothes that flashed like
5 lightning. The women were terrified, and they bowed down to the ground.

"Why do you look among the dead for Him who is alive?"
6 they asked the women. ǀ "He is not here; He has risen! Remember
7 what He told you while He was still in Galilee, 'The Son of Man

must be handed over to sinful men, be crucified, and rise on the third day.' "

They remembered what He said. They left the grave, went 24:8-9 back, and reported all this to the eleven and all the others. It 10 was Mary from Magdala, Johanna, Mary the mother of James, and the other women with them that told the apostles about it.

The apostles thought it was nonsense and wouldn't believe 11 them.

But Peter started out and ran to the grave. He bent down 12 and saw only the linen cloths. Then he went home, amazed at what had happened.

On the Way to Emmaus

On the same day, two of them were going to a village called 13 Emmaus, about seven miles from Jerusalem. They were talking 14 about everything that had happened.

While they were talking and discussing, Jesus Himself joined 15 them and walked with them. They saw Him but were kept from 16 knowing who He was.

"What are you discussing as you're walking along?" He asked 17 them.

They stood still and looked gloomy. ¦ "Are you the only 18 stranger living in Jerusalem," the one by the name of Cleopas asked Him, "who doesn't know what happened there these days?"

"What do you mean?" He asked. 19

"All about Jesus from Nazareth," they told Him, "who was a prophet, mighty in what He did and said before God and all the people, and how our high priests and rulers handed Him 20 over to be condemned to death and crucified Him. But we were 21 hoping He would be the One to free Israel. What is more, this is now the third day since it happened. And then some of our 22 women startled us. They went to the grave early this morning ¦ and didn't find His body. They came and told us they had even 23 seen a vision of angels who said He is alive. Some of our men 24 went to the grave and found it as the women had said; and they didn't see Him."

"How foolish you are," He told them, "and how slow to be- 25 lieve everything the prophets said! Didn't the promised Savior 26 have to suffer this and so go to His glory?" Then He explained to 27 them, starting with Moses and all the prophets, what they said about Him in all their writings.

And so they came near the village where they were going, and
29 He acted as if He were going farther. "Stay with us," they urged
Him. "It's getting late, and the day is almost gone." So He
went in to stay with them.

30 While He was at the table with them, He took the bread,
31 blessed and broke it, and gave it to them. Then their eyes were
opened, and they knew who He was. But He vanished from them.

32 "Didn't our hearts glow," they said to each other, "as He
was talking to us on the way and explaining the Bible to us?"

33 That same hour they started out, went back to Jerusalem, and
found the eleven and those who were with them all together.
34 These said, "The Lord really did rise, and Simon saw Him."

35 Then the two men told what had happened on the way and
how they had recognized Him while He was breaking the bread.

Behind Locked Doors

36 While they were talking about what had happened, Jesus
37 stood among them. "Peace to you!" He said to them. They were
startled and terrified and thought they were seeing a ghost.

38 "Why are you troubled?" He asked them. "And why do
39 doubts come into your minds? Look at My hands and My feet:
it is I Myself. Feel Me and see. A ghost doesn't have flesh
40 and bones as you see Me have." As He said this, He showed
them His hands and His feet.

41 They were so happy — they thought it was too good to be
true — and they were surprised. "Do you have anything here
42 to eat?" He asked them. They gave Him a piece of broiled fish.
43 He took it and ate it while they watched Him.

44 "While I was still with you," He said to them, "I told you
that everything written about Me in the Law of Moses, the
45 prophets, and the Psalms must come true." Then He opened their
46 minds to understand the Bible. "This," He told them, "is what
is written: The promised Savior will suffer, rise from the dead on
47 the third day, and in His name you will preach to all people,
beginning at Jerusalem, that they repent of their sins so that they
48 will be forgiven. You will testify of these things."

Jesus Goes Up to Heaven

49 "I am sending you Him whom My Father promised. Wait
here in the city till you are armed with power from above."

50 He took them out to a place where Bethany lay ahead of

them. Then He raised His hands and blessed them. While He was blessing them, He parted from them and was taken up to heaven.

They knelt and worshiped Jesus. And then they went back 52 to Jerusalem very happy. And they were always in the temple praising God.

OLD TESTAMENT REFERENCES

1. Dan. 10:12
2. Gen. 17:19
3. Num. 6:3;
   Judges 13:4
4. Mal. 4:5-6
5. Is. 7:14
6. 2 Sam. 7:12-14, 16;
   Is. 9:7; Micah 4:7;
   1 Chron. 17:12-14
7. Gen. 18:14
8. 1 Sam. 2:1;
   Hab. 3:18
9. 1 Sam. 1:11
10. Ps. 111:9; Is. 57:15
11. Ps. 103:17
12. Ps. 89:10
13. Job 12:19; 5:11;
    Ezek. 21:26
14. Ps. 107:9
15. Is. 41:8-9
16. Ps. 98:3
17. Gen. 17:7;
    Micah 7:20
18. Ps. 41:13; 72:18;
    89:52; 106:48
19. Ps. 111:9
20. 1 Sam. 2:10;
    Ps. 18:2; 132:17
21. Ps. 106:10
22. Micah 7:20
23. Gen. 22:16-17;
    Lev. 26:42; Ps.
    105:8-9; 106:45
24. Mal. 3:1
25. Ps. 107:10; Is. 9:2
26. Is. 59:8
27. Lev. 12:6
28. Ex. 13:12
29. Lev. 5:7, 11; 12:8;
    Num. 6:10

30. Is. 40:5; 52:10
31. Is. 42:6; 46:13;
    49:6
32. 1 Sam. 2:26
33. Is. 40:3-5
34. Ps. 2:7; Is. 42:1
35. Deut. 8:3
36. Deut. 6:13
37. Ps. 91:11-12
38. Deut. 6:16
39. Is. 58:6; 61:1-2
40. 1 Kings 17:9
41. 2 Kings 5:14
42. Lev. 13:7, 49
43. Lev. 24:5-8;
    1 Sam. 21:6
44. 1 Kings 17:23
45. Is. 29:18; 35:5;
    61:1
46. Ex. 23:20;
    Mal. 3:1
47. Is. 6:9
48. Ps. 2:7; Is. 42:1;
    Deut. 18:15
49. 2 Kings 1:10, 12
50. Is. 14:13, 15
51. Ps. 91:13
52. Deut. 6:5
53. Lev. 19:18
54. Lev. 18:5
55. Micah 7:6
56. Ps. 104:12;
    Ezek. 17:23; 31:6
    Dan. 4:12, 21
57. Ps. 6:8
58. Mal. 1:11
59. Jer. 12:7; 22:5
60. Ps. 118:26

61. Gen. 7:6-7
62. Gen. 19:24-25
63. Gen. 19:17, 26
64. Ex. 20:12-16;
    Deut. 5:16-20
65. Ezek. 34:16
66. Ps. 118:26
67. Ps. 137:9
68. Is. 56:7
69. Jer. 7:11
70. Is. 5:2
71. Ps. 118:22
72. Gen. 38:8;
    Deut. 25:26
73. Ex. 3:6
74. Ps. 110:1
75. Dan. 2:28
76. Is. 19:2;
    2 Chron. 15:6
77. Deut. 32:35;
    Hos. 9:7
78. Is. 63:18;
    Zech. 12:3
79. Ps. 65:7
80. Is. 34:4
81. Dan. 7:13
82. Is. 24:17
83. Ex. 24:8; Jer.
    31:32; Zech. 9:11
84. Is. 53:12
85. Dan. 7:13
86. Ps. 110:1
87. Hos. 10:8
88. Ps. 22:18
89. Ps. 22:7
90. Ps. 69:21
91. Ps. 31:5
92. Ps. 38:11

THE GOOD NEWS

as it was told by

JOHN

¹ IN THE BEGINNING WAS THE WORD, and the Word was with God,
² and the Word was God. He was in the beginning with God.

³ Everything was made by Him, and not one thing that was made was made without Him.

⁴⁻⁵ In Him was life, and the Life was the Light of men. The Light is shining in the dark, and the darkness has not put it out.

⁶⁻⁷ A man came — God sent him — his name was John. He came to tell the truth about the Light to help everyone believe.
⁸ He was not the Light but came to tell the truth about the Light.

⁹ The true Light that gives light to everyone was coming into
¹⁰ the world. He was in the world, and He made the world, and
¹¹ the world didn't know Him. He came to His own, and His own
¹² people didn't welcome Him. But to all who welcomed Him, who believe in His name, He gave the power to become God's chil-
¹³ dren. They have been born, not of the blood of parents or of a sexual desire or of a man's desire but of God.

¹⁴ And the Word became flesh and lived among us as in the tabernacle, and we saw His glory, a glory of the only Son from His Father, full of love and truth.

¹⁵ John told the truth about Him when he called: "This is the One of whom I said, He who is coming after me is ahead of me because He was before me."

¹⁶ All of us have taken from all that is in Him — gift after gift
¹⁷ of His love. The Law was given through Moses, but Jesus Christ
¹⁸ brought love and truth. ᐦNobody has ever seen God. The only Son who is God and close to the Father's heart has told us about Him.

The Lamb of God

When the Jews in Jerusalem sent priests and Levites to John 1:19
to ask him, "Who are you?" this was John's testimony. He con- 20
fessed and didn't deny. He confessed: "I'm not the promised
Savior."

"What are you then?" they asked him. "Are you Elijah?" 21
"I am not," he said.
"Are you the Prophet?"
"No," he answered.

Then they asked him, "Who are you? We want to bring an 22
answer to those who sent us. What do you say about yourself?"

He said: "I am *someone calling in the wilderness, 'Make* 23
straight the way for the Lord,' [1] as the prophet Isaiah said."

Some who had been sent belonged to the Pharisees. They 24-25
asked him, "Why, then, do you baptize if you're not the promised
Savior or Elijah or the Prophet?"

"I baptize with water," John answered them. "There is 26
standing among you Someone you don't know, the One who is 27
coming after me. I'm not good enough to untie His shoe strap."

This happened at Bethany on the other side of the Jordan, 28
where John was baptizing.

The next day John sees Jesus coming toward him. And he 29
says, "Look at the Lamb of God who takes away the sin of the
world. He is the One I meant when I said, 'A Man is coming 30
after me but is ahead of me, because He was before me.' Even 31
I didn't know who He was, but I came and baptized with water
to show Him to Israel."

John testified: "I saw the Spirit come down from heaven as 32
a dove and stay on Him. I didn't know who He was, but He who 33
sent me to baptize with water told me, 'When you see the Spirit
come down on Someone and stay on Him, He is the One who
baptizes with the Holy Spirit.' I saw it and testified, 'This is the 34
Son of God.' "

The First Disciples

The next day, while John was again standing with two of his 35
disciples, he saw Jesus passing by. "Look at the Lamb of God!" 36
he said. When the two disciples heard him say this, they fol- 37
lowed Jesus.

Jesus turned around and saw them following. "What are you 38
looking for?" He asked them.

165

"Rabbi" (which means Teacher), "where are You staying?" they asked Him.

1:39   "Come and you'll see," He told them. So they came and saw where He was staying, and they stayed with Him that day. It was about ten in the forenoon.

40   One of the two who heard John and then followed Jesus was
41   Andrew, Simon Peter's brother. He first found his own brother Simon and told him, "We have found the promised Savior."
42   (The Greek word for Him is Christ.) ¹ He brought him to Jesus.

Looking at him, Jesus said, "You are Simon, John's son. Your name will be Cephas" * (which means Peter *).

43   The next day Jesus wanted to go to Galilee. He found
44   Philip. "Follow Me!" Jesus told him. ¹ Philip was from Beth-saida, the home town of Andrew and Peter.

45   Philip found Nathanael and told him, "The One Moses wrote about in the Law, and the prophets too — we've found Him, Jesus, Joseph's Son from Nazareth."

46   "Nazareth — can anything good come from there?" Nathanael asked him.

"Come and see!" Philip told him.

47   Jesus saw Nathanael coming toward Him. "Here's a real Israelite in whom there is no deceit," He said of him.

48   "Where did You get to know me?" Nathanael asked Him.

"Before Philip called you," Jesus answered him, "when you were under the fig tree, I saw you."

49   "Master," Nathanael answered Him, "You are God's Son! You are Israel's King!"

50   "You believe because I told you I saw you under the fig
51   tree," Jesus answered him. "You will see greater things than that." And He said to him, "I tell you people the truth, you will see *heaven* opened *and God's angels going up and coming down* ² on the Son of Man."

Jesus Changes Water to Wine

2   Two days later there was a wedding in Cana in Galilee, and
2   Jesus' mother was there. Jesus and His disciples had also been invited to the wedding.

3   When the people were out of wine, Jesus' mother said to Him, "They don't have any wine."

* Cephas in Aramaic and Peter in Greek both mean "rock."

"Will you leave that to Me, woman?" Jesus asked her. "It isn't the right time yet."

His mother told the waiters, *"Do anything He tells you."* [3] 5

Six stone water jars were standing there for the religious 6 washings of the Jews. Each jar held eighteen to twenty-seven gallons.

"Fill the jars with water," Jesus told them. And they filled 7 them to the top. "Now take some of it," He told them, "and 8 bring it to the manager of the dinner." So they brought it to him.

When the manager tasted the water that had been changed 9 to wine, he didn't know where it was from; only the waiters who had dipped the water knew. So the manager called the groom. "Everybody serves his good wine first," he told him, "and when 10 people have. drunk much, then the poorer wine. You've kept the good wine till now."

Jesus did this, the first of His miracles, in Cana in Galilee. 11 He showed His glory, and His disciples believed in Him.

After this He, His mother, His brothers, and His disciples 12 went down to Capernaum and stayed there a few days.

Jesus Cleans the Temple

The Jewish Passover was near, so Jesus went up to Jerusalem. 13

In the temple He found men selling cattle, sheep, and pigeons, 14 and the money changers were sitting there. So He made a whip 15 of small ropes and with their sheep and cattle drove them all out of the temple. He scattered the coins of the money changers and upset their tables.

"Take these away!" He told those who sold pigeons. "Don't 16 make My Father's house a place for business."

His disciples had to think of what the Bible said: *The zeal for* 17 *Your house will consume Me.*[4]

Then the Jews came back at Him by asking, "By what miracle 18 can You prove to us You may do this?"

"Tear down this temple," Jesus answered them, "and I will 19 raise it in three days."

"It took forty-six years to build this temple," said the Jews, 20 "and You'll raise it in three days?"

But the temple He spoke of was His own body. After He 21-22 rose from the dead, His disciples remembered He had said this, and they believed the Bible and what Jesus had said.

John

Nicodemus

2:23   Now, while He was in the crowd at the Passover in Jerusalem,
many believed in His name when they saw the miracles He was
24   doing. Jesus, however, wouldn't trust them, because He knew
25   everybody. He didn't need to be told about anyone, because He
knew what was in him.

3   Now, there was a Pharisee by the name of Nicodemus, a mem-
2   ber of the Jewish court. ¹ He came to Jesus one night. "Master,"
he said to Him, "we know You're a teacher who has come from
God. Nobody can do these miracles You do unless God is with
him."

3   "I tell you the truth," Jesus answered him, "if anyone isn't
born from above, he can't see God's kingdom."

4   "How can anyone be born when he's old?" Nicodemus asked
Him. "He can't go back into his mother's womb and be born
again, can he?"

5   "I tell you the truth," Jesus answered him, "if anyone isn't
born of water and the Spirit, he can't get into God's kingdom.
6   Anything born of the flesh is flesh, but anything born of the Spirit
7   is spirit. Don't be surprised when I tell you you must all be born
8   from above. The wind blows where it pleases and you hear the
sound of it, but you don't know where it's coming from or
where it's going. So it is with everyone born of the Spirit."

9   "How can that be?" Nicodemus asked Him.

10   "You are the teacher in Israel," Jesus said to him, "and
11   don't know this? I assure you, We tell what We know, and We
testify to what We have seen. But you people don't accept Our
12   testimony. If you don't believe the earthly things I told you, how
13   will you believe Me if I tell you heavenly things? No one has
gone up to heaven except the One who came down from heaven —
the Son of Man.

14   "As Moses lifted up the snake in the desert, so the Son of
15   Man must be lifted up ¹ so that everyone who believes in Him
16   has everlasting life. God so loved the world that He gave His
only Son so that everyone who believes in Him doesn't perish
17   but has everlasting life. You see, God didn't send His Son into
the world to condemn the world but to save the world through
18   Him. ¹ If you believe in Him, you're not condemned. But if you
don't believe, you're already condemned because you don't believe
19   in the name of God's only Son. This is why people are condemned: The Light came into the world, but people have loved

darkness instead of the Light because they have been doing
wrong. Everyone who does wrong hates the Light and will not 3:20
come to the Light — he doesn't want his works to be seen in
the light. But anyone who lives in the truth comes to the Light 21
so that his works may be seen to have been done in God."

John Is Happy in Jesus

After this, Jesus and His disciples went into the country of 22
Judea, and there He spent some time with them and baptized.

John, too, was baptizing in Aenon, near Salim, because there 23
was much water there. So people came and were baptized.
John had not yet been put in prison. 24

John's disciples started a discussion with a Jew about religious 25
cleansing, [1] and they came to John. "Teacher," they told him, "He 26
who was with you on the other side of the Jordan and to whom
you gave your testimony — He's here. He's baptizing, and everybody's going to Him."

"A man can get only what Heaven has given him," John 27
answered. "You yourselves are witnesses that I said I'm not the 28
promised Savior but am sent ahead of Him.

"The One who has the bride is the Bridegroom. The Bride- 29
groom's friend stands and listens to Him. And when the Bridegroom speaks, He makes His friend very happy. Now, this is
my happiness, and it's complete. He must grow while I must 30
become less. The One who comes from above is above all 31
others.

"Anyone who comes from the earth is earthly and talks about
earthly things. The One who comes from heaven is above all
others. He tells the truth of what He has seen and heard, and 32
nobody accepts the truth He tells. But anyone who has accepted 33
the truth He tells has stamped with his seal of approval that
God tells the truth. The One whom God has sent says what 34
God says because God gives Him His Spirit without a limit.
The Father loves the Son and has put everything in His hands. 35
[1] Anyone who believes in the Son has everlasting life. But anyone 36
who will not listen to the Son will not see life, but God will
always be angry with him."

The Samaritan Woman

The Lord found out that the Pharisees had heard, "Jesus is 4
making and baptizing more disciples than John," although it 2

4:3 wasn't really Jesus but His disciples who baptized. Then He
4 left Judea and started back on the way to Galilee, and He had to
5 go through Samaria. He came to a town in Samaria by the name
of Sychar, near the piece of land Jacob gave his son Joseph.
6 ¹Jacob's Well was there. So Jesus, tired as He was from traveling,
sat down by the well. It was about six in the evening.

7 A woman of Samaria came to draw water. "Give Me a drink,"
8 Jesus said to her. His disciples had gone into the town to buy
food.

9 The Samaritan woman asked Him: "How can You, a Jew,
ask me, a Samaritan woman, for a drink?" Jews, you see, don't
drink from the same jar with Samaritans.

10 "If you knew what God is giving," Jesus answered her, "and
who it is that says to you, 'Give Me a drink,' you would have
asked Him, and He would have given you living water."

11 "Sir, You have nothing to draw water with," she told Him,
"and the well is deep. Where can You get living water from
12 a spring? Are You greater than Jacob, our ancestor, who gave
us the well? He himself drank from it, and also his sons and his
animals."

13 "Everyone who drinks this water," Jesus answered her, "will
14 get thirsty again. Anyone who drinks the water I'll give him will
never get thirsty again. But the water I'll give him will be in him
a spring of water bubbling up to everlasting life."

15 "Sir, give me this water," the woman told Him. "Then I won't
get thirsty or have to come out here to draw water."

16 "Go, call your husband," Jesus told her, "and come back
here."

17 "I don't have any husband," the woman answered Him.
"You're right when you say, 'I don't have any husband,'"
18 Jesus told her. "You've had five husbands, and the man you have
now isn't your husband. You've told the truth!"

19-20 "Sir," the woman said to Him, "I see You're a prophet! Our
ancestors worshiped on this mountain, but you say, 'The place
where people must worship is in Jerusalem.'"

21 "Believe Me, woman," Jesus told her, "the time is coming
when you will not be worshiping the Father on this mountain or
22 in Jerusalem. ¹You don't know what you're worshiping. We
know what we're worshiping, because salvation comes from the
23 Jews. But the time is coming, and it is here now, when real
worshipers will worship the Father in spirit and in truth. You

see, the Father is looking for such people to worship Him. God is a spirit, and those who worship Him must worship in spirit and in truth."

The woman said to Him, "I know that the promised Savior" (who is called Christ) "is coming. When He comes, He'll tell us everything."

"I am He — I who am talking to you," Jesus told her.

Just then His disciples came and were surprised to find Him talking to a woman. But none of them asked, "What do you want?" or, "Why are You talking to her?"

Then the woman left her water jar and went back into the town. "Come," she told the people, "see a Man who told me everything I've done. Could He be the promised Savior?" ¹ They left the town and were coming to Him.

Meanwhile the disciples were urging Him, "Master, eat."

He told them, "I have food to eat which you don't know about."

"Could anyone have brought Him something to eat?" the disciples asked one another.

"My food is to do what He wants who sent Me," Jesus told them, "and to finish His work.

"Don't you say, 'Four more months and we'll cut the grain'? I tell you, look and see how the fields are white and ready to be cut. Already the reaper is getting paid and is gathering grain for everlasting life, so that the sower is happy with the reaper. Here the saying is true, 'One man sows, and another cuts the grain.' I sent you to cut grain where you had not worked before. Others have done the hard work, and you have succeeded them in their work."

Many Samaritans in that town believed in Him because the woman had declared, "He told me everything I've done." When the Samaritans came to Him, they asked Him to stay with them. And He stayed there two days. ¹ Then many more believed because of what He said. "We no longer believe on account of what you said," they told the woman. "Now we heard Him ourselves and know He certainly is the Savior of the world."

After two days He left and went to Galilee.

An Officer's Son

Jesus Himself declared a prophet is not honored in his own country. Now, when He came to Galilee, the people in Galilee

171

welcomed Him. They had seen all He did at the festival in Jerusalem, since they, too, had gone to the festival.

4:46 Then Jesus went again to Cana in Galilee, where He had changed water to wine.

One of the king's officers lived at Capernaum. Now, his son 47 was sick. When he heard Jesus had come from Judea to Galilee, he went to Him and asked Him to come down and heal his son, who was dying.

48 "If you don't see wonderful proofs and miracles," Jesus told him, "you won't believe."

49 "Lord, come down," the officer asked Him, "before my little boy dies."

50 "Go," Jesus told him, "your boy is well." The man believed what Jesus told him and left.

51 On his way back his slaves met him and told him his boy 52 was well. So he asked them what time he got better. They told 53 him, "Yesterday at seven in the evening the fever left him." Then the father knew it was the same hour when Jesus had told him, "Your boy is well." And he and everybody at his house believed.

54 This was the second miracle Jesus did after He had come from Judea to Galilee.

Sick for 38 Years

5 After this there was a Jewish festival, and Jesus went up to Jerusalem.

2 Near the Sheep Gate in Jerusalem there's a pool that the 3 Jews call Bethesda. It has five porches. In them there used to lie a crowd of people who were sick, blind, lame, and para-
5 lyzed. One man who was there had been sick thirty-eight years.
6 Jesus saw him lying there and found out he had been sick a long time. "Would you like to get well?" He asked him.

7 "Lord," the sick man answered Him, "I don't have anybody to put me into the pool when the water is stirred. And while I'm trying to get there, somebody else steps in ahead of me."

8 "Get up," Jesus told him, "pick up your bed, and walk."
9 Immediately the man got well, picked up his bed, and walked.
10 That day was a Sabbath. "Today is the day of rest," the

* Our oldest manuscripts, including Papyrus 75 and Papyrus 66, do not have vv. 3b-4: "waiting for the water to be stirred. At a certain time the Lord's angel would come down into the pool and stir the water. After the stirring of the water, the first to step in got well, whatever disease he was suffering from."

Jews told the man who had been healed. "It's wrong for you to carry your bed."

He answered them, "The One who made me well told me, 5:11 'Pick up your bed and walk.'"

They asked him, "Who is the man that told you, 'Pick it up 12 and walk'?" But the man who had been healed didn't know who 13 He was, because Jesus had disappeared in the crowd that was there.

Later Jesus found him in the temple and said to him, "Look, 14 you're well now. Don't sin any more, or something worse may happen to you."

The man went back and told the Jews it was Jesus who made 15 him well.

God's Son

Because Jesus was doing such things on a Sabbath, the Jews 16 started to persecute Him. But Jesus answered them, "My Father 17 has been working until now, and so I am working."

Then the Jews were all the more eager to kill Him, because 18 He wasn't only abolishing the Sabbath but even calling God His own Father, making Himself equal to God.

"I tell you the truth," Jesus answered them, "the Son can 19 do nothing by Himself but only what He sees the Father doing. ' You see, the Son does exactly what the Father does. ' The Father 20 loves the Son and shows Him everything He is doing. And He will show Him even greater works than these so that you'll be surprised. As the Father wakes up the dead and makes them 21 live, so the Son makes alive whom He wants to make alive.

"The Father doesn't judge anyone but has entrusted the judg- 22 ment entirely to the Son ' so that all should honor the Son as they 23 honor the Father. Anyone who doesn't honor the Son doesn't honor the Father who sent Him. I tell you the truth: If you 24 listen to what I say and believe Him who sent Me, you have everlasting life, and you will not be judged, but you have come from death to life.

"Let me assure you, the hour is coming and is here now 25 when the dead will hear God's Son calling them, and those who hear Him will live. As the Father has life in Himself, so He has 26 given the Son the power of having life in Himself.

"He has also given Him power to judge because He is the 27 Son of Man. This should not surprise you, because the hour is 28

173

coming when all who are in their graves will hear Him calling
5:29 and will come out. Those who have done good will rise to
live; those who have done evil will rise to be condemned.
30 ¹I can do nothing by Myself. I judge only as I'm told to do,
and so My judgment is just, because I'm not trying to do what
I want but what He wants who sent Me.

31 "If I alone testify about Myself, My testimony isn't depend-
32 able. There's Someone else testifying about Me, and I know
33 what He testifies about Me is true. You sent to John, and he
34 testified to the Truth. Not that I get My testimony from a man,
35 but I say this to save you. John was a lighted lamp that shone,
36 and for a while you wanted to enjoy his light. But I have a greater
testimony than John had. The works the Father gave Me to
37 finish, these works that I do testify the Father sent Me. The
Father who sent Me — He testified about Me. You never heard
38 His voice or saw His form. You don't keep His Word within
39 you because you don't believe Him whom He sent. You search
the Scriptures because you think you have everlasting life in
40 them; and yet they testify about Me! But you don't want to
come to Me to have life.

41-42 "I don't get glory from men. But I know in your hearts you
43 don't love God. I have come in My Father's name, and you
don't accept Me. If someone else comes in his own name, you'll
44 accept him. How can you believe while you accept honor from
one another but are not eager to have the honor that comes from
the only God?

45 "Don't think that I will accuse you before the Father. There
is already one who accuses you — Moses, whom you trust.
46 If you really believe Moses, you would believe Me, because
47 he wrote about Me. But if you don't believe what he wrote,
how will you believe what I say?"

Jesus Feeds Five Thousand

6 Some time later Jesus crossed over to the other side of the
2 Lake of Galilee, which is the Lake of Tiberias. A large crowd
was following Him because they saw the miracles He did on
3 the sick. Jesus went up the hill and sat down there with His
4 disciples. The Jewish festival of the Passover was near.

5 As Jesus looked up, He saw a large crowd coming to Him.
He turned to Philip: "Where should we buy bread for these

people to eat?" He asked this only to test him, since He knew what He was going to do.

"Two hundred denarii,*" Philip answered, "wouldn't buy 7 enough bread for each of them to get just a little."

One of His disciples, Andrew, Simon Peter's brother, told 8 Him, "There's a boy here who has five barley loaves and two 9 fish. But what is that among so many?"

"Have the people sit down," Jesus said. There was much 10 grass at the place. So they sat down. There were about five thousand men.

Then Jesus took the loaves, gave thanks, and distributed them 11 to the people who were sitting down, and in the same way as much of the fish as they wanted.

When they had enough, He told His disciples, "Gather the 12 pieces that are left so that nothing will be wasted." They gathered 13 them and filled twelve baskets with pieces of the five barley loaves left by those who had eaten.

Seeing the miracle He did, the people said, "This certainly 14 is the Prophet who is coming into the world."

Jesus Walks on Water

When Jesus learned that the people meant to come and take 15 Him by force and make Him king, He went back again to the hill by Himself. Meanwhile, as it got late, His disciples went 16 down to the lake, stepped into a boat, and were on their way 17 across the lake to Capernaum. By this time it was dark, and Jesus hadn't come to them yet. A strong wind started to blow 18 and stir up the lake.

After they had rowed three or four miles, they saw Jesus 19 walking on the lake and coming near the boat, and they were terrified.

"It is I," He told them. "Don't be afraid." 20

They wanted to take Him into the boat. And in a moment 21 the boat came to the shore where they were going.

Bread from Heaven

The next day the people were still lingering on the other side 22 of the lake. They had noticed only one boat was there and Jesus had not stepped into that boat with His disciples but they had gone away without Him. Other boats came from Tiberias near 23

---

* A denarius was a day's pay.

6:24 the place where they had eaten the bread after the Lord gave thanks. When the people saw that neither Jesus nor His disciples were there, they stepped into these boats and came to Capernaum,

25 looking for Jesus. They found Him on the other side of the lake and asked Him, "Master, when did You get here?"

26 "Surely, I tell you," Jesus answered them, "you're not looking for Me because you've seen miracles but because you've eaten

27 some of the bread and been well fed. Don't work for the food that spoils but for the food that keeps for everlasting life, which the Son of Man will give you because God the Father has sealed in Him the power to give it."

28 "What are the works God wants us to do?" they asked Him.

29 "What God wants you to do," Jesus answered them, "is to believe in Him whom He sent."

30 "What miracle can You do?" they asked Him. "Let us see

31 it, and we'll believe You. What can You do? ¹ Our fathers ate the manna in the desert, as it is written: *He gave them bread from heaven to eat.*" ⁵

32 "I tell you the truth," Jesus said to them, "Moses didn't give you the bread from heaven, but My Father gives you the

33 real bread from heaven. God's bread is coming down from heaven and giving life to the world."

34 "Lord," they said to Him, "always give us this bread."

35 "I am the Bread of Life," Jesus told them. "Come to Me, and you will never be hungry. Believe in Me, and you will never

36 be thirsty. But I have told you, 'You have seen Me, and you

37 don't believe!' Everything the Father gives Me will come to Me,

38 and anyone who comes to Me I will never turn away, ¹ because I came down from heaven, not to do what I want but what He

39 wants who sent Me; and He who sent Me doesn't want Me to lose any of those He gave Me but to raise them on the last day.

40 Yes, My Father wants everyone who sees the Son and believes in Him to have everlasting life, and He wants Me to raise him on the last day."

41 Then the Jews grumbled because He said, "I am the Bread

42 that came down from heaven." "Isn't this Jesus, Joseph's son," they asked, "whose father and mother we know? Then how can He say, 'I came down from heaven'?"

43 "Don't grumble among yourselves," Jesus answered them.

44 "A person can come to Me only if the Father who sent Me

45 draws him. Then I will raise him on the last day. ¹ The prophets

wrote, *God will teach everyone.*[6] Everyone who listens to the
Father and learns from Him comes to Me. Not that anyone 6:46
has seen the Father; only He who comes from God has seen 47
the Father. I tell you the truth, if you believe, you have everlasting life.

"I am the Bread of Life. Your fathers ate the manna in the 48-49
desert, and they died. But this is the Bread coming down from 50
heaven so that anyone may eat it and not die. I am the living 51
Bread that came down from heaven. If anyone eats this Bread,
he will live forever. The bread I'll give to bring life to the world
is My flesh."

Then the Jews argued with one another: "How can He give 52
us His flesh to eat?"

"I tell you the truth," Jesus answered them, "unless you 53
eat the flesh of the Son of Man and drink His blood, you don't
have any life in you. If you eat My flesh and drink My blood, 54
you have everlasting life, and I will raise you on the last day.
My flesh is a real food, and My blood is a real drink. If you eat 55-56
My flesh and drink My blood, you stay in Me and I in you.
As the living Father sent Me and I live because of the Father, 57
so if you eat Me, you will live because of Me. This is the Bread 58
that came down from heaven. It isn't like the bread the fathers
ate. They died. Eat this Bread, and you will live forever."

He said this while He was teaching in a synagog in Caper- 59
naum. When they heard it, many of His disciples said, "This 60
is hard to take. Who can listen to Him?"

Inwardly aware that His disciples were complaining about 61
this, Jesus asked them, "Does this upset you? What if you 62
see the Son of Man go up where He was before? The Spirit 63
makes alive; the flesh doesn't help. The words I spoke to you
are Spirit, and they are life. But some of you don't believe."
Jesus knew from the beginning who wouldn't believe and who 64
would betray Him. So He added, "That is why I told you a per- 65
son can come to Me only if the Father gives him the power."

As a result many of His disciples went back to their old life 66
and wouldn't go with Him anymore. Then Jesus asked the 67
twelve, "Do you want to leave Me too?"

"Lord, to whom should we go?" Simon Peter answered Him. 68
"You have words of everlasting life. And we have come to be- 69
lieve and know You are God's Holy One."

"Didn't I choose the twelve of you," Jesus asked, "and one 70 of you is a devil?" He meant Judas, the son of Simon, the man from Kerioth. He was going to betray Him — one of the twelve.

To Jerusalem

7 Later Jesus went around in Galilee. He didn't want to travel in Judea because the Jews were trying to kill Him.

2-3 The Jewish festival of Booths was near. So His brothers told Jesus, "Leave this place, go to Judea, and there let Your disciples

4 see the works You're doing. Nobody goes on doing things secretly when he wants to be known publicly. If You do these

5 things, let the world see You." Not even His brothers believed in Him.

6 "It isn't the right time for Me yet," Jesus told them, "but

7 any time is right for you. The world can't hate you, but it hates

8 Me because I tell the truth about it that it is doing wrong. You go up to the festival. I'm not going up to this festival right now, because it isn't the right time for Me yet."

9-10 After telling them this, He did stay in Galilee. But after His brothers had gone up to the festival, He went up too, not publicly but without being seen.

At the Festival of Booths

11 So the Jews were looking for Jesus in the crowd at the festival.

12 "Where is He?" they kept asking. ¹ And there was much whispering about Him in the crowds. "He's a good man," some said;

13 but others, "No, He deceives the people." Yet nobody would talk about Him in public because everybody was afraid of the Jews.

14 But when the festival was already half over, Jesus went up

15 to the temple and started to teach. The Jews were surprised. "How can He know so much," they asked, "when He hasn't been in the schools?"

16 "What I teach doesn't come from Me," Jesus answered them,

17 "but from Him who sent Me. If anyone wants to do His will, he'll know whether My teaching is from God or I speak My own

18 thoughts. Anyone who speaks his own thoughts tries to glorify himself. But He who wants to glorify the One who sent Him

19 tells the truth, and there's nothing wrong in Him. Didn't Moses give you the Law? Yet none of you does what the Law tells you. Why do you want to kill Me?"

"There's a devil in You," the crowd answered. "Who wants to kill You?"

"I did one thing," Jesus answered them, "and you're all surprised about it. Moses gave you circumcision (not that it came from Moses but from our ancestors), and you circumcise a person on a Sabbath. If a child is circumcised on a day of rest to keep the Law of Moses, do you feel bitter toward Me because I made all of a man well on a Sabbath? Don't judge by what you see, but be fair when you judge."

Then some of the men from Jerusalem said, "Isn't He the man they want to kill? But here He speaks in public, and they don't say a thing to Him! Surely the rulers haven't found out He's the promised Savior, have they? Now, we know where this One comes from. But when the promised Savior comes, nobody knows where He's from."

"You know Me," Jesus called aloud as He was teaching in the temple, "and you know where I come from. I didn't by Myself decide to come, but there's One who is real who sent Me. You don't know Him, ¹ but I know Him because I come from Him and He sent Me."

Then they tried to arrest Him, but nobody laid a hand on Him, because the right time hadn't come yet for Him.

But many in the crowd believed in Him. "When the promised Savior comes," they asked, "will He do more miracles than this One has done?"

The Pharisees heard the people muttering such things about Him. So the ruling priests as well as the Pharisees sent their men to arrest Him.

"I'll be with you just a little longer," said Jesus; "then I go to Him who sent Me. You'll be looking for Me and won't find Me; and where I am, you can't come."

The Jews asked one another, "Where's He intending to go, saying we won't find Him? He doesn't intend to go to our people scattered among the non-Jews and teach the non-Jews, does He? What does He mean by saying, 'You'll be looking for Me and won't find Me,' and, 'Where I am, you can't come'?"

On the last day, the great day of the festival, as Jesus was standing there, He called out loud, "If you're thirsty, come to Me and drink. If you believe in Me, streams of living water will flow from you, as the Bible has said." By this He meant the Spirit, whom those who believed in Him were to receive.

The Spirit hadn't come yet, because Jesus hadn't been glorified yet.

7:40   After they heard Him say this, some of the people said,
41 "This is certainly the Prophet." Others said, "This is the promised Savior." Still others asked, "What! Does the promised Sav-
42 ior come from Galilee? Doesn't the Bible say, 'The promised Savior *will come from the descendants of David* and *from* the little
43 town of *Bethlehem*,⁷ where David lived'?" So the people were
44 divided over Him. Some of them wanted to arrest Him, but nobody laid hands on Him.

45   When the men who had been sent went back to the ruling priests and Pharisees, these asked them, "Why didn't you bring Him?"

46   "Nobody ever spoke like this Man," the men answered.

47   "You haven't been deceived too, have you?" the Pharisees
48 asked them. "No ruler or Pharisee has believed in Him, has he?
49 But this crowd, which doesn't know the Bible, is cursed."

50   One of them, Nicodemus, who had once come to Jesus, asked
51 them, "Does our Law condemn anyone without first hearing what he has to say and finding out what he's doing?"

52   "Are you from Galilee too?" they asked him. "Search and see; the Prophet doesn't come from Galilee."

The Adulteress *

53 8   Then everyone went home. But Jesus went to the Mount
2 of Olives. Early in the morning He came back into the temple. All the people came to Him, and He sat down and taught them.

3   The Bible scholars and the Pharisees brought to Him a woman who had been caught in adultery and had her stand in the middle.
4 "Teacher," they told Him, "this woman was caught in the act
5 of adultery. In the Law, Moses ordered us to stone such women.
6 Now, what do You say?" ¹ They asked this to test Him. They wanted to find something to accuse Him of.

    Jesus bent down and with His finger wrote on the ground.
7 But when they kept on asking Him, He got up. "Anyone that's without sin among you," He said, "should be the first to throw
8 a stone at her." Then He bent down again and wrote on the ground.

9   Convicted by their conscience as they heard Him, they went

---

* Our best manuscripts, including the two oldest papyri (P⁶⁶ and P⁷⁵, dated about A. D. 200), omit this story. It is most likely a true story in the life of Jesus but not a part of the Gospel that John wrote.

out one by one, beginning with the older men, till all had gone
and Jesus was left alone with the woman in the middle of the
place. Jesus got up. "Woman, where are they?" He asked her. 8:10
"Didn't anyone condemn you?"

"No one, Lord," she said.

"I don't condemn you either," Jesus said. "Go, from now 11
on don't sin anymore."

Jesus Argues with the Jews

Jesus spoke to them again, "I am the Light of the world. 12
Follow Me, and you will never wander in the dark but will have
the Light of Life."

"You testify about Yourself," the Pharisees said to Him. "We 13
can't depend on Your testimony."

"Even if I testify about Myself," Jesus answered them, "you 14
can depend on My testimony, because I know where I came
from and where I'm going; but you don't know where I came
from or where I'm going. You judge in a human way, a way in 15
which I don't judge anybody. But whenever I judge, you can 16
depen on My judgment because I am not alone, but I'm with
the Father who sent Me. In your own Law it is written the testi- 17
mony of two men is valid. I testify about Myself, and the Father 18
who sent Me testifies about Me."

"Where is Your Father?" they asked Him. 19

"You don't know Me or My Father," Jesus answered. "If you
knew Me, you would know My Father."

He said this in the room of the treasury while He was teaching 20
in the temple; nobody arrested Him, because the right time hadn't
come yet for Him.

"I'm going away," He said to them again, "and you'll be 21
looking for Me, but you will die in your sin. Where I'm going,
you can't come."

"Is He going to kill Himself?" the Jews asked. "Is that what 22
He means when He says, 'Where I'm going, you can't come'?"

"You're from below," He told them. "I'm from above. Your 23
home is in this world. My home is not in this world. That's 24
why I told you, 'You will die in your sins'; if you don't believe
I'm the One, you will die in your sins."

"Who are You?" they asked Him. 25

"What should I tell you first?" Jesus asked them. "I have 26
much to say about you and to condemn. But I tell the world

8:27 only what I heard from Him who sent Me, and He tells the truth." They didn't understand He was talking to them about the Father.

28 So Jesus told them, "When you have lifted up the Son of Man, you will know I am the One and I do nothing by Myself, 29 but I speak as My Father taught Me. And He who sent Me is with Me and has not left Me alone, because I always do what pleases Him."

30-31 As He was saying this, many believed in Him. Then Jesus said to those Jews who believed in Him, "If you live in My 32 Word, you are really My disciples, | and you will know the truth, and the truth will free you."

33 "We are Abraham's descendants," they answered Him, "and have never been anybody's slaves. How can You say, 'You'll be freed'?"

34 "I tell you the truth," Jesus answered them, "everyone who 35 lives in sin is a slave to sin. A slave doesn't stay in the home 36 forever. A son stays forever. | If, then, the Son frees you, you 37 will really be free. | I know you're Abraham's descendants. But you want to kill Me because My Word is not working in you. 38 I'm telling what I've seen, being with My Father, and you do what you've heard from your father."

39 "Abraham is our father," they answered Him.

"If you were Abraham's children," Jesus told them, "you 40 would do what Abraham did. But now you want to kill Me, a Man who told you the truth, which I heard from God. Abraham 41 didn't do that. You're doing what your father does."

"We weren't born outside of marriage," they said. "God alone is our Father."

42 "If God were your Father," Jesus told them, "you would love Me because I came from God, and as such I am here. I did not 43 by Myself decide to come, but He sent Me. Why don't you understand what I say? Because you can't listen to what I tell 44 you. Your father is the devil, and you want to do what your father wants. From the beginning he has been murdering people and hasn't stood in the truth, because there's no truth in him. When he tells a lie, he's telling it from his heart, because he's 45 a liar and the father of lies. Now, because I tell the truth, you 46 don't believe Me. Which of you can prove Me guilty of a sin? 47 If I tell the truth, why don't you believe Me? | A child of God

listens to what God says. You don't listen to Him because you're not God's children."

"Aren't we right," the Jews answered Him, "when we say ⁸:⁴⁸ You're a Samaritan and there's a devil in You?"

"There's no devil in Me," Jesus answered. "No, I honor My ⁴⁹ Father, but you dishonor Me. I'm not trying to get glory for ⁵⁰ Myself. There's One who wants Me to have it, and He's the Judge. Let me assure you: If you keep My Word, you will ⁵¹ never see death."

"Now we know there's a devil in You," the Jews told Him. ⁵² "Abraham died, and so did the prophets, but You say, 'If you keep My Word, you will never taste death.' Are You greater ⁵³ than our father Abraham? He died, and the prophets died. Who do You think You are?"

"If I glorify Myself," Jesus said, "My glory is nothing. It is ⁵⁴ My Father who glorifies Me, He of whom you say, 'He's our God.' You don't know Him, but I know Him. And if I would say ⁵⁵ I don't know Him, I'd be a liar like you. But I do know Him, and I obey His Word. Your father Abraham was delighted to ⁵⁶ know of My day; he saw it and was glad."

"You're not fifty years old yet," the Jews said to Him, "and ⁵⁷ Abraham has seen You?"

"I tell you the truth," Jesus told them, "I was before ⁵⁸ Abraham."

Then they picked up stones to throw at Him. But Jesus hid ⁵⁹ Himself and left the temple.

A Blind Man Sees

As Jesus was passing by, He saw a man who had been blind **9** from his birth. "Master," His disciples asked Him, "why was **2** he born blind? Did he sin or his parents?"

"Neither he nor his parents," Jesus answered. "He is blind **3** to show what God can do with him. We must do the works **4** of Him who sent Me while it is day. The night is coming when nobody can work. As long as I'm in the world, I'm the Light of **5** the world."

After He said this, He spit on the ground and with the **6** spit made some mud and put the mud on the man's eyes. "Go," **7** He told him, "wash in the pool of Siloam" (the name means "sent"). He went and washed. And as he walked away, he could see.

Now, his neighbors and others who used to see him as a beggar asked, "Isn't this the man who used to sit and beg?"

9 "It is he," some said. Others said, "No, but he looks like him." But he himself said, "I'm the one."

10 Then they asked him, "How did you get your sight?"

11 "The man they call Jesus made some mud," he answered, "and put it on my eyes and told me, 'Go to Siloam and wash.' So I went and washed, and then I could see."

12 "Where is He?" they asked him.

"I don't know," he answered.

13 They brought him who had been blind to the Pharisees.
14 Now, it was a Sabbath when Jesus made the mud and gave him
15 his sight. So the Pharisees also asked him how he got his sight.

"He put mud on my eyes," the man told them, "and I washed them, and now I can see."

16 "This Man is not from God," said some of the Pharisees, "because He doesn't rest on a Sabbath." Others asked, "How can a sinful man do such miracles?" So they disagreed.

17 Then they asked the blind man again, "What do you say about Him, since He gave you your sight?"

"He's a prophet," he answered.

18 The Jews didn't believe the man had been blind and got his sight till they called the parents of the man who could see now.
19 "Is this your son who you say was born blind?" they asked them. "How does it happen he can see now?"

20 "We know he's our son," his parents answered, "and was
21 born blind. But we don't know how it is he can see now or who gave him his sight. Ask him; he's of age. He'll tell you about
22 himself." His parents said this because they were afraid of the Jews. The Jews had already agreed to put out of the synagog
23 anyone who confessed Jesus was the promised Savior. That is why his parents said, "He's of age; ask him."

24 So once again they called the man who had been blind. "Give glory to God," they told him. "We know this Man is a sinner."

25 "I don't know if He's a sinner," he answered. "I know only one thing — I used to be blind, and now I can see."

26 "What did He do to you?" they asked him. "How did He give you your sight?"

"I've already told you," he answered them, "and you heard it. Why do you want to hear it again? You don't want to be His disciples too, do you?"

"You're His disciple," they answered him scornfully, "but we're Moses' disciples. We know God spoke to Moses, but this Fellow — we don't know where He's from."

"Well, that's strange!" the man answered them. "You don't know where He's from, and yet He gave me my sight. We know that God doesn't hear sinners but hears anyone who worships God and does what He wants. Nobody has ever heard of anyone giving sight to a man born blind. If this One were not from God, He couldn't do anything."

"You were altogether born in sins," they answered him, "and are you trying to teach us?" Then they put him out of the synagog.

Jesus heard they had put him out. Finding him, He asked him, "Do you believe in the Son of Man?"

"Who is He, sir?" he asked. "I want to believe in Him."

"You've seen Him," Jesus told him. "It is He who is now talking to you."

"I do believe, Lord," he said and bowed down to worship Him.

Then Jesus said, "I've come into this world to judge men, so that those who don't see may see and those who see may turn blind."

Some Pharisees who were near Him heard this. "We aren't blind, are we?" they asked Him.

"If you were blind," Jesus told them, "you wouldn't be sinning. But now you say, 'We see,' and you go on sinning."

The Good Shepherd

"I tell you the truth: The man who doesn't come into the sheepfold through the door but climbs over somewhere else, is a thief and a robber. But the one who comes in through the door is the shepherd of the sheep. The doorkeeper opens the door for him, and the sheep listen to his voice. He calls his own sheep by their names and leads them out. When he has brought out all his own sheep, he walks ahead of them, and the sheep follow him because they know his voice. They will not follow a stranger but will run away from him because they don't know the voice of strangers."

This was the illustration Jesus used in talking to them, but they didn't know what He meant. So Jesus spoke again: "I tell

10:8 you the truth: I am the Door for the sheep. All who came before Me were thieves and robbers, but the sheep didn't listen to them.

9 ¹ I am the Door. If anyone comes in through Me, he will be saved and will go in and out and find pasture.

10 "A thief comes only to steal and kill and destroy. I came so that they will have life and have it overflowing in them.

11 ¹ I am the Good Shepherd. The Good Shepherd gives His life for
12 the sheep. When a hired man, who isn't a shepherd and doesn't own the sheep, sees a wolf coming, he leaves the sheep and runs
13 away — and the wolf carries them off and scatters them — ¹ because he works for money and doesn't care about the sheep.
14 I am the Good Shepherd, and I know My own and My own
15 know Me, as the Father knows Me and I know the Father.
16 And I give My life for the sheep. ¹ I have other sheep too, that are not in this fold. I must lead those too, and they will listen to My voice, and so they will become one flock with *One*
17 *Shepherd.*⁸ The Father loves Me because I give My life in order
18 to take it back again. ¹ Nobody takes it from Me. No, of My own free will I am giving it. I have the power to give it, and I have the power to take it back again. This is what My Father ordered Me to do."

19-20 These words again caused a split among the Jews. Many of them said, "There's a devil in Him and He's crazy. Why do
21 you listen to Him?" Others said, "Nobody talks like this when there's a devil in him. Can a devil give sight to the blind?"

"I and the Father Are One"

22 Then came the festival of Dedication in Jerusalem. It was
23 winter, and Jesus was walking in Solomon's porch in the temple.
24 ¹ There the Jews surrounded Him. "How long will You keep us in suspense?" they asked Him. "If You're the promised Savior, tell us frankly."

25 "I did tell you," Jesus answered them, "but you don't be- lieve it. The works I do in My Father's name tell the truth
26 about Me. But you don't believe, because you're not My sheep.
27 My sheep listen to My voice, and I know them, and they follow
28 Me, ¹ and I give them everlasting life. They will never be lost,
29 and nobody will tear them out of My hand. My Father, who gave them to Me, is greater than all others, and nobody can tear
30 them out of My Father's hand. I and the Father are one."

31-32 Again the Jews picked up stones to stone Him. Jesus answered them, "I have shown you many good works that come from the Father. For which of these works are you trying to stone Me?"

"We're stoning You," the Jews answered Him, "not for a good 10:33 work but for blasphemy because You, a man, claim to be God."

Jesus said to them, "Isn't it written in your Bible, *I said,* 34 *'You are gods'?* [9] If it called them gods to whom God's Word 35 came — and the Bible can't be set aside — [1] do you say to Me, 36 whom the Father appointed for His holy purpose and sent into the world, 'You're blaspheming,' because I said, 'I'm God's Son'? If I'm not doing My Father's works, don't trust Me. But if I do 37-38 them, even if you don't trust Me, trust My works so as to learn and understand the Father is in Me and I am in the Father."

Again they tried to arrest Him, but He escaped from their 39 hands. He went back across the Jordan to the place where John 40 had been baptizing earlier, and He stayed there.

Many came to Him. "John did no miracle," they said, "but 41 everything John said about this One is true." And many be- 42 lieved in Him there.

Jesus Raises Lazarus

Then Lazarus was sick. He was in Bethany, the village 11 where Mary and her sister Martha were living. Mary was the 2 one who poured perfume on the Lord and wiped His feet with her hair. It was her brother Lazarus who was sick.

So the sisters sent someone to tell Jesus, "Lord, the one 3 You love is sick."

When Jesus heard it, He said, "The purpose of this sickness 4 isn't death but to show God's glory; it is to glorify God's Son."

Jesus loved Martha and her sister and Lazarus. Now, when 5-6 He heard Lazarus was sick, He stayed two days where He was. After that He said to His disciples, "Let us go back to Judea." 7

"Master," the disciples said to Him, "the Jews have just 8 been wanting to stone You, and You're going back there?"

"Aren't there twelve hours in a day?" Jesus answered. "If 9 you walk during the day, you don't stumble, because you see the light of this world. But if you walk at night, you stumble, 10 because you have no light."

After He said this, He told them, "Our friend Lazarus 11 has gone to sleep, but I'm going there to wake him up."

"Lord, if he has gone to sleep," His disciples said to Him, "he'll get well."

13 Jesus meant he was dead, but they thought He meant he was
14 only sleeping. Then Jesus told them in plain words, "Lazarus
15 died. And I'm glad I wasn't there; it will help you believe. But let us go to him."

16 Then Thomas, who was called Twin, said to his fellow disciples, "Let us go, too, and die with Him."

17 When Jesus got there, He found that Lazarus had been in the grave four days already.

18-19 Bethany was near Jerusalem, not quite two miles away, and many Jews had come to Martha and Mary to comfort them about their brother.

20 Now, when Martha heard, "Jesus is coming," she went to
21 meet Him, while Mary stayed at home. "Lord, if You had been
22 here," Martha told Jesus, "my brother wouldn't have died. But even now I know God will give You anything You ask Him."

23 "Your brother will rise again," Jesus told her.

24 "I know he'll rise again," Martha answered Him, "in the resurrection on the last day."

25 "I am the Resurrection and the Life," Jesus said to her.
26 "Anyone who believes in Me will live even if he dies. Yes, anyone who lives and believes in Me will never die. Do you believe that?"

27 "Yes, Lord," she told Him, "I believe You are the promised Savior, God's Son, who is coming into the world."

28 After she said this, she went to call her sister Mary. "The Teacher is here," she whispered, "and is calling for you."

29-30 When Mary heard it, she got up quickly to go to Him. Jesus hadn't come to the village yet but was still where Martha had
31 met Him. Now, the Jews who were in the house with Mary to comfort her saw her get up quickly and leave. So they followed
32 her, thinking she was going to the grave to weep there. When Mary came where Jesus was and saw Him, she bowed down at His feet and said, "Lord, if You had been here, my brother wouldn't have died."

33 When Jesus saw her weeping, and the Jews weeping who came with her, He groaned deeply and was troubled.

34 "Where did you lay him?" He asked.

"Lord, come and see," they answered Him.

Jesus burst into tears. "See how He loved him," the Jews said. But some of them asked, "He gave sight to the blind man — couldn't He have kept this man from dying?"

Groaning deeply again, Jesus went to the grave. It was a cave, and a stone was laid against it. "Move the stone away," said Jesus.

Martha, the dead man's sister, told Him, "Lord, he smells already. He's been dead four days."

Jesus said to her, "Didn't I tell you, 'If you believe, you will see God's glory'?" So they moved the stone away.

Jesus looked up and said, "Father, I thank You for hearing Me. I I knew You always hear Me. But I spoke so that the people standing around Me will believe You sent Me." After He had said this, He called out loud, "Lazarus, come out!"

The dead man came out, his feet and hands wrapped in bandages and his face wrapped in a cloth. "Unwrap him," Jesus told them, "and let him go."

Then many of the Jews who had come to Mary and had seen what He did believed in Him. But some of them went to the Pharisees and told them what Jesus had done. Then the ruling priests and the Pharisees called a meeting of the council. "What are we doing?" they asked. "This Man is doing many miracles. If we let Him go on like this, everybody will believe in Him, and then the Romans will come and take away our place and our nation."

But one of them, Caiaphas, who was high priest that year, told them, "You don't know anything, I and you don't consider it is better for you that one man dies instead of the people and the whole nation doesn't perish." He didn't think of this himself, but being high priest that year, he prophesied Jesus was going to die for the nation, and not only for this nation but also to bring God's scattered children together and make them one.

From that day on they planned to kill Him. So Jesus no longer walked in public among the Jews but left and went into the country near the wilderness, to a town called Ephraim and stayed there with His disciples.

Mary Anoints Jesus

The Jewish Passover was near, and many came from the country to Jerusalem before the Passover to purify themselves. They were looking for Jesus and asking one another as they stood

11:57 in the temple, "What do you think? He isn't coming to the festival, is He?" The ruling priests and the Pharisees had given orders if anyone found out where He was he should report it so that they might arrest Him.

12 Six days before the Passover, Jesus came to Bethany, where
2 Lazarus was, whom Jesus had raised from the dead. There a dinner was prepared for Him. Martha served, and Lazarus was one of those eating with Him.

3 Then Mary took a pound of perfume, real nard and very expensive, and poured it on Jesus' feet and dried His feet with her hair. The fragrance of the perfume filled the house.

4 Judas (the man from Kerioth, one of His disciples, who was
5 going to betray Him) asked, "Why wasn't this perfume sold for
6 three hundred denarii and the money given to the poor?" He didn't say this because he cared about the poor but because he was a thief and used to steal what was put in the money box he carried.

7-8 "Let her do it for the day of My burial," Jesus said. "The poor you always have with you, but you don't always have Me."

9 A large crowd of the Jews found out He was there, and they came, not only on account of Jesus but also to see Lazarus,
10 whom He had raised from the dead. But the ruling priests de-
11 cided to kill Lazarus too, because he was the reason many Jews were going over to Jesus and believing in Him.

The King Comes to Jerusalem

12 The next day the large crowd that had come to the festival
13 and heard, "Jesus is coming to Jerusalem," ¹ took branches from the palm trees and went out to meet Him, shouting:
"Our Savior!
Blessed is He who is coming in the Lord's name, ¹⁰
The King of Israel!"

14 Jesus found a donkey and sat on it, as it is written:
15 *Don't be afraid, daughter of Zion!*
Look! Your King is coming, riding on a donkey's colt! ¹¹

16 At that time His disciples didn't know what it meant, but after Jesus was glorified, they remembered this was written about Him and was done to Him.

17 The people who had been with Him when He called Lazarus out of the grave and raised him from the dead were telling what

they had seen. Because the crowd heard He had done this
miracle, it came to meet Him.

Then the Pharisees said to one another, "You see, you're not ¹⁹
getting anywhere. Look! The world is running after Him."

Death and Glory

Among those who came up to worship at the festival were some ²⁰
Greeks. They went to Philip (who was from Bethsaida in Galilee) ²¹
and told him, "Sir, we want to see Jesus." Philip went and told ²²
Andrew. Andrew and Philip went and told Jesus.

Jesus answered them, "The time has come for the Son of ²³
Man to be glorified. Surely, I tell you, if a kernel of wheat ²⁴
doesn't fall into the ground and die, it will be just one kernel.
But if it dies, it produces much grain. Love your life and lose it, ²⁵
but hate your life in this world, and you will keep it for an everlasting life. If you serve Me, follow Me; and where I am, there ²⁶
My servant will be. If you serve Me, the Father will honor you.

"I am deeply troubled ¹² now. But what should I say? Father, ²⁷
save Me from what is going to happen? No! I came to suffer
this now. Father, glorify Your name." ²⁸

Then a voice came from heaven: "I have glorified My name
and will glorify it again."

The crowd, which stood there and heard it, said it had ²⁹
thundered. Others said, "An angel talked to Him." Jesus ex- ³⁰
plained: "That voice did not come for My benefit but for yours.

"Now this world is being judged; now the ruler of this world ³¹
will be thrown out. And once I have been lifted up from the ³²
earth, I will draw all people to Me." He said this to indicate ³³
how He was going to die.

Then the crowd answered Him, "We've heard from the Bible ³⁴
the promised Savior lives forever. How, then, can You say the
Son of Man must be lifted up? Who is this Son of Man?"

"The Light will be with you just a little longer," Jesus an- ³⁵
swered them. "Walk while you have the Light, or darkness will
overtake you. If you walk in the dark, you don't know where
you're going. While you have the Light, believe in the Light in ³⁶
order to become enlightened people."

After Jesus had said this, He went away and hid from them.
Although they had seen Him do so many miracles, they wouldn't ³⁷
believe in Him — what the prophet Isaiah said had to come true: ³⁸

> *Lord, who has believed what we preach?*
> *And to whom has the Lord's arm been uncovered?* ¹³

12:39 And so they couldn't believe, because Isaiah also said,

40
> *He blinded their eyes*
> *And dulled their minds*
> *So that their eyes don't see,*
> *Their minds don't understand,*
> *And they don't turn and let Me heal them.*[14]

41 Isaiah said this because he saw His glory and spoke of Him.
42 And yet even many of the rulers believed in Him but wouldn't say so publicly, because the Pharisees would have put them out
43 of the synagog. Yes, they loved to be praised by men more than by God.

44 Then Jesus called out, "If you believe in Me, you don't believe
45 only in Me but in Him who sent Me. And if you see Me, you
46 see Him who sent Me. I have come as a light into the world so that anyone who believes in Me will not have to stay in the dark.
47 If anyone hears what I say but doesn't keep it, I don't condemn him, because I didn't come to condemn the world but to save the
48 world. If anyone rejects Me and doesn't take to heart what I say, he has one that is condemning him. The Word that
49 I spoke will condemn him on the last day, because what I said didn't come from Me, but the Father who sent Me ordered Me to
50 say and tell it. I know what He orders is everlasting life. And so, whatever I say, I say it just as the Father told Me."

Jesus Washes the Disciples' Feet

13 Before the Passover festival Jesus knew the time had come for Him to leave this world and go to the Father. He had loved His own who were in the world, and now He loved them to the end.

2 It was during the supper. The devil had already put the idea of betraying Jesus into the mind of Judas, the son of Simon from Kerioth.

3 Jesus knew the Father put everything in His hands and He had come from God and was going back to God.

4 So Jesus rose from supper, laid aside His outer garment,
5 took a towel, and tied it around Him. Then He poured water into a basin and started to wash the disciples' feet and to dry them with the towel that was tied around Him.

6 And so He came to Simon Peter. "Lord," Peter asked Him, "are You going to wash my feet?"

7 "You don't know now what I'm doing," Jesus answered him. "But later you will understand."

"No!" Peter told Him. "You'll never wash my feet."

"If I don't wash you," Jesus answered him, "you have no share in Me."

"Lord," Simon Peter told Him, "not only my feet but also ⁹ my hands and my head."

"Anyone who has bathed needs only to have his feet washed," ¹⁰ Jesus told him. "He's clean all over. You're clean, but not all of you." ¹ He knew who was betraying Him. That's why He said, ¹¹ "Not all of you are clean."

After He had washed their feet and put on His garment, He ¹² lay down again. "Do you know what I've done to you?" He ¹³ asked them. "You call Me Teacher and Lord, and you're right because I am that. Now if I, the Lord and the Teacher, have ¹⁴ washed your feet, you, too, should wash one another's feet. I've given you an example so that you will do as I did to you. ¹⁵ Surely, I tell you, a slave is no greater than his Master, and if ¹⁶ you're sent, you're no greater than He who sent you. If you ¹⁷ know this, you're happy if you do it.

"I'm not talking about all of you. I know whom I've chosen. ¹⁸ But what the Bible says has to come true: *He who eats My bread kicks Me.*¹⁵ From now on I'm telling you these things ¹⁹ before they happen so that when they happen you believe I am the One.

"Let Me assure you, if you receive anyone I send, you re- ²⁰ ceive Me, and if you receive Me, you receive Him who sent Me."

"Is It I?"

After saying this, Jesus was deeply troubled. "I tell you the ²¹ truth," He declared, "one of you is going to betray Me!"

The disciples started to look at one another, wondering whom ²² He meant.

One of His disciples, the one Jesus loved, was lying close ²³ to Jesus' bosom. Simon Peter motioned to him to ask whom ²⁴ He meant.

Leaning back, where he was, against Jesus' breast, he asked ²⁵ Him, "Lord, who is it?"

"I'll dip this piece of bread and give it to him," Jesus an- ²⁶ swered. "He's the one." Then he dipped it and gave it to Judas, the son of Simon from Kerioth.

After Judas took the piece of bread, the devil went into him. ²⁷

193

13:28 So Jesus told him, "What you're doing, do quickly." [1] What He
29 meant by telling him this, nobody at the table knew. Some
thought, since Judas had the money box Jesus was telling him,
"Buy what we need for the festival," or that he should give
something to the poor.

30 Right after taking the piece of bread Judas went outside.
And it was night.

31 When Judas had gone out, Jesus said, "Now the Son of Man
32 is glorified, and in Him God is glorified. God will also glorify Him
in Himself; yes, He will glorify Him now."

Jesus Warns Peter

33, 31, 33 "Children," Jesus said, "I'm with you just a little longer.
You will look for Me, but as I told the Jews, so I tell you now:
Where I'm going, you can't come.

34 "I'm giving you a new order: Love one another! Love one
35 another as I have loved you. By your loving one another everybody will know you're My disciples."

36 "Lord, where are You going?" Simon Peter asked Him.
"Where I'm going you can't follow Me now," Jesus answered
him; "but you will follow Me later."

37 "Lord, why can't I follow You now?" Peter asked Him.
"I'll give my life for You."

38 "You'll give your life for Me?" Jesus asked. "I tell you the
truth: The rooster will not crow till you've denied Me three
times."

"I Am Going Away"

14 "Don't feel troubled. Believe in God, and believe in Me.
2 [1] In My Father's house there are many rooms. If it were not so,
I would have told you, because I go to prepare a place for you.
3 And when I have gone and prepared a place for you, I'll come
4 again and take you home with Me so you'll be where I am. You
know the way to the place where I'm going."

5 "Lord, we don't know where You're going," Thomas said to
Him. "So how can we know the way?"

6 "I am the Way, the Truth, and the Life," Jesus answered
7 him. "No one comes to the Father except by Me. [1] If you have
learned to know Me, you'll know My Father too. From now on
you know Him and have seen Him."

8 Philip said to Him, "Lord, show us the Father; that's
enough for us."

"I've been with all of you so long," Jesus answered him, "and you don't know Me, Philip? If you have seen Me, you have seen the Father. How can you say, 'Show us the Father'? Don't you believe I am in the Father and the Father is in Me? What I tell you doesn't come from Me, but the Father, who lives in Me, is doing His works. Believe Me, I am in the Father, and the Father is in Me. Or else believe Me on account of My works.

"I tell you the truth, if you believe in Me, you'll do the works I'm doing, and you'll do greater works than these, because I'm going to the Father, and I will do anything you ask in My name in order that the Son may glorify the Father. If you ask Me for anything in My name, I'll do it.

"If you love Me, you will do what I order. And I will ask the Father, and He will give you another Comforter to be with you forever. He is the Spirit of truth, whom the world cannot receive, because it doesn't see or know Him. You know Him, because He lives with you and will be in you.

"I will not leave you orphans; I'm coming back to you. Only a little while and the world won't see Me any more. But you will see Me, because I live, and you, too, will live. On that day you will know I'm in My Father and you in Me and I in you. If you have My commandments and obey them, you love Me. And if you love Me, My Father will love you, and I will love you and show Myself to you."

Judas (not the man from Kerioth) asked Him, "Lord, what has happened that you're going to show yourself to us and not to the world?"

Jesus answered him, "If you love Me, you'll do what I say, and My Father will love you, and We will come to you and live with you. Anyone who doesn't love Me doesn't do what I say. And you are hearing, not what I say but what the Father says who sent Me.

"I've told you this while I'm still with you. But the Comforter, the Holy Spirit, whom the Father will send in My name, will teach you everything and remind you of everything I told you.

"I leave peace with you; I give you My peace. I don't give it to you as the world gives it. Don't feel troubled or afraid. You heard Me tell you, 'I'm going away, but I'm coming back to you.' If you loved Me, you'd be glad I'm going to the Father, because the Father is greater than I.

"I've told you this now before it happens, so that when it
30 happens, you believe. I won't say much to you any more, because the ruler of the world is coming. He has no claim on Me.
31 But I want the world to know I love the Father and am doing
just what the Father ordered Me to do.

"Come, let us go away."

The Vine and the Branch

15 "I am the real Vine, and My Father takes care of the vine-
2 yard. He cuts away any branch of Mine that bears no fruit, and
He trims any branch that bears fruit to make it bear more fruit.

3 "What I have said to you has already made you clean. Stay
4 in Me, and I will stay in you. A branch can't bear any fruit by
itself — if it doesn't stay in the vine. Neither can you if you
5 don't stay in Me. I am the Vine, you are the branches. If you
stay in Me and I in you, you bear much fruit. Without Me you
6 can't do anything. If anyone doesn't stay in Me, he's thrown
away like a branch and dries up. Such branches are gathered,
7 thrown into the fire, and burned. If you stay in Me and what
I say stays in you, ask for anything you want, and it will be done
8 for you. You glorify My Father when you bear much fruit and
9 so prove to be My disciples. As the Father has loved Me, so
10 I have loved you. Stay in My love. If you obey My commandments, you'll stay in My love, as I have obeyed My Father's
11 commandments and stay in His love. I told you this so that My
12 joy will be in you and you will be very happy. This is what
I order you to do: Love one another as I have loved you.
13 No one has a greater love than he who gives his life for his
14 friends. You're My friends if you do what I order you to do.
15 I don't call you servants any more, because a servant doesn't
know what his master is doing. But I've called you friends be-
16 cause I've told you everything I heard from My Father. You
didn't choose Me, but I chose you and appointed you to go and
bear fruit that doesn't pass away and to have the Father give
17 you anything you ask Him in My name. This is what I order you
to do: Love one another.

18-19 "If the world hates you, you know it hated Me first. If you
belonged to the world, the world would love you as its own.
But you don't belong to the world; I took you away from the
20 world; that's why the world hates you. Remember what I told
you: a slave is no greater than his Master. If they persecuted

Me, they'll persecute you. If they did what I said, they'll do what you say. Now they will do all this to you on account of 15:21 Me, because they don't know Him who sent Me. If I hadn't 22 come and spoken to them, they wouldn't be sinning, but now they have no excuse for their sin. Anyone who hates Me hates 23 My Father. If I hadn't done among them the works no one 24 else has done, they wouldn't be sinning. But now they have seen and hated Me and My Father. What is written in their Bible has 25 to come true: *They will hate Me without any reason.*[16]

"When the Comforter comes, whom I'll send you from the 26 Father, the Spirit of truth, who comes from the Father, He'll tell the truth about Me. And you, too, tell the truth, because 27 you've been with Me from the beginning."

Sorrow Will Turn to Joy

"I told you this so that nothing will upset your faith. You **16** 1-2 will be put out of the synagog. Yes, the time will come when anyone who murders you will think he's serving God. Men will 3 do these things because they didn't get to know the Father or Me. But I told you this so that when it happens you'll remember I told 4 you about it. I didn't tell you this at first, because I was with you.

"Now I'm going to Him who sent Me, and none of you asks 5 Me, 'Where are You going?' But because I told you this, you feel 6 very sad. But I tell you the truth, it's good for you that I go 7 away. If I don't go away, the Comforter will not come to you. But if I go, I'll send Him to you. He will come and convince 8 the world of sin, righteousness, and judgment: of sin because 9 they don't believe in Me; of righteousness because I'm going to the 10 Father and you won't see Me any more; of judgment because 11 the ruler of this world is judged.

"I have much more to tell you, but it would be too much for 12 you now. When the Spirit of truth comes, He will lead you into 13 the whole truth. What He will say will not come from Himself, but He'll speak what He hears and tell you what is coming. He will glorify Me, because He'll take from what is Mine and 14 tell it to you. Everything the Father has is Mine. That is why 15 I said, 'He takes from what is Mine and will tell it to you.'

"A little while and you'll not see Me any more; and again 16 a little while and you'll see Me."

Then some of His disciples asked one another, "What does 17 He mean when He tells us, 'Just a little while and you'll not see

16:18 Me; and again only a little while and you'll see Me,' and 'I'm going to the Father'?" So they were asking, "What does He mean when He says, 'A little while'? We don't know what He means."

19 Jesus knew they wanted to ask Him something. "Are you trying to find out from one another," He asked them, "what I meant by saying, 'A little while and you'll not see Me; and 20 again a little while and you'll see Me'? I tell you the truth, you will cry and mourn, but the world will be glad. You will have 21 sorrow, but your sorrow will turn to joy. When a woman is going to have a child, she has pains because her time has come. But after the child is born, she's so happy a child was brought 22 into the world she doesn't remember her pains any more. You, too, are sad now; but I'll see you again, *and then you'll be glad,*[17] 23 and nobody will take your joy away from you. Then you won't ask Me any questions. I tell you the truth, if you ask the Father 24 for anything, He will give it to you in My name. So far you haven't asked for anything in My name. Ask and you will receive and be very happy.

25 "I used veiled speech in telling you these things. The time is coming when I won't use veiled speech any more in talking to 26 you, but I'll tell you about the Father in plain words. Then you will ask in My name, and I don't tell you I'll ask the Father for 27 you. The Father Himself loves you because you have loved Me 28 and believe that I came from the Father. I left the Father and came into the world; and now I'm leaving the world again and going to the Father."

29 "Yes, now You're talking in plain words," His disciples said, 30 "and using no veiled speech. Now we know You know everything and don't need to have anyone ask You anything. That's why we believe You've come from God."

31-32 "Now you believe," Jesus answered them. "The hour is coming, in fact, it's here now, when you'll be scattered, everyone to his home, and you'll leave Me alone. But I'm not alone, because 33 the Father is with Me. I told you this so you will have peace in Me. In the world you have trouble. But have courage; I've conquered the world."

Jesus Prays

17 After saying this, Jesus looked up to heaven and said:
"Father, the time has come. Glorify Your Son so that Your

Son will glorify You, since You have given Him power over all
men, to give everlasting life to all whom You gave Him. This is 3
everlasting life — to know You, the only true God, and Jesus
Christ, whom You sent. I have glorified You on earth by finishing 4
the work You gave Me to do. And now, Father, glorify Me at 5
Your side with the glory I had with You before the world began.

"I made Your name known to the people You gave Me out 6
of the world. They were Yours, and You gave them to Me, and
they have kept Your Word. Now they know everything You 7
gave Me comes from You, because I gave them the message You 8
gave Me. And they have accepted it and learned the truth that
I came from You, and have believed You sent Me.

"I pray for them. I don't pray for the world but for those 9
You gave Me, because they are Yours. All that is Mine is 10
Yours, and what is Yours is Mine. And I am glorified in them.
I am no longer in the world, but they are in the world, and I am 11
coming to You. Holy Father, keep them in Your name, which
You gave Me, so that they will be one as We are one. While I was 12
with them, I kept them safe in Your name, which You gave Me.
I watched over them, and none of them was lost except that
lost one — what the Bible says had to come true.

"But now I am coming to You, and I say this while I am in 13
the world so that they will feel all My joy in their hearts.
ᴵI gave them Your Word. But the world has hated them because 14
they don't belong to the world any more than I belong to the
world. I'm not asking You to take them out of the world, but 15
to keep them from the evil one. They don't belong to the world 16
any more than I belong to the world.

"Make them holy by the truth; Your Word is truth. As You 17-18
sent Me into the world, I sent them into the world. In this holy 19
way I give Myself for them to make them holy, too, by the truth.
I'm not asking for them only but also for those who through 20
their word believe in Meᴵ that they all be one. As You, Father, 21
are in Me and I in You, let them be in Us so that the world may
believe You sent Me. I gave them the glory You gave Me to 22
make them one as We are one. I am in them, and You are in 23
Me to make them perfectly one that the world may know You
sent Me and loved them as You loved Me.

"Father, I want those You gave Me to be with Me where 24
I am and to see My glory that You gave Me because You loved
Me before the world was made. Righteous Father, the world 25

didn't know You, but I knew You, and these have learned to
know You sent Me. I told them and I am going to tell them
Your name, so that the love You have for Me will be in them
and I will be in them."

The Arrest

18   After Jesus said this, He took His disciples to the other side
of the Kidron valley where there was a garden. He and His disciples went into it.

2   Judas, who was betraying Him, also knew the place because
3   Jesus and His disciples often got together there. So Judas took
the troop of soldiers and servants from the ruling priests and
Pharisees and came there with lanterns and torches and weapons.

4   Then Jesus went out, knowing exactly what was going to
happen to Him. "Whom are you looking for?" He asked them.

5   "Jesus from Nazareth," they answered Him.

"I am He," Jesus told them.

6   Judas, ready to betray Him, was standing with them. ' When
Jesus told them, "I am He," they went backward and fell to the
ground.

7   He asked them again, "Whom are you looking for?"

"Jesus from Nazareth," they said.

8   "I told you I am He," Jesus answered. "So if I'm the One
9   you want, let these others go." This was to make good what He
had said: "I lost none of those You gave Me." *

10   Then Simon Peter, who had a sword, drew it, struck the
high priest's slave, and cut off his right ear. The slave's name
was Malchus.

11   "Put your sword into its scabbard," Jesus told Peter. "The cup
My Father gave Me — shouldn't I drink it?"

12   So the troop of soldiers, the tribune, and the attendants of
13   the Jews arrested Jesus, bound Him, ' and took Him first to
Annas, because he was the father-in-law of Caiaphas, who was
14   high priest that year. It was Caiaphas who advised the Jews, "It
is better that one man dies instead of the people."

Peter Denies Jesus

15   Now, Simon Peter and another disciple were following Jesus.
The other disciple was known to the high priest and went with
Jesus into the high priest's courtyard. But Peter was standing

* John 6:39; 17:12

outside the door. So the other disciple, whom the high priest
knew, went out and talked to the girl watching the door and
brought Peter in.

This doorkeeper asked Peter, "You aren't one of this Man's ¹⁷
disciples too, are you?"

"I'm not," he answered.

The slaves and the attendants were standing around and had ¹⁸
made a heap of burning coals because it was cold. As they warmed
themselves, Peter was standing with them warming himself.

Before Annas

Then the high priest asked Jesus about His disciples and His ¹⁹
teaching.

"I have spoken publicly to the world," Jesus answered him. ²⁰
"I have always taught in a synagog or in the temple, where all
the Jews gather, and I haven't said anything in secret. Why do ²¹
you ask Me? Ask those who heard Me what I said to them;
they know what I said."

When He said this, one of the attendants standing near Jesus ²²
slapped His face. "Is that how You answer the high priest?" he
asked.

"If I said anything wrong," Jesus answered him, "tell us what ²³
was wrong. But if I told the truth, why do you hit Me?"

Then Annas sent Him, still bound, to Caiaphas, the high ²⁴
priest.

Peter Denies Again

Simon Peter continued to stand and warm himself. So the ²⁵
men asked him, "You aren't one of His disciples too, are you?"

He denied, saying, "I'm not!"

One of the high priest's slaves, a relative of the man whose ²⁶
ear Peter had cut off, asked, "Didn't I see you with Him in the
garden?"

Again, Peter denied, and just then a rooster crowed. ²⁷

Before Pilate

The Jews took Jesus from Caiaphas to the governor's palace. ²⁸
It was early in the morning.

To keep from getting unclean (they wanted to celebrate the
Passover), the Jews themselves didn't go into the governor's
palace. So Pilate came out to them. "What accusation are you ²⁹
bringing against this Man?" he asked.

"If He weren't a criminal," they answered him, "we wouldn't have handed Him over to you."

31 "Take Him yourselves," Pilate therefore told them, "and judge Him according to your law."

"We're not allowed to kill anyone," the Jews answered him. 32 And so what Jesus said when He predicted how He would die was to come true.

33 Pilate went back into the palace and called for Jesus. "Are You the King of the Jews?" he asked Him.

34 "Did you think of that yourself," Jesus asked, "or did others tell you about Me?"

35 "Am I a Jew?" Pilate asked. "Your own people and the ruling priests handed You over to me. What did You do?"

36 "My kingdom is not of this world," Jesus answered. "If My kingdom were of this world, My servants would fight to keep Me from being handed over to the Jews. But now My kingdom is not of this world."

37 "Then You are a king?" Pilate asked Him.

"Yes, I am a king!" Jesus answered. "I was born and came into the world to testify to the truth. Everyone who lives in the truth listens to Me."

38 Pilate said to Him, "What is truth?" After saying this, he went to the Jews again and told them, "I don't find this Man guilty of anything.

39 "You have a custom that I set someone free for you at the Passover. So would you like me to set the King of the Jews free for you?"

40 Then they yelled: "Not this One but Barabbas!" Now, Barabbas was a robber.

"Look at the Man!"

19 1-2 Then Pilate took Jesus and had Him scourged. The soldiers twisted some thorns into a crown and placed it on His head and 3 put a purple garment on Him. They went up to Him and said, "Hail, King of the Jews!" and slapped His face.

4 Pilate went outside again. "I'm bringing Him out to you," he told them, "to let you know I don't find Him guilty of any- 5 thing." Jesus came outside wearing the crown of thorns and the purple cloak. "Look at the Man!" Pilate said to them.

6 When the ruling priests and the servants saw Him, they shouted, "Crucify, crucify Him!"

"Take Him yourselves," Pilate told them, "and crucify Him. I don't find Him guilty of anything."

"We have a law," the Jews answered him, "and according to the law He must die. He has claimed to be God's Son." 19:7

When Pilate heard them say that, he was frightened more than ever. ¹He went into the palace again. "Where are You from?" he asked Jesus. But Jesus didn't answer him. 8 9

"Don't You speak to me?" Pilate then asked Him. "Don't You know I have the power to free You or to crucify You?" 10

"You wouldn't have any power over Me," Jesus answered him, "if it hadn't been given to you from above. That is why the man who handed Me over to you is guilty of a greater sin." 11

This made Pilate anxious to let Him go, but the Jews shouted, "If you let Him go, you're no friend of Caesar. Anyone who makes himself a king is against Caesar." 12

When Pilate heard this, he took Jesus outside and sat in the judge's seat at a place called Stone Pavement, or Gabbatha in the Jewish language. It was the Friday of the Passover and about six o'clock. 13 14

"Look at your King!" he said to the Jews.

Then they shouted, "Away with Him! Kill Him! Crucify Him!" 15

"Should I crucify your King?" Pilate asked them.

"We don't have any king but Caesar," the ruling priests answered.

Then Pilate handed Jesus over to them to be crucified. 16

"They Crucified Him"

So they took Jesus, ¹and He, carrying His cross, went out to what was called Skull Place, which the Jews call Golgotha. There they crucified Him with two others, one on each side and Jesus in the middle. 16-17 18

Pilate also wrote a notice and put it on the cross. It read: JESUS FROM NAZARETH, THE KING OF THE JEWS. Many Jews read this notice, because the place where Jesus was crucified was near the city, and it was written in Aramaic, Latin, and Greek. 19 20

Then the high priests of the Jews told Pilate, "Don't write, 'The King of the Jews,' but, 'He said, "I am the King of the Jews." ' " 21

Pilate answered, "What I've written I've written." 22

When the soldiers had crucified Jesus, they took His clothes 23 and divided them into four parts, one for each soldier, and the tunic was left over. The tunic was without a seam, woven in one

19:24 piece from top to bottom. "Let's not tear it," they said to one another, "but let's throw lots and see who gets it" — what the Bible said had to come true: *They divided My clothes among them, and for My garment they threw lots.*[18] So that's what the soldiers did.

Mary

25   Now, His mother and her sister, Mary the wife of Clopas, and Mary from Magdala were standing near Jesus' cross.

26   Jesus saw His mother and the disciple He loved standing near. "Woman," He said to His mother, "there is your son!" Then He said to the disciple, "There is your mother!"

27   The disciple took her and from that time on had her in his home.

Jesus Dies

28   After this, knowing everything had now been done, and to have the words of the Bible come true, Jesus said, *"I am thirsty."*

29   A jar full of *sour wine*[19] was standing there. So they put a sponge soaked in the wine on a hyssop stem and held it to His mouth.

30   When Jesus had taken the wine, He said, *"It is finished."*[20] Then He bowed His head and gave up His spirit.

No Bone Broken

31   Since it was Friday and the Jews didn't want the bodies to stay on the crosses on Saturday, because that Sabbath was an important day, they asked Pilate to have the legs of the men

32   broken and the bodies taken away. So the soldiers came and broke the legs of the first man and then of the other who had been crucified with Him.

33   But when they came to Jesus and saw He was dead already,

34   they didn't break His legs, but one of the soldiers stuck a spear

35   into His side, and immediately blood and water came out. He who saw it has testified about it, and his testimony is true, and he knows he is telling the truth so that you, too, will believe.

36   In this way what the Bible said had to come true: *None of*

37   *His bones will be broken.*[21] And it says in another place, *They will look at Him whom they pierced.*[22]

Jesus Is Buried

Later Joseph from Arimathea — who was a disciple of Jesus, 19:38
but secretly because he was afraid of the Jews — asked Pilate to
let him take Jesus' body away. Pilate let him have it. So he
came and took His body away. Then came also Nicodemus, 39
who had first come to Jesus at night. He brought a mixture of
myrrh and aloes, about seventy-two pounds.

They took Jesus' body and wrapped it with the spices in 40
linen according to the Jewish custom of burying the dead.

There was a garden at the place where Jesus was crucified, 41
and in the garden was a new grave, in which no one had yet been
laid. Here, then — because it was Friday (when the Jews got 42
ready for the Sabbath) and the grave was near — they laid
Jesus.

Peter and John

Early on Sunday morning while it was still dark Mary from 20
Magdala went to the grave and saw the stone had been taken
away from the grave. So she ran and came to Simon Peter and 2
the other disciple, whom Jesus loved. "They've taken the Lord
out of the grave," she told them, "and we don't know where they
laid Him."

So Peter and the other disciple started out for the grave. 3
The two were running side by side, but the other disciple ran 4
faster than Peter and got to the grave first. He looked in and 5
saw the linen wrappings lying there but didn't go in.

When Simon Peter got there after him, he went into the 6
grave. He saw the linen wrappings lying there, | also the cloth 7
that had been on Jesus' head, not lying with the linen wrappings
but rolled up in a place by itself. Then the other disciple, who 8
got to the grave first, also went in, saw it, and believed. They 9
didn't know yet what the Bible meant when it said He had to
rise from the dead.

So the disciples went home again. 10

"Mary!"

Mary stood outside, facing the grave and crying. As she 11-12
cried, she looked into the grave and saw two angels in white
clothes sitting where Jesus' body had been lying, one at the head
and the other at the feet. "Woman, why are you crying?" they 13
asked her.

"They've taken my Lord away," she told them, "and I don't know where they laid Him."

20:14 After she said this, she turned around and saw Jesus stand-
15 ing there but didn't know it was Jesus. "Woman, why are you crying?" Jesus asked her. "Whom are you looking for?"

"Sir," she said to Him, thinking He was the gardener, "if you carried Him away, tell me where you laid Him, and I will take Him away."

16 Jesus said to her, "Mary!"

She turned. "Rabboni!" she said to Him in the Jewish language. (The word means "Teacher.")

17 "Don't hold on to Me," Jesus told her. "I didn't go up to the Father yet. But go to My brothers and tell them, 'I am going up to My Father and your Father, to My God and your God.' "

18 Mary from Magdala went and told the disciples, "I saw the Lord," and that He said this to her.

Behind Locked Doors

19 That Sunday evening the doors were locked where the dis-
ciples were, because they were afraid of the Jews. Then Jesus came and stood among them and said to them "Peace to you!"
20 When He said this, He showed them His hands and His side. Then the disciples were delighted to see the Lord.

21 "Peace to you!" Jesus said to them again. "As the Father
22 sent Me, so I send you." When He had said this, He breathed
23 on them and said, ¹ "Receive the Holy Spirit. If you forgive sins, they are forgiven; if you don't forgive them, they're not forgiven."

Thomas Sees Jesus

24 But Thomas, one of the twelve, who was called Twin, was not
25 with them when Jesus came. So the other disciples told him, "We saw the Lord."

"Unless I see the marks of the nails in His hands," he told them, "and put my finger in the marks of the nails and put my hand in His side, I won't believe it."

26 A week later His disciples were again in the house, and Thomas was with them. The doors were locked, but Jesus came
27 and stood among them. "Peace to you!" He said. ¹ Then He told Thomas, "Put your finger here, and look at My hands — and

take your hand and put it in My side. And don't doubt but
believe."

"My Lord and my God!" Thomas answered Him.   20:28

"Do you believe because you've seen Me?" Jesus asked him.   29
"Blessed are those who didn't see Me and still believed."

Much More

His disciples saw Jesus do many other miracles that are not   30
written in this book. But these things are written so that you 31
believe Jesus is the promised Savior, God's Son, and by believing
have life in His name.

Breakfast with Jesus

After this, Jesus showed Himself again to the disciples at the 21
Lake of Galilee. This is how He showed Himself.

Simon Peter, Thomas (called Twin), Nathanael from Cana in   2
Galilee, Zebedee's sons, and two other disciples of Jesus were
together. Simon Peter said to the others, "I'm going fishing."   3

"We're going with you," they told him.

They went out and got into the boat. But that night they
caught nothing. When morning came, Jesus stood on the shore.   4
But the disciples didn't know it was Jesus.

"Boys, you don't have any fish, do you?" Jesus asked them.   5
They answered Him, "No."

"Drop the net on the right side of the boat," He told them,   6
"and you will find some." So they dropped it. And now they
couldn't pull it in, there were so many fish.

The disciple whom Jesus loved said to Peter, "It is the Lord."   7
When Simon Peter heard him say, "It is the Lord," he put on
the coat he had taken off, fastened it with his belt, and jumped
into the lake. But the other disciples, who were not far from   8
the shore, only about a hundred yards, came in the small boat,
dragging the net full of fish.

As they stepped out on the shore, they saw burning coals   9
there with fish lying on them, and bread.

"Bring some of the fish you just caught," Jesus told them.   10
Simon Peter got into the small boat and pulled the net on the   11
shore. It was filled with a hundred and fifty-three big fish.
Although there were so many, the net wasn't torn.

"Come, have breakfast," Jesus told them. None of the dis-   12
ciples dared to ask Him, "Who are You?" They knew it was the

Lord. Jesus came, took the bread, and gave it to them, and also the fish.

14 This was the third time Jesus showed Himself to the disciples after He rose from the dead.

"Do You Love Me?"

15 When they had eaten breakfast, Jesus asked Simon Peter, "Simon, son of John, do you love Me more than these do?"

"Yes, Lord," he answered Him, "You know I love You."

"Feed My lambs," Jesus told him.

16 "Simon, son of John," He asked him a second time, "do you love Me?"

"Yes, Lord," he answered Him, "You know I love You."

"Be a shepherd of My sheep," Jesus told him.

17 "Simon, son of John," He asked him a third time, "do you love Me?"

Peter felt sad because He asked him a third time, "Do you love Me?" "Lord, You know everything," he answered Him, "You know I love You."

18 "Feed My sheep," Jesus told him. "I tell you the truth: When you were younger, you used to fasten your belt and go where you wanted to. But when you're old, you'll stretch out your hands, and someone else will tie you and take you where 19 you don't want to go." He said this to show by what kind of death Peter would glorify God. After saying this, He told him, "Follow Me."

20 Peter turned and saw the disciple whom Jesus loved following them. He was the one who at the supper leaned against Jesus' breast and asked, "Lord, who is going to betray You?" 21 When Peter saw him, he asked Jesus, "Lord, what about him?"

22 "If I want him to stay till I come," Jesus asked him, "what is 23 that to you? You follow Me." And so it was said among the Christians, "That disciple will not die." But Jesus didn't say, "He will not die," but, "If I want him to stay till I come, what is that to you?"

24 This is the disciple who testified about these things and wrote this. And we know what he testifies is true.

Much More

25 Jesus also did many other things. If every one of these were written, I suppose the world would not have room for the books that would be written.

OLD TESTAMENT REFERENCES

1. Is. 40:3
2. Gen. 28:12
3. Gen. 41:55
4. Ps. 69:9
5. Ex. 16:4, 15;
   Ps. 78:24
6. Is. 54:13
7. 2 Sam. 7:12;
   Micah 5:2
8. Ezek. 34:23
9. Ps. 82:6
10. Ps. 118:25-26
11. Is. 40:9; 62:11;
    Zech. 9:9
12. Ps. 6:3
13. Is. 53:1
14. Is. 6:10
15. Ps. 41:9
16. Ps. 35:19; 69:4
17. Is. 66:14
18. Ps. 22:18
19. Ps. 69:21
20. Ps. 22:31
21. Ex. 12:46; Num.
    9:12; Ps. 34:20
22. Zech. 12:10

L U K E

writes

THE ACTS

1 IN MY FIRST BOOK, Theophilus, I wrote about everything Jesus
2 did and taught ¹ till the day He was taken up to heaven after
giving orders by the Holy Spirit to the apostles He had chosen.

Jesus Goes Up to Heaven

3 After His suffering Jesus in many convincing ways proved to
the apostles He was alive as He showed Himself to them during
forty days and talked about God's kingdom.

4 When He met with them, He ordered them not to leave
Jerusalem but to wait for what the Father had promised: "You
5 heard Me tell about Him: John baptized with water, but in a few
days you will be baptized with the Holy Spirit."

6 When they came together, they asked Him, "Lord, are You
now going to make Israel an independent kingdom again?"

7 "It isn't for you to know," He told them, "what times or
8 periods the Father has set by His own authority. But when the
Holy Spirit comes on you, you will receive power and will
testify of Me in Jerusalem, in all Judea and Samaria, and to the
farthest parts of the world."

9 When He had said this and while they were watching Him,
He was lifted up, and a cloud took Him away so they couldn't
see Him anymore.

10 As He was going and they were gazing up into the sky, two
11 men in white clothes were standing right beside them. "Men of
Galilee," they asked, "why are you standing here looking up to
heaven? This Jesus, who was taken away from you to heaven,
will come back the same way you saw Him go to heaven."

12 Then they went back to Jerusalem from the Mount of Olives,
as it was called (it's near Jerusalem, only half a mile away).

There Must Be Twelve

When they came into the city, they went to the second-floor 1:13
room where they were staying — Peter, John, James, and Andrew;
Philip and Thomas; Bartholomew and Matthew; James, the son
of Alphaeus, Simon the Zealot, and Judas, the son of James.
¹ With one mind these all kept praying together. With them were 14
the women, including Jesus' mother Mary, and His brothers.

In those days Peter got up among the disciples (a crowd of 15
them was there, about a hundred and twenty), and he said,
"Brothers, long ago the Holy Spirit spoke through David about 16
Judas, who led the men that arrested Jesus. And what He wrote
had to come true. Judas was one of us twelve and was given 17
a share in the work we're doing. With the money he got for his 18
crime he bought a piece of land; and falling on his face, he burst
in the middle, and all his intestines poured out. Everybody living 19
in Jerusalem heard about it. And so that piece of land is called
Akeldama" in their language; the word means place of blood.
"It is written in the book of Psalms: *His home should be deserted,* 20
*and nobody should live there.*¹ *And somebody else should take*
*over his office.*² Then someone should be added to our number 22
as a witness of His resurrection. He should be one of these men 21
who went with us all the time the Lord Jesus went in and out
among us, from John's baptism to the day He was taken up 22
from us."

The disciples named two: Joseph (called Barsabbas; he was 23
also called Justus) and Matthias. Then they prayed, "Lord, You 24
know the hearts of all. Show us which of these two You have
chosen ¹ to serve in this office of apostle, which Judas left to go 25
where he belonged."

They provided lots for them, and so Matthias was chosen and 26
added to the eleven apostles.

The Holy Spirit Comes

The day of Pentecost * came, and they were all together in 2
one place. Suddenly a sound like a violent blast of wind came 2
from heaven and filled the whole house where they were sitting.
They saw tongues like flames that separated, and one rested on 3
each of them. They were all filled with the Holy Spirit and 4
started to speak in other languages as the Spirit gave them the
ability to speak.

* A festival on the 50th day after the Passover.

Jews who feared God had come from every nation under
6 heaven to live in Jerusalem. When that sound came, the crowd
gathered and was dumfounded because each one heard the
7 disciples speak his own language. Amazed and wondering, they
asked, "Don't all these who are speaking come from Galilee?
8 And how does every one of us hear his own language he was
9 born in — Parthians, Medes, Elamites, and people living in Mesopotamia, Judea and Cappadocia, Pontus and the province of Asia,
10 Phrygia and Pamphilia, Egypt and the country near Cyrene in
11 Libya, the visitors from Rome, Jews and those who have accepted
the Jewish religion, people from Crete and Arabia? In our own
languages we hear them tell about God's wonderful things."
12 They were all amazed and puzzled. "What can this mean?" they
13 asked one another. Others sneered: "They're full of new wine."

Peter's Pentecost Sermon

14 Then Peter got up with the eleven, raised his voice, and ad-
dressed them:

"Jews and all you who live in Jerusalem, understand this,
15 and listen to what I say. These men are not drunk, as you sup-
16 pose. Why, it's only nine in the morning. No, this is what the
17 prophet Joel spoke about: 'In the last days,' *God says, 'I will pour
out My Spirit on all people. Then your sons and your daughters
will speak God's Word, your young men will have visions, and
18 your old men will have dreams. In those days I will pour out
My Spirit on My servants, both men and women,* and they will
19 speak God's Word. *I will give you startling wonders in the sky
20 above and marvelous signs on the earth below: blood and fire
and a cloud of smoke; the sun will turn dark and the moon to
blood before the coming of the Lord's great and splendid day.
21 Then everyone who calls on the Lord's name will be saved.'* [3]
22 "Men of Israel, listen to what I have to say: Jesus from
Nazareth — God showed you who the Man is by doing miracles,
startling wonders, and signs through Him among you, as you know.
23 God definitely planned and intended to have Him betrayed, and
so you had wicked men nail Him to a cross, and you killed Him.
24 But God set aside the pains of death and raised Him — death
could not hold Him.

25 "David says of Him, '*I always see the Lord before Me. He is
26 at My right side so that I will not be shaken. And so My heart
is glad, and My tongue rejoices, yes, even My body will rest*

*hopefully, because You will not leave Me in the grave or let
Your Loved One experience decay. You show Me ways of life.
You will fill Me with joy by being with Me.'* [4]

"Fellow Jews, I can tell you frankly our ancestor David died [29]
and was buried, and his grave is here to this day. He was [30]
a prophet and knew *God had sworn to him to put one of his
descendants on his throne.*[5] David saw what was ahead and said [31]
the promised Savior would rise again: *He was not deserted when
He was dead,* and His body *did not experience decay.*[6] God has [32]
raised this Jesus — we're all witnesses of that. Lifted up to God's [33]
right side and receiving from the Father the promised Holy Spirit,
He has poured out what you see and hear. David didn't go up [34]
to heaven, but he says, *'The Lord says to my Lord, "Sit at My
right*[1] *till I make Your enemies Your footstool." '*[7] [35]

"Then all the people of Israel should know it's true that God [36]
made Him Lord and Christ — this Jesus whom you crucified."

When the people heard this, they felt crushed. They asked [37]
Peter and the other apostles, "Fellow Jews, what should we do?"

Peter answered them, "Repent and be baptized, every one of [38]
you, in the name of Jesus Christ so that your sins will be forgiven, and you will be given the Holy Spirit. What is promised [39]
belongs to you, to your children, and to all *who are far away,*[8]
all *whom the Lord* our God *will call."* [9]

He said much more to warn them. "Let yourselves be saved [40]
from these crooked people," he urged them. Those who accepted [41]
what he said were baptized, and that day about three thousand
persons were added.

How Christians Lived

They were loyal to what the apostles taught, in their fellowship, [42]
in eating together, and in praying. Awe came on everybody — [43]
the apostles were doing many wonders and miracles. All who [44]
believed were together and shared everything with one another.
They would sell their lands and other property and distribute [45]
the money to anyone as he needed it. All were one at heart as [46]
they went to the temple regularly every day. They had their
meals in their homes and ate their food with glad and simple
hearts, praising God and having the good will of all the people. [47]
And every day the Lord added to their number those who were
being saved.

The Cripple

3 Peter and John were going up to the temple for the hour
2 of prayer at three in the afternoon. Now there was a man who
had been a cripple from his birth. Men would carry him and
lay him every day at the temple gate called Beautiful so he could
3 beg the people for gifts as they went into the temple. When
he saw Peter and John were going into the temple, he asked
them for a gift.

4 Peter and John looked at him. "Look at us!" Peter said.
5 He looked at them, expecting to get something from them.
6 "I don't have any silver or gold," Peter said, "but I'll give you
what I have. In the name of Jesus Christ from Nazareth, walk!"
7 ¹ He took hold of his right hand and raised him up. Immediately
8 his feet and ankles were made strong. He jumped up, stood, and
started to walk. And he went with them into the temple, walking,
jumping, and praising God.

9-10 When all the people saw him walking and praising God, they
knew he was the man who used to sit and beg at the Beautiful
gate of the temple, and they were very much surprised and amazed
11 to see what had happened to him. As he clung to Peter and
John, all the people came running together to them in Solomon's
Porch, as it was called. They were dumfounded.

12 When Peter saw the people, he said to them, "Men of Israel,
why are you wondering about this, or why are you staring at us
13 as if by our own power or piety we had made him walk? *The
God of Abraham, Isaac, and Jacob,*¹⁰ the God of our fathers,
has *glorified His Servant* ¹¹ Jesus, whom you delivered and denied
14 before Pilate when he had decided to let Him go. You denied
the holy and righteous One and asked to have a murderer given
15 to you. ¹ You killed the Lord and Giver of life. But God raised
16 Him from the dead — we're witnesses of that. His name, because
we believe in it, made this man strong whom you see and know.
The faith that Jesus works has given him this perfect health right
in front of all of you.

17 "And now, fellow Jews, I know that like your rulers you
18 didn't know what you were doing, but in this way God did what
He predicted by all the prophets — His Christ had to suffer.
19-20 Repent then, and turn, to have your sins wiped out ¹ that a time
may come when the Lord refreshes you and sends Jesus, whom
21 He appointed to be your Savior ¹ and whom heaven had to receive

until the time when everything will be restored, as God said long ago by His holy prophets.

"Moses said, *The Lord* our *God will raise one of your people* 3:22 *to be a Prophet to you like me. Listen to everything He tells* 12 you. *And destroy anyone among the people who will not listen* 23 *to that Prophet.*13 Samuel and all the other prophets after him, 24 as many as have spoken, told about these days. You are the 25 heirs of the prophets and of the covenant God made with our fathers when He said to Abraham, *And in your Descendant all the people on earth will be blessed.*14 Now that God has given 26 His Servant, He sent Him first to you to bless you by turning every one of you from your wicked ways."

In Court

While they were talking to the people, the priests, the captain 4 of the temple, and the Sadducees stepped up to them, ¹ much an- 2 noyed because they were teaching the people and preaching that in Jesus the dead rise. They arrested them, and since it was 3 already evening, they put them in prison till the next day.

But many of those who had heard the Word believed, and 4 the number of the men grew to about five thousand.

The next day their rulers, elders, and Bible scholars met in 5 Jerusalem ¹ with Annas the high priest, Caiaphas, John, Alex- 6 ander, and all the others of the high priest's family. And they 7 had the two men stand before them. "By what power or name did you do this?" they asked.

Then Peter was filled with the Holy Spirit. "Rulers of the 8 people and elders," he said to them, ¹ "if we're questioned today 9 about helping a cripple, how he was made well, ¹ all of you and 10 all the people of Israel should know this man stands healthy before you by the name of Jesus Christ from Nazareth, whom you crucified but God raised from the dead. He is *the Stone* 11 *rejected* by you *builders and has become the Cornerstone.*15 No one else can save us, because in all the world there is only 12 one name given us by which we must be saved."

When they found out Peter and John had no education or 13 training, they were surprised to see how boldly they spoke. Then they realized these men had been with Jesus. ¹ And seeing 14 the healed man standing with them, they couldn't say anything against them. So they ordered them to leave the court and 15

215

4:16 talked the matter over among themselves: "What should we do with these men? They've done a miracle; everybody living in

17 Jerusalem can see it clearly, and we can't deny it. But to keep this from spreading any more among the people, let's warn them never again to speak to anyone in this name."

18 They called Peter and John and ordered them not to say or teach anything in the name of Jesus.

19 Peter and John answered them, "Does God consider it right
20 to listen to you and not to God? Judge for yourselves. ¹ We can't stop telling what we've seen and heard."

21 Once more they threatened them and then let them go. They couldn't find any way to punish them, because all the
22 people were praising God for what had happened; the man who had been healed by this miracle was over forty years old.

❧ The Church Prays

23 When Peter and John were free again, they went to their friends and told them everything the high priests and elders had
24 said. When they heard it they all raised their voices together to God and said, "Lord, You *made heaven and earth, the sea, and*
25 *everything in them.*¹⁶ You said by the Holy Spirit through our ancestor, Your servant David:

> *Why do the nations rage*
> *And the people plan in vain?*
26 > *The kings of the earth stand ready,*
> *And the rulers get together*
> *Against the Lord and His Anointed.*¹⁷

27 "Herod and Pontius Pilate *certainly got together* with *non-Jews and the people* of Israel in this city against Your holy
28 Servant Jesus, *whom You anointed,*¹⁷ ¹ to do everything You by Your will and power long ago decided should be done.

29 "And now, Lord, see how they're threatening, and grant that
30 Your servants speak Your Word very boldly ¹ as You stretch out Your hand to heal and do miracles and wonders by the name of Your holy Servant Jesus."

31 When they had prayed, the place where they were meeting was shaken, and they were all filled with the Holy Spirit and boldly spoke God's Word.

Sharing

The whole group of believers was one in heart and soul. 4:32
And nobody called anything he had his own, but they shared
everything.

With great power the apostles told the truth that the Lord 33
Jesus had risen, and much good will rested on all of them.

None of them was in need, because all who had land or 34
houses would sell them and bring the money they got for them
and lay it at the apostles' feet. Then it was distributed to each 35
one as he needed it. There was Joseph, for example, a descendant 36
of Levi, born on Cyprus. The apostles called him Barnabas,
which means "a man of comfort." He had some land and sold it 37
and brought the money and laid it at the apostles' feet.

Ananias and Sapphira

But a man by the name of Ananias and his wife Sapphira 5
sold some property; he kept some of the money for himself — and 2
his wife knew about it — and some of it he brought and laid at
the apostles' feet.

"Ananias," Peter asked, "why did the devil fill your heart so 3
that you should lie to the Holy Spirit and keep back some of the
money you got for the land? While you had the land, wasn't it 4
your own? And after it was sold, couldn't you have done as you
pleased with the money? How could you think of doing such
a thing? You didn't lie to men but to God!"

When Ananias heard him say this, he fell down and died. 5
And all who heard of it were terrified. The young men got up, 6
wrapped him up, carried him out, and buried him.

About three hours later his wife came in. She didn't know 7
what had happened. "Tell me," Peter asked her, "did you sell 8
the land for that price?"

"Yes, that was the price," she answered.

"Why did you two agree to put the Lord's Spirit to a test?" 9
Peter asked her. "There at the door are the feet of those who
buried your husband, and they'll carry you out."

Immediately she fell down at his feet and died. When the 10
young men came in, they found her dead and carried her out and
buried her beside her husband. The whole church and all others 11
who heard about it were terrified.

Many Miracles

5:12   Many miracles and startling wonders were done among the
13 people by the apostles' hands. And they were all together in
Solomon's Porch. None of the others dared to come too near
14 them. But the people thought very highly of them, ¹ and still more
believers, a large number of men and women, were added to the
15 Lord. As a result people carried their sick out into the streets
and laid them down on cots and mats, to have at least Peter's
16 shadow fall on someone of them when he went by. Even from
the towns around Jerusalem crowds would gather, bringing their
sick and those who were troubled by unclean spirits, and they
were all made well.

In Court

17   The high priest and all who were with him, that is, the party
18 of the Sadducees, got very jealous. They went ¹ and arrested the
apostles and put them in the public prison.

19   But at night the Lord's angel opened the prison doors and
20 brought them out. "Go," he said, "stand in the temple, and keep
21 on telling the people everything about this life." After they had
heard him, they went into the temple early in the morning and
started to teach.

    The high priest and those who were with him came and called
the council and all the elders of Israel together and sent men
22 to the prison to get the apostles. But when the men got there,
23 they didn't find them in prison. They came back and reported,
"We found the prison very securely locked and the guards standing at the doors, but when we opened them, we found nobody
24 inside." When the captain of the temple and the high priests heard
this, they were puzzled as to what could have happened to them.
25   Then somebody came and told them, "The men you put in
prison are standing in the temple teaching the people."
26   Then the captain and his men went and got them, but without
using force, because they were afraid the people would stone
27 them. They brought them and had them stand before the council.
28   The high priest questioned them and said, ¹ "We gave you
strict orders not to teach in this name, and here you have filled
Jerusalem with your teaching. And you want to get us punished
for killing this Man."
29   Peter and the other apostles answered, "We must obey God
30 rather than men. *You hanged* Jesus *on a cross* ¹⁸ and murdered

Him. But the God of our fathers raised Him ¹ and took Him up
to His right side as Leader and Savior in order to have the
people of Israel repent and to forgive their sins. We are wit- ³²
nesses of these things — we and the Holy Spirit, whom God has
given those who obey Him."

When they heard this, they got furious and wanted to kill ³³
them. But a Pharisee in the court by the name of Gamaliel, ³⁴
a teacher of the Law, highly respected by all the people, got up
and ordered the men taken outside a little while.

"Men of Israel," he said to them, "consider carefully what ³⁵
you're going to do with these men. Sometime ago Theudas ap- ³⁶
peared, claiming to be somebody, and about four hundred men
joined him. He was killed, and all who followed him were scattered, and they disappeared.

"After him, at the time of the census, came Judas from ³⁷
Galilee and got people to follow him in a revolt. He perished too,
and all who followed him were scattered.

"And now I tell you, keep away from these men and let them ³⁸
alone. If it's only men planning or doing this, it will break down,
¹ but if it's God, you won't be able to stop them. You may even be ³⁹
fighting against God."

They took his advice. ¹ They called the apostles, beat them, ⁴⁰
ordered them not to speak in the name of Jesus, and let them go.
The apostles left the court, happy to have been thought worthy ⁴¹
to suffer shame for Jesus. And every day, in the temple and ⁴²
from house to house, they kept right on teaching and telling the
good news: Jesus is the promised Savior.

Seven Helpers

In those days, as the number of the disciples grew larger and 6
larger, a complaint was brought against those who spoke Aramaic
by those who spoke Greek that every day, when the food was
handed out, their widows were being neglected.

The twelve called the whole group of disciples together and 2
said, "Nobody likes it if we give up teaching God's Word and
serve at tables. Now, fellow disciples, appoint seven men among 3
you whom people speak well of, who are full of the Spirit and
wisdom, and we'll put them in charge of this work. Then we'll 4
devote ourselves to praying and to serving by speaking the
Word."

The whole group liked the idea. So they chose Stephen, a man 5 full of faith and of the Holy Spirit, Philip, Prochorus, Nicanor, Timon, Parmenas, and Nicolaus (who had become a Jew in 6:6 Antioch). They had these men stand before the apostles, who prayed and laid their hands on them.

7   God's Word kept on spreading, and the number of disciples in Jerusalem was getting very large. Even a large crowd of the priests came to believe and obey the Word.

Stephen Is Arrested

8   Stephen, full of God's gifts and power, was doing great won-
9 ders and miracles among the people. Some men of the Synagog of the Freedmen, as it was called, and of men from Cyrene and Alexandria, and men from Cilicia and Asia got up to argue with
10 Stephen. But they couldn't resist the wisdom and the Spirit by whom he spoke.

11   Then they secretly got some men to say, "We heard him
12 slander Moses and God." They stirred up the people, the elders, and the men of the Law, and rushing at him, took him by force
13 and brought him before the court. There they had witnesses stand up and lie, "This man won't stop talking against the holy
14 place and the Law. We heard him say, 'This Jesus from Naz-areth will tear this place down and change the customs Moses gave us.' "

15   All who sat in the court stared at him and saw his face — it was like an angel's face.

Stephen Defends Himself

7   Then the high priest asked, "Is this so?"

2   He answered, "Fellow Jews and fathers, listen. *The God of glory* [19] appeared to our father Abraham while he was in
3 Mesopotamia before he lived in Haran. *'Leave your country and your relatives,'* God told him, *'and come to the country I will show you.'* [20]

4   "Then Abraham left the country of the Chaldeans and lived in Haran. After his father died, God had him move from there
5 to this country where you live now. He *gave* him nothing to call his own, *not even enough to set his foot on,* [21] but prom-ised *to give it to him as his own and to his descendants after*
6 *him,* [22] although he had no child. This is what God said: *His descendants would be strangers in a foreign country, and its peo-ple would make slaves of them and mistreat them four hundred*

years. 'But I will punish the people whom they will serve,' God said, 'and after that they will leave.²³ and worship Me in this ²⁴ place.' ¹ He gave him a *covenant* of *circumcision*.²⁵ And so, when ⁸ his son Isaac was born, *he circumcised him on the eighth day*.²⁶ Isaac did the same to his son Jacob, and Jacob to his twelve sons, the ancestors of our tribes.

"These ancestors *were jealous of Joseph and sold him into* ⁹ *Egypt*,²⁷ but *God was with him*.²⁸ He rescued him from all his ¹⁰ troubles *and gave him the good will* ²⁹ *of Pharaoh the king of Egypt, and wisdom as he stood before him* ³⁰ — *Pharaoh made him ruler of Egypt and of his whole palace*.³¹ But a *famine* with ¹¹ much misery *came over* all Egypt and *Canaan*,³² and our ancestors couldn't find any food. When *Jacob heard there was grain in* ¹² *Egypt*,³³ he sent our ancestors on their first trip. On the second, ¹³ *Joseph told his brothers who he was*,³⁴ and Pharaoh learned about the family from which Joseph came. Joseph sent and had ¹⁴ his father Jacob come to him, and all his relatives — *seventy-five persons*. ¹ And so *Jacob went down to Egypt*.³⁵ Then he and ¹⁵ our ancestors died ¹ and *were brought* to *Shechem* and *laid* in the ¹⁶ tomb *Abraham bought* for a sum of money *from Hamor's sons at Shechem*.³⁶

"When the time that God set in His promise to Abraham had ¹⁷ almost come, the people *had grown and their number had become very large* in Egypt. And now *a different king who knew nothing* ¹⁸ *of Joseph became ruler of Egypt*. He *was shrewd in scheming* ¹⁹ *against* our people, and he *mistreated* ³⁷ʲ our fathers. He wanted to put away their babies so they wouldn't live.

"At that time Moses was born, and he was a *beautiful* child ²⁰ before God. For *three months* ³⁸ he was cared for in his father's home. When he was set out, *Pharaoh's daughter took him up* ²¹ and raised him *as her son*.³⁹ Moses was educated in all the wisdom ²² of the Egyptians and became a great man in what he said and did. When he was forty years old, he thought he would *visit* ²³ *his own people, the Israelites*. There he saw a man wronged and ²⁴ defended him. He avenged the man who was mistreated, by *striking down the Egyptian*. He thought his own people would ²⁵ understand he was the one by whom God was freeing them, but they didn't understand. *The next day he came* to them *as they* ²⁶ *were fighting*,⁴⁰ and he tried to make peace between them. 'Men, you are brothers,' he said. 'Why are you doing wrong to one another?'

"But *the man who was doing wrong to his neighbor* pushed Moses away. *'Who made you ruler and judge over us?'* he asked.
28 *'Do you want to kill me as you killed the Egyptian yesterday?'*
29 When he said that, *Moses fled and became a stranger in the land of Midian.* There he had *two sons.*⁴¹

30 "And so forty years passed. Then *an Angel appeared to him in the wilderness* of Mount Sinai *in the flames of a burning thorn-*
31 *bush.* ¹ Moses was surprised to see this. As *he went closer to*
32 *examine it, the Lord said,* ¹ *'I am the God of your fathers, the God of Abraham, Isaac, and Jacob.'* Moses started to tremble
33 and *didn't dare to look. The Lord told him, 'Take your shoes*
34 *off; the place where you're standing is holy ground. I have seen how My people are mistreated in Egypt, I have heard their groan-ing and have come down to rescue them. And now come, I will send you to Egypt.'* ⁴²

35 "This Moses whom they rejected by saying, *'Who made you ruler and judge?'* ⁴³ this one God sent to rule and free them with
36 the help of the Angel he saw in the thornbush. He led them out, doing *startling wonders and miracles in Egypt,* at the Red Sea,
37 and *for forty years in the desert.*⁴⁴ It was this Moses who told the Israelites, *God will raise one of your people to be a Prophet*
38 *to you like me.*⁴⁵ Moses was in the congregation in the wilder-ness with the Angel who spoke to him on Mount Sinai and with
39 our fathers. He received living truths to give you, ¹ but our fathers refused to obey him. Yes, they rejected him, and their
40 hearts *turned away to Egypt.*⁴⁶ *'Make gods for us who will lead us,'* they told Aaron. *'This Moses who took us out of Egypt —*
41 *we don't know what happened to him.'* That was the time *they made a calf,. brought a sacrifice* to the idol, *and delighted* ⁴⁷ in what their hands had made.

42 "So God perverted and abandoned them to worship *the sun, the moon, and the stars,*⁴⁸ as it is written in the book of the prophets: *People of Israel, you didn't offer Me slaughtered ani-mals and sacrifices during the forty years in the desert, did you?*
43 *You even took along the tent of Moloch, the star of the god Rompha, and the images you made* in order to worship them. *And so I will send you away to live on the other side* ⁴⁹ of Babylon.

44 "In the desert our fathers had the tabernacle *in which God spoke to His people.*⁵⁰ It was built *like the model Moses had seen,*
45 just as He who *spoke to Moses* had ordered him *to make* ⁵¹ it. From him our fathers received it, and they brought it here under

Joshua when they took the country from the nations God drove out before our fathers, and here it was till the time of David. He found God was kind to him and asked that *he might find* 7:46 *a home for the God of Jacob.*[52] And *Solomon built Him a* 47 *temple.*[53]

But the Most High God doesn't live in anything made by 48 human hands, as the prophet says, *'Heaven is My throne, and the earth My footstool. What kind of temple will you build Me,* 49 *the Lord asks, or what place is there where I can rest? Didn't My* 50 *hand make all this?'* [54]

"*How stubborn you are and pagan at heart and deaf to the* 51 *truth!* [55] You're always *opposing the Holy Spirit.*[56] Your fathers did it, and so do you! Was there ever a prophet your fathers 52 didn't persecute? They killed those who announced, 'The Righteous One will come!' and now you betrayed and murdered Him. Angels were ordered to give you the Law, but you didn't keep it!" 53

Stoning Stephen

While they were listening, the men of the court got furious 54 and ground their teeth at him. But he, full of the Holy Spirit, 55 gazed up to heaven and saw God's glory and Jesus standing at God's right side. "Look!" he said, "I see heaven opened and the 56 Son of Man standing at God's right side."

But they yelled at the top of their voices, held their ears shut, 57 and all together rushed at him. They threw him out of the city 58 and started to stone him. The witnesses had laid their outer clothes at the feet of a young man — his name was Saul.

While they were stoning Stephen, he called, "Lord Jesus, 59 receive my spirit." Then, kneeling, he called out loud, "Lord, 60 don't hold this sin against them." When he had said this, he fell asleep.

And Saul also approved of their killing him. 8

That day a great persecution broke out against the church in Jerusalem, and all except the apostles were scattered over the open country of Judea and Samaria.

God-fearing men buried Stephen and mourned loud for him. 2

The Samaritans Believe

Saul was trying to destroy the church. Going into one house 3 after another and dragging off men and women, he put them in prison.

So the people who were scattered went from place to place
5 telling the good news. Philip went down to the city of Samaria
6 and preached Christ to the people. When they heard him, all
listened eagerly to what Philip had to say, especially when they
7 saw the miracles he did. There were those who were plagued
by unclean spirits; many came screaming out of them. And
8 many who were paralyzed and lame were made well. So there
was great joy in that city.

9   There was in the city a man by the name of Simon who was
practicing witchcraft and amazing the people of Samaria, claiming
10 to be a great man. Everybody from the least to the greatest
listened eagerly to him, saying, "He's God's power; people call
11 it great." They were so interested in him because he had for
12 a long time amazed them by his witchcraft. But when Philip
told the good news of God's kingdom and of the name of Jesus
13 Christ, men and women believed him and were baptized. Even
Simon believed, and when he wäs baptized, he stayed with
Philip. He was amazed to see the miracles and wonderful works
that were done.

14   When the apostles in Jerusalem heard Samaria had accepted
15 God's Word, they sent Peter and John to them. These two went
down and prayed that the people would receive the Holy Spirit.
16 He had not come on any of them yet; but they had only been
17 baptized into the name of the Lord Jesus. Then Peter and John
laid their hands on them, and they received the Holy Spirit.

18   Simon saw the Spirit was given when the apostles laid their
19 hands on anyone. So he offered them money. I "Give me this
power," he said, "that anyone I lay my hands on receives the
Holy Spirit."

20   "Your money perish with you," Peter told him, "because you
21 meant to buy God's gift with money. You have no part or share
22 in this because your *heart isn't right with God.*[57] Now repent of
this wickedness of yours, and ask the Lord if He will perhaps
23 forgive you for thinking such a thing. I see you're turning to
bitter poison [58] and being *chained by wickedness.*" [59]

24   "You ask the Lord for me," Simon answered, "that none of
the things you said may happen to me."

25   After they had testified and spoken the Lord's Word, they
also brought the good news to many Samaritan villages on their
way back to Jerusalem.

The Treasurer from Ethiopia

The Lord's angel said to Philip, "Get up and go south to the 8:26
road going from Jerusalem down to Gaza." It is a deserted road.

He got up and went. Here there was a man from Ethiopia, 27
a eunuch and high official of Candace, queen of the Ethiopians,
in charge of all her treasures. He had come to Jerusalem to worship ¹ and was on his way home, sitting in his chariot and reading 28
the prophet Isaiah.

The Spirit said to Philip, "Go over to that chariot and keep 29
close to it."

Philip ran up to it and there heard him reading the prophet 30
Isaiah. "Do you really understand what you're reading?" he asked.

"Why, how can I without somebody to guide me?" he asked, 31
and he urged Philip to come up and sit with him.

This was the part of the Bible he was reading: 32

He will be led away like a sheep to be slaughtered,
And as a lamb is dumb before the man who cut off her wool,
So He will not open His mouth.
When He humbles Himself, His condemnation will be taken 33
away.
Who will describe the people of His time?
*His life will be cut off from the earth.*⁶⁰

"I ask you," the eunuch said to Philip, "whom is the prophet 34
talking about — himself or somebody else?"

Then Philip spoke. Starting with this statement of the Bible, 35
he told him the good news of Jesus. 'As they were going along 36
the road, they came to some water. "Here is water," the eunuch
said. "What keeps me from being baptized?" *

He ordered the chariot to stop, and both Philip and the eunuch 38
stepped down into the water, and Philip baptized him. When 39
they had stepped out of the water, the Lord's Spirit suddenly took
Philip away, and the eunuch, happily going his way, didn't see
him again.

But Philip found himself in Ashdod. He went through all 40
the towns, bringing them the good news, till he came to Caesarea.

Jesus Changes Paul

And Saul, still breathing threats and murder against the 9
Lord's disciples, went to the high priest and asked him for letters 2

---

* Our oldest manuscripts do not have v. 37: " 'If you believe with all
your heart,' Philip said, 'you may.' He answered, 'I believe Jesus Christ is
God's Son.' "

to the synagogs in Damascus, in order to bring any of Jesus' followers he might find there, men or women, back to Jerusalem in chains.

9:3   On his way, as he was coming near Damascus, suddenly
4   a light from heaven flashed around him. He fell to the ground and heard a voice saying to him, "Saul! Saul! Why are you persecuting Me?"

5   "Who are You, Lord?" he asked.

6   "I am Jesus," He said, "whom you are persecuting. | But get up, go into the city, and you will be told what you should do."

7   Meanwhile the men traveling with him were standing speechless. They heard the voice but didn't see anyone.

8   Saul got up from the ground. When he opened his eyes, he couldn't see anything. So they took him by the hand and led
9   him into Damascus. For three days he couldn't see and didn't eat or drink.

Ananias Comes to Saul

10   In Damascus there was a disciple by the name of Ananias. The Lord said to him in a vision: "Ananias!"

   "Yes, Lord," he answered.

11   "Get up," the Lord told him, "go to the street called Straight, and in the home of Judas look for a man from Tarsus by the
12   name of Saul. You see, he's praying. | And in a vision he has seen a man by the name of Ananias come in and lay his hands on him so he will see again."

13   "Lord," Ananias answered, "I've heard many tell how much
14   wrong this man has done to Your holy people in Jerusalem, and he's here with authority from the high priests to put in chains all who call on Your name."

15   "Go," the Lord told him, "he's an instrument I have chosen to bring My name before the Gentiles, before kings, and the
16   people of Israel. I will show him how much he has to suffer for Me."

17   Ananias went. When he came into the house, he laid his hands on Saul. "Brother Saul," he said, "the Lord sent me — Jesus, whom you saw on your way here — so that you will see again and be filled with the Holy Spirit."

18   Immediately something like scales fell from his eyes, and he
19   saw again. He got up and was baptized. | Then he had something to eat and was strengthened.

Paul Preaches Jesus

While Saul was with the disciples in Damascus several days, ⁹:²⁰
he immediately started to preach in the synagogs: "Jesus is God's
Son." ¹ All who heard him were amazed. "Isn't this the man," ²¹
they asked, "who in Jerusalem destroyed those who call on this
name, and didn't he come here to bring them in chains to the
high priests?"

But Saul grew more and more powerful and bewildered the ²²
Jews living in Damascus by proving "He is the promised Savior."
After some time the Jews plotted to murder him, but Saul was ²³
told about their plot. When they were even watching the gates ²⁴
day and night to murder him, his disciples took him one night and ²⁵
let him down through an opening in the wall by lowering him
in a basket.

He went to Jerusalem and there tried to join the disciples. ²⁶
But they were all afraid of him because they wouldn't believe
he was a disciple.

Then Barnabas took him, brought him to the apostles, and ²⁷
told them how Saul saw the Lord on the road and the Lord spoke
to him and how in Damascus Saul boldly preached in Jesus'
name. Then he went in and out among them in Jerusalem, ²⁸
preaching boldly in the Lord's name.

He was talking and arguing with the Greek-speaking Jews. ²⁹
But they were trying to kill him. ¹ As soon as the other disciples ³⁰
found out about it, they took him down to Caesarea and sent him
away to Tarsus.

So the church all over Judea, Galilee, and Samaria had peace ³¹
and was built up. Living in the fear of the Lord and in the
comfort of the Holy Spirit, it grew larger and larger.

Aeneas — Tabitha

Now when Peter was going around among all the disciples, ³²
he also came down to the holy people living in Lydda. There he ³³
found a man by the name of Aeneas who was paralyzed and had
been lying on a mat for eight years.

"Aeneas," Peter said to him, "Jesus Christ makes you well. ³⁴
Get up and make your bed." And immediately he got up.

All who lived in Lydda and Sharon saw him and turned to ³⁵
the Lord.

9:36   In Joppa there was a disciple by the name of Tabitha,* which in Greek is Dorcas.* She was always doing good works and giv-
37 ing things to the poor. Just at that time she got sick and died; so she was washed and laid in a room upstairs.

38   Lydda is near Joppa. When the disciples heard Peter was in Lydda, they sent two men to him and urged him: "Come to us without delay!"

39   Peter went with them. When he came there, they took him upstairs. There all the widows stood around him; they were crying and showing all the inner and outer garments Dorcas made while she was still with them.

40   But Peter made them all leave the room.

He knelt and prayed. Then, turning toward the body, he said, "Tabitha, get up!"

41   She opened her eyes, and seeing Peter, she sat up. He gave her his hand and helped her stand up. Then he called the holy people, and especially the widows, and gave her back to them alive.

42   The news spread all over Joppa, and many believed in the Lord.

Cornelius Sees a Vision

43   Peter stayed for some time with Simon, a tanner, in Joppa.
10   Now, there was a man in Caesarea by the name of Cornelius,
2 a captain in the troop called Italian. He was a religious man, who with all those in his home feared God. He gave much to the poor among the people and was always praying to God.

3   One day about three in the afternoon he had a vision in which he clearly saw God's angel come to him and say to him, "Cornelius!"

4   He stared at the angel and was terrified, "What is it, Lord?" he asked him.

"Your prayers and your gifts to the poor," the angel answered him, "have come up before God as an offering He remembers.
5 And now send men to Joppa, and get Simon, who is also called
6 Peter. He is a guest of Simon, a tanner, whose house is by the sea."

7   When the angel who was speaking to him had left, he called two of his slaves and a God-fearing soldier, one of those who
8 served him regularly. After telling them everything he sent them to Joppa.

* Both names mean gazelle.

Peter Sees a Vision

The next day about noon, while they were on their way and getting near the town, Peter went up on the roof to pray. But he got hungry and wanted to eat. While the food was being prepared, he fell into a trance. He saw heaven opened and something like a large linen sheet coming down, being let down by its four corners to the ground. In it were all kinds of animals, four-footed ones and those that creep on the ground, and birds of the air.

"Get up, Peter," a voice told him, "kill and eat."

"Oh no, Lord!" Peter answered, "I've never eaten anything common or unclean."

A voice spoke to him a second time: "Don't make unclean what God has made clean."

This happened three times, then the sheet was quickly taken up to the sky.

While Peter was still puzzling over the meaning of the vision he had seen, the men sent by Cornelius asked for Simon's house and came to the gate. They called and asked, "Is Simon, who is called Peter, staying here?" Peter was still thinking about the vision when the Spirit said, "There are three men looking for you. Now come, go down, and go with them. Don't treat them as different people, because I sent them."

So Peter went down to the men. "I'm the man you're looking for," he said. "What brings you here?"

They answered, "Cornelius is a captain, a righteous man who fears God, and all the Jewish people speak well of him. A holy angel told him to bring you to his home and hear what you have to say."

Peter asked them to come in, and they were his guests.

Peter and Cornelius

The next day he left with them, and some fellow disciples from Joppa went along. The following day he came to Caesarea. Cornelius was expecting them and had called his relatives and close friends together.

When Peter was about to go in, Cornelius met him, bowed down at his feet, and worshiped him. But Peter made him stand up. "Get up," he said. "I'm only a man."

Talking with him, he went in and found many people had gathered. "You understand," he said to them, "how wrong it is

10:29 for a Jew to live with or visit anyone who's not a Jew. But God has taught me not to call anyone common or unclean. That's why I didn't object to coming here when you sent for me. Now I want to know: Why did you send for me?"

30 "Three days ago," Cornelius answered, "I was at home praying till this hour, at three in the afternoon, when a man in shining
31 clothes stood in front of me. 'Cornelius,' he said, 'God has
32 heard your prayer and remembers your gifts to the poor. Now send to Joppa and ask Simon, who is called Peter, to come to you.
33 He's a guest in the home of Simon, a tanner, by the sea.' So I sent to you immediately, and it was good of you to come. We're all here before God now, ready to hear everything the Lord has ordered you to say."

34 Then Peter spoke: "Now I really understand that *God doesn't*
35 *prefer one person to another.*[61] It doesn't matter what people you belong to; if you fear Him and do what's right, He accepts you.
36 *He sent His Word*[62] to the people of Israel to *bring the news*
37 *of peace*[63] in Jesus Christ — He is Lord of all! You know what happened in the whole country of the Jews, how after the baptism
38 that John preached, *God anointed* Jesus from Nazareth *with the* Holy *Spirit*[64] and power, and Jesus, beginning in Galilee, went around doing good and healing all who were under the tyranny
39 of the devil, because God was with Him. We have seen everything He did in the land of the Jews and in Jerusalem, and we can tell about it. Men *hanged Him on a cross*[65] and killed Him.
40 But God raised Him on the third day and showed Him to us —
41 not to all our people but to us whom God had chosen to be witnesses and who ate and drank with Him after He rose from
42 the dead. He ordered us to preach to the people and warn them
43 that God has appointed Him to judge the living and the dead. All the prophets declare that through His name everyone who believes in Him has his sins forgiven."

44 While Peter was still speaking, the Holy Spirit came down on
45 all who heard the Word. All the Jewish believers who had come with Peter were surprised the gift of the Holy Spirit had been
46 poured out also on people who were not Jews. They heard them speaking in other languages and praising God.

47 Then Peter asked, "Can anyone keep the water from baptizing these people? They have received the Holy Spirit just as

we did." And he ordered them baptized in the name of Jesus
Christ.

Then they asked him to stay several days.

Peter Defends Himself

The apostles and other disciples in all Judea heard: "The 11
non-Jewish people, too, have accepted God's Word." But when 2
Peter went up to Jerusalem, those who still believed in circumcision disagreed with him. "You went to visit uncircumcised men," 3
they said, "and you ate with them."

Then Peter explained to them point by point what had hap- 4
pened. "I was in the town of Joppa praying," he said, "when 5
in a trance I saw a vision: Something like a large linen sheet
was coming down. It was lowered by its four corners from the
sky, and came down to me. Looking in, I examined it and saw 6
four-footed animals of the earth, wild animals, reptiles, and birds
of the air. I also heard a voice telling me, 'Get up, Peter, kill 7
and eat.'

"But I answered, 'Oh no, Lord. Nothing common or unclean 8
has ever come into my mouth.'

"A voice spoke from heaven a second time, 'Don't make 9
unclean what God has made clean.' This happened three times. 10
Then all of it was pulled up to the sky again.

"At that moment three men, sent to me from Caesarea, came 11
to the house we were in. The Spirit told me to go with them 12
and not treat them as different people. These six fellow disciples
went with me, and we came into the man's home.

"He told us how he had seen the angel standing in his home 13
and saying, 'Send to Joppa and get Simon, who is called Peter.
What he will tell you will save you and everybody in your home.' 14

"While I was speaking, the Holy Spirit came down on these 15
people as He originally came on us, and I had to think of what 16
the Lord had said: 'John baptized with water, but you will be
baptized with the Holy Spirit.' Now if God gave them the same 17
gift He gave us when we began to believe in the Lord Jesus Christ,
who was I — could I stop God?"

When the others heard this, they kept quiet. And they praised 18
God, saying, "Then God has given repentance also to the non-
Jewish people so that they will live."

The New Church in Antioch

11:19   The people scattered by the persecution that broke out over Stephen went as far as Phoenicia, Cyprus, and Antioch, and they 20 spoke the Word only to the Jews. But among them were some men from Cyprus and Cyrene who came to Antioch and started talking also to the non-Jews, telling them the good news of the 21 Lord Jesus. The Lord's hand was with them, and a large number believed and turned to the Lord.

22   The church in Jerusalem heard the news about them, and they 23 sent Barnabas to Antioch. When he came there, he was delighted to see what God's love had done, and he urged them all with 24 a hearty determination to be faithful to the Lord. He was a good man, full of the Holy Spirit and faith. And a large crowd was brought to the Lord.

25-26   Then Barnabas left for Tarsus to look for Saul. He found him and brought him to Antioch. And they were guests of the church for a whole year and taught a large crowd. — It was in Antioch the disciples were first called Christians.

27   At that time some prophets came from Jerusalem down to 28 Antioch. One of them by the name of Agabus got up and by the Spirit predicted there would be a big famine all over the 29 world (it came while Claudius was emperor). Every one of the disciples decided, as he was able, to send relief to the fellow 30 Christians living in Judea. They did this by sending Barnabas and Saul to bring it to the elders.

An Angel Frees Peter

12   At that time King Herod arrested some members of the 2 church in order to mistreat them. He killed John's brother James with a sword. When he saw how the Jews liked that, he arrested 3 Peter too. It happened during the Passover days of bread without 4 yeast. When he arrested Peter, he put him in prison and had sixteen soldiers in squads of four guard him. He wanted to bring 5 him before the people after the Passover. So Peter was kept in prison.

6   But the church was earnestly praying to God for him. The night before Herod was going to bring him before the people, Peter, bound with two chains, was sleeping between two soldiers, and guards in front of the door were watching the prison.

Suddenly the Lord's angel stood near him, and a light shone in his cell. He struck Peter on his side, woke him, and said, "Get up! Quick!" Peter's chains dropped from his wrists.

"Fasten your belt," the angel told him, "and tie on your sandals!" He did this. "Put on your garment," the angel told him, "and follow me." [8]

Peter followed him outside, not realizing the angel was actually doing this. He thought he was seeing a vision. They passed through the first guards and the second guards and came to the iron gate leading into the city. It opened by itself before them, and they went outside and up the street. There the angel suddenly left him. [9] [10]

"Now I'm sure the Lord sent His angel," Peter said when he was himself again, "and He rescued me from Herod and from everything the Jewish people were expecting." [11]

Peter Comes to His Friends

When he realized what had happened, He went to the home of Mary (the mother of John — the one called Mark), where many had gathered and were praying. He knocked at the entrance gate, and a maid by the name of Rose came to answer. Recognizing Peter's voice, she was so happy she didn't open the gate but ran in and announced, "Peter is standing at the gate!" [12] [13] [14]

"You're crazy!" they told her. But she insisted it was so. "It's his angel," they said. [15]

But Peter kept on knocking. When they opened the gate, they were surprised to see him. He waved his hand to quiet them down and told them how the Lord had taken him out of the prison. "Tell James and the other Christians about this," he said. Then he left and went to another place. [16] [17]

In the morning the soldiers were very much upset as they asked, "What happened to Peter?" Herod searched for him but didn't find him. So he examined the guards and ordered them executed. [18] [19]

Herod Dies

Then Herod left Judea, went down to Caesarea, and stayed there awhile. [19]

He had a violent quarrel with the people of Tyre and Sidon. So they came to him in a body. After they had won over Blastus, [20] who took care of the king's bedroom, they asked for peace because the king's country provided food for their country.

12:21 On a day that was set, Herod put on his royal robe, sat on **22** the platform, and made a speech to them. The people shouted, "It's a god speaking, not a man!"

23 Immediately the Lord's angel struck him because he didn't give glory to God. He was eaten by worms, and he died.

24 But God's Word continued to spread and win many followers.

On Cyprus

25 After Barnabas and Saul had delivered the offering for relief, they came back from Jerusalem, bringing with them John, also called Mark.

13 The following were prophets and teachers in the church at Antioch: Barnabas, Symeon, called Black, Lucius from Cyrene, Manaen, who had been raised with Herod the governor, and Saul.

2 While the Christians were worshiping the Lord and fasting, the Holy Spirit said, "Set Barnabas and Saul apart for Me to do the work I called them for."

3 Then they fasted and prayed, laid their hands on them, and **4** let them go. And so they, sent by the Holy Spirit, went down to **5** Seleucia and from there sailed to Cyprus. They came to Salamis and there started to preach God's Word in the synagogs of the **6** Jews. They also had John to help them. ' They went through the whole island as far as Paphos. There they found a Jewish sor- **7** cerer and false prophet by the name of Barjesus, who was with the proconsul Sergius Paulus, an intelligent man. He sent for **8** Barnabas and Saul and wanted to hear God's Word. But Elymas, the sorcerer (that was what his name meant), opposed them and tried to turn the proconsul away from the faith.

9 But Saul (who was Paul), filled with the Holy Spirit, looked **10** steadily at him ' and said, "O you who are full of every treachery and villainy, you son of the devil, enemy of all that is right! Won't **11** you stop twisting *the Lord's right ways?* [66] And now the Lord's hand is on you: You'll be blind and not see the sun for a while."

At that moment a mist and a darkness came over him, and he went around looking for people to take his hand and lead **12** him. When the proconsul saw what had happened, he believed. The Lord's teaching amazed him.

At Antioch near Pisidia

Paul and his men took a ship from Paphos and came to Perga 13:13
in Pamphylia. There John * left them and went back to Jerusalem. But they went on from Perga and came to Antioch near 14
Pisidia. On Saturday they went into the synagog and sat down.

After the reading of the Law and the prophets, the synagog 15
leaders had a man go and tell them, "Fellow Jews, if you have
anything to say to encourage the people, speak."

Paul got up and motioned with his hand. "Men of Israel," he 16
said, "and you others who fear God, listen to me. The God of 17
this people Israel chose our fathers and made them a great
people while they lived as strangers in Egypt, and *with an
uplifted arm He led them out of it.*[67] About forty years *He put* 18
up with them in the desert.[68] Then *He destroyed seven nations* 19
in Canaan and gave their *country* to His people *as an inheritance.*[69]
| He did all this in about 450 years. After that He gave them 20
judges till the time of the prophet Samuel.

"Then the people demanded a king, and God gave them Saul 21
for forty years. He was a son of Kish, a man of the tribe of
Benjamin. But God took the throne away from him again and 22
made David their king. In regard to him he declared, *'I found
David*, Jesse's son, *to be a man after My own heart,*[70] who *will
do everything I want him to do.'* [71]

"As He had promised, God had a Savior — Jesus — come 23
from David's descendants to Israel. When He came into the 24
world, John went ahead of Him as herald to tell all the people
of Israel to repent and be baptized. As John was finishing his 25
work, he said, 'Who do you think I am? I'm not the One. No,
there's Someone coming after me, and I don't deserve to untie
the shoes on His feet.'

"Fellow Jews, Abraham's descendants, and you others who 26
fear God, *the message* of this salvation *was sent* [72] to us. Not 27
knowing who Jesus was or what the prophets meant that are
read every Saturday, the people in Jerusalem and their rulers by
condemning Jesus did what their prophets predicted. Although 28
they found no good reason to kill Him, they asked Pilate to
have Him killed. When they had done everything that was 29
written about Him, they took Him down from the cross and laid
Him in a grave. But God raised Him from the dead, and for many 30-31
days He was seen by those who had come with Him from Galilee

* Mark

up to Jerusalem. They are now telling the people the truth about

13:32-33 Him. And we are bringing you the good news: What God promised the fathers He did for our children by raising Jesus, as it is written in the second Psalm:

You are My Son,
Today I am Your Father.[73]

34 "He raised Him from the dead, never to suffer *decay,* as He said, 'I will give *you what I gave David — mercies You can*
35 *trust.'* [74] Another Psalm says, '*You will not let Your Loved One*
36 *experience decay.'* [75] When *David* had served the people of his time, he by God's will *went to his rest* and was laid away *with*
37 *his fathers.*[76] His body decayed, but the body of Him whom God raised did not decay.

38 "And so you should know, my fellow men — we are an-
39 nouncing to you this Jesus forgives your sins and makes everyone
38 who believes righteous and free from everything from which Moses' Law couldn't free you.

40 "Now be careful, or what the prophets said will happen to
41 you: *Look, you scorners, then wonder and perish, because I'm doing something in your days that you would never believe if anyone told you.*" [77]

42 As Paul and Barnabas were going out, the people urged them
43 to tell them the same things the next Saturday. When the meeting of the synagog broke up, many Jews and others who had come to fear God followed Paul and Barnabas, who talked to them and urged them to stay in God's love.

44 The next Saturday almost the whole town was there to hear
45 God's Word. When the Jews saw the crowds, they got very jealous. They contradicted what Paul said and abused him.

46 Paul and Barnabas boldly declared: "We had to speak God's Word to you first, but since you reject it and judge yourselves unworthy of everlasting life, we are now turning to the non-
47 Jews. That is what the Lord has ordered us to do: '*I have made you a light for the non-Jews, to save people all over the earth.*'" [78]

48 The non-Jews were delighted to hear what the Lord had said and praised Him for it, and all who had been appointed for ever-
49 lasting life believed. The Lord's Word spread all over the country.
50 But the Jews stirred up the noble women who worshiped with them, and the leaders of the town. These started a persecution against Paul and Barnabas and drove them out of their territory.

In protest against them Paul and Barnabas shook the dust off their feet and went to Iconium. Meanwhile the disciples con- 52 tinued to be full of joy and of the Holy Spirit.

In Iconium

The same thing happened in Iconium. Paul and Barnabas **14** went into the synagog of the Jews and spoke in such a way that a big crowd of Jews and non-Jews believed. But the Jews who 2 refused to believe stirred up the non-Jews and poisoned their minds against the Christians. For a long time Paul and Barnabas 3 continued to speak boldly, trusting in the Lord, who gave His approval to the words of His love by letting their hands do miracles and wonders. But the people of the town were divided — 4 some were with the Jews, others with the apostles.

But when non-Jews and Jews with their rulers planned to mis- 5 treat and stone them, they found out about it and escaped to 6 Lystra and Derbe, towns of Lycaonia, and to the surrounding territory. There they kept on telling the good news. 7

In Lystra

In Lystra there was a man sitting who couldn't use his feet. 8 He had been lame from his birth and had never walked. ' He was 9 listening to Paul as he spoke. Paul watched him, and when he saw the man believed he would be made well, he called out loud, 10 *"Stand up* straight *on your feet."* [79] The man jumped up and walked around.

The people who saw what Paul had done shouted in the 11 language of Lycaonia, "The gods have become like men and have come down to us." And they called Barnabas Zeus, and 12 Paul Hermes, because he was the main speaker. The priest of 13 the temple of Zeus in front of the town brought bulls and garlands to the gates. He and the crowd wanted to sacrifice.

When the apostles Barnabas and Paul heard of it, they tore 14 their clothes and rushed out into the crowd. "You men, why are 15 you doing this?" they shouted. "We're just human beings too, with experiences like yours and are telling you the good news to turn from these empty things to the living God, *who made heaven and earth, the sea, and everything in them.*[80] In the ages 16 that have gone by He let all people go their own ways; yet He 17 didn't fail to give evidence of Himself by doing good, giving you rains from heaven and crops in their seasons, filling you with food, and making you happy."

14:18 Even by saying this they could hardly keep the crowd from
19 sacrificing to them. But then some Jews came from Antioch and Iconium and won the people over. So they stoned Paul and
20 dragged him out of the town, thinking he was dead. But when the disciples came and stood around him, he got up and went into the town.

Derbe and Back Home

21 The next day he and Barnabas left for Derbe. As they were telling the good news in that town, they won many disciples.
22 Then they went back to Lystra, Iconium, and Antioch, ¹ strengthening the disciples and encouraging them to be loyal to the faith, saying, "We must suffer much to go into God's kingdom."
23 ¹ They appointed elders for them in each church. And with prayer and fasting they entrusted them to the Lord in whom they believed.

24 When they had gone through Pisidia, they came to Pamphylia.
25-26 They spoke the Word in Perga and went down to Attalia. From there they took a boat to Antioch, where they had been entrusted
27 to God's love for the work they now had finished. When they arrived, they called the church together and told them everything God had done with them and how He had opened the door for the people who were not Jews so that they, too, might believe.
28 Then they spent a long time with the disciples.*

Must Non-Jews Be Circumcised?

15 Some men came down from Judea and started to teach the Christians: "If you're not circumcised according to the custom
2 taught by Moses, you can't be saved." When Paul and Barnabas had no little conflict and argument with them, Paul and Barnabas and some of the others were appointed to go up to Jerusalem and see the apostles and elders about this question.

3 The church sent them on their way. As they were going through Phoenicia and Samaria, they told the whole story how the non-Jews were turning to God, and they made all the Christians very happy.

4 When they came to Jerusalem, they were welcomed by the church, the apostles, and the elders and told everything God

* At this time, late in A. D. 48, Paul wrote his letter to the Galatians. They were the people he had been with on his first journey.

had done with them. But some believers of the party of the
Pharisees got up and said, "We must circumcise people and order
them to keep the Law of Moses."

The apostles and elders met to look into this matter. After 6-7
much discussion Peter got up. "Fellow Christians," he said to
the others, "you know in the early days God chose me to be the
one among you to tell the good news to the non-Jews so that
they would hear it and believe. And God, who knows our hearts, 8
showed them He approved by giving them the Holy Spirit as He
gave Him to us. And by cleansing their hearts by faith He has 9
declared we are not different from them. Now then, why do 10
you test God by putting on the disciples' neck a yoke neither
our fathers nor we could bear? No, by the love of the Lord 11
Jesus we believe in order to be saved; and so do they."

The whole crowd was silent. Then they heard Barnabas and 12
Paul tell about all the miracles and wonders God had done among
the non-Jews through them.

After they finished speaking, James said, "Fellow Christians, 13
listen to me. Simon has explained how God first came to the 14
non-Jews to get a people for Himself. This agrees with what the 15
prophets said. It is written: ¹ *'Afterwards I will come back* ⁸¹ *and* 16
build again David's hut that has fallen down. And its ruins
I will build and set up again, ¹ *so that the rest of the people, yes,* 17
all the nations who are called by My name, may search for the
Lord. The Lord says this and does this which was known long 18
ago.' ⁸² So it is my judgment that we should not trouble these 19
non-Jews who are turning to God ¹ but write them to keep away 20
from the unclean things of idols and from sexual sin and not eat
anything strangled or any blood. Ever since the earliest days 21
there are in each town those who preach Moses when he is read
in the synagogs every Saturday."

Then the apostles, the elders, and the whole church decided 22
to choose some of their men and send them with Paul and
Barnabas to Antioch: Judas, called Barsabas, and Silas — leaders
among the Christians. And they wrote this letter for them to 23
deliver:

"The apostles and elders, Christians, send greetings to their
non-Jewish fellow Christians in Antioch, Syria, and Cilicia.

"Since we heard that some men, coming from us without in- 24
structions from us, have said things to trouble you, and they
continue to upset you, we have unanimously decided to choose 25

Acts
15:26-27

men and send them to you with our dear Barnabas and Paul, who are living only for our Lord Jesus Christ. So we are sending Judas and Silas to talk to you and tell you the same things.

28 "The Holy Spirit and we have decided not to burden you
29 more than is necessary: Keep away from food sacrificed to idols, from blood, from the meat of strangled animals, and from sexual sin. Be careful to avoid these and you will be doing right. Farewell!"

30 So they were sent on their way and came to Antioch, where
31 they got the church together and delivered the letter. The people read it and were delighted with the encouragement it brought
32 them. And Judas and Silas, who also were prophets, said much to encourage and strengthen the Christians.

33 After they had stayed for some time, the Christians let Judas and Silas go back with a friendly greeting to those who had sent
* 35 them. But Paul and Barnabas stayed in Antioch and with the help of many others taught and told the Lord's good news.

Paul Takes Silas with Him

36 After a while Paul said to Barnabas, "Let's go back and visit our fellow Christians in every town where we told them the Lord's Word, and let's see how they are."

37 Barnabas wanted to take along John, who was called Mark.
38 But Paul thought it best not to take the man who had deserted them in Pamphylia and had not gone with them into the work.
39 They disagreed so sharply they separated, and Barnabas, taking
40 Mark along, sailed away to Cyprus. But Paul chose Silas and started out, his fellow Christians entrusting him to the Lord's love.

Timothy Joins Paul in Lystra

41 He went through Syria and Cilicia, strengthening the churches.
16 ¹ He came down to Derbe, then to Lystra. Here there was a disciple by the name of Timothy. His mother was a Jewish Christian,
2 but his father was a Greek. The Christians in Lystra and Iconium
3 spoke well of him. Paul wanted him to go with him, so he took him and circumcised him on account of the Jews who were in those places, because everybody knew his father was a Greek.

4 As they went through the towns, they delivered the decisions the apostles and elders in Jerusalem had made and the people

* Our two oldest manuscripts do not have v. 34: "But Silas decided to stay there, and Judas left alone."

were to keep. So the churches were strengthened in the faith and grew in number more and more every day.

The Call to Europe

They went through the region of Phrygia and Galatia because the Holy Spirit kept them from speaking the Word in the province of Asia. They came as far as Mysia and tried to get into Bithynia, but the Spirit of Jesus did not let them. So they passed through Mysia and went down to Troas.

One night Paul saw a vision — a man from Macedonia was standing there and urging him, "Come over to Macedonia and help us!"

As soon as he had seen the vision, we looked for a way to get to Macedonia since we concluded God had called us to tell them the good news.

At Philippi

Sailing from Troas, we went straight to Samothrace, the next day to Neapolis, and from there to Philippi, a leading city in that part of Macedonia and a colony of Rome. We stayed in that city for some days.

On Saturday we went out of the gate and along the river, where we thought there was a place for prayer. We sat down and started to talk to the women gathered there. There was a woman by the name of Lydia, a dealer in purple goods, who came from the town of Thyatira. She worshiped God. As she listened, the Lord opened her heart to be interested in what Paul said. When she and her family were baptized, she urged us, "If you're convinced I believe in the Lord, come and stay at my home." And she made us come.

One day when we were going to the place of prayer, we met a slave girl with a spirit of fortune-telling in her; she made much money for her owners by telling the unknown. She would follow Paul and us and shout, "These men are servants of the most high God and are telling you how to be saved." She kept on doing this for many days until Paul, very much annoyed, turned to the spirit and said, "In the name of Jesus Christ I order you to go out of her!"

Then and there the spirit went out of her, and with it, as her owners realized, went their chance of making money. So they grabbed Paul and Silas, dragged them before the officers in the marketplace, and brought them before the highest Roman officials. "These men are stirring up a lot of trouble in our city," they said.

21 "They're Jews, ¹ and they're teaching religious ways that we as Romans aren't allowed to adopt or practice."

22 The crowd also joined in attacking them. Then the officials
tore the clothes off Paul and Silas and ordered them beaten
23 with rods. After striking them many times, the men put them
in prison and ordered the jailer to watch them and not let them
24 escape. He did as he was ordered and put them in the inner
cell and fastened their feet in the stocks.

25 About midnight Paul and Silas were praying and singing to
26 God, and the other prisoners were listening to them. Suddenly
the earth quaked so violently the foundations of the prison were
shaken, all the doors flew open, and everybody's chains were
unfastened.

27 The jailer woke up and saw the prison doors open. Thinking
the prisoners had escaped, he drew his sword and was going to
28 kill himself. But Paul called out loud, "Don't harm yourself!
We're all here!"

29 The jailer asked for lights, rushed in, and fell down trembling
30 before Paul and Silas. Then he took them outside and asked,
"Sirs, what do I have to do to be saved?"

31 "Believe in the Lord Jesus," they answered, "and you and
32 your family will be saved." They spoke the Lord's Word to him
and everyone in his home.

33 At that hour of the night he took them with him and washed
their wounds. And he and all who were with him were baptized
34 immediately. He took them up into his home and gave them
a meal. He and everyone in his home were very happy to have
found faith in God.

35 In the morning the officials sent attendants and said, "Let
those men go."

36 The jailer reported the message to Paul. "The officials sent
word to let you go," he said. "Come out now, and *go in peace*." ⁸³

37 But Paul told them, "They have beaten us publicly without
trying and condemning us, although we're Roman citizens, and
have put us in prison. And now they're trying to put us out
secretly? I should say not! They should come themselves and
take us out."

38 The attendants reported to the officials what Paul said. Hearing that Paul and Silas were Roman citizens, they were fright-

ened. So they came and pleaded with them, took them out, and
asked them to leave the city.

Leaving the prison, they went to Lydia, saw and encouraged 40
the Christians there, and then left.

In Thessalonica

Paul and Silas traveled through Amphipolis and Apollonia 17
and came to Thessalonica. Here the Jews had a synagog. Paul 2
went in as usual and on three Saturdays had Bible discussions
with them. He explained and showed them: "The promised 3
Savior had to suffer and rise from the dead, and this Savior is
the Jesus I'm telling you about."

He convinced some of the Jews, and they joined Paul and 4
Silas, and also a large crowd of the Greeks who worshiped God,
and many of the wives of the leaders.*

Then the Jews got jealous, took some wicked men in the 5
marketplace, formed a mob, and started a riot in the city. They
attacked Jason's home and searched for Paul and Silas to bring
them out to the people. When they didn't find them, they dragged 6
Jason and some other Christians before the city officials, shouting, "Those men who have made trouble all over the world are
here now and are Jason's guests. They're all going against the 7
emperor's decrees by saying there's another king — Jesus!"

Hearing this, the crowd and the officials were upset. But after 8-9
they had taken security from Jason and the others, they let
them go.

That same night the Christians sent Paul and Silas away to 10
Berea.

At Berea

When they came there, they went into the synagog of the
Jews. These people were nobler than those at Thessalonica — 11
they were very eager to get the Word and every day studied the
Bible to see if those things were so. And many of them believed, 12
also many noble Greeks, women as well as men.

But when the Jews at Thessalonica found out Paul had now 13
preached God's Word also in Berea, they came there to stir up

* About this time Timothy came to Paul bringing money and food
from Philippi. Paul says, "Even while I was in Thessalonica, you more
than once sent help for my needs." (Phil. 4:16; cp. v. 15; 1 Thess. 1:1;
2 Thess. 1:1)

trouble among the people. Immediately the Christians sent Paul away to the sea, but Silas and Timothy stayed there.

In Athens

15   Those who escorted Paul took him all the way to Athens. When they left, they took instructions to Silas and Timothy to come to him as soon as possible.

16   While Paul was waiting for them in Athens, he was inwardly stirred up when he saw how many idols there were in the city.

17   Then he had discussions in the synagog with Jews and others who feared God, and every day in the marketplace with those

18   who happened to be there. Some Epicurean and Stoic philosophers also debated with him, but some asked, "What is this fellow with his scraps of learning trying to say?" Others said, "He seems to be telling about foreign gods" — because he was telling the good news of Jesus and the resurrection.

19   Then they took him and brought him before the court of Mars' Hill and asked, "Could we know, what is this new thing

20   you teach? You bring some things that sound strange to us, and we want to know what they mean."

21   Now everybody in Athens, also the visitors staying there, used their time only to tell or hear the latest news.

22   Paul stood before the court of Mars' Hill and said, "Men of

23   Athens, I see how very religious you are in every way. As I went through your city and saw the things you worship, I found an altar with the inscription TO AN UNKNOWN GOD. Now I'm

24   telling you about what you don't know and yet worship. *The God who made* the world and everything in it is the Lord of *heaven and earth* and doesn't live in temples made by human hands,

25   and He isn't served by human hands as if He needed anything. He Himself *gives* everyone life and *breath* [84] and everything.

26   From one man He made every nation to have the people live all over the earth, setting the times allotted to them and the boun-

27   daries they live in, that they should look for God and perhaps feel their way to Him and find Him. He is never far

28   from any one of us, because we live and move and are in Him; as some of your poets * have said, 'You see, we are His

29   children.' Now, if we're God's children, we shouldn't think God is like gold, silver, or stone, carved by man's art and imagination.

* Aratus and Cleanthes wrote this about 270 B.C.

"While God overlooked the times when people were ignorant, He now tells all of them everywhere to be sorry for their sins, because He has set a day when *He is going to* have a Man *judge the world with justice.*[85] He has appointed Him for this. And by raising Him from the dead has given everyone a good reason to believe." 31

When they heard about a resurrection of the dead, some started to mock, while others said, "We'll hear you again about this." 32

And so Paul left the meeting. Some men joined him and believed. Among them were Dionysius, a member of the court, and a woman by the name of Damaris, and some others with them. 33-34

In Corinth

After that he left Athens and came to Corinth. There he found a Jew by the name of Aquila, born in Pontus, and his wife Priscilla. They had recently come from Italy because Claudius had ordered all Jews to leave Rome. Paul went to them, ¹ and because they made tents for a living just as he did, he stayed with them, and they worked together. 18 1-2

3

Every Saturday he would argue in the synagog and try to win Jews and Greeks. But when Silas and Timothy came down from Macedonia, Paul devoted himself entirely to teaching the Word as he solemnly assured the Jews, "Jesus is the promised Savior!" ¹ But they opposed him and abused him. In protest he shook the dust from his clothes and told them, "Your blood be on your own heads. I am innocent. From now on I'll go to the non-Jews." 4

5

6

Then he left the place and went to the home of a man by the name of Titius Justus, who worshiped God. His house was right beside the synagog. Now Crispus, the synagog leader, and all who were in his home believed in the Lord. And many other people in Corinth who heard Paul believed and were baptized. 7

8

One night the Lord spoke to Paul in a vision, *"Don't be afraid!* But speak, and don't be silent — ¹ *I am with you,*[86] and nobody will attack you so as to harm you, because I have many people in this city." 9

10

He stayed there a year and six months and taught God's Word among them.* 11

* In the year 50 Paul wrote the two letters to the Thessalonians.

But when Gallio was proconsul of Greece, the Jews united in an attack on Paul and brought him before Gallio as judge.

13 "This man," they said, "is persuading people to worship God in ways that are against the Law."

14 Just as Paul was going to answer, Gallio said to the Jews, "If this were a crime or vicious wrong, it would be only fair that 15 I listen to you Jews. But since we have questions here about words, names, and your own Law, see to it yourselves. I don't 16 want to be a judge of those things." And he drove them away from his platform.

17 Then all of them took Sosthenes, the synagog leader, and beat him in front of the judge's platform. But Gallio paid no attention to it.

Home

18 After staying there quite a while longer, Paul said good-by to the Christians. Priscilla and Aquila went with him. At Cenchrea he had his hair cut, since he had been under a vow. 19 They took a boat for Syria ¹ and came to Ephesus, where Paul left Priscilla and Aquila. There he went into the synagog and 20 had a discussion with the Jews. They asked him to stay longer, 21 but he refused. As he said good-by to them, he told them, "I will come back to you if God wants me to."

22 He sailed from Ephesus and landed at Caesarea. He went up, greeted the church, and then went down to Antioch.

Apollos

23 After staying there for some time, Paul left and went from place to place through the Galatian country and through Phrygia, strengthening all the disciples.

24 A Jew by the name of Apollos, who was born in Alexandria, came to Ephesus. He was a learned man and mighty in the 25 Bible. After he had been instructed in the Lord's way, he spoke with a glowing enthusiasm and taught correctly about Jesus but 26 knew only John's baptism. He started to speak boldly in the synagog. When Priscilla and Aquila heard him, they took him with them and explained God's way to him more accurately.

27 As he wanted to cross over to Greece, the Christians wrote to the disciples there urging them to welcome him. When he got there, he gave much help to those who by God's love were

now believers. Publicly and vigorously he proved the Jews were
wrong as he showed from the Bible that Jesus is the promised
Savior.

Paul in Ephesus

While Apollos was in Corinth, Paul traveled over the hills **19**
to get to Ephesus. Meeting some disciples there, he asked them, **2**
"Did you receive the Holy Spirit when you became believers?"

"No," they answered him, "we haven't even heard there is
a Holy Spirit."

"Into what then were you baptized?" he asked them. **3**

"Into John's baptism," they answered.

Paul said, "John baptized those who were sorry for their sins **4**
and told the people to believe in the One coming after him, that
is Jesus."

When they heard this, they were baptized into the name of **5**
the Lord Jesus. And as Paul laid his hands on them, the Holy **6**
Spirit came on them, and they started to talk in other languages
and to speak God's Word. There were about twelve men in **7**
the group.

He went into the synagog and spoke there boldly for three **8**
months, discussing and trying to convince people about God's
kingdom. When some got stubborn, refused to believe, and slan- **9**
dered the Christian religion before the crowd, he left them, took
his disciples away from them, and had daily discussions in the
lecture hall of Tyrannus. This went on for two years so that all **10**
who lived in the province of Asia, Jews and Greeks, heard the
Lord's Word.

God did extraordinary miracles by Paul's hands. When hand- **11-12**
kerchiefs and aprons that had touched his skin were taken to the
sick, their sicknesses left them, and the evil spirits went out
of them.

Some Jews who made it their business to go around and drive **13**
out evil spirits tried to use the name of the Lord Jesus over those
having the evil spirits. "I order you by that Jesus whom Paul
preaches," they said. Seven sons of Sceva, a Jewish ruling priest, **14**
were doing this.

But the evil spirit answered them, "I know Jesus, and I know **15**
Paul, but who are you?" Then the man with the evil spirit jumped **16**
on them, got the better of them, and overpowered them all so
that they ran naked and bruised out of that house.

All the Jews and Greeks living in Ephesus heard about it. **17**

19:18 They were all frightened and started to think very highly of the name of the Lord Jesus. Many believers came to confess and tell

19 about their magic spells. Many of those who had practiced magic gathered their books and burned them in front of everybody. They added up the cost of these books and found they were worth fifty

20 thousand denarii.* In that way the Lord's Word grew mightily and triumphed.**

21 After all these things had happened, Paul decided to go through Macedonia and Greece and then to Jerusalem. "When I get there,"

22 he said, "I must also see Rome." But he sent two of his helpers, Timothy and Erastus, to Macedonia, while he himself stayed in the province of Asia a while longer.

The Riot

23 During that time there was a big disturbance over the Christian religion.

24 A silversmith by the name of Demetrius provided a big income

25 for the skilled workers by making silver shrines of Artemis. He called a meeting of these and others who did similar work. "Men," he said, "you know we're getting a fine income from this business,

26 and you see and hear how this Paul has won and taken away a large crowd not only in Ephesus but almost all over the province of Asia by telling them, 'Gods made by human hands are no gods.'

27 There is a danger people will not only reject our line of business but will also think nothing of the temple of the great goddess Artemis, and then she whom all Asia and the world worship will be robbed of her glory."

28 When they heard this, they got furious and shouted, "Great

29 is Artemis of the Ephesians!" The confusion spread all over the city. And they all rushed into the theater together, dragging with them Gaius and Aristarchus, Paul's fellow travelers from Macedonia.

30 Paul wanted to go into the crowd, but the disciples wouldn't

31 let him. Even some officials of the province of Asia who were his friends sent men to him and urged him not to risk going into the theater.

32 Some were shouting one thing, some another. The crowd was

* A denarius was one day's pay.

** From Ephesus, during the time of A. D. 54—55, Paul wrote his first letter to the Corinthians. There are good reasons to believe that here he also wrote the letters to the Philippians, Philemon, Colossians, and Ephesians.

confused, and most of them didn't know why they were meeting. 19:33
Then the Jews pushed Alexander to the front, and some of the
crowd told him what to do. Alexander waved his hand to quiet
them and wanted to make a defense before the people. But when 34
they found out he was a Jew, they all started to shout in unison
and kept it up for about two hours, "Great is Artemis of the
Ephesians!"

Then the city secretary quieted the crowd. "Men of Ephesus," 35
he said, "who in the world doesn't know that this city of the
Ephesians is the keeper of the temple of the great Artemis and
of the statue that fell down from Zeus? Since nobody can deny 36
this, you must be quiet and not do anything reckless. The men 37
you brought here don't rob temples or insult our goddess. Now 38
if Demetrius and his workers have something against anyone,
we have special days and proconsuls to hold court; there they
should accuse one another. And if you want anything else, it 39
must be settled in a legal meeting. We're in danger of being 40
accused of a riot today for which there is no good reason. We'll
not be able to explain this mob." After saying this, he dismissed
the meeting.

When the uproar had died down, Paul sent for the disciples, 20
encouraged them, and saying good-by to them, left to go to
Macedonia.* He went through those parts of the country and 2
spoke much to encourage the people and then went to Greece
¹ and stayed there three months.** 3

At Troas

Just as Paul was going to sail for Syria, the Jews plotted against 3
him, so he decided to go back through Macedonia. Sopater from 4
Berea, the son of Pyrrhus, went with him; also Aristarchus and
Secundus from Thessalonica, and Gaius from Derbe, and Timothy,
but Tychicus and Trophimus were from the province of Asia; 5
they came and were waiting for us in Troas. After the Passover 6
days of bread without yeast we sailed from Philippi and in five
days came to them in Troas and stayed there seven days.

On Sunday, when we met for a meal, Paul spoke to the people. 7
Since he intended to leave the next day, he went on talking till
midnight. There were many lamps in the upstairs room where 8
we were meeting.

* From Macedonia in A. D. 55 Paul wrote his second letter to the
Corinthians.
** From Corinth in A. D. 56 Paul wrote his letter to the Romans.

A young man by the name of Eutychus, sitting in the window, was dropping off into a deep sleep as Paul talked on and on. Finally, overcome by sleep, he fell down from the third story and
10 was picked up dead. But Paul went down, lay on him, and took him into his arms. "Don't get excited," he said. "He's alive!"
11 Then he went upstairs again, broke the bread, and ate. And after a long talk that lasted till the sun rose, he left.

12 The people took the boy away alive and were very much comforted.

From Troas to Miletus

13 We went ahead to the boat and sailed to Assos. There we were going to take Paul into the boat; he had arranged it that
14 way, planning himself to go there on foot. When we met him
15 in Assos, we took him on board and went on to Mitylene. We sailed from there and on the following day came opposite Chios. The next day we crossed over to Samos and on the next came
16 to Miletus. Paul had decided to sail past Ephesus to avoid spending time in the province of Asia; he was in a hurry to get to Jerusalem for the day of Pentecost if possible.

With the Pastors of Ephesus

17 From Miletus he sent men to Ephesus to get the pastors of the
18 church. When they came to him, he said to them: "You know how I lived with you all the time from the first day I came into
19 the province of Asia; how I served the Lord very humbly, with tears, and in trials I endured as the Jews plotted against me;
20 how I didn't shrink from telling you anything that would help you or from teaching you publicly and from house to house;
21 and how I earnestly warned Jews and non-Jews to turn from sin
22 to God and believe in our Lord Jesus. And now, you see, the
23 Spirit compels me to go to Jerusalem. I don't know what will happen to me there, except that the Holy Spirit keeps warning me from town to town that chains and troubles are waiting for me.
24 I don't count my life worth anything. I just want to finish running my race and doing the work the Lord Jesus entrusted to me, declaring the good news of God's love.

25 "I went around among you preaching the Kingdom, and
26 now I know none of you will see me again. That is why I declare
27 to you today I am innocent of the blood of any of you, because I didn't shrink from telling you God's whole plan.

"Take care of yourselves and the whole *flock* in which the
Holy Spirit has made you overseers to be shepherds of *God's
church that He bought* [87] with His own blood. I know when I'm 29
gone fierce wolves will come among you and not spare the flock.
And even some of you men will start to tell perversions of the 30
truth to get the disciples to leave and follow you. So watch and 31
remember how for three years, day and night, I didn't stop warning everyone with tears. And now I entrust you to God and to 32
the Word of His love, which can build you up and give you *the
salvation to be shared by all who are made holy.*[88]

"I didn't want anyone's silver or gold or clothes. You know 33-34
these hands worked for what I needed and for the men with me.
In every way I showed you that by working hard as I do we 35
should help the weak and remember what the Lord Jesus said:
'We are happier when we give than when we get something.' "

When he had said this, he knelt down with all of them and 36
prayed. They wept very much, put their arms around Paul, and 37
kissed him. It hurt them most of all that he had said they wouldn't 38
see him again. Then they took him to the ship.

At Tyre

When we had broken away from them, we sailed and followed **21**
a straight course to Cos and the next day to Rhodes and from
there to Patara. We found a ship going across to Phoenicia, went 2
on board, and sailed. We came in sight of Cyprus, and leaving it 3
on our left, sailed on to Syria and landed at Tyre because the
ship was to unload its cargo there.

We looked up the disciples and stayed there seven days. By 4
the Spirit they told Paul not to go up to Jerusalem. When our 5
time was up, we started on our way. All of them with their
wives and children accompanied us out of the city. There we
knelt on the beach and prayed and said good-by to one another.
Then we went on board the ship, and they went back home. 6

At Caesarea

We continued our sailing, going from Tyre to Ptolemais. 7
There we greeted our fellow Christians and spent a day with
them. The next day we left and came to Caesarea. We went 8
into the home of Philip the evangelist, one of the seven, and
stayed with him. He had four unmarried daughters who spoke 9
God's Word.

21:10   While we were staying there longer than we had expected,
11   a prophet by the name of Agabus came down from Judea. He
came to us, took Paul's belt, tied his own feet and hands, and
said, "The Holy Spirit says, 'This is how the Jews in Jerusalem
will tie the man this belt belongs to and hand him over to the
non-Jews.' "

12   When we heard this, we and those living there urged him not
to go up to Jerusalem.

13   Then Paul answered, "What are you doing — crying and
making me weak in my purpose? I'm ready not only to be bound
but even to die in Jerusalem for the name of the Lord Jesus."

14   When he would not be persuaded, we were silent and could
only say, "The Lord's will be done."

In Jerusalem

15   After those days we got ready and started for Jerusalem.
16   Some of the disciples from Caesarea came with us and took us
to the home of Mnason to be his guests. He was from Cyprus
17   and was one of the first disciples. When we came to Jerusalem,
our fellow Christians eagerly welcomed us.

18   The next day we went with Paul to James, and all the elders
19   came there too. After greeting them, Paul told them everything
God had done through his work among the non-Jews.

20   When they heard about it, they praised God. They told him,
"You see, brother, how many tens of thousands among the Jews
21   now believe, and all are zealous for the Law. They've been told
you teach all the Jews living among the non-Jews to turn away
from Moses and tell them not to circumcise their children or
22   follow the customs. ¹ What should we do about it? They will
23   certainly hear you have come. ¹ So do what we tell you. We have
24   four men who are under a vow. Take them, purify yourself with
them, and pay their expenses so that they may shave their heads.
Then everybody will know there's nothing in what they've told
25   about you but you live strictly according to the Law. About
the non-Jews who now believe, we wrote in a letter we decided
they should keep away from food sacrificed to idols, from blood,
from the meat of strangled animals, and from sexual sin."

26   Then Paul took the men and the next day purified himself
with them and went to the temple to announce when, with the
bringing of the sacrifice for each of them, *the days* of purification
would be over.[89]

In Chains

When the seven days were almost over, the Jews from the province of Asia, seeing him in the temple, stirred up the whole crowd. They grabbed him, yelling, "Men of Israel, help! This is the man who in his teaching everybody everywhere is against our people, the Law, and this place. And now he has even brought non-Jews into the temple and made this holy place unclean." They had seen Trophimus from Ephesus with him in the city and thought Paul had taken him into the temple.

The whole city was aroused and the people rushed together. They took Paul, dragged him out of the temple, and immediately the doors were shut.

They were trying to kill him when it was reported to the tribune who was in charge of about six hundred soldiers: "All Jerusalem is stirred up!" Immediately he took soldiers and captains and ran down to them. When they saw the tribune and the soldiers, they stopped hitting Paul. Then the tribune went to him, arrested him, and ordered him bound with two chains.

He asked who he was and what he had done. Some in the crowd shouted this and some that. There was such a noisy confusion he couldn't get the facts, so he ordered Paul to be taken to the barracks. When Paul came to the stairs, the crowd was so violent the soldiers had to carry him. The mob was right behind them, yelling, "Kill him!"

Paul Defends Himself

Just as he was going to be taken into the barracks, Paul asked the tribune, "May I say something to you?"

"Can you talk Greek?" he asked. "Aren't you the Egyptian who sometime ago got four thousand dagger-men to rebel and follow him into the wilderness?"

"I'm a Jew," Paul answered, "from Tarsus in Cilicia, a citizen of an important city. Now I'm asking you, let me talk to the people."

And he let him. Then Paul, standing on the stairs, waved his hand to quiet the people. When there was a hush all around, he spoke to them in the Jewish language: "Brothers and fathers, listen as I now defend myself before you."

When they heard him call to them in their own language, they quieted down still more.

Then he said: "I'm a Jew, born in Tarsus in Cilicia but raised in this city, trained at the feet of Gamaliel in the strict ways of the Law of our fathers, as zealous for God as all of you are today. I hunted to their death men and women who believed as I do now, tying them up and putting them in prisons, ¹ as the high priest and the whole council of elders can tell about me. From them I got letters to our fellow Jews in Damascus and was going there to bind those who were there and bring them to Jerusalem to be punished. But as I was on my way and coming near Damascus, suddenly about noon a bright light from heaven flashed around me. I fell to the ground and heard a voice asking me, 'Saul! Saul! Why are you persecuting Me?'

"I asked, 'Who are You, Lord?'

" 'I am Jesus from Nazareth,' He told me, 'whom you are persecuting.' The men who were with me saw the light but didn't understand the voice of Him who was talking to me.

"Then I asked, 'What should I do, Lord?'

"The Lord told me, 'Get up, go into Damascus, and there you will be told everything you are ordered to do.'

"That light was so bright I couldn't see anything. So the men who were with me took me by the hand and led me into Damascus.

"There was Ananias, a man who feared God according to the Law, and all the Jews living there spoke well of him. He came to me and stood by me. 'Brother Saul,' he said to me, 'see again!' Immediately I could see him.

"He said, 'The God of our fathers chose you to learn what He wants, to see the Righteous One and hear Him speak to you, because you must be His witness and tell everybody what you've seen and heard. ¹ And now, what are you waiting for? Get up, and calling on His name, have yourself baptized and your sins washed away.'

"I came back to Jerusalem. While I was praying in the temple, I fell into a trance ¹ and saw Him. 'Hurry,' He told me, 'and get out of Jerusalem quickly because they will not accept the truth you tell about Me.'

" 'Lord,' I said, 'they know I went from synagog to synagog and put in prison and beat those who believe in You. And when the blood of Your witness Stephen was being poured out, I was standing by, approving, and watching the clothes of those who were murdering him.'

" 'Go,' He told me. 'I will send you far away to people who are not Jews.' "

They listened to him till he said that. Then they shouted, ²²
"Kill him! Rid the world of such a fellow! He's not fit to live!"

While they were yelling, tossing their clothes around, and ²³
throwing dust in the air, the tribune ordered him taken to the ²⁴
barracks and told his men to get information from Paul by
whipping him. He wanted to find out why the people were yelling
at him like this. But when his men had stretched him out with ²⁵
the straps, Paul asked the captain standing near, "Is it right for
you to whip a Roman citizen who hasn't been condemned?"

When the captain heard this, he went and told the tribune ²⁶
about it. "What are you going to do?" he asked. "This man is
a Roman citizen."

The tribune went and asked Paul, "Tell me, are you a Roman ²⁷
citizen?"

"Yes," he said.

The tribune declared, "I had to pay a lot of money to be ²⁸
a citizen."

"But I was born a citizen," Paul said.

Immediately those who were going to examine him withdrew ²⁹
from him. When the tribune found out Paul was a Roman citizen,
he was frightened because he had tied him up.

Paul Before the Council

The next day, since he wanted to find out exactly what the ³⁰
Jews were accusing Paul of, he untied him and ordered the high
priests and the whole council to meet. Then he brought Paul
down and had him stand before them.

Paul looked earnestly at the council and said, "Fellow Jews, **23**
I have lived before God with a very good conscience till this day."

The high priest Ananias ordered the men standing near him ²
to strike him on the mouth. Then Paul said to him, "God will ³
strike you, you whitewashed wall! Do you sit there to judge me
according to the Law and yet break the Law by ordering them
to strike me?"

The men standing near him asked, "Do you insult God's ⁴
high priest?"

"Fellow Jews," Paul answered, "I didn't know he's the ⁵
high priest. The Bible does say, *Don't speak evil of a ruler of
your people.*" ⁹⁰

When Paul saw that some of them were Sadducees and others Pharisees, he called out in the council, "Fellow Jews, I'm a Pharisee and a son of Pharisees. I'm on trial for my hope that the dead will rise."

7 When he said that, the Pharisees and Sadducees started to
8 quarrel, and the men in the meeting were divided. The Sadducees say the dead don't rise and there is no angel or spirit, while the
9 Pharisees believe in all these things. So there was some loud shouting. Some of the Bible scholars who belonged to the party of the Pharisees got up and argued vehemently: "We find nothing wrong with this man. Suppose a spirit spoke to him, or an angel —."

10 The quarrel was getting violent, and the tribune was afraid they would tear Paul to pieces. So he ordered the soldiers to go down, take him away from them by force, and bring him to the soldiers' quarters.

11 That night the Lord stood near him and said, "Keep up your courage! As you have told the truth about Me in Jerusalem, so you must tell it in Rome."

The Plot to Kill Paul

12 In the morning the Jews banded together and vowed God should punish them if they ate or drank anything before they had
13 killed Paul. There were more than forty who swore to carry out this plot.

14 They went to the high priests and elders and said, "We have vowed God should punish us if we taste any food before we
15 have killed Paul. Now then, you and the council tell the tribune to bring him down to you as if you meant to get more exact information about him. We're ready to kill him before he gets to you."

16 But the son of Paul's sister heard about the ambush. He
17 came and got into the barracks and told Paul. Then Paul called one of the captains and told him, "Take this young man to the tribune. He has something to tell him."

18 He took him to the tribune and said, "The prisoner Paul called me and asked me to bring this young man to you. He has something to tell you."

19 The tribune took him by the arm and stepping aside to be alone with him, he asked him, "What have you to tell me?"
20 "The Jews," he answered, "have agreed to ask you to bring

Paul down to the council tomorrow as if they meant to get more exact information about him. Now, don't you listen to them. 23:21 More than forty of them are ambushing him. They have vowed God should punish them if they eat or drink anything before they have murdered him. They're ready now, just waiting for you to promise them."

The tribune dismissed the young man. "Don't tell anybody 22 you reported this to me," he ordered.

Then he called two of his captains and said, "Get two hundred 23 soldiers to go to Caesarea, and seventy on horses, and two hundred with spears, and have them ready to start at nine tonight." They were also to provide animals for Paul to ride on and so to 24 take him safely to Governor Felix. The tribune wrote a letter 25 with this message:

"Claudius Lysias sends greetings to the excellent Governor 26 Felix.

"The Jews had seized this man and were going to murder 27 him, but when I found out he was a Roman citizen, I came with the soldiers and rescued him. I wanted to know what they had 28 against him; so I took him down to their council ¹ and found their 29 accusations had to do with questions about their Law, but there was none for which he deserved to die or be in chains. Since I'm 30 informed they're plotting against the man, I'm quickly sending· him to you and also ordering his accusers to state before you what they have against him."

So the foot soldiers, as they were ordered, took Paul and 31 brought him to Antipatris during the night. The next day they 32 returned to their barracks, letting the men on horses ride on with him. When these came to Caesarea, they delivered the letter 33 to the governor and handed Paul over to him.

After he read the letter, he asked which province he was from 34 and found out he was from Cilicia. "I will hear your case," 35 he said, "when your accusers come." And he ordered him kept in Herod's palace.

Before Felix

Five days later the high priest Ananias came down with some 24 elders and Tertullus, an attorney, and they reported to the governor what they had against Paul.

When Paul had been called, Tertullus started to accuse him, 2 saying, "Excellent Felix, you have brought us much peace, and

24:3 your foresight has given these people reforms ⸀ in every way and in every place. We appreciate them and thank you very much.
4 Not to keep you too long — I ask you to listen in your kindly
5 way to what we briefly have to say. We have found this man a pest who starts quarrels among all the Jews in the world, and
6 he is a ringleader of the sect of the Nazarenes. He even tried
* 8 to pollute the temple, and so we arrested him. When you examine him yourself, you will be able to find out from him everything of which we accuse him."

9 The Jews supported his attack by declaring these things were so.

10 The governor nodded to Paul to speak, and he answered, "For many years you have been a judge of this nation.
11 Knowing that, I'm glad to defend myself. ⸀ Only eleven days ago, as you can find out for yourself, I went up to Jerusalem
12 to worship. They didn't find me arguing with anyone in the temple or stirring up a crowd in the synagogs or in the city;
13 and they can't prove to you the things they're now accusing me of.
14 But I confess to you that according to the way they call a sect I worship the God of our fathers. I believe everything written
15 in the Law and the prophets ⸀ and trust God for the same thing they're looking for, that the dead will rise, the righteous and the
16 wicked. That's why I'm doing my best always to have a clear
17 conscience before God and men. After some years I came to my
18 people to bring gifts for the poor and offerings. They found me busy with these and purified in the temple, but there was no
19 crowd or noisy mob. There were some Jews from the province of Asia, who should be here before you to accuse me if they
20 have anything against me. Or these men should tell what wrong
21 they found in me as I stood before their court, unless it's the one thing I shouted when I stood among them: 'I'm on trial before you today in regard to the resurrection of the dead.' "

22 But Felix, who knew the Christian religion rather well, told them to wait for a decision. "When Tribune Lysias comes down,"
23 he said, "I will decide your case." He ordered the captain to guard him but to let him have some liberty and not keep any of his friends from helping him.

24 Some days later Felix came again. His wife Drusilla, who

* Our oldest manuscripts do not have vv. 6b-8a: "And we wanted to try him under our Law. But Tribune Lysias came along and with much force took him out of our hands, ordering his accusers to come before you."

was a Jew, was with him. He sent for Paul and heard him tell about faith in Christ Jesus. As he spoke of righteousness, self- 24:25 control, and the coming judgment, Felix was frightened and answered, "Go now. When I get a chance, I'll send for you." ¹ At the same time he expected Paul to give him money. And so 26 he used to send for him often and talk with him.

Two whole years passed. Then Porcius Festus succeeded 27 Felix. Since Felix wanted the Jews to remember him for a kindness, he left Paul in prison.

Paul Appeals to the Emperor

Three days after Festus took over his duties in the province **25** of Judea he went from Caesarea up to Jerusalem. The high 2 priests and the leaders of the Jews reported to Festus what they had against Paul. They urged ¹ and begged him to do them 3 a favor and have Paul brought to Jerusalem. They were laying an ambush to kill him on the way.

But Festus answered that Paul would be kept in Caesarea 4 and he himself would be going there soon. "Those of you who 5 have the authority," he said, "come down with me, and if the man has done anything wrong, accuse him."

He stayed with them no more than eight or ten days and then 6 went down to Caesarea. The next day he sat on the judge's chair and ordered Paul brought in.

When Paul came in, the Jews who had come down from 7 Jerusalem surrounded him and were accusing him of many serious wrongs that they couldn't prove. Paul defended himself: "I have 8 in no way sinned against the Law of the Jews or the temple or the emperor."

But Festus wanted the Jews to remember him for a kindness. 9 So he asked Paul, "Do you want to go up to Jerusalem to be tried there before me in regard to these things?"

"I'm standing before the emperor's judgment seat," Paul said, 10 "and there I must be tried. I haven't done the Jews any wrong, as you, too, know very well. Now if I'm guilty and have done 11 something to deserve to die, I don't refuse to die. But if their accusations are nothing, nobody can hand me over to them. I appeal to the emperor!"

Festus talked it over with his council and then answered, 12 "You appealed to the emperor; you will go to the emperor!"

Some time later King Agrippa and Bernice came down to 13

Caesarea to welcome Festus. When they stayed there a number of days, Festus laid Paul's case before the king.

"There's a man here whom Felix left in prison," he said.
15 "When I went up to Jerusalem, the high priests and elders of the Jews informed me about him and asked me to condemn him.

16 "I answered them, 'It isn't customary for Romans to hand over a man before he has faced his accusers and had a chance to defend himself against their accusation.'

17 "They came here with me, and the next day without any delay I sat down in the judge's chair and ordered the man to 18 be brought. When his accusers got up, they didn't accuse him 19 of the crimes I was suspecting. But they disagreed with him about their own religion and about a certain Jesus who died; 20 Paul claimed He is alive. I was puzzled how I should look into this and asked if he would like to go to Jerusalem and be tried 21 there in regard to these things. But Paul appealed. He wanted to be held and have Augustus * decide his case. So I ordered him to be kept in prison till I send him to the emperor."

22 Agrippa told Festus, "I myself would like to hear the man."

"Tomorrow," he answered, "you will hear him."

Before Agrippa

23 The next day Agrippa and Bernice came with great pomp and went with the tribunes and leading men of the city into the hall. Then Festus gave the order, and Paul was brought in.

24 "King Agrippa and all you men here with us," Festus said, "you see this man about whom all the Jewish people in Jerusalem and here have appealed to me, shouting he mustn't live any 25 longer. I found he hasn't done anything to deserve to die, but 26 when he appealed to Augustus, I decided to send him. I don't have anything reliable to write our lord about him. So I have brought him before you, and especially before you, King Agrippa, so we could examine him and I'll have something to write. 27 It makes no sense to me to send a prisoner without reporting what he's accused of."

26 Agrippa said to Paul, "You may speak for yourself."

Then Paul, stretching out his hand, began to defend himself:

2 "King Agrippa, I think I'm fortunate I'm going to defend

* Another title for Nero.

myself today before you in regard to everything the Jews accuse me of, because you are so very familiar with all the Jewish customs and problems. So I ask you to listen to me patiently.

"The Jews all know how I lived from my youth, from my 4 earliest days, among my people in Jerusalem. They have known 5 long ago, if they want to tell the truth, that I lived the life of a Pharisee, the strictest party of our religion.

"And now I'm on trial here because I trust the promise God 6 made to our fathers. Our twelve tribes, worshiping zealously 7 day and night, expect to see this promise come true. This is the hope, King, in regard to which some Jews accuse me. Why do 8 you think it incredible that God raises the dead?

"Once I believed I had to work hard against the name of 9 Jesus from Nazareth. I did that in Jerusalem. By the power 10 I got from the high priests I locked up many of the holy people in prison, and when they were to be killed, I voted against them. And many a time in every synagog I would punish them to make 11 them blaspheme, and raging furiously against them, I hunted them down even to foreign cities.

"That is how I came to be traveling to Damascus, authorized 12 and appointed by the high priests, when on the way, King, at 13 noon I saw a light brighter than the sun, flashing from heaven around me and those who were going with me. All of us fell to 14 the ground, and I heard a voice asking me in the Jewish language, 'Saul, Saul! Why are you persecuting Me? You're only hurting yourself by kicking against the goads.'

"I asked, 'Who are you, Lord?' 15

" 'I am Jesus,' the Lord answered, 'whom you are persecuting. But get up and *stand on your feet*.[91] I showed Myself to you to 16 appoint you to serve Me and tell the truth of what you have seen and what you will see whenever I appear to you. *I will* 17 *rescue you* from your people and *from the non-Jews to whom I'm sending you*,[92] *to open their eyes* and turn them *from dark*- 18 *ness to light* [93] and from the devil's control to God to have their sins forgiven and get a share of what the people enjoy who are made holy by believing in Me.'

"And so, King Agrippa, I didn't disobey what I saw from 19 heaven, but first I told the people in Damascus and Jerusalem, 20 then the whole country of the Jews, and the other nations to turn from sin to God and do the works that show they have repented.

For this the Jews grabbed me in the temple and tried to murder me.

22   "God has helped me to this day, and so I have been standing and telling the truth to high and low, stating only what the
23   prophets and Moses said would happen, that Christ had to suffer and by being the first to rise from the dead would announce light to our people and the other nations."

24   As he was defending himself in this way, Festus shouted, "You're crazy, Paul! Your great learning is driving you crazy!"

25   "I'm not crazy, excellent Festus," Paul said, "but I'm telling
26   the sober truth. The king knows about these things, and I'm talking boldly to him. I'm sure he hasn't missed any of them, since
27   this wasn't done in a corner. King Agrippa, do you believe the prophets? I know you believe them!"

28   "You're trying to persuade me," Agrippa said to Paul, "that with a little effort you've made me a Christian!"

29   "I wish to God," Paul said, "that with little or much effort not only you but all who hear me today would become what I am — except for these chains!"

30   The king, the governor, Bernice, and those who sat with them
31   got up ¹ and left and said to one another, "This man isn't doing anything to deserve to die or be in chains."

32   "This man could be free," Agrippa told Festus, "if he hadn't appealed to the emperor."

Paul Sails for Rome

27   When it was decided we should sail to Italy, Paul and some other prisoners were turned over to a captain by the name of
2   Julius, of the troop of Augustus. We boarded a ship from Adramyttium that was going to sail to the ports on the coast of the province of Asia, and we started out. Aristarchus, a Macedonian from Thessalonica, went with us.

3   The next day we landed at Sidon, where Julius treated Paul kindly and let him go to his friends to get any care he needed.
4   Leaving Sidon, we sailed on the sheltered side of Cyprus be-
5   cause the winds were against us. We crossed the sea off Cilicia
6   and Pamphylia and landed at Myra in Lycia. There the captain of the soldiers found a ship from Alexandria sailing to Italy and
7   put us on it. We were sailing slowly for a number of days and

had some difficulty getting near Cnidus. The wind wouldn't let us go on, and so, starting at Cape Salmone, we sailed on the sheltered side of Crete. Hugging the coast, we struggled on to 27:8 a place called Fair Havens, near the town of Lasea.

We had lost a lot of time, even the day of fasting * had 9 already gone by, and sailing was now dangerous. So Paul ad- 10 vised them: "Men, I see that in this sailing we're going to suffer hardship and a heavy loss not only of the cargo and ship but also of our lives." But the captain of the soldiers listened to 11 the pilot and the captain of the ship and not to what Paul said. Since that harbor was not a good place to spend the winter, the 12 majority decided to sail away, hoping they could somehow reach Phoenix to spend the winter there. It is a harbor of Crete facing southwest and northwest. When a gentle breeze blew 13 from the south, they felt they could easily make it. They took up the anchor and sailed close to the shore of Crete.

But after a little while a hurricane, called the Northeastern, 14 dashed down from Crete. It caught the ship so that it couldn't 15 face the wind, and we gave up and were swept along. As we ran 16 into the shelter of a small island called Clauda, we managed with a struggle to get hold of the small boat. They pulled it up on 17 deck. Then they passed ropes around the ship to reinforce it. Fearing they would run on the great sandbank near Africa, they lowered the sail and so drifted along. We continued to be 18 tossed by the storm so violently that the next day the men started to throw the cargo overboard, and on the third with their own 19 hands they threw the ship's equipment overboard. For a number 20 of days we couldn't see any sun or stars and were in a great storm until at last we were giving up all hope of coming through alive.

Since hardly anybody wanted to eat, Paul stepped before 21 them and said, "Men, you should have listened to me and not have sailed from Crete. You would have avoided this hardship and damage. But now I urge you to cheer up because you will 22 lose no lives but only the ship. I am God's own and serve Him. 23 Last night His angel stood by me. ¹ 'Don't be afraid, Paul!' he 24 said. 'You must stand before the emperor, and now God has given you all who are sailing with you.' So, cheer up, men, 25 because I trust God it will be just as He told me. But we must 26 run on some island."

* The Day of Atonement, September 15, in the year 58.

The Shipwreck

27:27   It was the fourteenth night and we were drifting through the Adriatic Sea * when about midnight the sailors suspected land 28 was coming closer. They dropped the lead and found the water 120 feet deep. A little farther they dropped it again and found 29 it was 90 feet. Fearing we might run on rocks, they dropped four anchors from the back of the ship and prayed for morning to come.

30   Then the sailors tried to escape from the ship. They let the boat down into the sea, pretending they were going to take out the anchors from the front of the ship and let them down. 31 But Paul told the captain of the soldiers and his men, "If these 32 don't stay on the ship, you can't be rescued." Then the soldiers cut the ropes that held the boat and let it drift away.

33   Just before daybreak Paul was urging them all to eat something. "This is the fourteenth day you've waited and gone hungry 34 and not eaten a thing. ' So I urge you to eat something. It will help you come through this safely. None of you will lose a hair 35 of his head." After saying this, he took some bread, thanked God 36 in front of everybody, broke it, and started to eat. They were 37 all cheered up, and they too had something to eat. There were 38 276 of us in the ship. After they had eaten all they wanted, they lightened the ship by dumping the wheat into the sea.

39   In the morning they couldn't tell what land it was but gradually could see a bay with a beach on which they planned if 40 possible to run the ship ashore. They cut off the anchors and left them in the sea. At the same time they untied the ropes that held up the steering oars, spread out the foresail to catch 41 the wind, and steered the ship to the shore. They struck a bank in the water and ran the ship aground. The front of the ship stuck and couldn't be moved, while the back was being pounded to pieces by the sea.

42   To keep any of the prisoners from swimming away and 43 escaping, the soldiers planned to kill them, ' but the captain of the soldiers wanted to save Paul, so he kept them from doing this. He ordered those who could swim to jump out first and get 44 to the shore, ' and the rest to follow, some on planks and some on other pieces from the ship. In this way all of them came safely to the shore.

    * At that time the "Adriatic" Sea included the present Adriatic plus a large part of the Mediterranean Sea south of it.

Safe on Malta

Once we were safe on the shore, we recognized the island; **28**
it was called Malta. The natives were unusually kind to us. 2
It had started to rain and was cold, and so they made a fire and
welcomed all of us around it.

Paul gathered an armful of dry branches and put them on 3
the fire. The heat made a viper come out, and it bit his hand.
When the natives saw the snake hanging from his hand, they 4
said to one another, "This man certainly is a murderer! He did
escape from the sea, but Justice didn't let him live."

So he shook the snake into the fire and suffered no harm. 5
They were waiting for him to swell up or suddenly fall down 6
dead. But they waited long and saw nothing unusual happen
to him. Then they changed their minds and said he was a god.

The governor of the island, whose name was Publius, had 7
land around that place. He welcomed us and treated us kindly
while we were his guests for three days. The father of Publius 8
happened to be sick in bed with fever and dysentery. Paul went
to him, prayed, and laid his hands on him, and made him well.

After that had happened, the other sick people on the island 9
also came to him and were made well. They honored us in 10
many ways, and when we were going to sail, they put on board
whatever we needed.

From Malta to Rome

After three months we sailed on a ship from Alexandria that 11
had stopped at the island for the winter. It had in front a figure
of the Twin Sons of Zeus.* We stopped at Syracuse and stayed 12
there three days. From there we sailed around and came to 13
Rhegium. After a day a south wind started blowing, and on
the second day we came to Puteoli. There we found fellow 14
Christians who urged us to stay seven days with them.

And so we came to Rome. The fellow Christians in Rome, 15
who had heard about us, came as far as the Market Town of
Appius and the Three Shops to meet us. When Paul saw them,
he thanked God and felt encouraged.

In Rome

When we came into Rome, Paul was allowed to live by 16
himself with the soldier guarding him. After three days he called 17

* Castor and Pollux, the guardian gods of sailors.

the leaders of the Jews together. When they came, he said to them, "Fellow Jews, although I haven't done anything against our people or the customs of our fathers, I'm a prisoner from 28:18 Jerusalem who was handed over to the Romans. They examined me and wanted to let me go because I had done no wrong to 19 deserve to die. But the Jews objected and forced me to appeal to the emperor — not that I'm accusing my people of anything. 20 That's why I asked to see you and talk to you, since it is for the hope of Israel I wear this chain."

21 "We have had no letters from Judea about you," they told him, "and no Jew coming here has reported or said anything 22 bad about you. We would like to hear from you what you think, because we know that everywhere people are talking against this sect."

23 They set a day to meet with him, and more of them came to him where he was staying. From morning till evening he explained the matter to them, earnestly telling the truth about God's kingdom and trying to convince them about Jesus from 24 the Law of Moses and the prophets. Some of them were convinced by what he said, but others wouldn't believe.

25 They disagreed with one another as they were leaving, and Paul added a statement: "The Holy Spirit spoke the truth to 26 your fathers through the prophet Isaiah ¹ when he said, *Go to these people and say.*

> *You will hear and never understand,*
> *look and never see,*
27 *Because these people have become dull at heart*
> *and hard of hearing*
> *and have shut their eyes,*
> *So that their eyes don't see,*
> *their ears don't hear,*
> *their minds don't understand,*
> *And they don't turn to Me and let Me heal them.*⁹⁴

28 "You should know that *God's salvation* has been sent *to the*
* *non-Jews,*⁹⁵ and they will listen."

30 For two whole years he lived in his own rented place and 31 welcomed all who came to him. He preached God's kingdom and very boldly taught the truth about the Lord Jesus Christ, and nobody stopped him.

* Our oldest manuscripts do not have v. 29: "And after he said this, the Jews left, arguing vigorously among themselves."

OLD TESTAMENT REFERENCES

1. Ps. 69:25
2. Ps. 109:8
3. Joel 2:28-32
4. Ps. 16:8-11
5. Ps. 89:3-4; 132:11
6. Ps. 16:10
7. Ps. 110:1
8. Is. 57:19
9. Joel 2:32
10. Ex. 3:6
11. Is. 52:13
12. Deut. 18:15, 18-19
13. Lev. 23:29; Deut. 18:19
14. Gen. 12:3; 18:18; 22:18; 26:4; 28:14
15. Ps. 118:22
16. Ex. 20:11; Ps. 146:6; Neh. 9:6
17. Ps. 2:1-2
18. Deut. 21:22
19. Ps. 29:3
20. Gen. 12:1
21. Deut. 2:5
22. Gen. 12:7; 13:15; 17:8; 48:4
23. Gen. 15:13-14; Ex. 2:22; 12:40
24. Ex. 3:12
25. Gen. 17:10
26. Gen. 21:4
27. Gen. 37:11, 28; 45:4
28. Gen. 39:2-3, 21
29. Gen. 39:21
30. Gen. 41:46
31. Gen. 41:40-41, 43; Ps. 105:21
32. Gen. 41:54; 42:5
33. Gen. 42:2
34. Gen. 45:1
35. Gen. 46:6, 27; Ex. 1:5; Deut. 10:22
36. Gen. 50:13; Joshua 24:32
37. Ex. 1:7-8, 10-11
38. Ex. 2:2
39. Ex. 2:5, 10
40. Ex. 2:11-12
41. Ex. 2:13-15, 22; 18:3
42. Ex. 2:24; 3:1-8, 10; 4:19
43. Ex. 2:14
44. Ex. 7:3; Num. 14:33
45. Deut. 18:15, 18
46. Num. 14:3-4
47. Ex. 32:1, 23, 4, 6
48. Jer. 7:18; 19:13
49. Amos 5:25-27
50. Ex. 27:21
51. Ex. 25:1, 40
52. Ps. 132:5
53. 1 Kings 6:1
54. Is. 66:1-2
55. Ex. 33:3, 5; Lev. 26:41; Jer. 9:26; 6:10
56. Num. 27:14; Is. 63:10
57. Ps. 78:37
58. Deut. 29:18
59. Is. 58:6
60. Is. 53:7-8
61. Deut. 10:17
62. Ps. 107:20; 147:18
63. Is. 52:7; Nah. 1:15
64. Is. 61:1
65. Deut. 21:22-23
66. Hosea 14:9
67. Ex. 6:1, 6; 14:8
68. Deut. 1:31
69. Deut. 7:1; Joshua 14:1
70. 1 Sam. 13:14; Ps. 89:20
71. Is. 44:28
72. Ps. 107:20
73. Ps. 2:7
74. Is. 55:3
75. Ps. 16:10
76. 1 Kings 2:10
77. Hab. 1:5
78. Is. 49:6
79. Ezek. 2:1-2
80. Ex. 20:11
81. Jer. 12:15
82. Amos 9:11-12; Is. 45:21
83. Judges 18:6
84. Is. 42:5
85. Ps. 9:8; 96:13; 98:9
86. Ex. 3:12; Joshua 1:5; Is. 41:10; 43:5; Jer. 1:8
87. Ps. 74:1-2
88. Deut. 33:3-4
89. Num. 6:13
90. Ex. 22:28
91. Ezek. 2:1-2
92. 1 Chron. 16:35; Jer. 1:7-8
93. Is. 35:5; 42:7, 16
94. Is. 6:9-10
95. Ps. 67:2; 98:2-3

PAUL

writes to the

ROMANS

CORINTH
A. D. 56

1 PAUL, SERVANT OF JESUS CHRIST, called to be an apostle and appointed to tell God's good news —

2 He promised it long ago through His prophets in the holy
3 Bible. It is about His Son, who was born a descendant of
4 David according to His flesh ‖ but according to His spirit of holiness was by a rising of the dead declared to be the mighty
5 Son of God. And He is our Lord Jesus Christ, ‖ who loved us and made us apostles so that people will believe and obey
6 and so glorify Him among all nations. This includes you who have been called to belong to Jesus Christ

7 — to all in Rome whom God loves and has called to be His holy people: May God our Father and the Lord Jesus Christ continue to love you and give you peace!

I Want to See You

8 First, I thank my God through Jesus Christ for all of you because the news of your faith is spreading all over the world.
9 God, whom I serve in my spirit by telling the good news of His
10 Son, knows how I never fail to mention you ‖ whenever I pray and to ask that somehow by God's will I will now at last succeed
11 in coming to you. I long to see you, to share a spiritual gift
12 with you to strengthen you. I mean when I'm with you I'll be
13 encouraged by your faith and you by mine. I want you to know, fellow Christians, so far I have been kept from coming to you, but I often planned to come in order to enjoy some results of working among you as I do among the other non-Jewish people.
14 I must help Greeks and non-Greeks, the wise and the foolish.
15 So I'm eager to bring the good news also to you in Rome.

268

I am not ashamed of the good news. It is God's power to save everyone who believes it, the Jew first and also the Greek. It reveals God's righteousness as being by faith and for faith, as the Bible says, *By faith you are righteous and you will live.*[1]

God Is Angry

God in heaven shows He is angry at all the ungodliness and wickedness of people who by their wickedness hold back the truth. What can be known about God is clear to them because God has made it clear to them. Ever since He made the world, they have seen the unseen things of God — from the things He made they can tell He has everlasting power and is God. Then they have no excuse. They knew God and didn't honor Him as God or thank Him, but their thoughts turned to worthless things, [1] and their ignorant hearts were darkened. Claiming to be wise, they showed how silly they are [1] when *for the glory* of God, who cannot die, *they substituted images* [2] of man, who dies, and of birds, four-footed animals, and reptiles. And so God, letting them follow the lusts of their hearts, gave them up to live immorally and dishonor their bodies [1] because they traded the true God for a lie, worshiped and served what the Creator made instead of the Creator, who is blessed forever. Amen! [1] That is why God gave them up to shameful lusts. Women have changed their natural way to an unnatural one. And men likewise have given up the natural relation with a woman and burned with lust for one another, men doing the shameful act with men and for their error getting punished in themselves as they must. As they refused to know God any longer, God gave them up so that their minds were degraded and they lived immorally. Their lives are full of all kinds of wrongdoing, wickedness, greed, malice. They are full of envy, murder, quarreling, treachery, viciousness. They gossip [1] and slander. They hate God. They are insulting, proud, boasting. They invent new sins. They disobey parents. [1] They are foolish. They break their promises. They have no love or mercy. Knowing God's righteous decree that those who do such things deserve to die, they not only do them but approve when others do them.

God Will Judge the Jews

So, whoever you are, if you condemn anyone, you have no excuse. What you condemn in anyone else you condemn in

2:2 yourself, since you, the judge, are doing the same things. We know God is right when He condemns people for doing such
3 things. When you condemn people for doing such things but do them yourself, do you think you will escape being condemned
4 by God? Or do you think lightly of God, who is very kind to you, patiently puts up with you, and waits so long before He punishes you? Can't you see God is kind to you to get you to feel sorry for your sins?

5 But you stubbornly refuse to turn from sin, and so you make God more and more angry with you till the day of His anger,
6 when God will show how righteous He is in judging you. *He will*
7 *give everyone according to what he has done:* [3] everlasting life to those who by patiently doing good look for glory, honor, and
8 immortality, | but anger and fury to those who, because they are
9 selfish and refuse to listen to the truth, follow wickedness. There will be sorrow and anguish for every human being doing wrong,
10 for the Jew first and also the Greek; but glory, honor, and peace for everyone doing good, for the Jew first and also the Greek.
11 God doesn't prefer one to another.
12 All who sin without having the Law will perish without the Law. And all who sin having the Law will be judged by the Law.
13 We aren't righteous before God if we only hear the Law, but if
14 we do what the Law says, we'll be righteous.* When people who are not Jews and don't have the Law do by nature what the Law
15 says, they who don't have the Law are a law to themselves. They show that what the law wants them to do is written in their hearts. Their conscience tells the same truth, and their thoughts between
16 themselves accuse them or defend them, as we'll see on the day when God through Christ Jesus judges the secrets of people according to the good news I tell.

Who Is a Jew?

17 Suppose you call yourself a Jew, rest comfortably in your
18 Law, feel proud of your God, | know what He wants, and approve
19 of the better things, being instructed in the Law, | and feel sure
20 you're a guide to the blind and a light to those in the dark, that you can train the foolish and teach children because you have in
21 the Law the body of knowledge and truth. You teach someone else — won't you teach yourself? You preach, "Don't steal" —
22 are you stealing? You say, "Don't commit adultery" — are you

* See note at 3:20.

doing it yourself? You are disgusted with idols .— are you robbing their temples? You feel proud of the Law — are you breaking 2:23 the Law and so dishonoring God? *You make the non-Jews slander* 24 *God's name,*[4] as the Bible says.

Circumcision helps you only if you do what the Law says. 25 If you are breaking the Law, you have lost your circumcision. If an uncircumcised man does what the Law demands, will he 26 not be considered circumcised? If a man who has never been 27 circumcised really does what the Law says, he will condemn you with your written Law and circumcision for breaking the Law. He is no Jew who is one only outwardly, nor is that circumcision 28 which is only outward and physical. But he is a Jew who is one 29 inwardly, and a man is circumcised in his heart by the Spirit, not just by doing what the words say. Such a person will not be praised by men but by God.

What is the advantage then of being a Jew? Or what good 3 is there in being circumcised? ' Much in every way! The most 2 important advantage is that God entrusted His Word to the Jews.

God Is Faithful

What if some were unfaithful? Will their unfaithfulness make 3 God unfaithful? ' Never! God must be true and *any man a liar,*[5] 4 as the Bible says,

> *That You may be right when You speak*
> *And prove You are superior when You judge.*[6]

But if our wrong shows how right God is, what'll we say? 5 Is God wrong (I'm talking like a man) when He's angry and He punishes? ' Never! Otherwise how could God judge the world? 6 But if my lie honors God by showing how much truth there's 7 in Him, why am I still condemned as a sinner? And "shouldn't 8 we do evil that good may come of it?" Some slander us and claim we say that. They are condemned as they deserve.

All Are Sinners

What then? Do we have any advantage? Not at all. We have 9 already accused everybody, Jews and Greeks, that they are under sin, ' as the Bible says: *No one is righteous, no, not one. No one* 10-11 *understands. No one is searching for God.* ' *All have turned away* 12 *and have one and all become worthless. No one is doing anything good, not a single one.*[7] ' *Their throats are an open grave. They* 13

have spoken to deceive.[8] *Their lips hide the poison of snakes.*[9]
3:14-15 *Their mouths are full of cursing and bitterness.*[10] *Their feet run*
16 *fast to pour out blood. Wherever they go, there is destruction and*
17-18 *misery. They have not learned the way of peace.*[11] *God does not*
terrify them.[12]

19   We know that everything the Law says it says to those who
are under the Law so that nobody can say anything and the whole
20 world must let God judge it. What *anyone* does to keep the Law
will not make him righteous * *before God,*[13] because the Law
shows us our sin.

God Makes Us Righteous

21   But now God has shown us His righteousness; the Law and
22 the prophets tell about it, but it is without the Law. God's righteousness comes to all who believe, just by their believing in
Jesus Christ.

23   There is no difference. All have sinned and are without God's
24 glory. They become righteous * by a gift of His love, by the
25 ransom Christ Jesus paid to free them. God set Him up publicly
to pour out His blood before God to take away sins through faith,
to show His righteousness even though He had patiently passed
26 by the sins done in the past. Now He wanted to show His righteousness, to be righteous Himself and make righteous * anyone
who believes in Jesus.

27   What then becomes of our pride? It is excluded. How? By
28 the way of works? No, by the way of faith. 'We are convinced
anyone is righteous * by faith without doing what the Law says.

29   Or is God only the God of the Jews? Isn't He also the God
30 of the non-Jews? Certainly also of the non-Jews. 'There is only
one God, and He will make the circumcised man righteous *
on the basis of faith and the uncircumcised by the same faith.

31   Do we then by faith cancel the Law? Never! We uphold
the Law.

If We Believe, We're Righteous

4   What should we say Abraham, our natural ancestor, found?
2   If he got to be righteous * by what he did, he had something to

---

* "Righteous" is a court term. God, who gives us the righteousness of
Christ (3:23-24; 4:5; Phil. 3:9), as a judge declares us righteous and by
His creative verdict makes us righteous.

be proud of. But he couldn't feel proud before God. | What does 4:3
the Bible say? *Abraham believed God and so he was counted*
righteous.[14]

If you work, your pay isn't considered a gift but a debt. But 4-5
if instead of working you believe in Him who makes the ungodly
righteous, your faith is counted as righteousness. So David calls 6
the man happy whom God counts righteous apart from what
he does: *Happy are you if your wrongs are forgiven and your sins* 7
are covered. Happy are you if the Lord doesn't count sins 8
against you.[15]

Can only a circumcised person be happy in this way or also 9
an uncircumcised person? We say, *Abraham's faith was counted*
as his righteousness.[14] | How was it counted? Was he circumcised 10
then, or not? He wasn't circumcised but uncircumcised. | And he 11
received *circumcision as a mark* to confirm the righteousness he
got by believing *before he was circumcised.*[16] He was to be the
father of all who without being circumcised believe *and so are*
counted righteous[14] | as well as the father of the Jews who are not 12
only circumcised but also walk in the footsteps of our father
Abraham by believing as he did before he was circumcised.

It wasn't by the Law that Abraham or his descendants got 13
the promise that the world should be theirs but by the righteousness of faith. If the Law is the way to get it, then faith 14
can't get anything and the promise can't give anything. No, the 15
Law brings God's anger on us, and only where there is no Law
there is no breaking of the Law. God promises to those who 16
believe, in order to bring them a gift of His love. And the
promise should hold for all descendants, not only those who cling
to the Law but also those who only believe as Abraham did.
He is the father of all of us, | as it is written, *I have made you* 17
a father of many nations.[17] Standing before God, Abraham believed God makes the dead live and calls into being that which
doesn't exist. Hoping contrary to what he could expect, he had 18
the faith to become *a father of many nations,*[17] as he had been
told, *So many descendants you will have.*[18] He didn't get weak 19
in faith, although he realized that, being about a hundred years
old, he couldn't have children any more, and Sarah couldn't have
any either. There was no unbelief to make him doubt what 20
God promised, but by faith he got strong and gave glory to God.
He was fully convinced God could do what He promised. That 21-22
is why *he was counted righteous.* But the words *he was counted* 23

4:24 *righteous* were written not only for him ¹ but also for us. We are to be *counted righteous* if we *believe* ¹⁴ in Him who raised
25 from the dead our Lord Jesus, who was *handed over to die* ¹⁹ for our sins and was raised to make us righteous.

Our Hope

5 Now that we who believe are righteous,* we have peace with
2 God through our Lord Jesus Christ, who gave us the way to come to God's love in which we stand. And we feel proud as we hope for God's glory.

3 More than that, we also feel proud of our sufferings. We
4 know suffering stirs up the power to endure, and if we endure, we prove our strength, and if we prove our strength, we have
5 hope. In this *hope we're not disappointed,*²⁰ because the Holy Spirit, who has been given to us, poured God's love into our hearts.

6 At the right time, while we were still helpless, Christ died
7 for the ungodly. A man will hardly die for a righteous person;
8 oh, for a kind person somebody may dare to die. But God shows how He loves us by this, that while we were still sinners Christ died for us.

9 Now that His blood has made us righteous,* we are all the
10 more certain He will save us from God's anger. If while we were His enemies we were made God's friends by the death of His Son, now that we are His friends we are all the more certain
11 He will save us by His life. More than that, we rejoice in God through our Lord Jesus Christ, who has now given us this friendship.

Adam and Christ

12 One man brought sin into the world, and his sin brought death. And so because all have sinned, death spread to all people.
13 There was sin in the world before the Law was given, but where
14 there is no Law, sin isn't counted. Still death ruled from Adam to Moses even over those who when they sinned didn't break a law as Adam did.

15 He was a picture of Him who was to come. ¹ But the gift is more than the sin. If one man's sin brought death to all people, we are all the more certain God's love and the free gift of His

* See note at 3:20.

love in one Man, Jesus Christ, have been richly poured out on all people. The gift also does more than that one man's sin. ^{5:16} The sentence, due to one man, condemns us, but the gift, following many sins, makes us righteous. If one man by his sin made ¹⁷ death a king, we, on whom God has poured His love and His gift of righteousness, are all the more certain the one Jesus Christ makes us live and be kings.

Now then, as by one sin all people were condemned, so by ¹⁸ one righteous work all people were judged to be righteous and alive. | When one man disobeyed, all were made sinners. So when ¹⁹ One obeyed, all will be made righteous. The Law came to mul- ²⁰ tiply sin, but where there was much sin, God's gift of love was so much greater | that, as sin ruled in its deadly way, so His love ²¹ is to rule, giving a righteousness by which we live forever through our Lord Jesus Christ.

Live for God

What does it mean? Should we go on sinning so that God ⁶ may love us all the more? Certainly not! | We died to sin. How ² can we live in it any longer?

Or don't you know that all of us who were baptized into ³ Christ Jesus by our baptism share in His death? Sharing in His ⁴ death by our baptism, we were buried with Him so that as the Father's glory raised Christ from the dead we, too, will live a new life. If we were united with Him to die as He did, then ⁵ we'll also rise as He did. We know our old self was nailed with ⁶ Him to the cross to stop our sinful body and keep us from serving sin any longer. When we're dead, we're free from sin. But if ⁷⁻⁸ we died with Christ, we believe we'll also live with Him | because ⁹ we know that Christ, risen from the dead, will not die again. . Death has no hold on Him any more. When He died, He died ¹⁰ to sin once, never to die again, and the life He lives He lives for God. So you, too, because you are in Christ Jesus, think of your- ¹¹ selves as dead to sin and living for God.

Then sin should no longer rule in your dying bodies and make ¹² you do what they wish. Don't let sin keep on using your organs ¹³ as tools for doing wrong. But as people who have come back from the dead and live, give yourselves to God, and let God use your organs as tools for doing what is right. Sin will never rule ¹⁴ over you, because you are not under the Law but under God's love.

What then? Are we going to sin because we are not under ¹⁵

6:16 the Law but under God's love? Certainly not! Don't you know if you give yourselves to anyone to obey him as slaves, you are his slaves? Either you are the slaves of sin and will die, or you
17 obey God and become righteous. But thank God! Although you once were the slaves of sin, you have heartily obeyed the pattern
18 of teaching to which you were entrusted. Freed from sin, you were made the servants of righteousness. I talk in a human way
19 because you are naturally weak. But just as you once let uncleanness and wickedness use your organs as slaves to do wrong, so now let righteousness use your organs as slaves in order to
20 live holy. When you were slaves of sin, you weren't free to serve
21 righteousness as your master. What was your advantage then in doing the things that make you blush now? Why, they end
22 in death. But now that you've been made free from sin and servants of God, your advantage is that you live holy and finally
23 have everlasting life. Sin pays off with death, but God gives everlasting life in Christ Jesus, our Lord.

7 Or don't you know, my fellow Christians — I'm speaking to people who know the Law — that you have to obey the Law
2 only as long as you live? The Law, for example, binds a married woman to her husband while he is living, but if her husband dies,
3 the Law doesn't bind her to her husband any more. So, while her husband is living, she will be called an adulteress if she lives with another man. But if her husband dies, she is free and no longer bound by the Law, and so she's no adulteress if she marries another man.

4 So you too, my fellow Christians, have through Christ's body died to the Law to marry Another — Him who rose from the
5 dead so that we will produce good things for God. While we were living in the flesh, the Law stirred the sinful lusts in our
6 organs into action to produce fruit for Death. But now that we have died to the Law which bound us, we are freed from it, not to serve in the old way under the Law but in the new way of the Spirit.

The Law Shows What Sin Is

7 What does it mean? Is the Law sin? Certainly not! But only by the Law did I learn what sin is. For example, only when the Law said, *Don't lust,*[21] did I know how wrong it is to lust.
8 Taking the commandment as a challenge, sin worked in me every
9 kind of wrong desire. Without the Law sin is dead. Once I was

alive without the Law, but when the commandment came, sin became alive, ' and I died. And the commandment which is to 7:10 bring life actually brought me death. Taking the commandment 11 as a challenge, sin seduced me and with the commandment killed me.

So the Law itself is holy, and the commandment is holy, right, 12 and good. ' Now, did this good thing kill me? Certainly not! But 13 sin, to be sin, clearly used this good thing to kill me so that sin would by the commandment become extremely sinful.

Struggling with Sin

We know the Law is spiritual, but I am flesh, sold to be 14 a slave of sin. I am doing something strange, because I don't 15 do what I like but what I hate. But if I do what I don't like, 16 I agree that the Law is right. It is really no longer I doing it, 17 but sin living in me. I know that nothing good lives in me, that 18 is, in my flesh. I'm willing, but I'm not doing what is right. 19 I don't do the good things I like, but I do the evil I don't like. Now if I do what I don't like, it is no longer I doing it but sin 20 living in me.

So I find it a rule: When I want to do what is right, evil is 21 there with me. In my inner being I delight in God's Law, but 22-23 all through my body I see another law fighting against the Law in my mind and making me a prisoner to the sin ruling my body. ' What a miserable man I am! Who will rescue me from the body 24 that brings me to this death? Thank God — He does it through 25 our Lord Jesus Christ! So I serve the Law of God with my mind but with my flesh the law of sin.

The Spirit Gives Life

Now those who are in Christ Jesus cannot be condemned. 8 The rule of the Spirit, who gives life, has in Christ Jesus freed 2 you from the rule of sin that kills. What the Law, weakened 3 by the flesh, could not do God has done by sending His Son to be like sinful flesh and to be a sacrifice for sin. He condemned sin in the flesh ' so that we who don't follow the flesh but the 4 Spirit will be as righteous as the Law demands. Those who 5 follow the flesh have their minds on the things of the flesh, but those who follow the Spirit have their minds on the things of, the Spirit. What the flesh thinks kills; what the Spirit thinks gives 6 life and peace. This is so because the fleshly mind hates God. 7

8:8 It refuses to obey God's Law because it can't obey it. ᴵ Those
9 who are in the flesh can't please God. You are not in the flesh
but in the Spirit if God's Spirit lives in you. But anyone who
10 doesn't have the Spirit of Christ doesn't belong to Him. But if
Christ is in you, even though your bodies are dead because you
11 were sinful, your spirits are alive because you are righteous. And
if the Spirit of Him who raised Jesus from the dead lives in you,
He who raised Christ Jesus from the dead will also make your
dying bodies alive by His Spirit living in you.

12 And so, fellow Christians, we don't owe it to the flesh to live
13 according to the flesh. If you live according to the flesh, you
will die. But if by the Spirit you kill the activities of the body,
14 you will live. All who are moved by God's Spirit are God's
15 children. You didn't receive the spirit of slaves to make you
feel afraid again, but you received the Spirit who makes us God's
16 children and moves us to call "Father!" This Spirit assures our
17 spirit we are God's children, ᴵ and if children, then heirs, God's
heirs, who share Christ's inheritance with Him — if we really
suffer with Him in order to be glorified with Him.

We Want to Be Free

18 I think what we suffer now isn't important when I compare
19 it with the glory to be revealed to us. Nature is waiting on tiptoe
20 to see the unveiling of God's family. Nature must waste away,
not because it wants to but because its Master would have it so,
21 but nature hopes ᴵ it, too, will be freed from the slavery that de-
22 stroys it, to share the freedom of God's family in glory. We know
that all nature has been groaning with the pains of childbirth
until now.

23 More than that. Since the Spirit whom we have is our first
taste of heaven, we, too, groan inwardly as we look ahead to
24 have our bodies freed and so to be His family. We are saved,
hoping for this. But if we hope for something we see, we really
25 don't hope. Why should we hope for what we can see? ᴵ But if
we hope for what we can't see, we wait for it patiently.

26 In the same way the Spirit helps us in our weakness, because
we don't know how we should pray, but the Spirit Himself pleads
27 for us with yearnings that can't find any words. He who searches
our hearts knows what the Spirit means to do, that in God's own
way He's pleading for the holy people.

God Gives Us Glory

We know that God helps us in every way to have what is 8:28 good, us who love Him and are called according to His plan. Those whom He chose from the first He also appointed long ago 29 to be thoroughly like His Son so He would be the firstborn among many brothers. Those whom He appointed long ago He called. 30 Those whom He called He made righteous. And those whom He made righteous * He glorified.

What does this mean? If God is for us, who can be 31 against us? He didn't spare His own Son but gave Him up 32 for all of us — He will certainly with Him give us everything. ' Who will accuse those whom God has chosen? It is God *who* 33 *makes* us *righteous.** ' *Who will condemn?* ²² Christ died, more 34 than that, He rose, He is at the right of God, and He prays for us. ' Who will separate us from God's love? Will sorrow, 35 hardship or persecution, hunger or nakedness, danger or a sword? ' So it is written, *For you we are being killed all day long. We* 36 *are considered sheep to be slaughtered.*²³ But in all this He 37 who loved us helps us win an overwhelming victory. I'm con- 38 vinced that no death or life, no angels or their rulers, nothing now or in the future, no powers, ' nothing above or below, or 39 any other creature can ever separate us from God, who loves us in Christ Jesus, our Lord.

God's People

I'm telling the truth in Christ, I'm not lying, as my conscience 9 by the Holy Spirit assures me, when I say I have a great sorrow 2 and in my heart a pain that never leaves me. I could wish myself 3 cut off from Christ and damned for my fellow Jews, my own flesh and blood. ' They are the people of Israel. They were made 4 God's family. They have the glory, the covenant, the Law, the worship, and the promises. They have the ancestors, and from 5 them according to His body came Christ, who is God over every- thing, blessed forever. Amen.

It doesn't mean God failed to do what He said. Not all who 6 are descended from Israel are .the real Israel, and not all who 7 are descended from Abraham are for that reason his real children. No, *Isaac's children will be called your descendants.*²⁴ ' This means 8 children born in a natural way are not God's children. Only

* See note at 3:20.

the children he had because God promised them are counted his descendants.

God's Right to Choose

9:9 God promised, *I will come back at the right time, and Sarah*
10 *will have a son.*[25] The same thing happened to Rebekah. She
11 was going to bear children for our ancestor Isaac. They had not been born yet or done anything good or bad. Even then — in order that God may carry out His purpose according to His
12 choice, which doesn't depend on anything we do but on Him who calls us — she was told, *The older will serve the younger.*[26]
13 And so the Bible says, *I loved Jacob, but I hated Esau.*[27]
14-15 Does this mean God is unjust? Never! ¹ He says to Moses, *I will be merciful to whom I want to be merciful; I will pity*
16 *whom I want to pity.*[28] Then it doesn't depend on anyone want-
17 ing it or trying hard but on God being merciful. The Bible says to Pharaoh, *I raised you to the throne to demonstrate My power*
18 *on you and to spread the news of Me all over the earth.*[29] So He pities whom He wants to pity and *makes stubborn* [30] whom He wants to make stubborn.

19 You will ask me, "Why does He still find fault with anyone?
20 Who can resist His will?" But now, who are you, man, to talk back to God? *Will anything shaped by a man say to him,*[31]
21 "Why did you make me like this?" Doesn't *a potter* have the right over *his clay* [32] to make out of the same mud one thing for a noble purpose and another for a lowly purpose?

22 God wanted to show people His anger and let them know His power, but He waited very patiently before He would *punish those who deserved it* and had prepared themselves *for destruc-*
23 *tion,*[33] so as to show the riches of glory He has in store for those
24 He's merciful to and long ago prepared for glory — I mean us whom He called not only from the Jews but also from the non-Jews.

God Chooses Non-Jews

25 So He says in Hosea, *Those who are not My people I will call My people, and those who are not loved I will call My loved ones,*
26 ¹ *and where they were told, "You are not My people," they will*
27 *be called sons of the living God.*[34] Isaiah exclaims in regard to Israel, *Though the people of Israel are as many as the sand by*
28 *the sea, only a remnant will be saved. The Lord will completely*

and decisively execute His sentence on the country.[35] So Isaiah
said long ago, *If the Lord of armies hadn't left us some survivors,
we would have become like Sodom and ended like Gomorrah.*[36]

What does it mean? Non-Jewish people who didn't search [30]
for righteousness found a righteousness we get by believing, while [31]
Israel, pursuing a Law with its righteousness, didn't find it. Why?
They didn't try to get it by faith but thought they could get it by [32]
works. They stumbled over *the stumbling block,* | as the Bible
says, *I'm putting in Zion a Stone they will stumble over and a Rock* [33]
*they will fall over. But if you believe in Him, you will not be
disappointed.*[37]

Jews Should Believe

Fellow Christians, my heart's desire and my prayer to God [10]
is to save the Israelites. I can testify they are zealous for God [2]
but don't understand. Not knowing the righteousness God gives, [3]
and trying to set up their own, they haven't submitted to God's
righteousness. You see, Christ is the end of the Law to give [4]
righteousness to everyone who believes.

Moses writes, *if you have done* the righteous things demanded [5]
by the Law, *you will find life in them.*[38] But the righteousness [6]
you get by faith says this: *Don't ask yourself,*[39] *Who will go up
to heaven?* which means, bring Christ down, | or, Who will *go* [7]
down into the depths? which means, bring Christ up from the
dead. But what does it say? *The word is near you, in your mouth* [8]
and in your heart.[40] This is the word of faith that we preach.
If with your mouth you confess, "Jesus is the Lord," and in [9]
your heart you believe "God raised Him from the dead," you
will be saved. With your heart you believe and become righteous; [10]
with your mouth you confess and are saved. *Anyone who believes* [11]
in Him, the Bible says, *will not be disappointed.*[41] There is no [12]
difference between Jew and Greek, because they all have the
same Lord, who gives His riches to all who call on Him. *Everyone* [13]
who calls on the Lord's name will be saved.[42]

But how can they call on Him if they haven't believed in Him? [14]
And how can they believe in Him if they haven't heard Him?
How can they hear if nobody preaches? | How can men preach [15]
if they're not sent? Just as the Bible says, *How beautiful is the
coming of those who bring good news!* [43]

But not all have obeyed the good news. Isaiah asks, *Lord,* [16] *who has believed what we told them?* **44** So when we tell people, they believe, and we tell them by letting Christ speak.

18   But I ask, didn't they hear it? Of course they did.
>   *Their voices have gone all over the earth*
>   *And their words to the farthest parts of the world.* **45**

19 Again I ask, didn't Israel know? Moses was the first to say,
>   *I will make you jealous of those who are not a nation,*
>   *I will make you angry with a people who don't under-*
>   *stand.*[46]

20 Then Isaiah boldly says,
>   *I will let those who don't look for Me find Me.*
>   *I will let those who don't ask for Me know Me.*

21 And He says about Israel, *All day long I have stretched out My hands to a people who disobey Me and oppose Me.*[47]

The Remnant

11   So I ask, "Has *God rejected His people?*" Certainly not —
I'm an Israelite myself, a descendant of Abraham and of the tribe
2 of Benjamin. *God has not rejected His people* [48] whom He chose
long ago. Or don't you know what the Bible says in the story
3 of Elijah when he pleads with God against Israel: *Lord, they
have killed Your prophets, they have torn down Your altars,*
4 *I am the only one left, and they are trying to kill me?* But
what did *God answer him? I have kept for Myself seven thousand*
5 *men who have not knelt to Baal.*[49] So there is right now, too,
6 a remnant God has chosen by His love. But if He was moved
only by His love, it couldn't have been due to what they have
done; otherwise it wouldn't be His unearned love anymore.
7   What does it mean? Israel didn't get what it wanted, but
those whom God chose did get it.

God's Way of Winning Jews

8   And the minds of the others were dulled, as the Bible says,
>   *God has given them a spirit of deep sleep,*
>   *eyes that should not see,*
>   *and ears that should not hear,*
>   *And so it has been until this day.*[50]

9 And David says,
>   *Let their table be a snare* and a trap,
>   *To make them fall and get what they deserve.*
10   *Let their eyes turn dark so they cannot see,*
>   *And bend their backs forever.*[51]

Did they stumble, I ask, to be lost altogether? Certainly not! By their error salvation has come to the non-Jews *to make the Jews jealous.*[46] And if their error made the world rich and their loss made the non-Jews rich, how much more certainly will that happen when their full number comes in! Now, I am speaking to you non-Jews. As I am sent to the non-Jews, I glorify my work. Perhaps *I* can *make* my fellow Jews *jealous*[46] and save some of them. When God rejects them, the world is reconciled to God; when God accepts them, what can it mean but that the dead will live?

If the first handful of dough is holy, so is the whole dough. If the root is holy, so are the branches. | But if some of the branches have been broken off, and you, a wild olive, have been grafted in among them, and the rich sap from the root of the olive tree nourishes you too, don't brag of being more than the other branches. If you brag, remember you don't support the root, but the root supports you. "Branches were cut off," you will say, "to graft me in." | Right! They were broken off because they didn't believe, but you stand by believing. Don't feel proud but be afraid. If God didn't spare the natural branches, He will not spare you. Now see how kind and how severe God can be — severe to those who fell but kind to you if you cling to His kindness; otherwise you, too, will be cut off.

And if the others will no more refuse to believe, they will be grafted in, because God can graft them in again. You have been cut from an olive tree that grows wild and have been unnaturally grafted into a cultivated olive; how much more likely it is that these natural branches will be grafted back into their own olive tree!

To keep you from thinking too well of yourselves, my fellow Christians, I want you to know this secret truth: The minds of a part of the Jews were dulled until the full number of the non-Jews comes in. And in this way all Israel will be saved, as the Bible says, *The Savior will come from Zion. He will get rid of ungodliness in Jacob. And this will be My covenant with them when I take away their sins.*[52]

God's rule in telling the good news is to treat them as His enemies to help you. But He chose them, and so He loves them on account of their fathers. God never changes His mind when He gives anything or calls anyone. Once you disobeyed God,

11:30 ⏐but now that the Jews have disobeyed, He has been merciful to
31 you. So they also have disobeyed now that when you enjoy His
32 mercy, they may have it too. You see, God has put all people
in a prison of disobedience in order to be merciful to all.

33   How deep are God's riches, wisdom, and knowledge, how
impossible it is to find out His decisions and trace His ways!
34 ⏐*Who has found out how the Lord thinks? Or who has become*
35 *His adviser?* 53 *Or who has first given Him something* for which
36 he must *be paid back?* 54 Everything is from Him, by Him, and
for Him. To Him be glory forever. Amen.

Live for God

12   I appeal to you, fellow Christians, by the mercies of God, to
give your bodies as a living sacrifice, holy and pleasing to God,
2 and so worship Him as thinking beings. Don't live like this
world, but let yourselves be transformed by a renewing of your
minds so you can test and be sure what God wants, what is good
and pleasing and perfect.

3   As God gave me His gift of love for every one of you, I tell
you, don't think too highly of yourselves, but take a sane view
of yourselves, everyone according to the amount of faith God
4 gave you. We have many parts in one body, and these parts
5 don't all do the same thing. In the same way, many as we are,
we are one body in Christ and individually parts of one another.
6 We have gifts that are different according to what His love
gave us. If you can speak God's Word, do it according to the
7 faith you have. ⏐If you can serve, then serve. If you can teach,
8 teach. ⏐If you can encourage, encourage. If you share, be generous. If you manage anything, do it eagerly. If you help people
in need, do it cheerfully.

Love

9-10   Love sincerely. Hate evil; cling to what is good. ⏐Love one
another tenderly as fellow Christians. Outdo one another in
11 showing respect. ⏐Don't be backward in zeal. Glow with the
12 Spirit. Serve the Lord. ⏐Be happy in your hope, patient in trouble,
13 and keep busy praying. Share what you have with the holy
people who need it. Eagerly welcome strangers as guests. ·

14   Bless those who persecute you, bless, and don't curse them.
15 Be happy with those who are happy, weep with those who weep.

¹ Live in harmony with one another. Don't be too ambitious, but go along with the humble ways of others. *Don't think you are wise.*⁵⁵

Don't pay back evil for evil. *Be concerned with things that* ¹⁷ *everybody considers noble.*⁵⁶ As much as you can, live in peace ¹⁸ with everybody. Don't take revenge, dear friends, but let God pun- ¹⁹ ish, because the Bible says, *I alone have the right to avenge. I will pay back,*⁵⁷ says the Lord. No, *if your enemy is hungry, feed* ²⁰ *him. If he is thirsty, give him a drink. If you do this, you'll heap burning coals on his head.*⁵⁸ Don't let evil conquer you, ²¹ but conquer evil with good.

Obey Your Government

Everyone should obey the government that is over him, be- **13** cause there is no government except that which is put there by God. God has ordered our government to be over us. ¹ Then ² anyone who is against the government opposes what God has ordered, and those who oppose will be condemned.

If you do right, you don't have to be afraid of those who ³ rule, but only if you do wrong. Would you like to live without being afraid of your government? Do what is right, and it will praise you. ¹ It is God's servant to help you. If you do wrong, you ⁴ should be afraid, because the government doesn't carry a sword without a purpose. It is God's servant, an avenger, who must punish anyone doing wrong. You must obey, then, not only ⁵ because God punishes wrong but also because your conscience tells you to obey.

That is why you also pay taxes. Men in the government serve ⁶ God and are busy doing their work. Pay to all whatever you ⁷ owe them. If you owe anyone tribute, pay tribute; if taxes, then taxes; if respect, then respect; if honor, then honor.

Love One Another

Don't owe anybody anything but to love one another. If you ⁸ love the other person, you have kept the Law. The command- ⁹ ments — *don't commit adultery, don't kill, don't steal, don't be greedy* ⁵⁹ — and any others are summed up in this: *Love your neighbor like yourself.*⁶⁰ Love does no wrong to another person. ¹⁰ So by love you keep the Law in every way.

Do this especially since you know the time we're living in. ¹¹

13:12 It's time now for you to wake up from sleep because we are now nearer being rescued than when we first believed. The night is almost over, and the day is dawning. Then let us put

13 away the works of darkness and put on the armor of light. Let us live nobly as in the daytime, not carousing or getting drunk, not sinning sexually or living wild, not quarreling or being

14 jealous. But put on the Lord Jesus Christ, and don't plan to have your fleshly desires aroused.

Weak Christians

14 Welcome a man who is weak in his faith and not just to
2 argue about different opinions. One person believes he can eat
3 anything, but a weak Christian eats only vegetables. If you eat, don't despise anyone who doesn't eat, and if you don't eat, don't criticize anyone who eats, because God has accepted him.
4 Who are you to criticize Someone else's servant? He belongs to the Lord, who is concerned whether he succeeds or fails. And he will succeed, because the Lord can make him succeed.

5 One man thinks one day is better than the other; another thinks they're all alike. Everyone should be thoroughly convinced
6 in his own mind. He who has a special day means to honor the Lord. He who eats does it for the Lord since he thanks God. And he who keeps from eating does it for the Lord, and
7 he thanks God. None of us lives for himself, and none dies
8 for himself. If we live, we live for the Lord; and if we die, we die for the Lord. So whether we live or die, we belong to the
9 Lord. Christ died and became alive again to be Lord of the dead and the living.

10 I ask one of you, "Why do you criticize your fellow Christian?" Or another, "Why do you despise your fellow Christian?"
11 We must all stand before God to be judged. It is written, *"As sure as I live," says the Lord,*[61] *"everyone will kneel to Me, and*
12 *every tongue will praise God."* [62] So each of us will have to give an account of himself to God.

13 Then let us stop criticizing one another. But instead decide not to lay any stumbling block or trap in the way of a fellow
14 Christian. I know and am convinced in the Lord Jesus nothing is unclean in itself. Anything is unclean only to him who thinks
15 it is unclean. But if what you eat hurts your fellow Christian, you're not living according to love anymore. By what you eat

don't ruin him for whom Christ died. You have something good ¹⁶
that nobody should say anything bad about. God's kingdom is ¹⁷
not eating and drinking but righteousness, peace, and joy in the
Holy Spirit. If you serve Christ in this way, God is pleased ¹⁸
with you, and people approve of you.

So we eagerly go after the things which mean peace and by ¹⁹
which we help one another grow. Don't ruin God's work just ²⁰
for food. Everything is clean, but it's wrong for you to eat if it
makes someone stumble. It is good not to eat meat, drink wine, ²¹
or do anything else that makes your fellow Christian stumble, sin,
or be weak in faith. The faith you have, have it between your- ²²
self and God. Happy are you if you never have to condemn
yourself in regard to anything you approve. If anyone doubts ²³
and still eats, he is condemned because he doesn't go by what
he believes. Anything that is not an act of faith is sin.

But we who are strong must be patient with the weaknesses **15**
of the weak and not just please ourselves. Every one of us should ²
please his neighbor for his good, to help him grow. Even Christ ³
didn't please Himself, but it happened to Him as it is written,
Those who insult You insult Me.[63]

Jews and Non-Jews

All that was written long ago was written to teach us by the ⁴
endurance and encouragement we get from the Bible to have
hope. May God, who helps you to endure and encourages you, ⁵
give you such harmony with one another as you follow Christ
Jesus ¹ that together with one voice you praise the God and Father ⁶
of our Lord Jesus Christ.

Then, as Christ has welcomed you, welcome one another in ⁷
order to glorify God. I tell you Christ became a servant to the ⁸
Jews to do what God promised the fathers — showing that He
tells the truth — and to have the other nations praise God for ⁹
His mercy, as it is written,

> *For this I will praise You among the nations*
> *And sing to honor Your name.*[64]

And again,

¹⁰

> *Be happy, you other nations, with His own people!* [65]

And again,

¹¹

> *All you nations, praise the Lord,*
> *And all the people should praise Him.*[66]

15:12 Again, Isaiah says,

> Jesse will have the Descendant
> Who will rise to rule the nations,
> And He will be the hope of the nations.[67]

13 The God of hope fill you with perfect happiness and peace as you believe, to make you overflow with hope by the power of the Holy Spirit.

New Fields

14 I am convinced, my fellow Christians, you are full of kind-ness, fully equipped with every kind of knowledge, and able to
15 correct one another. Just to remind you, I have written you a letter, part of which is rather bold because God has by a spe-
16 cial gift of His love I made me a servant of Christ Jesus among the non-Jewish nations, to work for God's good news as a priest and bring the nations as an offering made holy by the Holy
17 Spirit and accepted by God. So I can in Christ Jesus be proud
18 of what I'm doing before God I because I'll dare to tell only what Christ has done through me to make the nations obedient,
19 by my speaking and working, I by the power to do miracles and wonders, by the power of God's Spirit, so that I have finished telling the good news of Christ all the way from Jerusalem as far around as Illyricum.

20 But I was ambitious to tell the good news only where Christ's name wasn't known, so as not to build on any foundation others
21 had laid, but as it is written,

> Those who were never told about Him will see,
> And those who never heard will understand.[68]

I Hope to See You

22 That is why I have so often been kept from coming to you.
23 But now there is in this territory no more opportunity for me to
24 work, and for many years I have longed to come to you I on my way to Spain. I hope to see you when I pass through and after I have enjoyed being with you for a while to have you send me on my way there.

25 Right now I am going to Jerusalem to bring help to the holy
26 people there. You see, Macedonia and Greece decided to share their goods with the poor among the holy people in Jerusalem.
27 So they decided, and they really owe something to the Jews.

If the Jews have shared their spiritual goods with the non-Jews, the non-Jews owe it to them to serve them with their earthly goods. When that is done and I've brought them this contribution 15:28 with my seal on it, I will come to you on my way to Spain. I know when I come to you I'll bring a full blessing of Christ. 29

By our Lord Jesus Christ and the love we have from the 30 Spirit I urge you to join me in my struggle by praying for me to God ᴵ to rescue me from those in Judea who refuse to believe 31 and to have the holy people in Jerusalem welcome the help I bring ᴵ so that by God's will I'll come to you with joy and be 32 refreshed with you.

The God of peace be with you all. Amen. 33

Farewell

I'm introducing Phoebe, our fellow Christian, to you. She 16 is a worker in the church in Cenchreae. Welcome her in the Lord 2 as holy people should, and give her any help she may need from you, because she has become a protector of many, including me.

Greet Prisca and Aquila, my fellow workers in Christ Jesus, 3 ᴵ who risked their necks to save my life. Not only I but 4 all the churches among the non-Jews are thanking them. Greet also the church that meets at their home. 5

Greet my dear Epaenetus, who was the first in the province of Asia to turn to Christ.

Greet Mary, who has worked very hard for you. 6

Greet Andronicus and Junias, my fellow Jews, who went to 7 prison with me. They are outstanding among the apostles. They also came to Christ before I did.

Greet Ampliatus, who is dear to me in the Lord. 8

Greet Urban, our fellow worker in Christ, and my dear Stachys. 9

Greet Apelles, a veteran in Christ. 10

Greet those who belong to the family of Aristobulus.

Greet Herodian, my fellow Jew. 11

Greet those in the family of Narcissus who are in the Lord.

Greet Tryphaena and Tryphosa, who have worked hard for the 12 Lord.

Greet dear Persis, who has worked very hard for the Lord.

Greet Rufus, the chosen one in the Lord, and his mother — 13 who has been a mother to me too.

16:14 Greet Asyncritus, Phlegon, Hermes, Patrobas, Hermas, and the fellow Christians who are with them.

15 Greet Philologus, Julia, Nereus, and his sister, and Olympas, and all the holy people who are with them.

16 Greet one another with a holy kiss. All the churches of Christ greet you.

17 I urge you, fellow Christians, to watch those who cause disagreements and make people fall by going against the teaching
18 you learned. Turn away from them. ¹ Such men are not serving Christ, our Lord, but their own bellies and by their fine and
19 flattering talk are deceiving innocent people. Everybody has heard how you obey, and so I'm happy about you. I want you to be wise for anything good, and too innocent for anything
20 bad. — The God of peace will soon crush the devil under your feet.

The love of our Lord Jesus be with you!

21 Timothy, my fellow worker, greets you; so do Lucius, Jason, and Sosipater, my fellow Jews.

22 I, Tertius, who wrote this letter, greet you in the Lord.

23 Gaius, my host and the host of the whole church, greets you. Erastus, the city treasurer, greets you, and Quartus, our fellow
* Christian.

25 Now, to Him —

who can make you strong by the good news I bring and the preaching of Jesus Christ, by unveiling the mystery veiled in
26 silence for long ages ¹ but now brought to light and by the writings of the prophets, as the everlasting God ordered them, shown to all the nations to get them to believe and obey

27 — to the only wise God through Jesus Christ be glory forever. Amen.

* Our oldest manuscripts, including Papyrus 46, do not have v. 24: "The love of our Lord Jesus (Christ) be with you all. Amen." They have most of these words at the end of v. 20.

OLD TESTAMENT REFERENCES

1. Hab. 2:4
2. Ps. 106:20
3. Ps. 62:12;
   Prov. 24:12
4. Is. 52:5
5. Ps. 116:11
6. Ps. 51:4
7. Ps. 14:1-3; 53:1-3;
   Eccl. 7:20
8. Ps. 5:9
9. Ps. 140:3
10. Ps. 10:7
11. Is. 59:7-8
12. Ps. 36:1
13. Ps. 143:2
14. Gen. 15:6
15. Ps. 32:1-2
16. Gen. 17:11
17. Gen. 17:5
18. Gen. 15:5
19. Is. 53:12
20. Ps. 22:5; 25:3, 20
21. Ex. 20:17;
    Deut. 5:21
22. Is. 50:8
23. Ps. 44:22

24. Gen. 21:12
25. Gen. 18:10, 14
26. Gen. 25:23
27. Mal. 1:2-3
28. Ex. 33:19
29. Ex. 9:16
30. Ex. 4:21; 7:3;
    9:12; 14:4, 17
31. Is. 29:16; 45:9
32. Jer. 18:6
33. Is. 13:5; Jer. 50:25
34. Hos. 2:1, 23; 1:10
35. Is. 10:22-23; 28:22
36. Is. 1:9
37. Is. 8:14; 28:16
38. Lev. 18:5
39. Deut. 9:4
40. Deut. 30:12, 14;
    (Ps. 107:26)
41. Is. 28:16
42. Joel 2:32
43. Is. 52:7
44. Is. 53:1
45. Ps. 19:4
46. Deut. 32:21
47. Is. 65:1-2

48. 1 Sam. 12:22;
    Ps. 94:14
49. 1 Kings 19:10, 14,
    15, 18
50. Deut. 29:4;
    Is. 29:10
51. Ps. 69:22-23
52. Is. 59:20-21; 27:9
53. Is. 40:13
54. Job 35:7; 41:11
55. Prov. 3:7
56. Prov. 3:4, Greek
57. Deut. 32:35
58. Prov. 25:21-22
59. Ex. 20:13-15, 17;
    Deut. 5:17-19, 21
60. Lev. 19:18
61. Is. 49:18
62. Is. 45:23-24
63. Ps. 69:9
64. 2 Sam. 22:50;
    Ps. 18:49
65. Deut. 32:43
66. Ps. 117:1
67. Is. 11:1, 10
68. Is. 52:15

P A U L

writes the First Letter to the

CORINTHIANS

EPHESUS
SPRING OF A. D. 55

1 PAUL, APOSTLE OF CHRIST JESUS, called by God's will, and
2 Sosthenes, my fellow worker, ¹ to God's church in Corinth, made
holy by Christ Jesus and called to be holy, with all who anywhere call on the name of our Lord Jesus Christ, their Lord
3 and ours — may God our Father and the Lord Jesus Christ
love you and give you peace.

4   I am always thanking God for you, because He has loved
5 you in Christ Jesus ¹ and in Him made you rich in every way,
6 in speech and knowledge of every kind, ¹ as the truth of Christ
7 we spoke was confirmed in you. And so you don't lack any
gift as you eagerly look for our Lord Jesus Christ to appear
8 again. He will strengthen you to the end so that nobody can
accuse you of anything on the day of our Lord Jesus Christ.
9 You can depend on God, who called you to the fellowship of
His Son Jesus Christ, our Lord.

Everyone for Christ

10   Fellow Christians, by the name of our Lord Jesus Christ
I urge you all to agree and not be divided but perfectly united
11 in your understanding and judgment. Chloe's people told me
12 you are quarreling, my fellow Christians. I mean that each of
you says, "I belong to Paul," or, "I belong to Apollos," or,
13 "I belong to Peter," or, "I belong to Christ." Is Christ divided?
Was Paul crucified for you? Or were you baptized into Paul's
14 name? I thank God I didn't baptize any of you except Crispus
15 and Gaius. Then nobody can say you were baptized into my
16 name. ¹ I also baptized the family of Stephanas. I don't know if
17 I baptized anyone else. Christ didn't send me to baptize but

to tell the good news; nor to be a clever speaker, or the cross of Christ would lose its power.

God's Foolish Things

The story of the cross is something foolish to those who perish, but it is God's power to us who are saved. The Bible says, *I will destroy the wisdom of the wise and defeat the intelligence of the intelligent.*[1] *Where is the wise man? Where is the Bible scholar?*[2] Where is the debater of our time? Hasn't God *made foolish the wisdom*[3] of the world? Since by God's wisdom the world by its wisdom didn't get to know God, God decided to use our foolish preaching to save those who believe it. Now that Jews ask for wonderful proofs and Greeks look for wisdom, we preach a crucified Christ. The Jews stumble over Him, the Greeks think He's something foolish, but to those who are called, both Jews and Greeks, He is Christ, God's power and God's wisdom. The foolish thing God does is wiser than men, and the weak thing God does is stronger than men.

You see what happened, fellow Christians, when God called you. Not many of you are wise as the world judges, not many in positions of power, not many born of noble parents. No, God chose the foolish things in the world to make wise men feel ashamed. God chose the weak things in the world to make strong men feel ashamed. God chose the low things in the world, what it despises, what is nothing, to make what is something nothing — and to keep anybody from bragging before God. He gave you your life in Christ Jesus, whom God made our wisdom, righteousness, holiness, and ransom from sin, so that it may be as the Bible says, *If you feel proud, feel proud of the Lord.*[4]

When I came to you, fellow Christians, I didn't come to tell you God's truth with any extra-fine speech or wisdom. While I was with you, I was determined to know only Jesus Christ and Him nailed to a cross. I came to you weak and afraid and with much trembling. When I spoke and preached, I didn't use clever talk to persuade you, but I let the Spirit and His power prove the truth to you so that your faith will not depend on men's wisdom but on God's power.

But we do speak a wisdom to those who are ripe for it, a wisdom unknown to the world today and to its rulers who pass away. Yes, we tell about God's secret wisdom that was

293

2:8-9 kept hidden but that God before the world began planned for our glory. None of those who rule this world knew it. If they had known it, they would not have crucified the Lord of glory. But it is as the Bible says:

> No eye has seen,
> No ear has heard,
> And no mind has thought of
> What God has prepared for those who love Him.[5]

10 God has revealed it to us by His Spirit. The Spirit finds out
11 everything, even the deep things of God. Who knows what a man thinks except his own inner spirit? In the same way only God's
12 Spirit knows what God thinks. Now we were not given the spirit of the world but the Spirit who comes from God so that we
13 know the good things God gave us. And we tell about them in words not taught by human wisdom but taught by the Spirit as we explain the things of the Spirit to those who have the Spirit.

14 But a natural man doesn't welcome the things of God's Spirit. He thinks they are foolish and can't understand them, because
15 you must have the Spirit to see their real value. If you have the Spirit, you can find out the real value of everything, but nobody
16 can know your real value. Who has known the mind of the Lord so as to teach Him?[6] And we have the mind of Christ.

We Plant and Build

3 Fellow Christians, I couldn't talk to you as spiritual people but had to treat you as living in your weak flesh, as babies in
2 Christ. I gave you milk to drink, not solid food, because you
3 weren't ready for it. Why, you aren't ready for it even now yet, because you still live in your weak flesh.

When you are jealous, quarreling, and forming different parties, aren't you following your flesh and acting like other
4 people? When one of you says, "I belong to Paul," and another,
5 "I belong to Apollos," aren't you just ordinary people? What is Apollos anyhow? Or what is Paul? Men by whose help you came to believe, and each helped only as the Lord gave him
6 the ability. I planted, Apollos watered, but God made it grow.
7 Now then, the one who plants isn't anything, or the one who
8 waters, but God, who makes it grow. The man who plants and the one who waters are together, but each of us will get paid
9 for his own work. We are God's men, working together. You are God's field.

You are God's building. In His love God gave me a work to do, and so as an expert master builder I laid a foundation, and somebody else is building on it. Everyone should be careful how he builds on it. Nobody can lay any other foundation [11] than the one that is already laid, and that is Jesus Christ. If on [12] this foundation you build anything of gold, silver, fine stones, wood, hay, or straw, what each one does will be known. That [13] day will show what it is because the fire will reveal it and test it to show what kind of work everyone has done. If what you [14] built on the foundation stands the test, you will get paid. If your [15] work is burned, you will lose something, but you will be saved, though it will be like going through a fire.

Don't you know you are God's temple and God's Spirit lives [16] in you? If anybody destroys God's temple, God will destroy [17] him, because God's temple is holy. And you are that temple.

Don't deceive yourself. If any one of you imagines he is wise [18] in the ways of this world, he should become a fool to become really wise. God considers this world's wisdom to be foolish, [19] as the Bible says, *He catches the wise with their own trickery,*[7] and again, *The Lord knows that the planning of* the wise *is* [20] *useless.*[8]

So don't feel proud of men. You see, everything is yours — [21] Paul, Apollos, Peter, the world, life or death, present or future [22] things — everything is yours, but you belong to Christ, and [23] Christ to God.

We Are Managers

Think of us as servants of Christ and managers who distribute God's hidden truths. Now then, you demand of any [4] [2] manager that he can be trusted.

It means very little to me that you or any human judges [3] should examine me. I don't even examine myself. I don't know [4] of anything that is against me, but that doesn't make me righteous.* It is the Lord who examines me. So, don't judge any- [5] thing too early. Wait till the Lord comes. He will let the light shine on what is hidden in the dark and bring to the light the plans people have in their hearts. And then everyone will get his praise from God.

Fellow Christians, in a special way of speaking I have referred [6]

* See note at Rom. 3:20.

only to myself and Apollos, but I want you to learn from us not to get away from the Bible and not to brag about one man at the expense of another.

Not a King but a Father

4:7 Does anyone see anything special in you? What do you have that wasn't given to you? And if it was given to you, why do you brag as if it hadn't been given to you?

8 So you're already satisfied! You've already become rich! You've become kings without us! I only wish you had become kings — we would like to be kings with you.

9 I think God has had us apostles come last in the procession like men condemned to die because we have become a big show 10 for the world, for angels and people to see. We are fools for ·Christ's sake, but you are wise in Christ. We are weak, but 11 you are strong. You are honored, but we are despised. ¹ Up to this hour we are hungry, thirsty, poorly dressed, beaten, homeless, 12 ¹ and we wear ourselves out working with our hands. When we're insulted, we bless. When we're persecuted, we put up with it. 13 ¹ When slandered, we talk kindly. We have come to be the filth of the world, the scum of the earth, and we are that to this day.

14 I'm not writing this to make you feel ashamed, but I'm 15 warning you as my dear children. You may have ten thousand to guide you in Christ, but not many fathers, because in Christ 16 Jesus I became your father by telling you the good news. So 17 I urge you to become like me. That is why I sent you Timothy, who is my dear and dependable son in the Lord. He will help you keep in mind my ways in Christ Jesus, just as I teach them everywhere in every church.

18 Some of you are puffed up as though I were not coming to 19 you. But I'll come to you soon if the Lord wants me to, and then I will find out, not what these puffed-up fellows say but 20 what they can do. God's kingdom isn't just talk but power.

21 Which would you like? Should I come to you with a stick or with love and a gentle spirit?

Put Out the Wicked Man

5 We actually hear there is sexual sin among you, and such as isn't found even among the people of the world, that a man has 2 his father's wife. And you feel proud of yourselves! ¹ Shouldn't you rather have wept and put away from you the man who did

this? Although I'm away from you, I am with you in spirit, and being with you, I have already decided in regard to the man who did this. ¹ Call a meeting. My spirit and the power of our ⁴ Lord Jesus will be with you. Then in the name of our Lord Jesus ¹ hand such a person over to the devil, to destroy his sinful ways in ⁵ order to save his spirit on the Lord's day.

It isn't good for you to feel proud. Don't you know a little ⁶ yeast makes the whole dough sour? Get rid of the old yeast in ⁷ order to be a new dough, as you are really free from the old yeast, because our *Passover Lamb* was *sacrificed;*⁹ it is Christ. Let us, ᵗ⁸ then, celebrate our festival, not with old yeast, not with any yeast of vice and wickedness, but with the sweet bread of purity and truth.

In my letter I wrote you not to mix with those who live in ⁹ sexual sin. I didn't mean you should altogether keep away from ¹⁰ people who live in sexual sin in this world, from those who are greedy, who rob, or worship idols; then you would have to get out of this world. But now I write you: Don't mix with anyone ¹¹ who calls himself a Christian but lives in sexual sin or is greedy, worships idols, slanders, gets drunk, or robs. Don't even eat with such a person.

Is it my business to judge those who are outside the church? ¹² God judges those who are outside. Shouldn't you judge those ¹³, ¹² who are inside the church? *Put the wicked man away from you.*¹⁰ ¹³

Don't Sue One Another

When one of you has a case against another, do you dare ⁶ to bring it before a court of unrighteous men and not before the holy people? Or don't you know these holy people will judge ² the world? And if you judge the world, aren't you able to judge trifles? ¹ Don't you know we'll judge angels? Shouldn't we then ³ judge things of this life? If then you are having things of this ⁴ life decided, will you let men who count nothing in the church be your judges? ¹ I say this to make you feel ashamed. Really, ⁵ isn't any one of you wise enough to decide a matter between one Christian and another? No, one Christian sues another — ⁶ and before unbelievers!

Without going any further, suing one another means you have ⁷ utterly failed. Why don't you rather suffer wrong? Why don't you rather let yourselves be robbed? No, you do wrong, and ⁸ you rob, and you do it to your own fellow Christians.

297

You Are God's Temple

6:9   Or don't you know wicked people will have no share in God's kingdom? Don't be mistaken about this: Nobody who lives in sexual sin or worships idols, no adulterers or men who sin sexually

10 with other men, [1] who steal, are greedy, get drunk, slander, rob

11 will have a share in God's kingdom. Some of you used to do these things. But you have washed, you've been made holy and righteous * by the name of the Lord Jesus Christ and by the Spirit of our God.

12   I'm allowed to do anything, but not everything is good for us. I'm allowed to do anything, but I'll not be a slave of anything.

13 Food is for the stomach, and the stomach for food, but God will put an end to both of them. The body is not made for sexual

14 sin but for the Lord; and the Lord is for the body. And God, who raised the Lord, will also raise us by His power.

15   Don't you know your bodies are members of Christ? Now, should I take the members of Christ and make them members

16 of a prostitute? Never! [1] Or don't you know he who gives himself to a prostitute is one body with her? The Bible says, *The two*

17 *will be one flesh.*[11] But if you give yourself to the Lord, you are one spirit with Him.

18   Flee from sexual sin. Every other sin a man may do is outside his body. But if he sins sexually, he sins against his own

19 body. Or don't you know your body is a temple of the Holy Spirit, whom God gives you and who is in you? You don't

20 belong to yourselves, because you were bought for a price. Then glorify God with your bodies.

If You Are Married

7   Now about the things you wrote — it is good for a man not

2 to have sex relations with a woman. But to avoid sexual sins, every man should have his own wife, and every woman her own husband.

3   A husband should do for his wife what he owes her, and

4 a wife should do the same for her husband. A wife can't do as she likes with her body; her husband has a right to it. In the same way a husband can't do as he likes with his body; his wife

5 has a right to it. Don't deprive one another, unless you agree to do so for a while to take time to pray. And come together

    * See note at Rom. 3:20.

again, or the devil will tempt you because you cannot control yourselves. But as I say this, I'm yielding to you, not ordering you. 7:6

I would like everybody to be like myself, but each one has 7 only the gift God gave him, one this and another that. To those 8 who aren't married and to widows I say, It is good for you to stay single like myself, ¹ but if you can't control yourselves, get 9 married; it is better to marry than to burn with desire.

If you are married, I — that is, not I, but the Lord — order 10 a wife not to leave her husband. If she does leave him, she 11 should stay single or make up with her husband. And a husband should not divorce his wife.

If You're Married to an Unchristian

To the rest I say (not the Lord), if a Christian has a wife 12 who doesn't believe and she agrees to live with him, he should not divorce her. And if a wife has a husband who doesn't believe 13 and he agrees to live with her, she should not divorce her husband. An unbelieving man married to such a woman serves a holy pur- 14 pose, and an unbelieving wife married to a Christian serves a holy purpose. Otherwise your children would be unclean, but now they are holy. But if the unbelieving person leaves, let him go. 15 In such a case a Christian man or woman is not bound. But God called us to live in peace. You wife, what do you know — 16 you may save your husband. Or you husband, what do you know — you may save your wife.

Stay as God Called You

But everyone should live the life the Lord assigned to him 17 just as God called him. This is the rule I lay down in all the churches.

Were you circumcised when you were called? Don't try to 18 get rid of your circumcision. Were you uncircumcised when you were called? Don't be circumcised. ¹ Circumcision is nothing, and 19 the lack of it is nothing, but doing what God orders is every- thing. Everyone should stay as he was called. Were you a slave 20-21 when you were called? Don't let that trouble you. Of course, if you have a chance to get free, take it. If you are a slave 22 when you are called in the Lord, you are the Lord's free man. In the same way, if you are free when you are called, you are Christ's slave. You were bought for a price; don't become slaves 23 of men. My fellow Christians, everyone should stay with God 24 just as he was when he was called.

To Marry or Not to Marry

7:25   For the unmarried girls I have no order from the Lord, but the Lord's mercy made me one you can trust, and I'll tell you

26 what I think. On account of the troubles we're in I believe it is

27 good for anyone to stay as he is. ⏐Are you married? Don't look for a divorce. Are you separated from a wife? Don't look for

28 a wife. But if you get married, it's no sin, and if a girl gets married, it's no sin. But if you do, you'll have trouble in your life, and I'm trying to spare you.

29   I mean, my fellow Christians, the time has been shortened.

30 While it lasts, if you have a wife, live as if you had none. ⏐If you weep, as if you weren't weeping. If you're happy, as if you weren't

31 happy. If you buy anything, act as if you didn't have it. ⏐While you use the world, don't try to get out of it all you can, since this world in its present form is passing away.

32   I don't want you to worry. An unmarried man is concerned

33 about the Lord's things, how he can please the Lord. But once he's married, he worries about earthly things, how he can please

34 his wife. ⏐He's interested in two different things. An unmarried woman or girl is concerned about the Lord's things, to be holy in body and in spirit. But once she's married, she worries about

35 earthly things, how she can please her husband. I'm saying this to help you, not to hold you by a rope but to show you how to live nobly for the Lord without being troubled about other things.

36   If a man thinks he's not acting properly toward his girl, if his passion is too strong and it must be so, he should do what

37 he wants to — it's no sin — they should get married. But suppose a man has a strong character and the will power and feels no necessity but has made up his mind to keep his girl as she is,

38 he'll be doing right. If, then, he marries his girl, he's doing right. But if he doesn't marry her, he'll be doing better.

39   A wife is bound to her husband as long as he lives. If her husband dies, she's free to marry anyone she wants to, but it should be in the Lord. But she'll be happier if she stays as she is.

40 That is my judgment, and I think I, too, have God's Spirit.

Meat Sacrificed to Idols

8   About the meat sacrificed to idols.

    We know that all of us have some knowledge. Knowledge

2 puffs up, but love builds up. If anybody thinks he knows some-

thing, he still has something to learn. But if he loves God, God knows him.

Now about eating meat that was sacrificed to idols, we know ⁴ there is no real idol in the world and there is only one God. Even if there are so-called gods in heaven or on earth (as there ⁵ are many gods and many lords), ¹ yet we have one God, the ⁶ Father: From Him comes everything, and we live for Him. And one Lord, Jesus Christ: He made everything, and we live by Him.

But not everybody knows this. Some are still so used to an ⁷ idol they think of the meat they eat as sacrificed to the idol, and their conscience, being weak, is stained with guilt.

Food will not bring us closer to God. We lose nothing by ⁸ not eating and gain nothing by eating. But be careful, or weak ⁹ Christians may fall into sin because you do as you please. If ¹⁰ anybody sees you who knows better lying down to eat in the temple of an idol, won't you be encouraging him who has a weak conscience to eat the meat sacrificed to idols? Then your knowl- ¹¹ edge is ruining the weak fellow Christian for whom Christ died. But when you sin against your fellow Christians in this way and ¹² wound their weak consciences, you sin against Christ.

So if food makes my fellow Christian sin, I will never eat ¹³ meat — I don't want to give him a reason for sinning.

A Pastor's Pay

Am I not free? Am I not an apostle? Didn't I see Jesus, **9** our Lord? Aren't you my work in the Lord? ¹ If I'm not an ² apostle to others, I certainly am one to you. You are the Lord's seal that proves I'm an apostle. That's how I defend myself ³ before those who examine me. Don't we have the right to eat ⁴ and drink? Don't we have the right to take a Christian wife ⁵ with us like the other apostles, the Lord's brothers, and Peter? Or do only I and Barnabas have no right to stop working for ⁶ a living?

Does a soldier ever pay his own expenses? Does anyone ⁷ plant a vineyard and not eat its grapes? Or does anyone take care of a flock and not drink any milk from it? Am I stating only ⁸ a human rule? Doesn't the Law say the same thing? ¹ The Law ⁹ of Moses says, *Don't muzzle an ox when he's treading out grain.*¹² Is God here interested in oxen? ¹ Surely He has us in mind. This ¹⁰ was written to show us when we plow or thresh we should expect to get a share of the crop. If we have sown the spiritual life in ¹¹ you, is it too much if we'll reap your earthly goods? If others enjoy this right over you, don't we have a better claim? But we haven't made use of this right. No, we put up with anything in order not to hinder the preaching of Christ.

13 Don't you know that the men who work at the temple get their food from the temple? That those who help at the altar 14 get their share of what is on the altar? In the same way the Lord has ordered that those who tell the good news should get their living from the good news.

15 But I haven't used any of these rights. And I'm not writing this to get such things done for me. I'd rather die than let anyone 16 take away my boast. If I tell the good news, I have nothing to boast about. I must tell it. Woe to me if I don't tell the good 17 news! If I do it because I want to, I get a reward. But if I don't want to do it, I still have this work entrusted to me.

18 What then is my reward? Just this: When I tell the good news, I won't let it cost anybody anything, and so I won't take advantage of my right in telling the good news.

Everything to Everybody

19 Although I am free from all people, I made myself a slave 20 of all of them to win more of them. To the Jews I became like a Jew to win Jews; to those under the Law I became like a man under the Law — although I'm not under the Law — to win those 21 under the Law. To those who don't have the Law I became like a man without the Law — although I'm not outside the Law of God but under the law of Christ — to win those who don't 22 have the Law. To weak persons I became weak to win the weak. I've been everything to everybody to be sure to save some of them.

23 I'm doing everything for the good news in order to have a share 24 of what it gives. Don't you know that all who are in a race run 25 but only one wins the prize? Like them, run to win! Anyone who enters a contest goes into strict training. Now, they do it to win a wreath that withers, but we to win one that never withers. 26 So I run with a clear goal ahead of me. I fight and don't just 27 hit the air. No, I beat my body and make it my slave so that, when I've called others to run the race, I myself will not somehow be disqualified.

A Warning

10 I want you to know, fellow Christians, our fathers were all 2 under the cloud and all went through the sea, and by baptism

in the cloud and in the sea all were united with Moses, all ate
the same food of the Spirit, and all drank the same water of the 4
Spirit, because they drank from the spiritual Rock that went
with them, and that Rock was Christ. Yet God wasn't pleased 5
with most of them — *they were killed in the desert*.[13]

Now, this happened in order to warn us not *to long for* [14] 6
what is evil as they did. Don't worship idols as some of them 7
did, as the Bible says, *The people sat down to eat and drink
and got up to play*.[15] Let us not sin sexually as some of them 8
did — 23,000 died on one day. Let us not go too far in testing 9
the Lord's patience as some of them did — the snakes killed
them. Don't complain as some of them did — the angel of death 10
killed them. These things happened to them to make them a lesson 11
to others and were written down to warn us who are living when
the world is coming to an end. So if you think you can stand, 12
be careful you don't fall.

You haven't been tempted more than you could expect. And 13
you can trust God He will not let you be tested more than you
can stand. But when you are tested, He will also make a way
out so that you can bear it.

Meat Sacrificed to Idols

And so, my dear friends, keep away from the worship of idols. 14
I'm talking to sensible people. Judge for yourselves what 15
I say. When we drink the blessed cup that we bless, don't we 16
share the blood of Christ? When we eat the bread that we break,
don't we share the body of Christ? All of us are one body, 17
because there is one bread and all of us share that one bread.

See how the Jews do it. Don't those who eat the sacrifices 18
share the altar? [1] What do I mean by this? That a sacrifice made 19
to an idol is something or that an idol really is something?
No, these *sacrifices* of the non-Jews *are made to devils and not* 20
to God.[16] I don't want you to be partners of devils. [1] You can't 21
drink the Lord's cup and the cup of devils. You can't share
the *Lord's table* [17] and the table of devils. Or are we *trying to* 22
make the Lord jealous? [18] Are we stronger than He?

We are allowed to do anything, but not everything is good 23
for others. We are allowed to do anything, but not everything
helps them grow. Nobody should look for his own good, but 24
everybody for the good of the other person. Eat anything sold 25
in the market, and don't ask any questions or let your conscience

10:26 trouble you, because *the earth and everything in it belong to the*
27 *Lord.*[19] If any of the unbelievers invites you and you want to go,
eat anything they serve you, and don't ask any questions or let
28 your conscience trouble you. But if somebody tells you, "This
was sacrificed," don't eat it, keeping in mind him who told you,
29 and conscience — I don't mean yours but the other one's conscience. What good is there in doing what I please if someone
30 else's conscience condemns it? If I give thanks for what I eat,
why should I let myself be denounced for eating what I thank
31 God for? So, whether you eat or drink or do anything else, do
32 everything to glorify God. Don't be the reason for others to sin,
33 whether they are Jews, Greeks, or God's church. So I try to
please everybody in every way and don't look for my advantage
11 but for that of many people so that they may be saved. Imitate
me as I imitate Christ.

Long Hair and Hats

2   I praise you for thinking of me in every way and for keeping
the truths as I delivered them to you.

3   I want you to know that the head of every man is Christ,
the head of a woman is her husband, and the head of Christ is
4 God. Any man who keeps his head covered when he prays or
5 speaks God's Word dishonors his head. But any woman who
prays or speaks God's Word with nothing on her head dishonors
her head. She's exactly like the woman whose head is shaved.
6 If a woman wears nothing on her head, she should also get her
hair cut. But if it is a disgrace for a woman to get her hair cut
7 or shaved off, she should keep her head covered. A man shouldn't
cover his head, because he is *God's image* [20] and glory; but
8 a woman is a man's glory. The man wasn't made from the
9 woman but the woman from the man, and the man wasn't made
10 for the woman but the woman for the man. That's why a woman
should wear something on her head to show she is under authority,
out of respect for the angels.

11   Yet in the Lord a woman needs a man, and a man needs
12 a woman. As the woman was made from the man, so a man
is born of a woman, and it all comes from God.

13   Judge for yourselves. Is it proper for a woman to pray to
14 God with nothing on her head? Doesn't nature itself teach you
15 it's disgraceful for a man to have long hair ᐟ but that it's a woman's
glory to wear her hair long? Her hair is given her as a covering.

But if anybody means to argue about it — we don't have such a custom, nor do God's churches.

How to Go to the Lord's Supper

While I'm giving these instructions, I'm not praising you for [17] doing harm instead of good at your meetings. In the first place, [18] I hear that when you meet as a church you are divided, and some of it I believe is true. Of course there must be divisions [19] among you to show clearly which of you can stand the test.

When you meet, you can't be eating the Lord's Supper. [20] Everyone eats his own supper ahead of the others, and then [21] one is hungry and another gets drunk. Don't you have homes [22] where you can eat and drink? Or do you despise God's church and humiliate those who don't have anything? What should I say to you? Should I praise you? I won't praise you for this.

The Lord gave me what I taught you, that the night He was [23] betrayed the Lord Jesus took bread. He gave thanks, broke it, [24] and said, "This is My body, which is for you. Do this to remember Me." He did the same with the cup after the supper. [25] He said, "This cup is the new *covenant* in My *blood*.[21] Every time you drink it, do it to remember Me."

Every time you eat this bread and drink the cup, you are [26] telling how the Lord died, till He comes. Then anyone who eats [27] the bread or drinks the Lord's cup in an unworthy way is sinning against the Lord's body and blood. Examine yourself and then [28] eat some of the bread and drink from the cup. Anyone who eats [29] and drinks without seeing that the body is there is condemned for his eating and drinking.

That is why many of you are sick and ailing and a number [30] are dead. If we would look at ourselves critically, we would not [31] be judged. But if the Lord judges us, He corrects us to keep us [32] from being condemned with the world.

So then, my fellow Christians, when you get together to eat, [33] wait for one another. If you are hungry, eat at home, so you [34] will not meet just to be condemned.

About the other things I'll give directions when I come.

The Spirit's Gifts

Fellow Christians, I want you to know about the gifts of the [12] Spirit. You know that when you were people of the world, you [2] were led away to the idols, that can't talk, as you felt yourselves

12:3 moved. So I tell you, if you are moved by God's Spirit, you don't say, "Jesus is cursed," and only if you are moved by the Holy Spirit can you say, "Jesus is the Lord."

4 Now gifts are given to different persons but by the same
5 Spirit. Ways of serving are assigned to them but by the same
6 Lord. Powers are given to them, but the same God works
7 everything in all people. Now, the Spirit shows Himself to each
8 one to make him useful. The Spirit gives one person the ability
9 to speak of wisdom. To another the same Spirit gives the ability to speak intelligently. To another the same Spirit gives faith.
10 To another that same Spirit gives the ability to heal. ¹ Another can work miracles. Another can speak God's Word. Another can tell the true Spirit from evil spirits. Another can talk strange
11 languages. Another can tell the meaning of languages. ¹ One and the same Spirit works all these things and gives as He wishes to each in his own way.

12 As the body is one and yet has many parts, and all the parts
13 of the body, many as they are, form one body, so is Christ. By one Spirit all of us — Jews or Greeks, slaves or free — were baptized to form one body, and that one Spirit was poured out for all of us to drink.

14-15 Not one part but many make up the body. Suppose a foot says, "I'm not a hand, and so I'm not a part of the body"; it is
16 still a part of the body. Or suppose an ear says, "I'm not an eye, and so I'm not a part of the body"; it is still a part of the body.
17 ¹ If the whole body were an eye, how could we hear? If it were
18 all hearing, how could we smell? As it is, God arranged the parts, fitting each of them into the body as He wanted it to be.
19-20 If all of it were one part, how could there be a body? As it is, there are many parts and one body.

21 The eye cannot say to the hand, "I don't need you," or the
22 head to the feet, "I don't need you." No, we really can't do
23 without the parts of the body that we think are weaker. And the parts of the body that we think less honorable we dress with special honor so that our shameful parts have a special nobility,
24 ¹ which our noble parts don't need. But God has put the body
25 together and given special honor to the part that lacks it, to keep the body from dividing and have the parts feel the same
26 concern for one another. If one member suffers, all the others suffer with it. If one is honored, all the others are happy with it.
27 Now, you are the body of Christ, and everyone has his place

in it. God has appointed in the church first apostles, next
preachers, third teachers, then miracle workers, then healers,
helpers, managers, and those who can talk strange languages.
| Are all apostles? Are all preachers? Are all teachers? Can 29
all do miracles? | Can all heal? Can all talk strange languages? 30
Can all tell what they mean? No, | but try to have the better gifts. 31

Love

And now I'll show you the best way of all. 31

If I speak the languages of men and of angels but don't have 13
any love, I've become a loud gong or a clashing cymbal. Even 2
if I speak God's Word and know every kind of hidden truth and
have every kind of knowledge, even if I have all the faith to
move mountains but don't have any love, I'm nothing. Even 3
if I give away all I have to feed the hungry and give up my body
but only to boast and don't have any love, it doesn't help me.

Love is patient. Love is kind. Love isn't jealous. It doesn't 4
brag or get conceited. | It isn't indecent. It isn't selfish. It doesn't 5
get angry. It *doesn't plan to hurt anyone.*[22] | It doesn't delight in 6
evil but is happy with the truth. It bears everything, believes 7
everything, hopes for everything, endures everything.

Love never dies. If there are prophecies, they will come to 8
an end. Or strange languages, they will stop. Or knowledge,
it will vanish. We learn only a part of anything and prophesy only 9
a part. But when that which is perfect comes, what is only a part 10
will vanish. When I was a child, I used to talk like a child, 11
think like a child, plan like a child. Now that I'm a man, I've
given up the ways of a child. Now we see by a mirror and are 12
puzzled, but then we'll see face to face. Now I learn only a part
of anything, but then I'll know as He has known me.

And now these three, faith, hope, and love, go on, but the 13
most important of these is love.

Speak to Be Understood

Pursue love, be eager to have the gifts of the Spirit, and 14
especially to speak God's Word. When a man talks a strange 2
language, he doesn't talk to people but to God, because nobody
understands him; his spirit is talking mysteries. But when you 3
speak God's Word, you talk to people to help them grow, to
encourage and comfort them. When you talk a strange language, 4
you encourage yourself. But when you speak God's Word, you

307

14:5 help the church grow. I want you all to talk strange languages, but I would rather have you speak God's Word. It is more important to speak God's Word than strange languages, unless **6** you explain what you say in order to help the church grow. Now, my fellow Christians, if I come to you and talk strange languages, how can I help you unless I tell you what God has told me and bring it as His Word or as something I know and teach?

7 Lifeless instruments such as a flute or a lyre produce sounds, but if there's no difference in the sounds, how can you tell what **8** is played on a flute or a lyre? And if the trumpet doesn't sound **9** a clear call, who will get ready for battle? In the same way, if you don't talk with a clear meaning, how will anyone know what **10** you're saying? You'll be talking into the air. There are, I suppose, ever so many different languages in the world, and none **11** is without meaning. Now if I don't know what a language means, I'll be a foreigner to him who speaks it, and he'll be a foreigner **12** to me. So you, too, since you are eager to have the Spirit's gifts, **13** try to be rich in them so as to build up the church. If then you talk a strange language, pray to be able to explain it.

14 If I pray in a strange language, my spirit prays, but my mind **15** isn't helping anyone. What then? I will pray in my spirit but also pray so as to be understood. I will sing praise in my spirit **16** but also sing so as to be understood. Otherwise, if you praise God only with your spirit, how can an ordinary person who is there say "Amen" to your prayer of thanks? He doesn't know **17** what you mean. It is good that you give thanks, but it doesn't **18** help the other person. I thank God I talk more in strange **19** languages than any of you, but in a church I would rather say five words that can be understood, in order to teach others, than ten thousand words in a language nobody understands.

20 Fellow Christians, don't be childish in your understanding. **21** In evil be babies, but grow up in your thinking. It is written in the Bible, *"In strange languages and by the mouth of foreigners I will speak to these people, but even then they will not listen* **23** **22** *to Me,"* says the Lord. Then strange languages are not meant to warn believers but unbelievers, while God's Word isn't meant **23** for unbelievers but for believers. Now if the whole congregation meets and all talk strange languages and then some ordinary people or unbelievers come in, won't they say you're crazy? **24** But if all speak God's Word and some unbeliever or ordinary person comes in, all convince him of his sin and all examine him.

The secrets of his heart are shown, and so he bows down with his face on the ground, worships ·God, and declares, *"God is certainly here among you."* [24]

Keep Order in Your Meetings

What should you do, then, my fellow Christians? When you [26] meet, everyone is ready with a song, something to teach, some truth from God, a strange language, or an explanation. Do it all to help one another grow. If you talk a strange language, [27] only two should talk, or three at the most, and one at a time, and somebody should explain. If there's nobody to explain what [28] you say, you shouldn't say anything in church but only talk to yourself and to God.

Two or three should speak God's Word, and the others should [29] decide whether they are telling it right or not. If God gives [30] a truth to another person who is seated, the first speaker should stop talking. You can all speak God's Word one after another [31] so that everybody learns something and is encouraged. Men [32] who speak God's Word control their own spirits. You see, God [33] is not a God of disorder but of peace.

As in all the churches of the holy people, ' the women should [34] be silent in church because they are not allowed to speak. They should submit, as the Law says. If there is something they want [35] to know, they should ask their husbands at home. It is a disgrace for a woman to speak in church.

Did God's Word first come from you? Or were you the only [36] ones to whom it came? If anyone thinks he speaks for God or [37] has the Spirit, he should know that what I write you is what the Lord orders. But if anyone ignores this, he should be ignored. [38]

So, my fellow Christians, be eager to speak God's Word, [39] and don't try to keep anyone from talking strange languages. But everything should be done in a fine and orderly way. [40]

Jesus Rose

My fellow Christians, I am telling you the good news I brought [15] you and you accepted. You stand in it ' and are saved by it if [2] you cling to the words I used in telling it to you — unless you were trifling when you believed. I brought you what I received — [3] something very important — that Christ died for our sins as the Bible said He would, ' He was buried, and He rose on the third [4] day as the Bible said He would. Peter saw Him, then the twelve, [5] ' then more than five hundred Christians at one time; most of [6]

15:6-7 these are still living, but some have gone to their rest. Then
8 James saw Him, then all the apostles. Last of all I saw Him,
9 I who 'am like an abortion, ' since I am the least of the apostles
and not fit to be called an apostle because I persecuted God's
10 church. God's love made me what I am, and His love wasn't
wasted on me. But I did far more work than all the others —
11 not I but God's love that was with me. Now, whether I did it
or they, this is what we preach, and this is what you believed.

We'll Rise

12 If we preach that Christ rose from the dead, how can some of
13 you say, "The dead don't rise"? If the dead don't rise, Christ
14 didn't rise. And if Christ didn't rise, our preaching means nothing,
15 and your faith means nothing. And we stand there as men who
lied about God, because we testified against God that He raised
Christ, whom He didn't raise if it is true that the dead don't rise.
16-17 You see, if the dead don't rise, Christ didn't rise. But if Christ
didn't rise, your faith can't help you, and you are still in your
18 sins. Then also those who have gone to their rest in Christ have
19 perished. If Christ is our hope only for this life, we should be
pitied more than any other people.

20 But now Christ did rise from the dead, the first in the harvest
21 of those who are sleeping in their graves. Since a man brought
22 death, a Man also brought the resurrection of the dead. As in
23 Adam all die, so in Christ all will be made alive. But everyone
in his own group: first Christ, then, when He comes, those who
belong to Christ.

24 Then the end will come when He hands over the kingdom to
God the Father after He has put an end to every other government,
25 authority, and power, ' since He must rule as King till *He puts* all
26 *enemies under His feet.*[25] The last enemy He will get rid of is
27 death. ' You see, *He puts everything under His feet.* When He
says, *Everything is put under Him,* this clearly doesn't include
28 Him who *puts everything under Him.* But when *everything has
been put under Him,* then the Son also will put Himself under
Him who *put everything under*[26] the Son so that God will be
everything in everything.

29 Otherwise, what will they do who are baptized for the dead? *
Why are they baptized for them if the dead don't actually rise?

* The relative of a Christian who had died may wish to be baptized
in order to see this Christian again in heaven. Or he may want to express
the hope that a Christian friend who has died will rise.

And why are we in danger every hour? As I'm proud of you, my fellow Christians, in Christ Jesus, our Lord, I assure you I'm facing death every day. If like other men I have fought with wild [32] animals in Ephesus, what good is it to me? If the dead don't rise, *let us eat and drink — tomorrow we die!* [27] Don't let anybody [33] deceive you. "Bad company ruins good habits." * Come back [34] to a sober and righteous life, and don't sin any more. Some people don't know God. I say this to make you feel ashamed.

Our Glorified Bodies

But somebody will ask, "How do the dead rise? And what [35] kind of body will they have when they come back?"

Just think a little! The seed you sow has to die before it is [36] made alive. And the seed you sow is not the body that it will be, [37] but a bare kernel, maybe wheat or something else. But God [38] gives it the body He wanted it to have, and to each kind of seed its own body. Not all flesh is the same. Human beings have one [39] kind of flesh, animals have another, birds have another, and fish have another kind of flesh. And so there are heavenly bodies [40] and earthly bodies. But the splendor of the heavenly bodies is different from that of the earthly bodies. The shining of the sun [41] is different from the shining of the moon, and the shining of the stars is different again. Even one star shines brighter than another.

That is how it will be when the dead rise. When the body is [42] sown, it decays; when it rises, it can't decay. When it is sown, [43] it isn't wonderful; when it rises, it is wonderful. It is sown weak; it rises strong. It is sown a natural body; it rises a body of the [44] Spirit. Just as there is a natural body, so there is a body of the Spirit.

That is what the Bible says: *Adam, the first man, was made* [45] *a natural living being;* the last Adam became a Spirit who makes alive. That which has the Spirit doesn't come first, but the natural; [46] then that which has the Spirit. The first *man is made of the soil* [47] *of the ground;* [28] the Second Man is from heaven. The people [48] of the ground are like the man from the ground; the people of heaven are like the Man from heaven. Just as we have been like [49] the man from the ground, let us be like the Man from heaven. I tell you, fellow Christians, flesh and blood can't have a share [50] in God's kingdom, or decay have what doesn't decay.

* Menander.

15:51　　　Now I'll tell you a secret. We're not all going to die, but
52　we're all going to be changed — in a moment, in the twinkling
of an eye when the last trumpet sounds. It will sound, and the
53　dead will rise immortal, and we'll be changed. This decaying
body must be made one that can't decay, and this dying body
54　must be made one that can't die. When this decaying body is
made one that can't decay and this dying body is made one that
can't die, then will happen what is written: *Death is destroyed*
55　*in victory!* [29]

Where, Death, is your victory?
Where, Death, is your sting? [30]

56-57　Sin gives death its sting, and the Law gives sin its power. But
thank God! He gives us the victory through our Lord Jesus Christ.
58　　　Stand firm, then, my dear fellow Christians, and let nothing
move you. Always keep on doing a great work for the Lord
since you know in the Lord your hard work isn't wasted.

The Collection

16　　　About the collection for the holy people — do just as I ordered
2　the churches in Galatia to do. Every Sunday each of you should
at home lay aside some money he makes and save it so that none
3　will have to be collected when I come. But when I come, I will
send the men whom you approve with letters to take your gift
4　to Jerusalem. If it is worthwhile for me to go, too, I'll go
with them.

I Am Coming

5　　　I will come to you when I go through Macedonia. I am going
6　through Macedonia, and probably will stay with you or even spend
the winter with you so that you will send me on my way wherever
7　I'm going. I don't want to see you now just in passing, because
I hope to stay with you for some time if the Lord will let me.
8-9　But I'll be staying in Ephesus till Pentecost, because a door has
opened wide for me to do effective work, and many are opposing me.

Timothy, Apollos, and Others

10　　　If Timothy comes, see to it he's not afraid when he's with
11　you. He's doing the Lord's work just as I am. Nobody should
despise him. Send him on his way in peace so he will come to
me, because I'm expecting him with the other Christians.

312

As for Apollos, our fellow worker — I tried hard to get him to go to you with the other Christians, but God didn't at all want him to go now. He will come when the time is right.

Watch, stand firm in your faith, *be men, be strong.*[31] Do everything with love.

You know that the family of Stephanas was the first to be won in Greece, and they gave themselves to the service of the holy people. I urge you, my fellow Christians, ' let such people and anyone else who works hard with you lead you. I'm glad Stephanas, Fortunatus, and Achaicus came here, because they have made up for your absence: They have refreshed me — and you too. You should appreciate men like that.

Greetings

The churches in the province of Asia greet you. Aquila and Prisca and the church at their home send you hearty greetings in the Lord. ' All the Christians greet you. Greet one another with a holy kiss. Here is the greeting that I, Paul, write with my own hand.

If anyone doesn't love the Lord, a curse on him! Our Lord, come!

May the Lord Jesus love you! My love be with you all in Christ Jesus. Amen.

OLD TESTAMENT REFERENCES

1. Is. 29:14; Ps. 33:10
2. Is. 19:12; 33:18
3. Is. 44:25
4. Jer. 9:24
5. Is. 64:4
6. Is. 40:13
7. Job 5:13
8. Ps. 94:11
9. Ex. 12:21
10. Deut. 17:7; 19:19; 22:21, 24; 24:7
11. Gen. 2:24
12. Deut. 25:4
13. Num. 14:16
14. Num. 11:4, 34
15. Ex. 32:6
16. Deut. 32:17; Ps. 106:37
17. Mal. 1:7, 12
18. Deut. 32:21
19. Ps. 24:1
20. Gen. 1:27
21. Ex. 24:8; Zech. 9:11
22. Zech. 7:10; 8:17
23. Is. 28:11-12
24. Is. 45:14
25. Ps. 110:1
26. Ps. 8:6
27. Is. 22:13
28. Gen. 2:7
29. Is. 25:8
30. Hos. 13:14
31. Ps. 31:24

PAUL

writes the Second Letter to the

CORINTHIANS

MACEDONIA
A. D. 55

1 PAUL, APOSTLE OF CHRIST JESUS by God's will, and Timothy, our fellow worker, to God's church in Corinth and to all the **2** holy people everywhere in Greece — may God our Father and the Lord Jesus Christ love you and give you peace!

God Comforts and Rescues Us

3 Let us praise the God and Father of our Lord Jesus Christ, **4** the Father of mercy and the God of every comfort. He comforts us in all our suffering to make us able to comfort others in all their suffering with the same comfort with which God comforts us. **5** As Christ's sufferings overflow to us, so Christ makes our comfort **6** overflow. If we suffer, it helps us to comfort and save you. If we are comforted, it helps us to comfort you effectively when you **7** endure the same sufferings as we do. Our hope for you is unshaken because we know as you share our sufferings you share our comfort.

8 Fellow Christians, we want you to know our suffering in the province of Asia was so extreme, so much more than we could **9** stand, we even despaired of living. Yes, we felt sentenced to death. We were not to trust ourselves but God, who raises the **10** dead. He rescued us from such a death, and He who is our hope **11** will rescue us again. He will continue to rescue us if you, too, will help us by praying — and have many people look up to God and thank Him for what He gave us.

We Were Sincere

12 This is what we're proud of. Our conscience tells us that with God's holiness and sincerity, without human cleverness but

314

with God's love, we have lived in the world and especially with 1:13
you. We are writing you only what you can read and understand.
And I hope you will understand till the end, ¹ as you have to some 14
extent understood us, that you can be proud of us as also we of
you on the day of our Lord Jesus.

Feeling sure of this, I wanted you to have the benefit of 15
a double visit. I planned to come to you first, ¹ go from you to 16
Macedonia, then come back again from Macedonia to you and
let you send me on to Judea.

When I wanted to do this, was I trifling? Or do I go on 17
making my plans any way I please so that I can say "Yes, yes"
and "No, no"? You can trust God that what we tell you isn't 18
yes and no. God's Son Jesus Christ, whom I, Silas, and Timothy 19
preached to you, wasn't yes and no, but in Him there has come
and is a yes. For all God's promises He is the Yes that makes 20
them come true. And so He makes it possible for us to give
glory to God by saying, "It is true."

It is God who makes us and you firm in the anointed Savior 21
and also has anointed us. He has put His seal on us and given 22
us the Spirit as a guarantee in our hearts.

I Don't Want to Hurt You

I call on God as a witness against me that I stayed away from 23
Corinth in order not to hurt you. I don't mean we're lords of 24
your faith, but we're working with you to make you happy. You
stand on your own feet in your faith.

I made up my mind not to come if I had to bring you grief 2
again. If I make you sad, who should make me happy but the 2
person I'm making sad? ¹ This is what I said in my letter. I didn't 3
want to come and be made sad by those who should have made
me happy. Feeling sure about all of you that what makes me
happy makes all of you happy too. I was deeply troubled and in 4
anguish when I wrote you with much weeping, not to make you
sad but to have you realize how very much I love you.

Forgive the Man Who Did Wrong

If someone caused grief, he didn't do it to me but to some 5
extent (not to make it too strong) to all of you. Most of you 6
have punished him; that's enough for such a person. Now you 7
should turn around, forgive and comfort him, or too much grief
may overwhelm such a person. So I urge you to assure him of 8

2:9 your love. I wrote you to see if you would stand the test and obey in every way.

10 When you forgive anyone, I do too. If I forgave anything,
11 I did it in the presence of Christ to help you [1] and to keep the devil from getting the best of us. We know what he has in mind.

An Odor of Life

12 I went to Troas to tell the good news of Christ, and there
13 a door to do the Lord's work stood wide open for me, but my spirit couldn't get any relief because I didn't find Titus, my fellow worker. So I said good-by to the people and went to Macedonia.
14 But thank God! He always leads us on triumphantly in Christ and everywhere through us spreads the fragrance of knowing Him.
15 Yes, we are a fragrance of Christ to God among those who are
16 saved and among those who perish — to some an odor of death that kills, to others an odor of life that gives life.
17 And who is qualified for this? — At least we don't peddle an impure Word of God like many others, but in Christ we talk sincerely as men who come from God and stand before God.

3 Are we again recommending ourselves? Or do we, like some people, need letters of recommendation to you or from you?
2 You are our letter, written in our hearts, known and read by
3 everybody. Anyone can see you are Christ's letter, prepared by us, not written with ink but with the Spirit *of* the living *God,* not *on stone plates* but *on human hearts.*[1]

4-5 That is how Christ gives us confidence in God. We can't do anything by ourselves and so claim to produce it ourselves,
6 but God gives us our ability. He has made us able servants of a new covenant, not of a written Law but of the Spirit, because the written Law kills, but the Spirit makes alive.

The Glory of the New Covenant

7 Now if that service, engraved in stone and bringing death, came with such glory the people of Israel couldn't look at *Moses'*
8 *face* because it *shone with the glory* that was fading, how much
9 more certainly will the service of the Spirit have *glory?* If the service that condemns has *glory,* the service that gives righteous-
10 ness much more certainly overflows with *glory.* That which had
11 *glory* lost it because the other *glory* outshone it. If that which fades away had its *glory,* that which is permanent much more certainly has *glory.*

316

Because we expect this, we are very bold [1] and not like *Moses,*
who *wore a veil over his face* to keep the people of Israel from
seeing the last rays of the fading *glory.* But their minds have 14
been closed. To this day the same *veil* is still there on the reading
of the old covenant and isn't taken away, because it is put away
only in Christ. Yes, to this day, when they read Moses, a *veil* 15
lies on their hearts. But *whenever anyone turns to the Lord,* 16
the veil is taken away.[2]

The Lord is the Spirit, and where the Spirit of the Lord is, 17
there is liberty. And all of us, reflecting *the Lord's glory* [3] in our 18
unveiled faces, are changed from glory to glory to be like Him,
as we expect it from the Lord, who is the Spirit.

Treasure in Clay Jars

And so we who by God's mercy have this service don't get 4
discouraged. But we have renounced the secret ways that any- 2
body should feel ashamed of. We don't use trickery or falsify
God's Word. But by clearly telling the truth we recommend
ourselves to everyone's conscience before God.

If the good news we tell is veiled, it is veiled to those who 3
perish, [1] whose minds the god of this world has blinded — they 4
don't believe — to keep them from seeing the light of the good
news of the glory of Christ, who is God's image.

You see, we don't preach ourselves but Jesus Christ as the 5
Lord, and we are your servants for Jesus' sake. God, who said, 6
"*Let light shine* [4] out of the dark," has shone in our hearts to
bring you the light of knowing God's glory in the face of Jesus
Christ.

We have this treasure in clay jars to show that its extraordinary 7
power comes from God and not from us. In every way we are 8
hard pressed but not crushed, in doubt but not in despair;
[1] hunted but not forsaken; struck down but not destroyed. We are 9—10
in our bodies always being killed with Jesus so that you can see
in our bodies the life of Jesus. While we're living, we're always 11
being given up to die for Jesus so that you can see in our dying
bodies the life of Jesus. So death is working in us, but life is 12
working in you.

· It is written, *I believed and so I spoke.*[5] Having the same 13
spirit of faith, we also believe and so we speak, [1] because we 14
know that He who raised the Lord Jesus will also raise us with
Jesus and bring us with you before Him.

All this is to help you so that God's love, as it spreads will move more and more people to overflow with thanks to God's 16 glory. That is why we are not discouraged. No, even if we out- 17 wardly perish, inwardly we're renewed from day to day. The light trouble of this moment is preparing for us an everlasting 18 weight of glory, greater than anything we can imagine. We don't look at the things that are seen but at the things that are not seen. What we see lasts only a while, but what we don't see lasts forever.

We Long for a Heavenly Body

5 If the earthly tent we live in is torn down, we know we'll get one from God, not made by human hands but lasting forever 2 in heaven. In this body we sigh as we long to put on and live 3 in the body we get from heaven. Of course, if we put that on, 4 we'll not be found without a body. So while we are in this tent, we sigh, feeling oppressed because we don't want to put off this body but put on the other and have life swallow up our death. 5 It is God who has prepared us for this and given us His Spirit as a guarantee.

6 And so we always feel confident. We know that as long as 7 we are living in this body we are living away from the Lord. We 8 live by trusting Him, without seeing Him. We feel bold and prefer 9 to move out of this body and move in with the Lord. Now, whether we live here or move out, we try hard to please Him. 10 We must all appear before the judgment seat of Christ each to get paid for what he has done with his body, good or bad.

Christ Compels Us

11 Since we know the terror of the Lord, we're trying to win the confidence of people. God already knows what we really are, 12 and I hope you, too, are clearly conscious of it. We are not recommending ourselves to you again but giving you a reason to be proud of us so that you can answer those who boast about 13 outward things but nothing in the heart. If we were crazy, it 14 was for God. If we're sane, it is for you. The love of Christ compels us because we're convinced One died for all and so all 15 have died. He died for all that those who live should no longer live for themselves but for Him who died and rose for them.

16 And so from now on we don't think of anyone only as a human being. Once we thought of Christ only as a man, but not now any-

more. [|] So if anyone is in Christ, he is a new being. The old things have passed away. They have become new.

Be God's Friends

But God has done it all. When we were His enemies, **18** through Christ He made us His friends and gave us the work of making friends of enemies. In Christ, God was getting rid of the **19** enmity between Himself and the people of the world by not counting their sins against them, and He has put into our hands the message how God and men are made friends again. Since **20** God is pleading through us, we are ambassadors for Christ. We ask you for Christ, "Come and be God's friends." God made **21** Him who did not know sin to be sin for us to make us God's righteousness in Him.

As men who are working with God we plead with you: **6** Don't let God's love be wasted on you. He says, **2**

> *When the time comes to be kind, I will answer you,*
> *And when the time comes to save, I will help you.*

You know

> Now is *the time when He welcomes* us,
> Now is *the time when He saves* [6] us.

So We Endure

We're not in any way giving people a reason to turn away, to **3** keep them from finding fault with our work. Instead we're in **4** everything showing we're God's good workers by great endurance in suffering, in need, and in hardships; when we're beaten or put in **5** prison; in riots; when we're overworked and go without sleep and food; by being pure, by knowledge, by patience and kindness; **6** by the Holy Spirit; by sincere love; [|] by telling the truth; by God's **7** power; with the weapons of righteousness in the right hand and the left; when we're honored or dishonored, blamed or praised. **8** Treated as deceivers, we are honest; [|] as unknown, we are well **9** known; as *dying,* and you see, we go on *living;* as *corrected but not killed;* [7] [|] as sad, we're always glad; as beggars, we're mak- **10** ing many rich; as having nothing, we really have everything.

We have talked frankly to you Corinthians. Our *hearts are* **11** *wide open.*[8] There's plenty of room in them for you, but you're **12** narrow in your feelings toward us. I ask you as my children: **13** Treat me as I treat you, and open your hearts wide, too.

Don't Touch Anything Unclean

6:14   Don't be yoked with unbelievers. How can right and wrong be partners? Or how can light have anything to do with dark-
15   ness? ¹ How can Christ agree with the devil? Or what does
16   a believer have in common with an unbeliever? How can God's temple agree with idols? Now, we are the temple of the living God, as God said, *I will live and walk among them, and I will be*
17   *their God, and they will be My people.* So, *come out of them, and separate from them,* says the Lord, *and don't touch anything*
18   *unclean. Then I will welcome you,* ¹ *and I will be* your *Father,* and you *will be My sons* and daughters, says *the Almighty Lord.*⁹

7   Since we have such promises, dear friends, let us cleanse ourselves from everything that soils body and spirit as we try to be perfectly holy in the fear of God.

You Encouraged Us

2   Make room in your hearts for us. We haven't wronged any-
3   one, ruined anyone, gotten the best of anyone. I'm not saying this to condemn you. I've told you before, you are in our hearts
4   to die together and to live together. I have much confidence in you. I'm very proud of you. I'm very much encouraged. I'm overjoyed in all our troubles.

5   Even when we came to Macedonia, our bodies got no rest. We were in every kind of trouble, outwardly fighting and in-
6   wardly afraid. But *God,* who *comforts those who feel miserable,*
7   *comforted* ¹⁰ us by the coming of Titus, ¹ and not only by his coming but also by the way you encouraged him. He told us how you long for me, how sorry you are, and how eager to take my side, and this made me happier still.

8   I'm not sorry if my letter made you sad. Even if I did feel sorry when I saw that letter make you sad, though only for
9   a while, ¹ I'm glad now, not that you were sad but that your sad-ness led you to feel sorry for sin. You were sad in God's way.
10   And so we haven't done you any harm. ¹ Being sad in God's way makes you feel sorry for sin so as to save you — you can't
11   regret that. But the sorrow of the world brings death. ¹ See how eager God's sorrow has made you, how ready to clear yourselves, how disgusted with wrong, how alarmed you were, what longing and zeal you felt, and how ready you were to punish! In every

way you've shown you're innocent in this matter. Although
I wrote you, I didn't have in mind the man who did wrong or
him who was wronged, but I wanted to show you before God
how zealous you are for us. This is what encouraged us. 13

While we were encouraged, we were much more delighted to
see how happy Titus was because all of you had cheered him up.
If I boasted to him about you, you didn't disappoint me. But 14
just as everything we told you was true, so what we had proudly
told Titus proved to be true. And his heart goes out to you, 15
all the more as he recalls how ready all of you were to do what
he asked and how you welcomed him with respect and trembling.
I'm glad I can in every way feel confident about you. 16

Finish Your Collection

Fellow Christians, we want you to know what God's gift 8
of love has done in the churches of Macedonia. While they were 2
severely tested by trouble, their overflowing joy and their deep
poverty have yielded a richly overflowing generosity. I assure 3
you they have given all they could, yes, more than they could
give, of their own free will, and with much pleading they begged 4
us for the privilege of sharing in the help given the holy people.
They did more than we expected: they gave themselves to the 5
Lord first and then to us, doing just what God wanted.

This led us to urge Titus, as he had started it, to finish in 6
you, too, this work of love. As you are rich in everything, in 7
faith, speech, knowledge, every kind of zeal, and in the love we
stirred up in you, we want you also to be rich in this work
of kindness.

I'm not ordering you but testing you by the zeal of others 8
to see how real your love is. You know the love of our Lord 9
Jesus Christ — He was rich, but became poor for you to make
you rich by His poverty.

I'm telling you what I think you should do about this, be- 10
cause it is best for you. Last year you were the first not only
to do something but to want to do something. Now finish the 11
job — you were eager to undertake it — in the same way finish
it as well as you can. If you're eager to give, God accepts you 12
according to what you have, not according to what you don't
have.

We don't mean to bring relief to others and hardship to you 13

321

8:14 but to be fair. Right now what you don't need should relieve their need so that what they will not need will relieve your need,

15 and so it will be fair, ¹ as it is written: *Anyone who got much didn't have too much, and anyone who got little didn't have too little.*¹¹

16 We thank God for making Titus just as eager to help you as
17 I am. ¹ He welcomed my request. He's very eager and is by his own choice coming to you.

18 We're sending with him the fellow Christian whom all the
19 churches praise for his telling the good news. More than that, the churches appointed him to travel with us in this work of love we're doing to honor the Lord and show we're willing to help.

20 We're trying to avoid any criticism of the way we're handling
21 this great gift. We *intend to do what's right not only before the Lord but also before other people.*¹²

22 We are also sending with them our fellow Christian whom we have often tested in many ways and found zealous and now more eager than ever because he has so much confidence in you.

23 As for Titus, he is my partner and fellow worker among you. And our fellow Christians, the messengers of the churches, are
24 the glory of Christ. Show the churches how you love them and how right we were when we boasted to them about you.

How to Give

9 I really don't need to write you about helping the holy people,
2 ¹ because I know how eager you are. That's what I'm telling the people in Macedonia in boasting about you, "Greece has been ready since last year," and your enthusiasm has stirred up
3 most of them. Now I'm sending my fellow workers so that we may not have been wrong in boasting about you on this point
4 but that you may be ready as I said. Otherwise, if any Macedonians come with me and find you aren't ready, you would make us (to say nothing of yourselves) feel ashamed of being
5 so confident. So I thought it necessary to urge these fellow workers to go to you ahead of me, arrange in advance the gift you promised and have it ready as money that was gladly given and not forced out of you.

6 Remember this: *If you sow little, you won't get much grain.*
7 But *if you sow generously, you will get much grain.* ¹ Everyone

should do what he has made up his mind to do, not with regret or being forced, because *God* loves *anyone who gives gladly.*¹³

God Blesses You

God can pour out every gift of His love on you so you will ⁹:⁸ always in every way have all you need and plenty to do any good work. The Bible says of such a person, *He scatters his* ⁹ *gifts to the poor. His righteousness goes on forever.*¹⁴ ¹ He who ¹⁰ gives *seed to the sower and bread to eat,*¹⁵ will give you seed and multiply it and make *your righteous grain* ¹⁶ grow. You ¹¹ will get rich in everything so you can give generously in every way; through us this will make people thank God. This work ¹² you do in serving others doesn't only supply the needs of the holy people; it makes them pour out many thanks to God. As ¹³ you prove by this service what you are, they praise God that you submit to the good news of Christ which you confess and that you freely share with them and with everybody. While ¹⁴ they pray for you, they long for you because they see what an extraordinary gift God's love has brought you. Thanks be to ¹⁵ God for His gift that is more than we can tell.

I Am Bold

I myself, Paul, plead with you with the gentleness and kind- ¹⁰ liness of Christ — I who am humble when I'm face to face with you but get bold toward you when I'm away! I beg you that ² when I come I don't have to be as confident and bold as I think I'll dare to be against some men who think we're living accord- ing to the flesh. Of course, we're living in the flesh, but we're ³ not fighting in a fleshly way. The weapons we fight with are not ⁴ those of the flesh but have the power before God to tear down fortresses. With them we tear down arguments ¹ and everything ⁵ raising its proud head against the knowledge of God and make every opposing thought a prisoner and have it obey Christ. We're ready to punish every disobedience when you are com- ⁶ pletely obedient.

You see things as they are outwardly. If anyone feels sure he ⁷ belongs to Christ, he should remind himself that we belong to Christ just as he does. If I boast a little too much about our ⁸ authority, which the Lord gave us to build you up and not to tear

10:9 you down, I will not have to feel ashamed. I don't want to seem to scare you with my letters.

10 "His letters are impressive and strong," somebody says, "but when he's with us, he's weak, and people despise what he says." 11 Such a person should understand: When we come, we'll act exactly the way we express ourselves in letters when we're away.

We Are Proud of Our Work

12 We don't dare to put ourselves in a class or compare ourselves with some of those who speak highly of themselves, but when they measure themselves by their own yardstick and compare themselves with themselves, they don't show good sense. 13 Now we'll limit our boasting. Our limit is the field of work to which God has bound us. This includes coming to you. 14 It is not as though we were not coming to you and so we are reaching beyond our limit. We were the first to reach you with 15 the good news of Christ. We are not going beyond our limit and boasting of work done by others, but we expect your faith to grow so as to enlarge the work in our field in your area till it 16 goes beyond you, and so we'll tell the good news in the countries beyond you without boasting of work already done in another man's field.

17 But *if anyone feels proud, he should feel proud of the Lord.*[17] 18 Not the man who approves of himself is really approved but he of whom the Lord approves.

I Am Jealous

11 I wish you would put up with a little foolishness of mine. 2 Yes, do put up with me. I am jealous of you with God's own jealousy. I promised you in marriage, to bring you as a pure 3 bride to one husband — to Christ. But I'm afraid that as *the snake* by its trickery *seduced*[18] Eve, your minds may somehow be corrupted and you may lose your simple and pure loyalty to 4 Christ. When somebody comes along and preaches a different Jesus whom we didn't preach or gives you a different spirit you didn't get before or a different gospel you didn't receive before, you put up with it well enough.

5 I don't think I'm in any way less than your "super" apostles. 6 Even if I'm no trained speaker, I know what I'm talking about. In every way we have shown you this before everybody.

7 Did I do wrong when I humbled myself so you would be

lifted up, when I charged you nothing for bringing you God's good news? I robbed other churches, taking pay from them in 11:8 order to serve you. When I was with you and needed anything, 9 I didn't bother anyone to help me, because our fellow workers * who came from Macedonia supplied all I needed. I kept myself from being a burden to you in any way, and I'll continue to do so. As the truth of Christ is in me, this boast of mine will not be 10 silenced anywhere in Greece. Why? Because I don't love you? 11 God knows I do. And I will go on doing as I do, to take away 12 the opportunity of those who want it to get others to think they are like us in the work they're boasting about. Such men are 13 false apostles, deceitful workers masquerading as apostles of Christ. And no wonder, when the devil himself masquerades as 14 an angel of light. So it isn't surprising if his servants also 15 masquerade as servants of righteousness. In the end they'll get what they deserve for what they're doing.

I Will Boast

Again I say nobody should think I'm a fool. But if you do, 16 then let me come to you as a fool and also boast a little. What 17 I say when I boast so confidently is not the Lord's way of speaking but a fool's. Since many brag in a human way, I will, too, 18 because you, being wise, like to put up with fools. You put up 19-20 with anyone who makes you his slaves or devours what you have or traps you or lords it over you or slaps your face. I'm 21 ashamed to admit it: As you say, we have been too weak.

But what anyone else dares to claim — I'm talking like a fool — I can claim too. Are they Jews? So am I! Do they 22 belong to the people of Israel? So do I! Are they descended from Abraham? So am I! Are they servants of Christ? I'm mad 23 to talk like this, but I'm a better one! I've done much more hard work, been in prison much more, been beaten very much more, and often faced death. Five times the Jews gave me 24 thirty-nine lashes, three times I was beaten with a stick, once I was stoned, three times I was in a shipwreck, a night and 25 a day I drifted in the water. I've traveled much and faced 26 dangers of flooded streams and of robbers, dangers from Jews and non-Jews, dangers in the city, in the wilderness, and on the sea, dangers from false friends. I have toiled and struggled, 27 often sleepless, hungry and thirsty, often starving, cold, and

* Silas and Timothy. (Acts 18:5; 2 Cor. 1:19)

11:28 naked. Besides everything else, I have a daily burden — I'm
29 anxiously concerned about all the churches. When anyone is
weak, am I not weak too? When anyone is led into sin, don't
30 I feel a burning shame? If I have to boast, I'll boast of the
31 things that show how weak I am. The God and Father of the
Lord Jesus, who is blessed forever, knows I'm not lying.
32 In Damascus the governor under King Aretas had the city of
33 Damascus watched to catch me, but through an opening in the
wall I was let down in a basket, and I escaped.

Caught Up to Paradise

12 I have to boast. It doesn't do any good, but I'll go on with
2 what the Lord has shown and told me. I know a man in Christ;
fourteen years ago — whether in his body or outside it, I don't
know, God knows — that man was caught up to the third
3 heaven. I know that such a man — whether in his body or out-
4 side it, I don't know, God knows — was caught up to Paradise
5 and heard what no human being can or may tell. About such
a man I will boast, but as to myself, I will boast only of my
weaknesses.
6 But if I would want to boast, I wouldn't be a fool, because
I'd be telling the truth. But I'm not going to do it, in order to
keep anyone from thinking more of me than he judges me to be
by seeing me or hearing me.
7 To keep me from feeling proud because such wonderful things
were revealed to me, a thorn was put into my flesh, the devil's
8 messenger to plague me and keep me from getting proud. Three
9 times I begged the Lord to have him leave me alone, but He told
me, "My love is enough for you. When you are weak, My
power is doing its best work." So I'll delight rather to feel proud
of my weaknesses in order to have Christ's power rest on me.
10 That's why I'm glad to be weak and mistreated, to suffer hardships,
to be persecuted and hard pressed for Christ. You see, when
I'm weak, then I'm strong.

I Will Be No Burden

11 I've become a fool. You forced me to it. Really, you should
have spoken well of me. Even if I'm nothing, I wasn't in any
12 way inferior to your "super" apostles. The miracles that prove
I'm an apostle were very patiently done among you — miracles,
wonders, and works of power.

How were you treated worse than the other churches except that I didn't burden you? Forgive me this wrong! Here I'm ready to come to you a third time, and I'm not going to be a burden, because I don't want your things but you. Children shouldn't save up for their parents but parents for their children. And I'll be very glad to spend what I have and myself, too, to help you. Do you love me less because I love you so much?

But granting I was no burden to you, was I a clever fellow who trapped you with some trick? Did I take advantage of you through any of the men I sent you? I urged Titus to go to you, and I sent the fellow worker with him. Titus didn't take advantage of you, did he? Didn't both of us act in the same spirit? And do exactly the same things?

Have you been thinking all along we're only defending ourselves before you? We are speaking before God in Christ, and everything, dear friends, is meant to help you.

Will There Be Trouble?

I'm afraid I may come and find you different from what I want you to be, and you may find me different from what you want me to be. And there may be quarreling, jealousy, angry feelings, selfishness, slander, gossip, proud and disorderly behavior. When I come, my God may again humble me before you, and I may have to weep over many who formerly lived in sin and haven't felt sorry for the unclean, sexual, and lustful things they did.

This will be the third time I'm coming to you. **13**

Everything must be proved by two or three witnesses. When I was with you the second time as well as now when I'm not with you, I warned and I still warn you who formerly lived in sin and all you others: When I come again, I won't spare you — seeing that you want proof that Christ is speaking through me. He's not weak in dealing with you but powerful in you. He died on a cross in weakness, but He lives by God's power. We, too, are weak in Him, but with Him we'll live by God's power as it comes to you.

Examine yourselves to see if you really believe. Test yourselves. Don't you know Jesus Christ is in you — unless you fail in your test? I hope you'll see we haven't failed in our test. We pray God you will do no wrong — not to show we haven't failed, but we want you to do what is right even if we may seem to have

327

13:8 failed. We can't do anything against the truth but only work
9 for it. ¹ We are glad when we're weak and you're strong. And we're praying that you may grow to be perfect.
10 Here's the reason I'm writing this while I'm not with you: When I come, I don't want to be sharp in using the authority the Lord gave me to build you up and not to tear you down.

Farewell

11 Finally, fellow Christians, farewell! Keep on growing to be perfect. Take encouragement from me. Agree with one another, live in peace, and the God of love and peace will be with you.
12 ¹ Greet one another with a holy kiss. All the holy people greet you.
13 The grace of the Lord Jesus Christ, the love of God, and the Holy Spirit as you share Him be with you all!

OLD TESTAMENT REFERENCES

1. Ex. 24:12; 31:18;
   Prov. 3:3; Ezek.
   11:19; 36:26
2. Ex. 34:29-30, 33-35
3. Ex. 16:7, 10; 24:17
4. Gen. 1:3
5. Ps. 116:10
6. Is. 49:8
7. Ps. 118:17-18
8. Ps. 119:32
9. Lev. 26:11-12;
   2 Sam. 7:7, 14;
   Is. 52:11;
   Jer. 32:38; 51:45;
   Ezek. 20:34, 41;
   37:27; Amos
   4:13
10. Is. 49:13
11. Ex. 16:18
12. Prov. 3:4
13. Prov. 22:8
14. Ps. 112:9
15. Is. 55:10
16. Hos. 10:12
17. Jer. 9:24
18. Gen. 3:4, 13
19. Deut. 19:15

P A U L

writes to the

GALATIANS

ANTIOCH, SYRIA
A. D. 48

PAUL, AN APOSTLE not sent from men or by any man but by **1**
Jesus Christ and by God the Father, who raised Him from the
dead, ¹ and all the Christians who are with me, to the churches **2**
in Galatia — love and peace to you from God the Father and **3**
our Lord Jesus Christ, who gave Himself for our sins to save **4**
us from this present wicked world according to the will of our
God and Father. To Him be glory forever! Amen. **5**

You Are Turning Away

I am surprised you are so soon leaving Him who called you **6**
by the love of Christ and are turning to another kind of good
news, ¹ which really is not another. But there are some men who **7**
are troubling you and want to change the good news of Christ.
But even if we or an angel from heaven would bring you any **8**
other good news than what we brought you, a curse be on him!
I say again what we said before: If anyone brings you any **9**
other good news than the one you received, a curse be on him!

Do I say this now to get the approval of men — or of God? **10**
Or am I trying to please men? If I were still trying to please
men, I wouldn't be a servant of Christ.

Jesus Gave Me the Good News

I tell you, my fellow Christians, the good news I told is not **11**
a human idea, ¹ because no man gave it or taught it to me, but **12**
Jesus Christ revealed it to me.

You have heard what I used to do when I still lived according **13**
to the Jewish religion, how violently I persecuted God's church
and tried to destroy it ¹ and how in this Jewish religion I was **14**
ahead of many of my own age among my people, so extremely
zealous was I for the traditions of my ancestors.

But God *had appointed me before I was born,*[1] and in His
16 love He called me. And when He kindly decided to show me
His Son so that I would tell the good news of Him among the
17 Gentiles, I didn't talk it over with other men [1] or go up to Jerusalem to see those who were apostles before me, but I went
immediately to Arabia * and then came back to Damascus.

18 After three years I went up to Jerusalem to get to know
19 Peter, and I stayed with him fifteen days. But I didn't see any
20 of the other apostles, only James, the Lord's brother. (And I de-
21 clare before God I'm writing you no lie.) Then I went to the
22 regions of Syria and Cilicia. In Judea the churches of Christ
23 didn't know me personally. They only heard people say: "The
man who used to persecute us is now preaching the faith he
24 once tried to destroy," and they praised God for what they
saw in me.

Fellowship with the Apostles

2 Fourteen years later I went up to Jerusalem again, this time
2 with Barnabas, and I also took Titus with me. (God had told
me to go.) Then I laid before the Christians, and privately before
the leaders, the good news I preach among the non-Jewish people.
I didn't in any way want to run or to have run in vain.

3 Titus was with me, and he's a Greek. But nobody forced
4 him to be circumcised [1] to please the false Christians who had
come in secretly. They sneaked in to spy out the liberty we have
5 in Christ Jesus and to make us slaves. Not for a moment did
we let them dictate to us, so that you will always have the real
good news.

6 I don't care what those leaders once were — *God doesn't
prefer one to another.*[2] Those leaders didn't teach me anything
7 new. On the contrary, they saw I had been entrusted with bringing the good news to the non-Jews as Peter was to bring it to the
8 Jews. He who had worked in Peter to make him an apostle to
the Jews had worked in me to make me an apostle to the non-
9 Jews. When James, Peter, and John, who were considered pillars,
saw what God's love had given me, they gave me and Barnabas
the right hand of fellowship with the understanding that we
10 work among the non-Jews and they among the Jews. All they
asked was that we remember the poor, and that I was eager to do.

* This part of Arabia may be near Damascus.

I Criticized Peter

But when Peter came to Antioch, I opposed him to his face   2:11
because he had shown how wrong he was. He had been eating   12
with the non-Jews before certain men came from James. But
when they came, he held back and kept away from non-Jews
because he was afraid of those who believed in circumcision.
And the other Jews acted just as insincerely as he did, so much   13
so even Barnabas was carried away to be a hypocrite with them.

But when I saw they were not doing right according to the   14
truth of the good news, I told Peter before everybody: "If you,
a Jew, don't live like a Jew but like a non-Jew, how can you
insist the non-Jews must live like Jews?

"We were born Jews and not Gentile sinners; yet we know   15-16
a person cannot become righteous * by doing what the Law says,
but only by believing in Jesus Christ. Even we came to believe
in Jesus Christ to become righteous * by believing in Christ
and not by doing what the Law says, because *no one will become
righteous* *³ by doing what the Law says.

"Now if we who want to be righteous in Christ are found   17
to be sinners like the non-Jews, does Christ encourage us to sin?
Never! ¹ But if I build up again what I've torn down, I make   18
myself a sinner. By the Law I died to the Law, to live for God.**   19
I was crucified with Christ, and I don't live any more, but Christ   20
lives in me. The life I now live in my body I live by believing
in the God and Christ who loved me and gave Himself for me.
¹ I don't reject God's gift of love. You see, if we could get right-   21
eousness through the Law, then Christ died for nothing."

The Believer Is Blessed

You foolish Galatians! Who has bewitched you — you who   3
saw Jesus Christ publicly pictured as crucified? I want you to   2
tell me just one thing: Did you get the Spirit by doing what the
Law says or by the truth you heard and believed? Are you so   3
foolish? You started with the Spirit; are you now going to finish
with the flesh? ¹ Did you experience so much for nothing? Perhaps   4

* See note at Rom. 3:20.

** The meaning of verses 17-19 is this: When we don't try to be
righteous by doing what the Law demands, we "tear down" the Law, and
the Jews may think we are just non-Jewish sinners. If to please the Jews,
we try again to do what the Law demands and so "build it up," the Law
only condemns us as sinners. The Law condemned Jesus for our sins
and killed Him, and us with Him. Now the Law can't demand any more
from us than from a dead person.

3:5 it really was for nothing! Does God give you the Spirit and make such powers active in you by your doing what the Law says or by the truth you hear and believe?

6 It was the same way with *Abraham*. He *believed God, and*
7 *so he was counted righteous.*[4] You see, then, that those who
8 believe are Abraham's real descendants. The Bible foresaw that God would make the nations righteous * by faith, and long ago He told Abraham the good news, *Through you all nations will*
9 *be blessed.*[5] So those who believe are blessed with Abraham, who believed.

10 There is a curse on all who depend on doing what the Law says, because it is written, *Cursed is everyone who doesn't follow*
11 *and do everything written in the book of the Law.*[6] It is clear the Law makes no one righteous * before God, because *if you believe,*
12 *you are righteous * and you will live.*[7] But the Law is not based on faith; no, it says, *If you do these things, you will find life in*
13 *them.*[8] Christ paid the price to free us from the curse of the Law when He was cursed for us (it is written, *Cursed is everyone*
14 *who hangs on a cross*[9]) so that in Jesus Christ Abraham's blessing would come to the nations and we by believing would get the promised Spirit.

The Promise Was First

15 My fellow Christians, let me use an example from daily life. Once a will is ratified, even if it's only a man's will, nobody sets
16 it aside or adds to it. Now the promises were made to Abraham and to his Descendant. He doesn't say, "and, by the descendants," in the plural, but in the singular, and *by your Descendant,*[10]
17 which is Christ. Now, I say this: First God confirmed His covenant; and the Law, which came 430 years later, doesn't set
18 aside and cancel its promise. If we get the inheritance by the Law, we don't get it by a promise; but God gave it to Abraham by a promise.

Our Guardian

19 Why, then, was the Law given? It was added to arouse transgressions ** until the Descendant would come to whom the promise was made. And it was given through angels in the hands

* See note at Rom. 3:20.

** The Law was like a stick with which a trainer stirs up a sleeping wild animal to show how terrible it is.

of a mediator. A mediator deals with more than one, but God is one.*

Is the Law, then, opposed to God's promises? Never! If [21] a law had been given that could make us alive, it certainly would have given us righteousness. But the Bible has condemned all [22] people as sinners so that believers by believing in Jesus Christ would get the promised blessing. Before faith came, we were [23] under the Law, guarded in prison for the faith that was to be revealed. Then the Law has been our guardian so that we would [24] come to Christ and become righteous by faith. But now that [25] faith has come, we are no longer under a guardian. You are [26] all God's children by believing in Christ Jesus, because all of [27] you who were baptized into Christ have put on Christ. There [28] is no Jew or Greek, no slave or free person, no man or woman — you're all one in Christ Jesus. If you belong to Christ, then you [29] are Abraham's descendants and heirs of the blessing God promised.

God's Sons

Now, I say that as long as the heir is a child, he is no better [4] than a slave, although he owns everything. He is under guardians [2] and managers till the day set by his father. So it is with us. [3] When we were children, we were slaves under the elementary ways of the world. But when the right time came, God sent His [4] Son, born of a woman, born under the Law, | to free those under [5] the Law and make us His sons. And because you are sons, [6] God sent into our hearts the Spirit of His Son, who cries, "Father!" | So you are no longer a slave but a son. And if you [7] are His son, God has made you His heir.

But when you didn't know God, you were slaves to gods who [8] really don't exist. Now that you know God — or rather, God [9] knows you — how can you turn back to those elementary ways, so weak and beggarly, and want to be slaves to them again? You [10] keep days, months, seasons, and years! I'm afraid the work I did [11] on you may have been wasted.

You Welcomed Me

I beg you, my fellow Christians, become like me, since I be- [12] came like you. You did me no wrong. | You know I brought you [13]

* God gave the Law to Moses, who brought it to the people, but God gave His promise directly to Abraham.

4:14 the good news the first time because I was sick.* Though my sick body was a test to you, you didn't despise or scorn me, but you welcomed me as if I were God's angel or Christ Jesus

15 Himself. You thought you were happy — what has become of that? I tell you, if possible, you would have torn out your eyes

16 and given them to me. Can it be I have become your enemy by telling you the truth?

17 Those men are making much of you without meaning well. They want to exclude you,** so that you will have to make much

18 of them. It is fine if somebody, meaning well, is always making much of you, not just while I'm with you.

19 My children, I'm suffering birth pains for you again till Christ

20 is formed in you. I could wish I were with you right now and could talk in a different tone of voice because I'm puzzled about you.

We Are like Isaac

21 Tell me, you who want to be under the Law, will you not

22 listen to what the Law says? It is written: Abraham had two sons; one was the son of the slave and the other the son of the free

23 woman. Now, the son of the slave was born like other children, but the son of the free woman by being promised.

24 This has a special meaning. The women are two covenants. The children of the covenant given on Mount Sinai are born to

25 be slaves; this is Hagar. "Hagar" in Arabia means Mount Sinai. She is like Jerusalem today, because she and her children are

26 slaves. But the Jerusalem that is above is free; and she is our

27 mother. It is written:

> Be glad, barren woman, you who don't have any children;
> Break into shouting, you who feel no pains of childbirth,
> Because the deserted woman has many more children
> Than the one who has the husband.[11]

28 Now you, my fellow Christians, like Isaac, are children born by a promise.

29 At that time the son born like other children persecuted the

30 son born by the Spirit. And so it is now. [1] But what does the

* It may have been malaria which forced Paul to leave the swampy country of Pamphylia and to go up into the mountains, 3,600 feet above sea level, and so to come to the Galatians. (Acts 13:13-14)

** Perhaps from Paul, who was anxious to win the non-Jews, and from happiness in Christ.

Bible say? *Put away the slave and her son, because the son of
the slave must not get any of the inheritance of the son* [12] of the
free woman. Now, then, fellow Christians, we are not children
of a slave but of a free woman.

Christ Freed Us

Christ has freed us so that we'll be free. Stand firm, then,   5
and don't get caught again under a yoke of slavery.

I, Paul, tell you, if you get circumcised, Christ will do you   2
no good. And again I warn everyone who gets circumcised he   3
must do everything the Law says. You who try to become   4
righteous by the Law have cut yourselves off from Christ and
lost God's love. But we who believe by the Spirit eagerly wait   5
for the hope of the righteous. In Christ Jesus no circumcision or   6
the lack of it can do anything but only faith that is active in love.

You were running well. Who has kept you from obeying   7
the truth? You were not persuaded by Him who called you.   8
A little yeast makes the whole dough sour. I'm convinced in the   9-10
Lord you'll think as I do, but anyone who troubles you will have
to take his punishment, whoever he may be. My fellow Christians,   11
if I'm "still preaching that people have to be circumcised," why
am I still persecuted? If I were preaching that, the Jews would
have no reason to oppose the Cross. I could wish the men who   12
upset you would castrate themselves.

You were called to be free, my fellow Christians. Only don't   13
use your freedom as a chance to sin as you like, but in love
serve one another. You keep the whole Law when you do one   14
thing — *love your neighbor like yourself*.[13] But if you bite and   15
eat one another, be careful, or you'll be devoured by one another.

I say, follow the Spirit, and you will not do what the flesh   16
wants. What the flesh wants is against the Spirit, and what the   17
Spirit wants is against the flesh, because they are opposed to
each other and so keep you from doing what you want to do.
But if the Spirit leads you, you are not under the Law.   18

Now, you know the works of the flesh. They are: sexual sin,   19
uncleanness, wild living, ' worshiping of idols, witchcraft, hate,   20
wrangling, jealousy, anger, selfishness, quarreling, divisions, ' envy,   21
drunkenness, carousing, and the like. I warn you, as I did before,
those who do such things will have no share in God's kingdom.

But the Spirit produces love, joy, peace. He makes us patient,   22

5:23 kindly, good, faithful, ¹ gentle, and gives us self-control. There's
24 no law against such things. But if we belong to Christ Jesus,
25 we have crucified the flesh with its passions and desires. If we
26 live by the Spirit, let us also follow the Spirit. Let us not get
conceited, challenge one another and get jealous of one another.

When Anyone Sins

6 My fellow Christians, if you find anyone doing wrong, you
who have the Spirit should set him right. But be gentle and keep
2 an eye on yourself; you may be tempted too. Help one another
carry these loads, and so do everything the Law of Christ demands.

3 If anyone thinks he's something when he's nothing, he's cheat-
4 ing himself. ¹ Everyone should examine his own work. Then he
will have something in himself that deserves praise, without com-
5 paring himself with anyone else. Everyone will have to carry
his own load.

We Reap What We Sow

6 If someone teaches you the Word, share all your good things
7 with your teacher. Don't make a mistake; you can't fool God.
8 Whatever you sow you'll reap. ¹ If you sow to please your own
flesh, you will from your flesh reap destruction. If you sow to
please the Spirit, you will from the Spirit reap everlasting life.
9 ¹ Let us not get tired of doing good. At the right time we'll reap
10 if we don't give up. So whenever we have a chance, let us do
good to everybody but especially to our family of believers.

The World Is Crucified to Me

11 See what big letters I make when I write to you with my
own hand.

12 These men who want to be popular in a worldly way are
insisting you must be circumcised only to keep themselves from
13 being persecuted for the Cross of Christ. Why, these who are
circumcised don't keep the Law themselves, but they want you
to be circumcised so they can boast of that physical fact
14 about you. May I never boast of anything but the Cross of our
Lord Jesus Christ, by whom the world is crucified to me and
15 I to the world. No circumcision or the lack of it is anything,
16 but only the new life that is created. *Peace* and mercy on all
who follow this rule, that is, *on* God's *Israel*.¹⁴

336

From now on nobody should make trouble for me, because
I have on my body the scars of a slave of Jesus.

The love of our Lord Jesus Christ be with your spirit, my 18
fellow Christians. Amen.

OLD TESTAMENT REFERENCES

1. Is. 49:1
2. Deut. 10:17
3. Ps. 143:2
4. Gen. 15:6
5. Gen. 12:3; 18:18;
   22:18; 26:4; 28:14
6. Deut. 27:26
7. Hab. 2:4
8. Lev. 18:5
9. Deut. 21:23
10. Gen. 22:18;
    26:4
11. Is. 54:1
12. Gen. 21:10
13. Lev. 19:18
14. Ps. 125:5;
    128:6

PAUL

writes to the

EPHESIANS

EPHESUS
SPRING OF A. D. 55

1 PAUL, APOSTLE OF CHRIST JESUS by God's will, to the people
2 who are holy and faithful in Christ Jesus: May God our Father
and the Lord Jesus Christ love you and give you peace.

What God Has Done

3   Let us praise the God and Father of our Lord Jesus Christ,
who in Christ has blessed us with every spiritual blessing in heaven.

5, 4   He has done what in His kindness He planned to do: Before
5 He made the world, He who loved us ' appointed us to be made
4 His sons by Jesus Christ. In Him He chose us to be holy and
6 blameless before Him ' in order to praise the glory of the love
7 He gave us in His dear Son, who bought us with His blood to
8 forgive our sins and set us free. So ' He poured out the riches
of His love on us, giving us every kind of wisdom and under-
9 standing ' as He told us the hidden meaning of His will.

10   It was His kindly purpose in Christ ' to manage everything in
heaven and on earth in such a way that when the right time
would come it would all be organized under Christ as its Head.

11   He who accomplishes everything just as He wants to plan it
long ago appointed us in Christ and chose us according to His
12 purpose ' that we, the first to find our hope in Christ, should live
13 to praise His glory. When you heard the message of the truth,
the good news that you were saved, and you believed in Him,
· you, too, were sealed in Him by the Holy Spirit — whom He
14 promised ' and who is now the Guarantee of our inheritance —
that He might free you to be His people and to praise His glory.

338

I'm Praying for You

That is why, since I heard how you believe in the Lord Jesus 1:15
and love all the holy people, I never stop thanking God for you 16
as I remember you in my prayers. I ask the God of our Lord 17
Jesus Christ, the Father of glory, to give you His Spirit to make
you wise and reveal the truth to you as you learn to know Him
better ¹ and to enlighten the eyes of your minds so that you know 18
the hope He called you to, the riches of the glory of the *inheritance*
He gives to *His holy people,*¹ and the vast resources of His power 19
working in us who believe. It is the same mighty power ¹ with 20
which He worked in Christ, raised Him from the dead, and *made
Him sit at His right* ² in heaven, ¹ above all rulers, authorities, 21
powers, lords, and any name that can be mentioned, not only in
this world but also in the next. And *He put everything under* 22
*His feet,*³ and gave Him as the Head of everything to the church,
¹ which is His body, having all that is in Him who fills everything 23
in every way.

God's Love Saved You

You, too, were dead in your transgressions and sins, ¹ in which 2 1-2
you once followed the ways of this present world and the ruler
whose power is in the air, the spirit who is now working in the
people who disobey. Among them all of us once lived in our 3
fleshly lusts, doing what our flesh and mind wanted to do, and
by nature we, like the others, were people with whom God
was angry.

But God, who is rich in mercy, loved us with such a great 4
love ¹ He made us who were dead in sins alive with Christ. (You 5
are saved by a gift of His love.) And since we are in Christ Jesus, 6
He raised us with Him and had us sit with Him in heaven ¹ to 7
show in the coming ages the immeasurable riches of His love by
being kind to us in Christ Jesus. You are saved by a gift of love 8
you get by faith. You didn't do it. It is God's gift. ¹ It isn't 9
because of anything you have done, or you might boast. He has 10
made us what we are, creating us in Christ Jesus to do good
works, which God long ago planned for us to live in.

Jews and Non-Jews

Remember, then, physically you once were Gentiles, and those 11
who call themselves "circumcised" (which is physical and done
by human hands) called you "uncircumcised." You were then 12

without Christ, excluded from being citizens of Israel and strangers to the covenants that had the promise. You had no hope or God in the world.

2:13   Once you were *far away,* but now in Christ Jesus the blood
14 of Christ has brought you *near.* [1] He is our *Peace:* [4] In His flesh He has made the Jew and the non-Jew one by breaking down
15 the wall of enmity that kept them apart and by putting away the Law with its rules and regulations, in order to make the Jew and the non-Jew in Himself one new man (so making peace)
16 and to make both in one body friends with God by His cross,
17 on which He killed the enmity. And He came with *the good news of peace* [5] *to* you *who were far away and to* us *who were*
18 *near,* [4] since by one Spirit He enables both to come to the Father.

19   Then you are no longer foreigners or strangers but fellow citizens, a part of God's holy people and members of His family.
20 You are built on the *foundation* of the apostles and prophets,
21 and Christ Jesus Himself is the *Cornerstone.* [6] In Him the whole building is fitted together and grows to be a holy temple in the
22 Lord. In Him you, too, are built up with the others to be God's home in the Spirit.

God's Purpose in Me

3   For this reason I, Paul, whom Christ Jesus made a prisoner
2 for you who are not Jews —* surely you've heard how God gave
3 me gifts of His love to bring you [1] and how He revealed to me
4 the hidden truth, as I have briefly written. When you read this,
5 you can see I understand the hidden truth of Christ. The people of other times weren't told about it as the Spirit now has revealed
6 it to His holy apostles and prophets, that in Christ Jesus the people who are not Jews have the same inheritance, belong to the same body, and have the same promise through the good news.

7   I was made a servant of it by the gift of love God gave me
8 by the working of His power. To me, the least of all His holy people, He gave this gift of His love: to bring the news of the
9 unsearchable riches of Christ to the non-Jews [1] and let everybody see clearly what God planned to do according to the truth hidden
10 from the beginning in God, who created everything, [1] so that through the church God's many-sided wisdom would now be

* Here Paul breaks off and doesn't take up the thought again until v. 14.

shown to the rulers and authorities in heaven. He planned it

through the ages and then did it in Christ Jesus, our Lord. In 12
Him, by believing in Him, we have confidence and can boldly
come to God. So I ask you not to get discouraged by what 13
I suffer for you. It is an honor to you.

How Christ Loves Me

For this reason I kneel before the "Father," from whom every 14-15
group in heaven and on earth gets the name of "family," * and 16
ask Him, as He is rich in glory, to give you this: that His Spirit
will inwardly strengthen you with power, Christ will live in your 17
hearts by faith, and you will be firmly rooted and built up in
love ¹ so that you and all the holy people can grasp how broad 18
and long and high and deep love is, and know how Christ 19
loves us — more than we can know — and so you will be filled
with all that is in God.

Now to Him who by the power working in us can do far, 20
far more than anything we ask or imagine, to Him be glory in 21
the church and in Christ Jesus to all ages forever. Amen.

We Are One

So I, a prisoner in the Lord, urge you to live as people whom 4
God has called should live. Be humble and gentle in every way, 2
be patient, and lovingly bear with one another. Do your best 3
to keep the oneness of the Spirit by living together in peace:
one body and one Spirit — even as you have been called to 4
share one hope — one Lord, one faith, one baptism, ¹ one God 5-6
and Father of all, who rules over us all, works through us all,
and lives in us all.

But each of us has been given the gift measured out by 7
Christ who gave it. So it says: He *went up on high, took prisoners,* 8
and gave *gifts to people.*⁷ Now what can "He went up" mean 9
but that He had gone down to the lower parts of the earth?
He who went down also "went up" above all the heavens to fill 10
everything. And He gave us some men to be apostles, some to 11
speak the Word, some to tell the good news, some to be pastors
and teachers, in order to get His holy people ready to serve as 12
workers and build the body of Christ ¹ till all of us get to be one 13

* "Family" (= clan) in Greek is the same word as "Father" with
a special ending.

4:14 as we believe and know God's Son, reach a mature manhood, and grow to the full height of Christ. We shouldn't be babies any longer, tossed and driven by every windy thing that is taught,

15 by the trickery of men and their clever scheming in error. Let us tell the truth with love and in every way grow up into Him

16 who is the Head — Christ. He makes the whole body fit together, unites it by every contact with its support, and to the extent that each part is working He makes the body grow and builds it up in love.

A New Life

17 So I tell you and call on you in the Lord not to live any more like the people of the world. Their minds are set on worthless

18 things. ' Their understanding is darkened. Their ignorance and their closed minds have made them strangers to the life God gives.

19 Having lost their sense of right and wrong, they've given themselves up to a life of lust to practice every kind of vice with greed.

20 But that is not what you learned when you got to know

21 Christ, if you have heard Him and in Him have been taught

22 the truth as it is in Jesus: Strip off your old self, which follows your former ways of living and ruins you as it follows the desires

23 that deceive you. Become new in the spirit of your minds,

24 ' and put on the new self, which is created to be like God, righteous and holy in the truth.

25 So don't lie any more, but *tell one another the truth,*[8] be-

26 cause we are members of one another. *Be angry but don't sin.*[9]

27 Don't let the sun go down on your anger. ' Don't give the devil a chance to work.

28 Anyone who has been stealing should not steal any more, but instead work hard, doing something good with his own hands

29 so that he has something to share with anyone in need. Don't say anything bad but only what is good, so that you help where there's a need and benefit those who hear it.

30 And don't grieve God's Holy Spirit, by whom you were sealed for the day when you will be set free.

31 Get rid of all bitter feelings, temper, anger, yelling, slander,

32 and every way of hurting one another. Be kind to one another and tenderhearted, and forgive one another as God in Christ has forgiven you.

You Are a Light

As God's dear children try to be like Him [1] and live in love   5 1-2
as Christ loved us and gave Himself for us as a *fragrant* [10] *offering
and sacrifice* [11] to God.

Sexual sins, anything unclean, or greed shouldn't even be   3
mentioned among you. This is the right attitude for holy people.
[1] No shameful things, foolish talk, or coarse jokes! These aren't   4
proper. Instead give thanks. [1] Be sure of this, that nobody who   5
is immoral, unclean, or greedy (a greedy person worships an idol)
has any share in the kingdom of Christ, who is God. Don't let   6
anybody fool you with meaningless words. These things bring
God's anger and punishment on those who don't obey the truth.
So don't share their ways.   7

Once you were darkness, but now you are light in the Lord.   8
Live as children of light, [1] since light produces everything good   9
and righteous and true. And test things to see if they please   10
the Lord. Don't have anything to do with the works of darkness,   11
from which no good can come. Instead show that they are
wrong. We're ashamed even to mention what such people do   12
secretly. When you show that anything is wrong, it is seen in   13
the light; anything you can see is as clear as light. So it says: 14
"Wake up, sleeper! Rise from the dead, and Christ will shine
on you."

Be very careful, then, how you live. Don't be unwise but   15
wise. And make the most of your opportunities because these   16
are evil days. So don't be foolish, but understand what the Lord   17
wants. [1] *Don't get drunk on wine,* [12] which means wild living. But   18
let the Spirit fill you [1] as you speak psalms, hymns, and songs to   19
one another, and with your hearts sing and play music to the
Lord, always thanking God the Father for everything in the name   20
of our Lord Jesus Christ.

Husband and Wife

As you respect Christ, submit to one another. You married   21-22
women, obey your husbands as you obey the Lord, [1] because   23
a husband is the head of his wife as Christ is the Head of the
church, which is His body that He saves. Yes, as the church   24
obeys Christ, so wives should obey their husbands in everything.

You husbands, love your wives, as Christ loved the church   25
and gave Himself for it [1] to make it holy by washing it clean with   26
water by the Word, to have the church stand before Him as   27

343

something wonderful, without a spot or a wrinkle or anything
5:28 like that; yes, it should be holy and without a fault. This is how husbands should love their wives, like their own bodies. A man
29 who loves his wife is loving himself. Nobody ever hated his own body. Everybody feeds it and treats it tenderly, as Christ does
30-31 the church ¹ because we are parts of His body. *This is why a man will leave his father and mother and live with his wife, and the*
32 *two will be one flesh.*¹³ There's a great truth hidden here — I mean
33 that of Christ and the church. But every one of you, too, love your wife as you love yourself. And a wife should respect her husband.

Children and Parents

6 Children, obey your parents in the Lord, because it is right.
2 *Honor your father and mother* — this is an important com-
3 mandment with a promise: *it will be well with you and you will live long on the earth.*¹⁴

4 And you fathers, don't make your children angry, but raise them by letting *the Lord train* ¹⁵ and correct them.

Slaves and Masters

5 You slaves, obey those who are your masters in this world, with respect and trembling and as sincerely as you obey Christ,
6 ¹ working not only while you are being watched, as if you merely wanted to please men, but as slaves of Christ who are glad to
7 do what God wants them to do. Serve eagerly as you would
8 serve the Lord and not merely men. You know that if you do a good thing, the Lord will pay you back whether you are a slave or a free man.

9 You masters, treat your slaves in the same way, and stop threatening them. You know that they and you have one Master in heaven, and He doesn't prefer one to another.

Put on the Whole Armor

10 Finally, let the Lord and His mighty power make you strong.
11 Put on God's whole armor, and you will be able to stand against
12 the devil's tricky ways. You're not fighting against flesh and blood but against the rulers, authorities, and lords of this dark
13 world, against the evil spirits that are above. This is why you should take God's whole armor; then you can resist when things are at their worst and having done everything, you can hold your

ground. Stand, then, *with truth as a belt fastened around* your
waist,[16] *with righteousness covering you as a breastplate,*[17] and
with shoes on your *feet,* ready to *bring the good news of peace.*[18]
Besides all these, take faith as the shield with which you can
put out all the flaming arrows of the evil one. And take *salvation
as your helmet,*[17] and the Spirit's *sword,*[19] which is God's Word.

Pray at all times in the Spirit, using every kind of prayer.
Be alert and keep at it continually as you pray for all the holy
people. For me, too, that when I start to talk I'll be told what
to say and will boldly tell the hidden truth of the good news
(for which I'm an ambassador in chains) just as boldly as I must
tell it.

Farewell

You should know what is happening to me and how I'm
getting along. And so Tychicus, our dear fellow Christian and
loyal helper in the Lord, will tell you everything. I'm sending
him to you to let you know about us and to encourage you.

May God the Father and the Lord Jesus Christ give our
fellow Christians peace and love with faith! His love be with
all who have an undying love for our Lord Jesus Christ.

OLD TESTAMENT REFERENCES

1. Deut. 33:3-4
2. Ps. 110:1
3. Ps. 8:6
4. Is. 57:19
5. Is. 52:7
6. Is. 28:16
7. Ps. 68:18
8. Zech. 8:16
9. Ps. 4:4
10. Ezek. 20:41
11. Ps. 40:6
12. Prov. 23:31
13. Gen. 2:24
14. Ex. 20:12
15. Prov. 3:11
16. Is. 11:5
17. Is. 59:17
18. Is. 52:7
19. Is. 49:2

P A U L

writes to the

PHILIPPIANS

EPHESUS
EARLY IN A. D. 55

1 PAUL AND TIMOTHY, servants of Christ Jesus, to all who are holy
in Christ Jesus in Philippi, especially to the pastors and helpers:
2 May God our Father and the Lord Jesus Christ love you and give
you peace.

You Are in My Heart

3-4 Every time I think of you, I thank my God. Every time
5 I pray for all of you, I always do it with joy ' because you have
6 shared in telling the good news from the first day till now. I'm
sure that He who started a good work in you will go on to
7 finish it till the day of Christ Jesus. And it is right for me to
feel like this about all of you. Whether I'm in my chains or
defending and confirming the good news, you're all in my heart
8 as sharing God's love with me. God knows how I long for you
all with the tenderness of Christ Jesus.

9 And I pray your love will still grow more and more in
10 knowledge and in every kind of understanding ' so that you approve the better things and are pure, harming nobody, till the
11 day of Christ, ' as Jesus Christ has filled your life with righteous
works by which you glorify and praise God.

If Only Christ Is Preached

12 I want you to know, my fellow Christians, that what hap-
13 pened to me actually helped spread the good news ' so that the
governor's whole palace and all the others have found out I'm
14 in chains for Christ. And so my chains have given most of our
friends the confidence in the Lord to speak God's Word more
boldly and fearlessly than ever.

Some men are moved by jealousy and rivalry to preach Christ, but others by good will. Those who love to preach Him know ¹⁶ I'm appointed to defend the good news. But the others preach ¹⁷ Christ selfishly, without a pure motive, and mean to stir up trouble for me even while I am in chains. But what does it ¹⁸ mean? Only this, that in one way or another, whether their motive is false or real, they preach Christ — and I'm glad of that.

Live or Die?

Yes, and I'm also going to be happy because I know that ¹⁹ your prayer and the help of the Spirit of Jesus Christ will make *this turn out victoriously for me* ¹ ǀ as I eagerly hope there will be ²⁰ nothing for me to be ashamed of. But by speaking very boldly I will now as always glorify Christ in my body by living or by dying ǀ since for me to live is Christ, and to die is gain. If I live ²¹⁻²² here in my body, I'll enjoy the results of my work. And which would I like best? I don't know. ǀ I find it hard to choose between ²³ the two. I want to leave and be with Christ; that is much better. ²⁴ But when I think of you, I feel a greater need to stay in my body. And since I feel convinced of this, I know I'll live and be with ²⁵ all of you to help you grow and be happy in your faith. And ²⁶ so by coming to you again I want to give you all the more reason to glory in Christ Jesus.

Fighting for the Faith

But live as citizens worthy of the good news of Christ so ²⁷ that, whether I come and see you or stay away, I will hear you are standing firm, one in spirit, and fighting side by side like one man for the faith in the good news. Don't let your enemies ²⁸ frighten you in any way. This is how you prove to them they will be destroyed and you will be saved, and this proof is from God. It is given to you to be for Christ, not only to believe in Him ²⁹ but also to suffer for Him ǀ as you have the same struggle you ³⁰ once saw me have and now hear that I have.

Live in Harmony

Now if you are encouraged in Christ, moved by comforting ² words of love, if you and we have the same Spirit, if you are tender and sympathetic, make me very happy — be one in ² thought and in love, live in harmony, keep one purpose in mind. Don't be selfish or proud, but humbly treat others as better than ³

2:4   yourselves. Each of you, be interested not only in your own things but also in those of others.

Be like Jesus

5-6   Think just as Christ Jesus thought: Although He was God, He decided not to take advantage of His being equal with God as 7 though it were stolen goods, ¹ but He emptied Himself, made Himself a slave, became like other human beings, and was seen to 8 have the ways of a man. He became obedient and humbled Himself till He died, yes, died on a cross. That is why God also raised 9 Him up on high and gave Him the name above every other 10 name ¹ that at the name of JESUS *everyone* in heaven and on 11 earth and under the earth *should kneel* ¹ and *everyone should confess,* "JESUS CHRIST IS *LORD!*" and so *glorify God* ² the Father.

Work Out Your Salvation

12   My dear friends, you have always obeyed, not only when I was with you but even more now that I'm away. And so work 13 out your salvation with fear and trembling ¹ since it is God who makes you willing and gives you the energy to do what He wants.

14-15   Do everything without complaining or arguing, so that you will be blameless and innocent, *God's children with whom nobody can find a fault* in the middle of *a crooked and perverted* 16 *people,* ³ among whom you shine like stars in the world ¹ as you cling to the Word of Life. Then I can boast on the day of Christ 17 I didn't run in vain or *work in vain.* ⁴ But even if my life is poured out while I bring your faith as a sacrifice and service to 18 God, I'm glad, and I'm happy with all of you. You, too, be glad and be happy with me.

Timothy and Epaphroditus

19   I hope in the Lord Jesus to send Timothy to you soon to get 20 news about you that will cheer me up too. You see, I don't have anybody who will take such a real interest in your welfare as 21 he will. All look after their own interests, not after those of 22 Jesus Christ. But you know how he has stood the test, how like a son helping his father he worked hard with me to tell the good 23 news. So I expect to send him as soon as I see what's going

to happen to me. And I trust the Lord that I'll be coming
soon too.

I feel I must send you Epaphroditus, my fellow Christian, 25
fellow worker, and fellow soldier, whom you sent to help me in
my needs, since he has been longing to see all of you and is feel- 26
ing troubled because you heard he was sick. He was sick and 27
almost died, but God had pity on him and helped him; not
only him but me, to keep me from having one sorrow after another. So I'm especially eager to send him and give you the joy 28
of seeing him again and to feel more relief myself. So give him 29
a very happy welcome in the Lord, ¹ and value men like him. For 30
the work of Christ he risked his life and almost died, to make
up for the service you couldn't give me.

Only Christ

Now, then, my fellow Christians, be happy in the Lord. It is 3
no trouble to write the same things to you, and it is necessary for
your safety. Look out for those dogs, look out for those who 2
do wrong, look out for the men who circumcise only their bodies.
We are really the circumcised people, we who worship by God's 3
Spirit, are proud of Christ Jesus, and don't trust anything
human, ¹ though I, too, have something human to trust. If any- 4
body else thinks he has anything human to trust, I have more.
I was circumcised on the eighth day, a descendant of Israel of 5
the tribe of Benjamin, a Hebrew son of Hebrew parents; in
regard to the Law, a Pharisee, ¹ so zealous I persecuted the 6
church and according to the Law so righteous nobody could
find any fault with me.

But any advantages I had I considered a loss for Christ. 7
Yes, I think it is all a loss because it is so much better to know 8
Christ Jesus, my Lord. For Him I have lost everything and consider it garbage in order to win Christ ¹ and find myself in Him, 9
not having my own righteousness based on the Law but the
righteousness that depends on faith, that God gives those who
believe in Christ. I want to know Him and the power of His 10
resurrection, to share His sufferings and be like Him in His
death ¹ if somehow I will get to be one of those who rise from 11
the dead.

I don't mean I have already reached this or am already at 12
the goal, but I eagerly go after it to make it mine because Christ
Jesus made me His own. Fellow Christians, I don't think I have 13

349

it in my hands. But one thing I do: I forget what is behind,
3:14 reach for what is ahead, ¹ and with my eyes on the mark I go
after the heavenly prize to which God has called us in Christ
15 Jesus. ¹ Let us all who are mature think this way. But if you
think differently about anything, God will reveal this to you too.
16 Only be guided by what we have learned so far.

Citizens of Heaven

17 My fellow Christians, all together imitate me more and more,
and watch those who live according to the example we're giving
18 you. As I have often told you and now tell you with tears,
19 many live as the enemies of the cross of Christ. In the end they
will be destroyed. Their god is their belly, they glory in their
20 shame, and their mind is on earthly things. But we are citizens
of heaven and look for the Lord Jesus Christ to come from
21 heaven as the Savior, who will change our humble bodies and
make them like His glorified body by the power by which He
4 can make everything serve Him. And so, my fellow Christians,
whom I love and long for, my joy and crown, stand firm in the
Lord, dear friends.

Two Women

2-3 I urge Euodia and Syntyche to agree in the Lord. And I beg
you, my true fellow worker, help them. They fought side by side
with me in telling the good news, and with Clement and the rest
of my fellow workers, whose names are in *the book of life*.⁵

Be Happy

4 Be happy in the Lord always! I'll say it again: Be happy!
5 ¹ Everybody should know how gentle you can be. The Lord is
6 near. Don't worry about anything, but in everything go to God,
and pray to let Him know what you want, and give thanks.
7 Then God's peace, better than all our thinking, will guard your
hearts and minds in Christ Jesus.

8 Finally, my fellow Christians, keep your minds on all that
is true or noble, right or pure, lovely or appealing, on anything
9 that is excellent or that deserves praise. Do what you have
learned, received, and heard from me and what you saw me do.
Then the God of peace will be with you.

Your Gift

It made me very happy in the Lord that now again you 4:10
showed a fresh interest in me. You were interested but didn't
have a chance to show it. [1] I'm not saying I need anything. I've 11
learned to have enough whatever my condition. I know how to 12
live with too little or too much. In every way of life I've learned
the secret of eating heartily and of being hungry, of having too
much and too little. I can do everything through Him who gives 13
me the strength.

But it was kind of you to share my trouble. You people at 14-15
Philippi know, too, that when I first told you the good news
and then left Macedonia, you were the only church to share
with me by an account of gifts and receipts. Even while I was 16
in Thessalonica, you more than once sent help for my needs.
It isn't the gift I want but to see the profits growing and credited 17
to you. You have paid me in full, and I have more than enough. 18
I am fully supplied, now that I received from Epaphroditus what
you sent. It is *a sweet odor,*[6] a sacrifice that God accepts and
is pleased with. And my God will give you all you need according 19
to His riches, in His glory, and in Christ Jesus. To our God and 20
Father be glory forever. Amen.

Greet everyone who is holy in Christ Jesus. The Christians 21
who are with me greet you. All the holy people greet you, espe- 22
cially those of the emperor's household. The love of our Lord 23
Jesus Christ be with your spirits. Amen.

OLD TESTAMENT REFERENCES

1. Job 13:16
2. Is. 45:23-24
3. Deut. 32:5
4. Is. 49:4; 65:23
5. Ps. 69:28
6. Ezek. 20:41

PAUL

writes to the

COLOSSIANS

EPHESUS
SPRING OF A. D. 55

1 PAUL, APOSTLE OF CHRIST JESUS by God's will, and our fellow
2 worker Timothy, to the holy and faithful fellow believers in
Christ at Colossae: May God our Father love you and give
you peace.

We're Praying for You

3 In our prayers for you we are always thanking God, the
4 Father of our Lord Jesus Christ, because we have heard how
5 you believe in Christ Jesus and love all the holy people ˡ and
what you hope for is stored up for you in heaven. You heard
6 of it before when you were told the truth of the good news ˡ that
has come to you. As it is producing fruit and growing all over
the world, so it did among you since the day you heard it and
7 got to know what it really means to have God love you, as you
learned it from Epaphras, our dear fellow servant, who is loyally
8 serving Christ in our place. And he's the one who told us about
your love in the Spirit.

9 That is why, since the day we heard of it, we haven't stopped
praying for you and asking God to fill you with a clear knowledge of His will by giving you every kind of spiritual wisdom
10 and understanding ˡ so that you live worthy of the Lord, aiming
to please Him in every way as you produce every kind of good
11 work and grow by knowing your God better. We ask Him
according to His wonderful might to strengthen you with all the
12 power you need to endure patiently whatever comes ˡ as you
joyfully thank the Father, who made you fit to share everything
the holy people have in the light.

God's Son Brought Peace

He rescued us from the tyranny of darkness and transferred 1:13
us into the kingdom of the Son He loves, who paid the ransom 14
to forgive our sins and set us free. He is the image of the in- 15
visible God, born before and above everything created, ' since in 16
Him was created everything you can see and cannot see in heaven
and on earth — thrones, lords, rulers, or powers — everything
was created by Him and for Him. He was before everything, and 17
He holds everything together. He is the Head of the church, 18
which is His body. He is the Beginning, the first among the dead
to become alive that He may be first in everything. God decided 19
to have His whole being live in Him ' and by Him to reconcile to 20
Himself * everything on earth and in heaven in a peace made
by the blood on His cross.

Our Work Among You

Once you were strangers to God and in your hearts His 21
enemies, doing wicked things, ' but now by dying in His human 22
body He has made of you enemies friends ' in order to have you 23
stand before Him without sin or fault or blame if, of course,
you continue in your faith to stand firm on the foundation and
are not moved from the hope of the good news you heard. This
has been preached to every creature under heaven, and I, Paul,
was made its servant.

I delight to suffer for you now and in my body am enduring 24
what still needs to be endured of Christ's sorrows for His body,
which is the church. God made me its servant when He gave 25
me this work among you in order to do everything God meant
to do by His Word. This was a mystery hidden from the people 26
of all the ages but now shown to His holy people, whom God 27
wanted to tell how rich among the non-Jews is the glory of this
hidden truth: Christ, the Hope of glory, is in you.

Him we preach, warning everyone and teaching everyone, 28
using every kind of wisdom, in order to present everyone perfect
in Christ. This is what I'm working for, struggling like an ath- 29
lete by His power that is working mightily in me.

I want you to know how much I'm struggling for you and 2
the people of Laodicea and all who haven't seen me face to face,
' to encourage you, as you're bound together by love, to be ever 2
so richly convinced in your understanding and to know well God's

* God and the world, who are enemies, become friends in Christ.

353

2:3 hidden truth, that is Christ, ¹ in whom are hidden all the treasures
⁴ of wisdom and knowledge. I say this so that nobody will mislead
⁵ you by fine-sounding arguments. Although I'm away from you,
I'm with you in spirit and delight to see how orderly and firm
you are in your faith in Christ.

You Live in Christ

⁶ Just as you accepted Christ Jesus as your Lord, so live in Him.
⁷ In Him be rooted, built up, and strengthened in your faith, as
you were taught, and overflow with thanksgiving.

⁸ Be careful or somebody will capture you by his philosophy,
tricking you with meaningless words, as he follows the traditions
of men and the elements of the world but not Christ.

⁹ God's whole being lives in Christ, that is, in His body.
¹⁰ And in Him, who is the Lord of all rulers and powers, you
¹¹ have a full life. In Him you also were circumcised, not by
human hands but by putting away the sinful body by the cir-
¹² cumcision of Christ ¹ since in baptism you were buried with Him
and raised with Him by believing in the power of God, who
raised Him from the dead.

¹³ Yes, you who were dead in sins and in your uncircumcised
bodies He has made alive with Him when He forgave us all our
¹⁴ sins, wiped out the Law's demands that were against us and
¹⁵ took them out of the way by nailing them to the cross. He
stripped rulers and powers of their armor and made a public
show of them as He triumphed over them in Christ.

Man-made Rules

¹⁶ Then nobody should say you are wrong in what you eat or
drink or do on a festival, on the first of the month, or on a Sab-
¹⁷ bath. These have been a shadow of the coming things, but the
real things are in Christ.

¹⁸ Nobody who likes to be humble and worship angels should
condemn you. Such a person goes on searching his visions and
¹⁹ without a reason is puffed up by his fleshly mind. He doesn't cling
to the Head, who by being in touch with the whole body nourishes
it and by its ligaments binds it together to make it grow as God
gives it growth.

²⁰ With Christ you have died to the elements of the world.
Then why, as though you were living with the world, do you
²¹ let others dictate to you: "Don't take hold, don't taste, and don't

touch"? These are rules about all such things as are meant to
be used up and pass away. You are doing *what men order and
teach,*[1] this looks like wisdom, with its self-imposed worship, 23
humble way, and harsh treatment of the body. But it lacks
honor — it serves the full enjoyment of the flesh.

In Christ We Put Away Sin

Now if you were raised with Christ, be eager for the things 3
that are above, where Christ is *sitting at the right of God.*[2] Keep 2
your mind on things above, not on earthly things. You see, you 3
have died, and your life is hidden with Christ in God. When 4
Christ, your Life, appears, then you, too, will appear with Him
in glory.

Kill, then, what is earthly in you: sexual sin, uncleanness, 5
passion, evil lust, and greed, which is idol worship; these are 6
bringing down God's anger. Once you also practiced them when 7
you lived in them. But now also get rid of all such things as 8
anger, rage, malice, slander, and dirty talk. Don't lie to one 9
another, seeing that you have put away your old self and its
ways [1] and have put on the new self, which is continually renewed 10
in knowledge *to be like Him who made him.*[3] Here there is no 11
Greek or Jew, circumcised or uncircumcised, barbarian, Scythian,
slave or free, but Christ is everything and in everything.

Live as God's People

Then, as holy people whom God has chosen and loved, be 12
tenderhearted, kind, humble, gentle, patient; bear with one an- 13
other and forgive one another if you have a complaint against
anyone. Forgive as the Lord forgave you. [1] With all this have 14
love, which binds it all together to make it perfect.

Let the peace of Christ, to which you were called as one 15
body, be in your hearts to decide things for you. And be
thankful. Let Christ's Word live richly in you as you teach and 16
warn one another, using every kind of wisdom. With thankful
hearts sing psalms, hymns, and spiritual songs to God. And 17
everything you say or do, do it in the name of the Lord Jesus,
and by Him give thanks to God the Father.

Parents, Children, and Slaves

You married women, submit to your husbands as it is right 18
in the Lord. You husbands, love your wives, and don't be harsh 19
with them.

3:20   You children, obey your parents in everything. This is
21 pleasant when it is done in the Lord. Parents, don't irritate your children, or they will get discouraged.

22   You slaves, obey your earthly masters in everything. Don't serve them only when they are watching you, as if you meant only to please them, but sincerely because you respect the Lord.
23 Whatever you do, work heartily as for the Lord and not for men,
24 because you know the Lord will give you the inheritance as
25 your reward. Serve the Lord Christ. ¹The man who does wrong will get paid for the wrong he has done, and there will be no exceptions.

4   You masters, be just and fair to your slaves because you know you, too, have a Master in heaven.

Winning the Others

2-3   Keep on praying, watch as you pray, and give thanks. At the same time also pray for us that God will open a door for the Word and let us tell the hidden truth of Christ, for which I am
4 in chains, that I may make it as well known as I should.

5   Be wise in the way you live with those who are outside, and
6 make the most of your opportunities. Always talk pleasantly, season your talk with salt so you will know how you should answer everyone.

Tychicus and Onesimus

7   Tychicus, a dear fellow Christian, loyal helper and fellow
8 servant in the Lord, will tell you all about me. I'm sending him to you to bring you the news about us and encourage you.
9 Onesimus, our loyal and dear fellow Christian who is one of you, is with him. They will tell you about everything that is happening here.

Greetings

10   Aristarchus, my fellow prisoner, sends greetings. So does Mark, the cousin of Barnabas. You received directions about
11 him. If he comes to you, welcome him. ¹Jesus, called Justus, also greets you. They are the only Jews working with me for
12 God's kingdom. They've been a comfort to me. Epaphras, one of your men, a servant of Christ Jesus, greets you. He is always wrestling in prayer for you that you will stand mature and con-
13 vinced in everything God wants. I assure you he works hard for

you and the people in Laodicea and Hierapolis. Luke, the doctor
and dear friend, and Demas greet you. Greet the fellow Christians
in Laodicea, and Nympha and the church that meets at her home.

When this letter has been read to you, have it read also in
the church at Laodicea, and see that you also read the letter
from Laodicea.

Tell Archippus, "See that you do all the work you were given
to do as the Lord's servant."

I, Paul, am writing this greeting with my own hand. Remember I'm in chains. May the Lord love you!

OLD TESTAMENT REFERENCES

1. Is. 29:13   2. Ps. 110:1   3. Gen. 1:26-27

P A U L

writes the First Letter to the

THESSALONIANS

CORINTH
A. D. 50

1 .PAUL, SILAS, AND TIMOTHY to the church of the Thessalonians which is in God the Father and the Lord Jesus Christ: Love to you and peace!

The Good News

2 We always thank God for all of you and mention you in our
3 prayers, never forgetting before our God and Father how your faith is working, your love is toiling, and your hope in our Lord
4 Jesus Christ is enduring. We know, fellow Christians, whom
5 God has loved, that He has chosen you, ˈ because the good news
6 we told wasn't just words to you, ˈ but it had power, the Holy Spirit, and a strong conviction; you know this is the kind of men we proved to be among you for your good. And you became just like us and like the Lord as you welcomed the Word, which brought you much suffering, with such joy in the Holy Spirit
7 that you became a model for all the believers in Macedonia
8 and Greece. Not only has the Lord's Word spread from you through Macedonia and Greece, but everywhere people have heard of your faith in God so that we don't need to say anything.
9 They tell how we came to you and you turned from the idols
10 to God, to serve a God who lives and is real ˈ and to wait for His Son to come from heaven — whom He raised from the dead — Jesus, who saves us from the punishment that is coming.

2 You know, my fellow Christians, our coming to you wasn't
2 in vain. We had suffered and been shamefully mistreated in Philippi, as you know. But then we took courage in our God to tell you God's good news though it meant a hard struggle.

358

Our appeal isn't based on error or an unclean desire, and 2:3
we aren't tricking you. No, we have God's approval to be 4
entrusted with the good news. And so we tell it, not to please
people but God, *who tests* our *hearts*.[1] We never flattered, as 5
you know, or found excuses to make money, as God knows,
nor did we try to get you or other people to praise us, although 6-7
we can claim respect as apostles of Christ.

You Are Dear to Us

But we became children when we were with you — and like
a mother tenderly caring for her children. So we longed for you 8
and were determined to share with you not only God's good
news but our own lives, so dear had you become to us. You 9
remember, my fellow Christians, how hard we worked and struggled. Night and day working for our living, not to burden
any of you, we preached God's good news to you. You are 10
witnesses and God too, how holy, righteous, and blameless we
proved to be to you who believe. As you know, like a father 11
urging his children we used to urge, encourage, and warn every 12
one of you to live worthy of God, who is calling you into His
kingdom and glory.

We continually thank God also for this, that when you accepted 13
God's Word, which you heard from us, you didn't accept it as
the word of men but as the Word of God, which it really is.
And it is working in you who believe.

You, our fellow Christians, became just like God's churches 14
in Christ Jesus that are in Judea, since you suffered the same
things from your own people as they did from the Jews. These 15
killed the Lord Jesus and the prophets and drove us out. They
don't please God, are opposed to everybody, and try to keep us 16
from talking to the non-Jews to save them, and so they always
fill up the cup of their *sins*.[2] Now God is angry with them forever.

My fellow Christians, when we were torn from you like 17
orphans for a little while — you were out of sight but not out
of mind — we were all the more eagerly and intensely longing to
see you. We wanted to come to you — I, Paul, wanted to again 18
and again — but the devil stopped us.

After all, who is our hope or joy or crown of glory before 19
our Lord Jesus when He comes? Aren't you that? Why, you 20
are our glory and joy!

We Long to See You

3 When we couldn't stand it any longer, we thought it best to
2 be left alone in Athens, and we sent Timothy, our fellow Christian
who works with God in telling the good news of Christ, to
3 strengthen you and encourage you in your faith, so that these
troubles will not disturb anyone, because you know they are
4 planned for us. When we were with you, we warned you, "We're
5 going to suffer." And so it happened, as you know. ¹ That's
why I couldn't stand it any longer, and I sent to find out about
your faith. I was afraid the Tempter had in some way tempted
you and our work was wasted.

6 But now Timothy came back to us from you and told us
the good news of your faith and love, also that you always think
7 kindly of us and long to see us as we long to see you. So you,
fellow Christians, by your faith have encouraged us in all our
8 distress and trouble. Now we live if you stand firm in the Lord.
9 How can we thank God for all the joy you give us before
10 our God ¹ as day and night we are most ardently praying to see
you face to face and to supply whatever is lacking in your faith?
11 May our God and Father Himself and the Lord Jesus lead us
to you.

12 The Lord make you grow in love and overflow with it for
13 one another and for everybody, just as we love you, ¹ and so may
He give you inward strength to be holy and without a fault before
our God and Father when our Lord Jesus comes with all His
holy ones! Amen.

Live to Please God

4 And now, my fellow Christians, this is what we ask and urge
you to do in the Lord Jesus. You learned from us how you
must live and please God, and that is how you are living. But
2 now do so more and more. You know what instructions we
3 gave you by the Lord Jesus. God wants you to be holy and
4 keep away from sexual sin. Every one of you should know how
5 to get a wife in a holy and honorable way ¹ and not in the way
of passionate lust like *the people of the world who don't know*
6 *God.*³ Nobody should wrong and cheat his fellow Christian in
business, because *the Lord avenges* ⁴ all these things, as we told
7 you and warned you before. God didn't call us to be unclean but
8 holy. Now, if anyone rejects this, he doesn't reject a man but
God, *who gives you His* Holy *Spirit.*⁵

You don't need anyone to write you about brotherly love, because God has taught you to love one another, and you are practicing it toward all the Christians all over Macedonia. But we urge you, my fellow Christians, grow more and more, ¹ do your best to live quietly, mind your own business, and work with your hands, as we ordered you to do, ¹ so that you live nobly with those who are not Christians — without needing anything.

Your Dead Will Rise

We want you to know about those who go to their rest, my fellow Christians, so you don't grieve like the others, who have no hope. We believe that Jesus died and rose again; then God will in the same way through Jesus bring with Him those who went to their rest. We tell you only what the Lord has told us: We who are left behind and are still living when the Lord comes will not get ahead of those who went to their rest. When the order is given and the archangel calls and God's trumpet sounds, the Lord Himself will come down from heaven, and the dead who are in Christ will rise first. Then we who are still living and left behind will be caught up with them in the clouds to meet the Lord in the air, and so we'll always be with the Lord. Now, then, comfort one another with what I have told you.

Watch!

You don't need anyone to write and tell you exactly when things will happen, my fellow Christians, ¹ because you know very well the Lord's day will come just like a thief in the night. When people say, "All's well and safe!" then destruction will come on them suddenly like pains on a woman who is going to have a baby, and they will not escape. But you, my fellow Christians, are not in the dark that you should let that day take you by surprise like a thief. You are all the children of light and of the day. We have nothing to do with night and darkness. ¹ Let us not sleep, then, like the others, but be awake and sober. People sleep at night and get drunk at night. But let us who live in the daylight be sober and *put on* faith and love *as a breastplate* and the hope of *salvation as a helmet*.⁶ God didn't appoint us to be punished by His anger but to be saved by our Lord Jesus Christ, ¹ who died for us so that, awake or asleep, we may live with Him. Then encourage one another and strengthen one another just as you are doing.

Some Last Words

5:12 We ask you, fellow Christians, to appreciate the men who
13 work with you and lead you in the Lord and warn you. Love them and think very highly of them on account of the work they're doing. Live in peace with one another.

14 We urge you, fellow Christians, warn those who are disorderly, cheer up those who are discouraged, help the weak, be patient
15 with everybody. Don't let anyone pay back wrong for wrong, but always be eager to help one another and everybody.

16-18 Always be happy. Never stop praying. Whatever happens, thank God, because that is what God in Christ Jesus wants you to do.

19-20 Don't put out the fire of the Spirit. Don't despise God's
21 Word when anyone speaks it. But test everything and cling to
22 what is good. *Keep away from every* kind of *evil.*[7]

23 The God of peace make you holy in every way and keep your spirit and life and body sound and without a fault when
24 our Lord Jesus Christ comes. You can depend on Him who calls you — He will do it.

25 My fellow Christians, pray for us.

26 Greet all the Christians with a holy kiss.

27 I order you by the Lord to read this letter to all the Christians.

28 The love of our Lord Jesus Christ be with you. Amen.

OLD TESTAMENT REFERENCES

1. Jer. 11:20
2. Gen. 15:16
3. Ps. 79:6; Jer. 10:25

4. Ps. 94:1
5. Ezek. 36:27; 37:14

6. Is. 59:17
7. Job 1:1, 8; 2:3

P A U L

writes the Second Letter to the

THESSALONIANS

CORINTH
A. D. 50

PAUL, SILAS, AND TIMOTHY to the church of the Thessalonians 1
in God our Father and the Lord Jesus Christ: Love to you and 2
peace from God our Father and the Lord Jesus Christ.

Look to God in Suffering

We always have to thank God for you, my fellow Christians. 3
It is the right thing to do because your faith is growing wonder-
fully and the love of every one of you for one another is increas-
ing, so much so that we're boasting about you in God's churches 4
how you endure and trust no matter how much you're persecuted and made to suffer. It shows how God judges righteously: 5
He means to make you worthy of His kingdom, for which you
are suffering; it really is just for God to pay back with suffering 6
those who make you suffer [1] and to give relief to you who suffer 7
and to us when the Lord Jesus will be revealed from heaven with
His mighty angels [1] *in a blaze of fire, to take vengeance* [1] *on* 8
those who don't know God [2] *and on those who will not obey* [3]
the good news of our Lord Jesus. They will be punished by 9
being taken *away from the Lord and from the glory of His*
power [4] to be destroyed eternally [1] when He comes on that Day [5] 10
to *be glorified in His holy people* [6] and *admired* [7] by all who
believed (you did believe the truth we told you). With this in 11
mind we're always praying for you that our God will make you
worthy of His calling and by His power accomplish every good
thing you decide to do and every work of faith, *so as to glorify the* 12
name of our Lord [8] Jesus among you, and you in Him, according
to the love of our God and Lord Jesus Christ.

363

The Man of Sin

2 Our Lord Jesus Christ is coming, and we'll be gathered to
² meet Him. But we ask you, fellow Christians, ¹ not to lose your
heads so quickly or get alarmed either by a "spirit" message or
by any word or letter that seemed to come from us, saying "The
³ day of the Lord has already come!" Don't let anybody deceive
you in any way. First there must be a revolt, and the man of
⁴ sin must be revealed, who is doomed to destruction, ¹ who opposes
and *sets himself above anyone* who is called *God* ⁹ or anything
we worship, so that *he sits in God's temple* and proclaims *he is
God.*¹⁰

⁵ Don't you remember I told you this when I was still with
⁶ you? And now you know what's holding him back so that he
⁷ will be revealed when his time comes. This wicked thing is
already working secretly, but only till he who is now holding
⁸ it back gets out of the way. Then the wicked one will be revealed, and the Lord Jesus *will destroy him with the breath of
His mouth* ¹¹ and wipe him out by coming and showing Himself.
⁹ The coming of this wicked one is the work of the devil who
¹⁰ uses every kind of false power, miracle, and wonder, ¹ and every
wicked way to deceive those who are perishing because they
¹¹ refused to love the truth and be saved. That is why God sends
¹² them a power to deceive them so they will believe the lie ¹ and
all will be condemned who did not believe the truth but delighted
in wrong.

God Has Chosen You

¹³ But we always have to thank God for you, my fellow Christians, whom *the Lord loves,*¹² because in the beginning God chose
you to be made holy by the Spirit, to believe the truth, and so to
¹⁴ be saved. For this purpose He called you by the good news we
tell; He wants you to have the glory of our Lord Jesus Christ.
¹⁵ Stand then, fellow Christians, and cling to the instructions
we gave you when we spoke to you or wrote to you.
¹⁶ Now our Lord Jesus Christ Himself and God our Father,
who loved us and by His love gave us an everlasting comfort
¹⁷ and a good hope, inwardly comfort and strengthen you to do
and say everything that is good.

Pray for Us

3 Finally, my fellow Christians, pray for us that the Lord's
² Word will run well and win glory as it did among you ¹ and we'll

364

be rescued from wrong-minded and wicked people. Not everybody has faith.

But the Lord is faithful. He will strengthen you and protect 3:3
you against the evil one. We are certain in the Lord you are doing 4
and will be doing what we order you to do. And may the Lord 5
lead you to realize how God loves you and how patiently Christ
suffered.

Work

Now we order you, fellow Christians, in the name of our 6
Lord Jesus Christ to keep away from any Christian who refuses
to live and work as we instructed you. You know how you 7
should imitate us. We were not idle when we were with you and 8
took no free meals from anyone but worked hard and struggled
day and night in order not to burden any of you. Not as though 9
we didn't have a right to get support. No, we wanted to give you
an example to imitate. And while we were with you, we gave 10
you the order, "If anyone doesn't want to work, he shouldn't eat."

We hear that some of you are living a lazy life, not doing 11
any work, but being busybodies. Such people we order and en- 12
courage by the Lord Jesus Christ to work quietly and eat their
own bread. And you, fellow Christians, don't get tired of doing 13
good.

If anyone will not listen to what we say in this letter, mark 14
him, and don't have anything to do with him, so he will feel
ashamed. Don't treat him like an enemy, but warn him like 15
a brother.

Farewell

The Lord of peace always give you peace in every way. The 16
Lord be with you all.

I'm writing this greeting with my own — that is, Paul's — 17
hand. By this you can recognize every letter: This is my handwriting.

The love of our Lord Jesus Christ be with you all! 18

OLD TESTAMENT REFERENCES

1. Is. 66:15
2. Ps. 79:6; Jer. 10:25
3. Is. 66:4
4. Is. 2:10, 19, 21
5. Is. 2:11, 17
6. Ps. 88:7; Is. 49:3
7. Ps. 68:35
8. Is. 66:5
9. Dan. 11:36
10. Ezek. 28:2
11. Job 4:9; Is. 11:4
12. Deut. 33:12

PAUL

writes the First Letter to

TIMOTHY

MACEDONIA
EARLY IN A. D. 63

1 PAUL, APOSTLE OF CHRIST JESUS by the order of God, our Savior,
2 and Christ Jesus, our Hope, ¹ to Timothy, my real son by faith:
Love, mercy, and peace from God the Father and Christ Jesus,
our Lord.

Teaching the Law

3   When I was going to Macedonia, I urged you to stay in
Ephesus. I wanted you to order certain men not to teach any-
4 thing different ¹ and not to busy themselves with stories and end-
less records of ancestors, that provide speculations but no divine
training in faith.

5   The goal of our instruction is love flowing from a pure heart,
6 from a good conscience, and from a sincere faith. Certain peo-
7 ple have failed to find this and have turned to silly talk. They
want to be teachers of the Law but don't understand what they say
or the things they so confidently express.

8   But we know the Law is good if it is used as it was meant
9 to be used, if we keep in mind that the Law is not meant for
a righteous man but for those who break the Law and rebel
against it, the ungodly and sinners, those who live unholy lives
and insult holy things, those who kill their fathers or mothers,
10 murderers, ¹ men who sin sexually with women or with other men,
slave dealers, those who lie or swear to lies — and anything else
11 that is contrary to sound teaching. This is according to the good
news of the glory of God, the Blessed, that was entrusted to me.

God Was Merciful to Me

12   I thank Christ Jesus, our Lord, whose power has been in me.
He thought I could be trusted and appointed me to do His work

366

¹ although I used to slander, persecute, and shamefully mistreat Him. But He was merciful to me because, when I didn't believe, I didn't know what I was doing. Our Lord poured His unde- ¹⁴ served kindness on me, bringing faith and love in Christ Jesus.

We can trust this statement and accept it absolutely: Christ ¹⁵ Jesus came into the world to save sinners. I am the worst of them, but God was merciful to me so that Jesus Christ would ¹⁶ first show in me all His long-suffering and make me an example to those who are going to believe in Him and live forever. To the ¹⁷ everlasting King, the immortal, invisible, and only God, be honor and glory forever. Amen.

Fight and Pray

I'm giving you these instructions, my son Timothy, according ¹⁸ to the prophecies made earlier about you. In the spirit of those prophecies fight a good fight ¹ with faith and a good conscience. ¹⁹ Some refused to listen to their conscience and suffered shipwreck in their faith. Among them are Hymenaeus and Alexander, ²⁰ whom I turned over to the devil to teach them not to slander holy things.

I urge you, as most important of all, to ask, pray, plead, and ² give thanks for all people, for kings and all who are over us, ² so that we may live quietly and peacefully and be godly and noble in every way. This is good and pleases God our Savior, who ³⁻⁴ wants all people to be saved and to come to know the truth.

There is one God, and One who brings God and men together, ⁵ the Man Christ Jesus, ¹ who gave Himself as a ransom to free ⁶ all people, and this was announced at the right times. For this ⁷ purpose I was appointed a preacher and an apostle (I'm telling the truth and not lying) to teach the non-Jews to believe the truth.

So I want the men to pray everywhere, lifting up holy hands, ⁸ not in a mood of anger or argument.

Women

Women should dress in decent clothes, modestly and prop- ⁹ erly, without braiding their hair, without gold, pearls, or expensive dresses ¹ but as it is proper for women who promise to worship ¹⁰ God with good works.

A woman should learn in silence, completely submitting her- ¹¹ self. I don't let a woman teach and have authority over a man; ¹²

2:13 she should keep silent. The reason is that Adam was formed
14 first, then Eve. And Adam wasn't deceived; the woman was
15 deceived and so fell into sin. But women, having children, will
be saved if they live in faith, love, and holiness, and use good
judgment.

Church Workers

3   You can depend on this: If anyone sets his heart on being
2 a pastor, he wants to do a noble kind of work. Now, a pastor
must be blameless, the husband of one wife, not drinking too
much wine, a man of good judgment and fine behavior, kind to
3 guests, able to teach, ¹ no drunkard, not violent but gentle, not
4 quarrelsome, not one who loves money. He should manage his
own family well and have his children obey him as he treats
5 them very seriously. If anyone doesn't know how to manage his
6 own family, how can he take care of God's church? He should
not be a person who has just been won, or he may feel proud and
7 so be condemned with the devil. The people outside the church
must speak well of him, or he may fall into disgrace and the
devil's snare.

8   In the same way the helpers in the church should be serious,
9 sincere in speech, not drinking a lot of wine, not greedy. With
a clear conscience they should keep the hidden truth they believe.
10 They, too, should first be tested; then if no fault is found in
11 them, they should serve. In the same way the wives should be
serious, not slandering, not drinking too much wine, but trust-
12 worthy in every way. A church worker should be the husband
of one wife and should manage his children and his home well.
13 When they have served well, they get a good standing and can
talk very confidently of their faith in Christ Jesus.

We Bring the Truth

14-15   I hope to come to you soon but am writing you this ¹ so that
if I'm delayed you know how people should behave in God's
family, which is the church of the living God, a pillar and support
of the truth.

16   It must be admitted the hidden truth of our religion is great —

> He appeared in flesh,
> Became righteous in spirit,
> Was seen by angels,

> Was preached among nations,
> Was believed in the world,
> Was taken up in glory.

Danger Ahead

The Spirit says clearly that in later times some will turn away **4** from the faith as they listen to spirits who deceive and to what devils teach and are taken in by the hypocrisy of liars branded in **2** their consciences as the devil's slaves, who order people not to **3** marry and to keep away from foods that God created to be eaten with thanks by those who believe and know the truth. Everything God created is good. We shouldn't reject any of it **4** but take it and thank God for it, because the Word of God and **5** prayer make it holy.

How to Serve Christ

Point these things out to our fellow Christians, and you will **6** be a good servant of Christ Jesus, nourished by the words of the faith and of the sound teaching you have followed. Don't have **7** anything to do with unholy stories such as old women tell. Train yourself for a godly life. Training the body helps a little, but **8** godliness helps in every way, having a promise of life here and hereafter (you can trust His Word and accept it absolutely); that **9-10** is what we work and struggle for, because our hope is in the living God, who is the Savior of all people, especially of those who believe.

Order them to do these things, and keep on teaching. **11**

Don't let anyone look down on you because you're young, **12** but be an example to those who believe, in speech, behavior, love, faith, and purity. Till I come, take care of the public reading, **13** encouragement, and teaching. Don't neglect the gift you have **14** which was given you by prophecy when the elders laid their hands on you. Practice these things, continue in them, so that every- **15** body can see your progress. Watch yourself and your teaching. **16** Keep right on in these things. If you do that, you will save your-self and those who hear you.

Don't be harsh with an older man, but encourage him like **5** a father, young men like brothers, older women like mothers, **2** younger women like sisters, keeping yourself altogether pure.

Take Care of Widows

Treat with respect widows who are all alone. If any widow **3-4** has children or grandchildren, these should learn as their first

duty to respect their own family and repay their parents, because
5:5 that pleases God. A widow who is all alone and forsaken trusts
6 the Lord and keeps on praying day and night. But one who
lives for pleasure is dead while she lives.

7 Order them to do these things so that they can't be criticized.
8 If anyone doesn't take care of his own relatives, especially his
family, he has denied the faith and is worse than an unbeliever.
9 Put a widow on your list if she isn't under sixty, if she was faith-
10 ful to her husband, if people tell about the good she has done,
if she raised children, welcomed strangers, washed the feet of
holy people, helped the suffering, and was busy doing every kind
11 of good work. But don't put younger widows on the list. When
they feel vigorous and turn against Christ, they want to marry
12 and so are guilty of breaking the pledge they made in the begin-
13 ning. At the same time they learn to be idle and go around in
the homes. And they're not only idle but gossiping and meddling,
saying things they shouldn't say.

14 So I want younger women to marry, have children, manage
their homes, and give the enemy no chance to slander them.
15-16 Some have already left us to follow the devil. If any believing
woman has widows, she should help them and not let them be
a burden to the church, so that the church may help those widows
who are all alone.

17 Pastors who lead well should be considered worthy of double
18 honor, especially if their work is preaching and teaching, because
the Bible says, *When an ox is treading out the grain, don't
muzzle him,*[1] and "a worker deserves his pay." *

19 Don't accept an accusation against a pastor unless *it is sup-
20 ported by two or three witnesses.*[2] Those who keep on sinning,
correct before everybody in order to make the others afraid.

21 I solemnly call on you before God and Christ Jesus and the
chosen angels to keep these things without a prejudice and without a preference for anyone in anything you do.

22 Don't be in a hurry to ordain anyone. Don't share in the sins
of others. Keep yourself pure.

23 Don't drink water only, but use a little wine for your stomach
because you are often sick.

24 Anybody can see the sins of some people as these sins go
ahead of them to judgment, but the sins of others follow them

* Matt. 10:10.

there. And so anybody can also see good works, and even when they can't be seen, they can't stay hidden.

Slaves and Masters

All who are under the yoke of slavery should think of their **6** masters as men who deserve every respect, so that God's name and what we teach isn't slandered. If you have masters who be- **2** lieve, don't think less of them because they are fellow Christians, but serve them all the better because those who get the benefit of your work are believers and dear to you.

Religion and Contentment

Teach and urge them to do these things. If anyone teaches **3** anything else and will not agree with the sound words of our Lord Jesus Christ and godly teaching, he is proud and doesn't **4** know anything; he has a morbid craving for debates and argu- ments, which produce jealousy, quarreling, insults, evil suspicions, | continued wrangling of people whose minds are corrupt, who have **5** lost the truth and think religion is a way to make money.

Of course, there's a big profit in religion if we're satisfied. **6** We didn't bring anything into the world, and we can't take any- **7** thing out. If we have food and clothing, we'll be satisfied. **8**

But people who want to get rich fall into temptation and **9** a snare and many foolish and harmful desires that drown them in destruction and ruin. Love of money is a root of all evils, and **10** some people, eager to get rich, have wandered away from the faith and pierced themselves with much pain.

Fight the Good Fight

But you, man of God, flee from these things. Be eager to be **11** righteous, godly, full of faith and love, able to endure, gentle. Fight the good fight of faith, take hold of the everlasting life **12** to which you were called when you made a good confession before many witnesses.

I order you before God, from whom comes all life, and before **13** Christ Jesus, who testified before Pontius Pilate and made a good confession, | that you do what you are ordered, without spot or **14** blame, till our Lord Jesus Christ appears. At His own right **15** time God will show Him to us — He, the blessed and only Ruler, the King of kings and Lord of lords, | who alone cannot die, who **16** lives in a light to which no one can come near, whom no one

371

has ever seen or can see. To Him be honor and power forever. Amen.

6:17 Tell those who are rich in this world not to feel proud and not to trust anything as uncertain as riches but to trust God, who

18 richly gives us everything to enjoy. Tell them to do good, to

19 be rich in good works, to be glad to give and share, [1] and so to store up for themselves a treasure, a good foundation for the future, and to take hold of the life that is real.

20 Timothy, guard what has been entrusted to you. Turn away from empty, unholy talk and contradictory statements of what

21 is falsely called knowledge. Some claim to have it and have lost their faith.

God's love be with you all!

OLD TESTAMENT REFERENCES

1. Deut. 25:4   2. Deut. 19:15

P A U L

writes the Second Letter to

TIMOTHY

ROME
A. D. 64

PAUL, APOSTLE OF CHRIST JESUS by God's will because God 1
promised life in Christ Jesus, 1 to Timothy, my dear son — God 2
the Father and Christ Jesus, our Lord, give you love, mercy,
and peace!

I thank God — whom I, like my fathers, serve with a clear 3
conscience — when I remember you in my prayers, as I never
fail to do day and night. Remembering your tears, I long to 4
see you and so to be perfectly happy. I recall how sincere your 5
faith was; just as it lived in your grandmother Lois and your
mother Eunice before you, so I am convinced it is in you too.

Stir Up God's Gift

That is why I remind you to stir into a flame God's gift that 6
is in you through the laying on of my hands. God didn't give us 7
a cowardly Spirit but a Spirit of power and love and good
judgment. So don't be ashamed to tell about our Lord, and 8
don't be ashamed of me, His prisoner, but with God's power
to back us, join me in suffering for the good news. He saved 9
us and called us to be holy, not because we did anything, but
because He planned a gift of His love and gave it to us in
Christ Jesus before the world began; it has now come to light 10
by the coming of our Savior Christ Jesus. He took away the
power of death and by the good news brought into the light the
life that can't be destroyed. To tell about it, I was appointed 11
a preacher, apostle, and teacher.

That is why I suffer as I do, but I'm not ashamed, because 12
I know Him whom I trust, and I'm sure He can keep for that
day what I have entrusted to Him.

With a faith and a love in Christ Jesus keep what you heard 13

1:14 me say as an example of sound teaching. With the help of the Holy Spirit living in us, guard the good thing entrusted to you.

Onesiphorus

15   You know how everybody in the province of Asia deserted me, including Phygelus and Hermogenes.

16   The Lord be merciful to the family of Onesiphorus because
17 he often cheered me up. He didn't feel ashamed of my being a prisoner, but coming to Rome, he searched hard for me and
18 found me. May the Lord let him find mercy from the Lord on that day. And you know very well all he did to help me in Ephesus.

Be a Good Soldier

2   You, my son, let God's love in Christ Jesus make you strong,
2 and what you heard me say before many witnesses entrust to faithful people who will be able to teach others.

3   Share hardships with me like a good soldier of Christ Jesus.
4 If you're in the army, you don't get tangled up with the ways of making a living; you want to please him who made you
5 a soldier. If you enter a contest, you win a prize only if you
6 compete according to the rules. If you work the ground, you
7 should be the first to get what grows on it. Try to understand what I say, because the Lord will give you understanding in everything.

8   Keep in mind Jesus Christ risen from the dead, a descendant
9 of David — this is the good news I tell. For this I'm suffering and am even chained like a criminal. But God's Word isn't
10 chained. That's why I can endure anything for the chosen people to have them get salvation in Christ Jesus and everlasting glory.
11 You can depend on this: If we have died with Him, we'll live
12 with Him. If we endure, we'll rule with Him. | If we disown Him,
13 He'll disown us. If we're disloyal, he stays loyal because He cannot be untrue to Himself.

14   Remind them of these things and warn them before the Lord not to fight about words; it doesn't do any good but only ruins those who are listening.

15   Do your best to come before God as one whom He approves, a worker who doesn't have to feel ashamed as he teaches the
16 Word of truth in the right way. Keep away from empty, unholy

talk, because such people get to be more and more ungodly, and their talk will spread like a cancer. Among them are 2:17 Hymenaeus and Philetus, who lost the truth by saying the 18 resurrection has already taken place. They're upsetting some people's faith.

But there stands God's solid foundation, and it has this seal: 19 *The Lord has chosen those who belong to Him,*[1] and: "Everyone who *calls on the Lord's name*[2] must give up doing wrong."

In a big house there are not only things of gold and silver 20 but also of wood and clay. Some are used in a noble way and some are not. Now if anyone will cleanse himself from bad ways, 21 he'll be ready for a noble purpose, purified, useful to the owner, and prepared to do any good work.

Flee from the lusts of young people, try to be righteous, 22 faithful, loving, peaceful with people who with pure hearts call on the Lord. Don't have anything to do with foolish and un- 23 intelligent arguments; you know they breed quarrels. A Lord's 24 servant must not quarrel but be kind to everyone. He should be a good teacher, ready to suffer wrong, and gentle in correcting 25 those who oppose him. Perhaps God will change their hearts and lead them to know the truth. Then they'll escape the snare of 26 the devil, who trapped them to do what he wants, and they'll come to their senses.

The Last Days

Understand this, that in the last days there will come times 3 of trouble. People will love themselves and money. They'll brag 2 and be proud. They'll blaspheme. They'll disobey parents. They'll be ungrateful and unholy, without love, never forgiving an enemy, 3 slandering. They'll be without control, wild, with no love for what is good. They'll be treacherous, reckless, proud. They'll 4 love pleasure and not God. They'll have the essence of godliness 5 but refuse to let it be a power. Keep away from such people. Some of them get into homes and captivate weak women, loaded 6 with sins, driven by all kinds of desires, always learning and never 7 able to understand the truth. Just as Jannes and Jambres opposed 8 Moses, so they oppose the truth. Their minds are corrupt, and their faith is no good. But they won't get very far; like Jannes 9 and Jambres, they will be seen by everybody to be the plain fools they are.

Teach the Truth

3:10 But you have followed closely my teaching, way of living, and
11 purpose, my faith, patience, love, and endurance, | my persecutions and sufferings, the things that happened to me in Antioch, Iconium, and Lystra, the persecutions I endured. The Lord
12 rescued me from everything. All who want to live a godly life in Christ Jesus will be persecuted.

13 But bad men and swindlers will get worse as they cheat and
14 are cheated. But you stay with what you've learned and found
15 to be true. You know from whom you learned it | and how since you were a little child you have known the Holy Scriptures, which can make you wise and save you if you believe in Christ Jesus.
16 All Scripture is inspired by God and helps us to teach, to show
17 what is wrong, to improve and train in right living | so that a man of God is ready and equipped for every good work.

4 Before God and Christ Jesus, who is going to judge the living and the dead, I solemnly call on you — in view of His coming
2 and ruling over us — preach the Word, keep at it at the right time and the wrong time, correct, rebuke, encourage, being very patient and thorough in your teaching.

3 A time will come when people will not listen to sound teaching but, craving to hear something different, will get more and more
4 teachers whom they like. They will refuse to listen to the truth and will turn to fictions.

5 But you, keep a clear head in everything, endure hardship, do your work of telling the good news, and everything else you should do as a pastor.

The Lord Will Deliver Me

6-7 I'm now being sacrificed, and it's time for me to leave. I fought
8 the good fight, I ran the race, I kept the faith. Now there is waiting for me the crown of righteousness which the Lord, the righteous Judge, will give me on that day, and not only me but all who love to see Him come again.

9-10 Do your best to come to me soon. Demas fell in love with this world, deserted me, and went to Thessalonica. Crescens went
11 to Galatia, Titus to Dalmatia. | Only Luke is with me. Get Mark and bring him with you, because he's a good help to me in my
12 work. I sent Tychicus to Ephesus.
13 When you come, bring the warm coat I left with Carpus in Troas, and the scrolls, especially the parchments.

Alexander the metalworker did me a lot of wrong. *The Lord will pay him back for what he did.*[3] Be on your guard against him, 15 because he was very much opposed to what we said.

The first time I had to defend myself nobody came to help me, 16 but everybody deserted me — may it not be held against them. But the Lord stood by me and gave me the strength to finish my 17 preaching so that all the non-Jews would hear it. *I was rescued from the lion's mouth.*[4] The Lord will rescue me from all the 18 evil that is done and will save me and take me to His heavenly kingdom. To Him be glory forever. Amen.

Greetings

Greet Prisca and Aquila and the family of Onesiphorus. 19 [|] Erastus stayed in Corinth. I left Trophimus sick in Miletus. 20 [|] Do your best to get here before the winter. Eubulus and Pudens 21 and Linus and Claudia and all the fellow Christians greet you.

The Lord Jesus Christ be with your spirit! God's love be 22 with you all!

OLD TESTAMENT REFERENCES

1. Num. 16:5
2. Is. 26:13

3. Ps. 62:12;
   Prov. 24:12

4. Ps. 22:21;
   Dan. 6:20, 27

P A U L

writes to

TITUS

MACEDONIA
A. D. 63

1 PAUL, SERVANT OF GOD and apostle of Jesus Christ —
sent to help God's chosen people to believe and know the
2 truth which promotes godliness, ᴵ hoping, as we do, for everlasting life, which God, who never lies, promised ages ago
3 ᴵ and at His own right times revealed in His Word by the
preaching entrusted to me by an order of God our Savior
4 — to Titus, my real son by the faith we share: May God the
Father and Christ Jesus our Savior love you and give you peace!

Appoint Good Pastors

5 I left you behind in Crete to make the improvements still
needed and to appoint pastors in every town as I directed you —
6 someone who is blameless, who has one wife, and believing
7 children not accused of wild living or disobedient. As a manager
appointed by God, a pastor should be blameless. He shouldn't
do as he pleases, get angry easily, drink too much, be quick to
8 strike anyone, or be greedy. He should welcome guests, love
anything good, use good judgment, live right and holy. He should
9 control himself. He should cling to the Word, which he can
depend on, just as he was taught, so that by sound teaching he
can encourage people and correct those who oppose him.

Correct Your Opponents

10 There are many who can't be controlled, who talk foolishly
11 and deceive, especially the Jews. ᴵ They must be silenced. They
are ruining whole families by teaching what they must not teach,
only to make money in such a shameful way.

12 One of their own men, their own prophet, said, "Men of

378

Crete are always liars, savage animals, lazy bellies." * That
statement is true. For that reason correct them sharply so that
they may be sound in their faith [|] instead of listening to Jewish 14
myths or orders given by men who reject the truth. Everything 15
is pure to those who are pure. But nothing is pure to the evil-
minded who don't believe — their minds and consciences are
unclean. They openly claim to know God but deny Him by
what they do. They're abominable, disobedient, and not fit to 16
do anything good.

Special Instructions

But you tell people what is right according to sound teaching. 2
Tell older men: Be sober, serious, sensible, and sound in 2
faith, love, and endurance.

In the same way tell older women: Behave as holy women 3
should behave. Don't slander. Don't be slaves to much wine.
Teach what is good, | in order to train young women to love their 4
husbands and their children, to use good judgment and be pure, 5
to keep house, to be good, to submit to their husbands, so that
people don't slander God's Word.

In the same way urge the young men to use good judgment. 6
| In everything be an example of good works. Don't let anything 7
corrupt your teaching. But be noble, | and give a sound message 8
that can't be condemned so that anyone who opposes us will feel
foolish because he can't say anything bad about us.

Tell slaves: Obey your masters in everything, please them, 9
| and don't talk back. Don't steal, but show you can be trusted 10
in every way, so that in everything you show the beauty of the
teaching of God, who saves us.

Jesus Is Coming

God has shown His love. It brings salvation to all people 11
| and trains us to say no to ungodliness and worldly lusts, to use 12
good judgment, and to live right and godly in this world | as we 13
look for the blessed One who is our hope, for our great God and
Savior Christ Jesus to show Himself in glory. He gave Himself 14
as *a payment* for us *to free* us *from all wickedness* ¹ and cleanse
us *to be His own people,*² eager to do good works.

Talk and urge these things, and correct with full authority — 15
nobody should ignore you.

* This may have been said by Epimenides about 500 B. C.

3 Remind people to submit to governments and authorities, to
2 obey, to be ready to do any good work, ¹ not to insult anyone or fight, but to yield and show themselves perfectly gentle to everyone.

What God Did for Us

3 Once we, too, were foolish, disobedient, led astray, slaves to many kinds of passions and pleasures. We lived in wickedness and jealousy, being hated and hating one another.

4 But when God our Savior showed how kind He is and how
5 He loves us, ¹ He saved us, not because of any good works we did but because He was merciful. He saved us by the washing in which the Holy Spirit gives us a new birth and a new life.
6 He poured a rich measure of this Spirit on us through Jesus
7 Christ our Savior, to make us righteous by a gift of His love
8 and, as we hope, heirs of everlasting life. You can depend on this statement.

And I want you to insist on these things so that those who believe in God have their minds on being busy with good works. This is good, and it helps other people.

9 But keep away from foolish arguments, lists of ancestors, quarreling, and fighting about the Law. These help nobody and
10 are worthless. A man who chooses to be different in his teaching warn once and a second time, and then don't have anything more
11 to do with him ¹ because you know such a man is set in his wrong way and is a sinner who condemns himself.

Farewell

12 When I send Artemas or Tychicus to you, hurry to come to
13 me at Nicopolis; I've decided to stay there for the winter. Do your best to help Zenas the lawyer and Apollos to get on their way; they should have everything they need.
14 Our people should learn to be busy with good works to help real needs and not waste their lives.
15 All who are here with me send greetings. Greet those who love us as fellow believers.

God's love be with you all!

OLD TESTAMENT REFERENCES

1. Ps. 130:8   2. Ex. 19:5; Deut. 14:2

P A U L

writes to

PHILEMON

EPHESUS
SPRING OF A. D. 55

PAUL, A PRISONER OF CHRIST JESUS, and Timothy, my fellow ¹
worker, to Philemon, our dear fellow worker, ¹ Apphia, our fel- ²
low Christian, Archippus, our fellow soldier, and to the church
that meets at your home: May God our Father and the Lord ³
Jesus Christ love you and give you peace!

I'm always thanking my God when I mention you in my ⁴
prayers, because I hear how you believe in the Lord Jesus and ⁵
love Him and all the holy people, ¹ so that, knowing every good ⁶
thing you have in Christ, you vigorously share your faith. Your ⁷
love delighted and encouraged me very much because you, my
fellow Christian, have refreshed the hearts of our holy people.

For that reason, although I feel bold enough in Christ to ⁸
order you to do what is right, I am moved by love just to urge ⁹
you. As Paul, an old man and now a prisoner of Christ Jesus,
¹ I appeal to you for my son Onesimus,* who became my son ¹⁰
while I have been in chains. Once he was useless * to you, ¹¹
but now he's quite useful * to you and me.

I'm sending him back to you — and my heart goes with him. ¹²
I would have liked to keep him with me and have him serve me ¹³
in your place while I'm in chains for the good news, but I don't ¹⁴
want to do anything without your approval. I don't want you to
be kind because you must but because you want to be. Perhaps ¹⁵
Onesimus left you for a while only to be yours again forever, no ¹⁶
longer a slave but more than a slave, a dear fellow Christian,
especially to me, but how much more to you, as a man and as
a Christian.

Now if you can think of me as your partner, welcome him ¹⁷
as you would welcome me. If he cheated you or owes you any- ¹⁸

* Onesimus means "useful."

¹⁹ thing, charge it to me. I, Paul, am writing this with my own hand — I'll pay it back. I don't want to mention that you owe ²⁰ me more than that — your own self. Yes, my fellow Christian, I want you to be useful to me in the Lord. Refresh my heart ²¹ in Christ. | As I write you, I'm sure you'll do this. I know you'll do even more than I ask.

²² One thing more: Have a guest room ready for me, because I hope by the prayers of all of you to be given back to you.

²³ Greetings to you from Epaphras, my fellow prisoner in Christ ²⁴ Jesus, | and from my fellow workers: Mark, Aristarchus, Demas, Luke.

²⁵ The love of the Lord Jesus Christ be with your spirits. Amen.

PERHAPS GREECE OR ASIA MINOR
BEFORE A. D. 70

LONG AGO GOD SPOKE to our fathers in many different ways 1
by the prophets, but in these last days He has spoken to us by 2
His Son, whom He made the heir of everything and by whom
He made the world. He who shines with God's glory and is the 3
copy of His being carries everything by His mighty Word. He
made a cleansing from sins, *sat down at the right* [1] of the Majesty
in heaven, and became as much greater than angels as the name 4
He has is better than theirs.

To which of the angels did God ever say, 5

> *You are My Son,*
> *Today I am Your Father?* [2]

Or again,

> *I will be His Father,*
> *And He will be My Son?* [3]

And when He again will bring the firstborn Son into the world, 6
He says,

> *All of God's angels should worship Him,* [4]

He says of the angels, 7

> *He makes His angels winds*
> *And His servants fiery flames.* [5]

But to the Son He says, 8

> *Your throne, O God, is forever,*
> *And You rule Your kingdom with a scepter of righteous-*
>   *ness.*
> *You have loved right and hated wrong.* 9
> *That is why God, Your God, has put You above your*
>   *companions by anointing You with the oil of joy.* [6]

383

And,

> Lord, in the beginning You laid the foundation of the earth,
> And Your hands made the heavens!

11
> They will perish,
> But You continue.
> They will all get old like a garment,

12
> You will roll them up like a blanket,
> And like a garment they will be changed.
> But You are the same,
> And Your years will never end.⁷

13 To which of the angels did He ever say, Sit at My right till
14 I make Your enemies a footstool for Your feet? ⁸ Aren't all angels spirits that serve Him and are sent to help those who are going to be saved?

Don't Neglect Your Salvation

2 That is why we should listen all the more carefully to what
2 we have been told, or we may drift away. If what God said through angels was valid, and every transgression and disobedience
3 got a just punishment, how can we escape if we neglect a salvation as great as this? First the Lord spoke of it, and then those
4 who heard Him guaranteed its truth to us, while God added His testimony by supernatural proofs, wonders, different kinds of miracles, and by giving the Holy Spirit as He wanted to give Him.

Lord of Everything

5 He didn't put the coming world that we're talking about under
6 the control of angels. But somewhere someone has declared,

> What is man that You should think of him?
> Or a son of man that You should come to help him?
> You make Him lower than the angels for a little while,

7
> Then crown Him with glory and honor
> And make Him Ruler over what Your hands have made
> And put everything under His feet.

8 Now when He put everything under His feet, He left nothing outside His control.

Jesus Died for Us

8-9 As it is, we do not yet see everything put under Him. But we do see Jesus, who for a little while was made lower than the

angels, now crowned with glory and honor [9] because He suffered
death in order by God's love to taste death for everyone. It fitted   2:10
Him well for whom and by whom everything exists that in
bringing many sons to glory He should make the One who gives
them salvation perfect through suffering.

He who makes men holy and those who are made holy all   11
have one Father. That is why He is not ashamed to call them
brothers. He says,   12

> *I will tell My brothers Your name,*
> *In the congregation I will sing Your praise.*[10]

| And again, *I will trust Him.*[11] And again, *Here am I and the*   13
children God has given Me.[12]

Now since all these *children* have flesh and blood, He in the   14
same way took on flesh and blood in order to die and so take
away all the powers of him who had the power of death, that is,
the devil, | and to free those who, terrified by death, had to be   15
slaves all their lives. It is clear He didn't *come to help* angels   16
but *Abraham's descendants.*[13] And so in every way He had to   17
become like His brothers to be merciful and faithful as high priest
before God and pay for the sins * of the people. Because He   18
Himself suffered when He was tested, He can help others when
they're tested.

Greater than Moses

And so, fellow Christians — you're holy, and heaven called   3
you as it called us — look at Jesus, the Apostle and High Priest
whom we confess, | being *faithful* to Him who appointed Him, just   2
as *Moses was faithful in God's whole family.* He deserves greater   3
glory than Moses, as the builder of a house is honored more than
the house. Every house is built by someone, but He who built   4
everything is God.

Now, *Moses was faithful in God's whole family* as *a servant*   5
who was to testify of what would be said later, but Christ was   6
faithful as the Son in charge of *God's family.*[14] We are His
family if to the end we continue unshaken in our courage and
in feeling proud of our hope.

* He wipes out our sins by His blood and so changes God's anger
to love.

Don't Close Your Minds

3:7　　And so, as the Holy Spirit says, *Today, if you hear Him*
8　*speak, don't close your minds as it happened when the people*
9　*provoked Me at the time they tested Me in the desert, where*
10　*your fathers put Me to a test* ⅼ *when for forty years they saw*
what I could do. That was why *I was angry with those people,*
and I said, "In their hearts they're always going wrong and haven't
11　*learned My ways." So because I was angry I swore they will never*
come to My place of rest!

12　　See to it, fellow Christians, that none of you has a wicked,
13　unbelieving heart that turns away from the living God. Yes,
encourage one another every day, as long as you can say *today,*
to keep sin from deceiving anyone of you with its pleasure and
14　*closing your mind* to the truth. We share in Christ if we only
keep our first confidence unshaken to the end.

15　　When it says, *Today, if you hear Him speak, don't close your*
16　*minds as it happened when the people provoked Me* — who were
those that heard Him and yet *provoked* Him? Were they not all
17　those Moses led out of Egypt? With whom was He *angry for*
forty years? ¹⁵ Was it not with those who sinned and whose
18　*bodies dropped dead in the desert?* ¹⁶ To whom did He *swear*
they would not come to His place of rest ¹⁵ if not to those who
19　disobeyed? So we see that they couldn't come there because
they didn't believe.

4　　We should be fearful then. While we still have the promise
of coming to His place of rest, someone of you may be judged
2　to have missed it. The good news came to us as it came to
them, but the message they heard didn't help them because
those who heard it didn't believe it and let it influence them.

There Is a Rest for Us

3　　We who have believed *go to a rest,* since He has said, *So*
*I swore in My anger they will never come to My place of rest.*¹⁵
4　And yet God finished His work when He made the world, ⅼ because
in one place He said about the seventh day, *On the seventh day*
5　*God rested from all He had done.*¹⁷ And here, too, He says,
6　*They will never come to My place of rest.* Now, it is still true
that some *will go to His rest,* and those who once heard the good
7　news didn't *go to* it because they disobeyed; so He sets another
day — *today* — when long afterwards He says in David's words,
already quoted, *Today if you hear Him speak, don't close your*

minds. If Joshua had given them rest, God wouldn't later have
spoken of another day. So there is still a sabbath of rest for 9
God's people, since anyone who *goes to his rest*[15] *finds rest* 10
after his work as *God* did *after His.*[17]

Let us then do our best to *come to* that *rest*[15] so that no 11
one may disobey and fall like those people.

The Living Word

God's Word lives and is active. It cuts better than any 12
two-edged sword. It pierces till it divides soul and spirit, joints
and marrow. And it can judge thoughts and purposes of the
heart. No creature can hide from Him. Everything is naked and 13
helpless before the eyes of Him to whom we must give account.

Our High Priest

Now that we have a great High Priest who has gone through 14
the heavens, Jesus, God's Son, let us cling to what we confess.
We have a High Priest who can sympathize with our weaknesses. 15
He was tempted in every way just as we are, only without sin.
So let us come boldly to God's throne of love to get mercy and 16
find love to help us when we need it.

Any high priest selected from men is appointed to represent 5
them before God and to bring gifts and sacrifices for sins. He 2
can be gentle with ignorant and erring people because he, too, is
troubled with weakness and for that reason must bring sacrifices 3
for sins for himself just as he does for the people.

No one takes the honor of this office, but God calls a man as 4
He called Aaron. So Christ didn't take the glory of being a high 5
priest but was given it by Him who said to Him,

> *You are My Son,*
> *Today I am Your Father.*[18]

And so He said in another place, *You are like Melchizedek* 6
a priest forever.[19]

In His humble life on earth Jesus came to Him who could 7
save Him from death and prayed and pleaded, crying loud with
tears, and because He feared God, He was heard. Although 8
Jesus is the Son, He found out from what He suffered what it
means to obey. And when He was finished, He became One who 9
gives *everlasting salvation*[20] to all who obey Him, being pro- 10
claimed by God a high *priest like Melchizedek.*[19]

More than ABC

5:11   We have much to say about this, but it's difficult to explain
12 because you have become too dull to understand. At a time
when you should be teachers you need someone to teach you
the ABC of God's Word again. It has come to this that you
13 need milk again instead of solid food. Anyone who lives on
milk, being a baby, doesn't have enough experience to talk of
14 what is right. But solid food is for grown-up people, whose
senses are trained by practice to tell good from bad.

6   Let us leave behind the ABC of Christ and not lay again
a foundation of repentance from dead works, faith in God,
2 ¹ teaching about baptisms, laying on hands, raising the dead, and
1, 3 everlasting judgment. But let us go on to be mature. We will
do this if God lets us.

4   When those who once had the light and tasted the gift from
5 heaven, who had the Holy Spirit just as others did ¹ and tasted
how good God's Word is and the powers of the coming world —
6 when those fall away, it is impossible to bring them back to
a new repentance because they to their own undoing again
7 crucify God's Son and hold Him up for mockery. When *ground*
drinks the rain that often falls on it and *produces plants* [21] that
can be used by those for whom it is worked, it is blessed by God.
8 ¹ But if *it produces thorns and thistles,* it is worthless. A *curse* [22]
hangs over it, and finally it will be burned.

9   Although we say this, we are convinced that for you, dear
10 friends, there are better things that mean salvation. God is
righteous to remember your work and the love you showed for
11 Him as you helped His holy people and still help them. But we
want every one of you to show the same zeal to make certain
12 of your hope till the end, and not get lazy but be like those who
by believing and being patient are getting what is promised.

13   God promised Abraham, and since He had no one greater
14 to swear by, He *swore by Himself* ¹ and said, *I will certainly bless*
15 *you and make you many people.*[23] And so, after waiting patiently,
Abraham got what God promised.

16   People swear by Someone greater to guarantee what they say
17 and to silence anyone who opposes them. So God, wanting to
make it perfectly clear, to those who would get His promise,
18 that He can't change His plan, bound Himself with an oath ¹ so
that we who have fled to Him would have two unchangeable
things, in which God cannot lie, to give us a strong encourage-

ment to take hold of the hope set before us. We have this hope like an anchor for our lives, sure and strong and *reaching behind the curtain,*[24] | where Jesus has gone for us, ahead of us, having become *like Melchizedek a* high *priest forever.*[19]

A Priest Forever

This *Melchizedek, king of Salem* and *priest of the most high* 7 *God met Abraham coming back from defeating the kings, and he blessed Abraham. And Abraham gave him a tenth of every-* 2 *thing.* His name, in the first place, means *king of righteousness,* but then he is also *king of Salem,* that is, *king of peace.*[25] He is 3 without father, mother, or line of ancestors. His life has no beginning or end. Like God's Son he continues *a priest forever.*[19]

See how great he was! *Abraham,* the father of the people, 4 *gave him a tenth* from the best of the spoils. And the Law 5 orders those descendants of Levi who become priests to take a tenth from the people, that is, from other Israelites, although they, too, have descended from Abraham. But this man, who 6 was outside their line of descent, took *a tenth* from *Abraham* and *blessed him* who had the promises. Nobody can deny the 7 higher one blesses the lower.

And here those who take a tenth are people who die, but 8 there we are assured it is one who lives. And we may say that 9 Levi, who takes a tenth, in *Abraham gave a tenth,* | since he was in 10 the body of his ancestor when *Melchizedek* [25] met him.

Levi's descendants were the priests; on this basis the people got 11 the Law. Now, if the priests who descended from Levi could have given us something perfect, why did another *priest* still need to come who is *like Melchizedek* and said to be different from Aaron? When a different person is made priest, the Law also 12 has to be changed. The One here spoken of belongs to a dif- 13 ferent tribe, which never had a priest serving at the altar. Every- 14 body knows our Lord came from Judah, but Moses said nothing about priests in this tribe. That point is much clearer still when 15 we see a different *Priest* coming *like Melchizedek,* not appointed 16 according to a Law that says he must be someone's descendant but by the power of a life that can't be destroyed. We are assured, *You are like Melchizedek a Priest forever.* The earlier 17-18 rule is canceled because it is weak and can't help us. The Law 19 made nothing perfect, but the coming of a better hope did — it brings us close to God.

When those men were made priests, there was no oath. But when Jesus was appointed, God swore as He said to Him *(The Lord has sworn and will not change His mind): You are a Priest* 20, 22 *forever.* Swearing to it [1] made the agreement Jesus guarantees so much the better.

23 Once many were made priests because death didn't let them 24 continue as priests. But because Jesus lives forever, He will 25 *always* be the *Priest.* And so He can forever save those who come to God by Him, because He always lives to pray for them.

26 Here is the High Priest we needed — holy, innocent, spotless, separated from sinners, and risen higher than the heavens, 27 who doesn't need to bring sacrifices every day like those high priests, first for His own sins, then for the sins of the people. 28 He did this only once when He sacrificed Himself. [1] The Law appointed weak men to be high priests, but when God speaks with *an oath* later than the Law, He appoints the *Son,*[26] who was made perfect *forever.*[19]

A Better Covenant

8 Now, this is my main point. We have such a High Priest, and He *sat down at the right* [27] of the throne of the Majesty 2 in heaven [1] to serve as priest in the holy place and in the real *taber-* 3 *nacle set up by the Lord* [28] and not by men. As every high priest is appointed to offer gifts and sacrifices, this One, too, had to bring some sacrifice.

4 If He were on earth, He wouldn't even be a priest, because 5 there are priests who offer the gifts demanded by the Law. They serve a copy and a shadow of what is in heaven, as God told Moses when he was going to make the tabernacle: *"Be careful to make* all of *it like the pattern you were shown on the mountain."* [29]

6 Now, the priestly work that Jesus was given to do is as much better as the covenant of which He is the Mediator is a better 7 one because God has based it on better promises. If that first covenant had been without a fault, nobody would have wanted 8 a second one. But God is finding fault with them when He says, *"See! The time is coming," says the Lord, "when I will set up a new covenant with the people of Israel and the people of Judah,* 9 *not like the covenant I made with their fathers when I took them by the hand to lead them out of Egypt, because they have not been loyal to My covenant. And so I turned away from them,"* 10 *says the Lord. "The covenant I will make with the people of*

*Israel after those days," says the Lord, "is this: I will put My
laws into their minds and write them on their hearts, and I will
be their God, and they will be My people. No more will anyone* 8:11
*teach his fellow citizen or his brother and say, 'Know the Lord!'
They will all know Me from the least to the greatest of them,
because I will forgive their wrongs and not remember their sins* 12
any more." ³⁰ By saying *a new covenant* He made the first one 13
old. When He treats it as old and it is getting old, it is ready
to vanish.

The Tabernacle

The first covenant had its regulations for worship and the 9
earthly holy place. ¹ A tabernacle was set up. In the first part were 2
the lampstand, the table, and the bread laid before God; this is
called the holy place. Behind the second curtain was the part of the 3
tabernacle called the most holy place ¹ with the golden altar of in- 4
cense and the ark of the covenant, completely covered with gold.
In the ark were the golden jar containing the manna, Aaron's rod
that had budded, and the tablets on which the covenant was
written. Above it were the angels of glory overshadowing the 5
cover on which the blood was sprinkled. — I can't tell about these
in detail now.

But that is how it was arranged. The priests are always going 6
into the first part of the tabernacle to serve God, but only the high 7
priest goes into the second part once a year with blood he offers
for himself and for the sins the people have done in ignorance.
And so the Holy Spirit clearly tells us that the way into the real 8
holy place had not yet been shown as long as the outer part of
the tabernacle was still standing.

This is a picture of our time: Gifts and sacrifices are brought 9
which can't make the worshiper feel perfect in his conscience
but deal only with gifts of food and drink and various baptisms, 10
which are regulations for the body imposed till the time when
things would be set right.

Jesus' Blood

But Christ came as a High Priest of the good things that have 11
come and went through that greater and more perfect tabernacle
not made by human hands (that is, not a part of our created
world). And He didn't use the blood of goats and calves but 12
His own blood to go only once into the holy place and pay a price

391

that frees us forever. Now, sprinkling the blood of goats and bulls and the ashes of a calf on unclean people makes them out-
14 wardly holy and clean. How much more will the blood of Christ, who by His everlasting spirit offered Himself without a spot to God, wash our consciences clean from dead works to worship the living God?

15 And He is the Mediator of a new covenant. By dying He paid the ransom to free people from the sins under the first covenant, and those who are called are to get the everlasting
16 inheritance promised them. Where there is a will, it must be
17 shown that the one who made it died, since a will takes effect only when a person is dead. It is not in force as long as the one
18 who made it is still living. That is why the first covenant was
19 also dedicated with blood. When *Moses* had told all the people every commandment of the Law, he *took the blood* of calves and goats and some water, scarlet wool, and hyssop *and sprinkled*
20 the scroll and *all the people. "This is the blood of the covenant,"*
21 he said, *"that God has ordered you* 31 to keep."* In the same way he sprinkled blood on the tabernacle and on everything used in the
22 worship. According to the Law almost everything is cleansed by blood, and if no blood is poured out, no sins are forgiven.

One Perfect Sacrifice

23 Now, the copies of the things in heaven had to be cleansed by these sacrifices, but the heavenly things themselves needed
24 better sacrifices. Christ didn't go into a holy place made by human hands and just a copy of the real thing but into heaven
25 itself, now to appear before God for us. And not to sacrifice Himself over and over again like that high priest going every year
26 into the holy place with blood that is not his own. Otherwise He would have had to suffer many times since the world was made. But as it is, He appeared only once at the end of the ages
27 to get rid of sin by His sacrifice. And as people are appointed
28 to die once and after that to be judged, so Christ also was sacri-ficed once to *take away the sins of many people,*32 but those who eagerly look for Him will see Him again, without sin, when He comes to save them.

10 The Law, having only a dim outline of the good things in the future and not their substance, can never by the same sacrifices, repeated endlessly year after year, make perfect those who come.
2 1 Otherwise wouldn't they have stopped bringing sacrifices? Once

cleansed, the worshipers would no longer be aware of any sins. No, year after year these sacrifices reminded people of their sins. The blood of bulls and goats can't take away sins.

That is why He says when He comes into the world, *You* *didn't like sacrifice and offering, but You prepared a body for Me. Burnt offerings and sacrifices for sin didn't* please *You. Then* *I said, "I have come (the writing in the scroll of the book tells about Me). I'm here to do what You want, O God."* First He says, *You didn't like and weren't* pleased *with sacrifices, offerings, burnt offerings, and sacrifices for sin* which are offered according to the Law. Then He says, *I have come and am here to do what* *You want.* He takes away the first to set up the second. *Doing* *God's will,* Jesus Christ *sacrificed* His *body* [33] only once and so made us holy.

Every other priest stands and serves day after day, and over and over again brings the same sacrifices, which can never take away sins. But He made one sacrifice for sins, good forever, *sat down at the right of God,* and since then is waiting *for His* *enemies to be made a footstool for His feet.*[34] By one sacrifice He forever made perfect those who are made holy.

The Holy Spirit assures us of this. First He says, *"This is* *the covenant I will make with them after those days," says the Lord: "I will put My laws on their hearts and write them on their minds."* Then *"I will not remember their sins and their wrongs* *any more."* [35] Now, where sins are forgiven, there is no more sacrificing for sin.

Fellow Christians, with the blood of Jesus we can now boldly go into the holy place by the new, living way He opened for us through the curtain, the way of His body, and we have a *great* *Priest* in charge of *God's family.*[36] Let us then come near God, sincere in our hearts and convinced in our faith, because our hearts were sprinkled to take away our guilty feelings, and our bodies were washed with clean water. Let us cling to the con- fession of our hope and not waver in it. We can trust Him who gave us His promise.

Give Up Sin

And let us consider how we can stimulate one another to love and to do good works. Let us not stay away from our meetings, as some are regularly doing, but let us encourage one another, all the more because you see the day coming nearer.

If we choose to go on sinning after we have learned the truth, ^{27} there is no more sacrifice for our sins, ¹ only a terrible waiting for judgment and *a fire that will be eager to devour the enemies.*^{37} ^{28} Anyone who violates the Law of Moses *dies* without pity *on the* ^{29} *testimony of two or three witnesses.*^{38} How much worse a punishment do you think he will deserve who tramples on God's Son, treats as an unholy thing *the blood of the covenant* ^{39} that made ^{30} him holy, and insults the Spirit of love? We know Him who said, *I have the right to punish; I will pay back,* and again, *The Lord* ^{31} *will judge His people.*^{40} It is terrible to fall into the hands of the living God.

Endure

^{32} Remember those early days, how after you received the light you successfully came through a hard and painful struggle. ^{33} Mocked and mistreated, you were made a public show, or you ^{34} shared the life of those who were treated that way. You sympathized with the prisoners, and when you were robbed of your property, you took it cheerfully because you knew you have something better that is permanent.

^{35} Then don't lose your courage. There's a great reward for it. ^{36} You need endurance to do what God wants and so to get what ^{37} He promised. *Soon, very soon,*^{41} *He who is coming will come* ^{38} *and will not delay,* ¹ *and by faith My righteous one will live. If he* ^{39} *shrinks back, I will not be pleased with him.* Now, we're not those who *shrink back* and so are lost, but we have *faith* ^{42} and so are saved.

Faith

11 Faith is being sure of the things we hope for, being convinced ^{2} of the things we can't see. The men of long ago won approval for their faith.

^{3} By faith we know God made the world by His Word so that what we see wasn't made of what can be seen.

^{4} By faith *A b e l brought* to God a better sacrifice than Cain and was declared to be righteous. *God* approved *his offerings.*^{43} He died, but by his faith he is still speaking to us.

^{5} By faith *E n o c h* was taken away without dying *and couldn't be found, because God had taken him.* We are assured *he pleased God* before he was taken. But you can't *please* ^{44} God without faith. If you come to God, you must believe He exists and will always reward those who search for Him.

By faith N o a h , when he was warned about the things 7 nobody could foresee, respected God and built an ark to save his family, and by such a faith he condemned the world and got the righteousness that is to be had by faith.

By faith *A b r a h a m* obeyed when he was called to *leave* 8 home and go to a place he would get as his own, and he *left* without knowing where he was going. By faith he *lived as* 9 *a stranger* [45] in the promised land, as though it belonged to someone else, and lived in tents with Isaac and Jacob, who had the same promise he had. He was looking for the city with 10 foundations, the one God built and made. By faith Sarah, even 11 though she was too old, got the strength to have a child because she believed she could trust Him who had promised. And so, 12 although he was as good as dead, one man had *many* descendants, *like the stars in the sky and the sand on the seashore that nobody can count.*[46]

All these died in faith without getting what was promised. 13 But they saw it far ahead and welcomed it, and they confessed they were *strangers who had no permanent home* [45] on earth. Those who talk that way show they're looking for a country of 14 their own. If their hearts had been in the country they left, they 15 could have found an opportunity to go back. Instead, they were 16 longing for a better country — I mean heaven. That is why God is not ashamed to be called their God, because He has prepared a city for them.

By faith *Abraham,* when he was *tested, offered Isaac.*[47] Yes, 17 this man, who received the promises [1] and was told, *Isaac's chil-* 18 *dren will be called your descendants,*[48] was sacrificing *his only* 17 *son,*[47] [1] thinking, "God can even raise him from the dead." And 19 in a way he did get him back from the dead.

By faith Isaac blessed Jacob and Esau in regard to their 20 future. By faith a dying Jacob blessed each of Joseph's sons and 21 *worshiped leaning on the top of his staff.*[49] By faith Joseph, when 22 his end was near, remembered how the Israelites would leave Egypt and gave directions for his burial.

By faith, when M o s e s was born, his parents *hid him three* 23 *months* because *they saw he was a fine baby* [50] and were not afraid of the king's order. By faith *Moses, when he grew up,*[51] 24 refused to be called a son of Pharaoh's daughter [1] and preferred 25

11:26 being mistreated with God's people to enjoying the short-lived pleasures of sin. He considered the *abuse suffered by Christ* [52] greater riches than the treasures of Egypt, because he was looking ahead to the reward.

27 By faith he left Egypt without fearing the king's anger. He persisted as one who was constantly seeing Him who can't be seen.
28 By faith he celebrated the *Passover* and put the *blood* on the doorposts to keep him who *destroyed* [53] the firstborn from touch-
29 ing his people. By faith they went through the Red Sea as if it were dry land. The Egyptians tried it, too, but were drowned.

30 By faith the walls of Jericho fell when the people marched
31 around them seven days. By faith the prostitute Rahab welcomed the spies as friends and didn't perish with her disobedient people.

32 And what more should I say? There will not be time enough for me to tell about Gideon, Barak, Samson, Jephthah, David,
33 Samuel, and the prophets, who by faith conquered kingdoms, did righteous works, got what was promised, shut the mouths of
34 lions, put out raging fires, escaped death by the sword, found strength when weak, proved to be mighty in battle, put foreign
35 armies to flight. Women got their dead back alive. Some were tortured; they refused to be freed, in order to rise to a better life.
36 Others suffered mocking and scourging and were even put in
37 chains and in prison. They were stoned, tempted, sawed in two, murdered with a sword. They went around in sheepskins and
38 goatskins, needy, oppressed, mistreated. The world wasn't worthy of them as they wandered around in deserts and in the hills, in caves and holes in the ground.

39 By faith all these won approval but didn't get what was
40 promised. God provided something better for us in order to have them reach their goal with us.

Run the Race

12 Now then, with all these witnesses around us like a cloud, let us get rid of every burden and the sin we easily fall into and
2 with endurance run the race laid out before us, looking to Jesus, who gives us our faith from start to finish. For the joy that was set before Him He endured the cross, thinking nothing of its shame, and *sat down at the right* [34] of God's throne.

3 Think of how sinners opposed Him and He endured it. It
4 will help you not to get tired and give up. In your struggle

against sin you haven't yet resisted till blood has flowed. And
you have forgotten the encouragement spoken to you as sons:

> *My son, don't think lightly of the Lord's training*
> *Or give up when He corrects you.*
> *The Lord corrects whom He loves,*   6
> *And He whips everyone He accepts as His son.*

What you endure is to *correct* you. God is treating you *as*   7
His *sons*. Is there a *son* whom his father doesn't *correct?* ¦ All   8
sons are corrected; if you're not *corrected,* you're *no sons* [54] but
bastards. Furthermore, our natural fathers used to correct us,   9
and we respected them. Shouldn't we much more submit to the
Father of spirits and live? They corrected us for a short time   10
as it seemed best to them. But He corrects us for our good, to
have us share His holiness. While we're being corrected, it always   11
seems unpleasant and painful. But after we've been trained, cor-
rection gives us the peaceful fruit of righteousness.

And so, *if your hands are letting go, take a firm hold; if you*   12
feel weak in your knees, stand firm;[55] and *march on without*
wavering.[56] Then a cripple will not be turned away but be   13
made well.

Try hard to live in peace [57] with everybody and to be holy.   14
Without holiness nobody will see the Lord. ¦ See to it that no one   15
loses God's love, *that no root with bitter fruit grows up to trouble*
you [58] and so defiles all of you, that nobody lives in sexual sin   16
or is unholy like *Esau,* who for one meal, *sold his rights as the*
firstborn.[59] You know that later, when he wanted to get the   17
blessing, he was rejected. He had no chance to change his mind
although he begged for it with tears.

You Have Come to God

You didn't come to anything you could touch, to *a blazing fire,*   18
darkness, gloom, a storm, ¦ *the blast of a trumpet,* or the speaking   19
of *a voice.* Those who heard that begged to be told no more,   20
because they couldn't endure the order that was given, *Even an*
animal, if it touches the mountain, must be stoned.[60] And the   21
sight was so terrible Moses said, "*I am terrified* [61] and trembling."

No, you have come to Mount Zion, the city of the living God,   22
the heavenly Jerusalem. Here are tens of thousands of angels,
the whole festival gathering ¦ and church of God's firstborn people   23
with their names written in heaven. Here is the Judge and God

of all. Here are the spirits of the righteous who have been per-
12:24 fected. And here is Jesus, who gave us a new covenant with God,
and the sprinkled blood that has better things to tell than Abel.

25   See that you don't refuse to listen to Him who is speaking.
If the others didn't escape when they refused to listen to Him
warning them on earth, much less will we if we turn away from
26 Him who warns us from heaven. Then His voice shook the
earth. But now He has promised, *Once more I will shake* not
27 only *the earth* but also *heaven.* The words *once more* show
clearly He will take away what is *shaken,* seeing He made it,
28 leaving what isn't *shaken* as permanent. Since we have received
a kingdom that can't be *shaken,*[62] let us thank God and so wor-
29 ship in a way that pleases Him, with fear and awe, | because our
God is a consuming fire.[63]

Live as Christians

13 1-2   Christians, keep on loving one another. Don't neglect to welcome guests. This is how some without knowing it had angels
3 as their guests. Remember those in prison as if you were in
chains with them, and those who are mistreated as if you could
feel it.

4   Everybody should think highly of marriage and keep married
life pure, because God will judge those who sin sexually whether
single or married.

5   Don't be greedy. Be satisfied with what you have, because
6 He said, *I will never leave you or desert you.*[64] And so we have
the courage to say, *The Lord is my Help. I will not be afraid.
What can man do to me?* [65]

Follow Your Teachers

7   Remember your leaders who told you God's Word. Consider
how their lives ended, and imitate their faith.

8   Jesus Christ is the same yesterday, today, and forever.

9   Don't get carried away with different kinds of strange teachings. It is good to be inwardly strengthened by God's love, not
by foods, which haven't helped those who make so much of them
10 in their lives. We have an altar, and those who still worship at
the Jewish tabernacle have no right to eat from this altar.

11   The high priest *brings the blood* of animals *into the holy place*
for sin, but the bodies of those animals are *burned outside the*

camp. And so Jesus suffered outside the gate to make the people holy by His own blood. Then let us go out to join Him *outside* 13 *the camp* [66] and bear the abuse He suffered. You see, we don't 14 have a permanent city here but look for the one that's coming. Through Jesus let us always *bring to God a sacrifice of praise,*[67] 15 that is, *the fruit of our lips,*[68] praising His name. And don't 16 forget to do good and to share; such sacrifices please God.

Your leaders, who have to give an account, watch over you. 17 Obey them and submit to them so that they may be happy in their work and not groaning, because that isn't good for you.

Pray for us as we're sure we have a good conscience and 18 want to live right in every way. I urge you the more earnestly 19 to do this that I may be brought back to you sooner.

Farewell

The God of peace *brought back* from the dead our Lord Jesus, 20 who by His *blood made an everlasting covenant* to become the great *Shepherd of the sheep* [69] — may He give you every good 21 thing you need, to do what He wants you to do, working in us through Jesus Christ what pleases Him. To Him be glory forever. Amen.

I urge you, fellow Christians, listen patiently to what I say 22 to encourage you, because I've written you a short letter. You 23 should know that Timothy, our fellow worker, is free again. If he comes here soon, he and I will see you.

Greet all your leaders and all the holy people. The Chris- 24 tians from Italy greet you.

God's love be with all of you. 25

OLD TESTAMENT REFERENCES

1. Ps. 110:1
2. Ps. 2:7
3. 2 Sam. 7:14
4. Deut. 32:43;
   Ps. 97:7
5. Ps. 104:4
6. Ps. 45:6-7
7. Ps. 102:25-27;
   Is. 50:9; 51:6
8. Ps. 110:1
9. Ps. 8:4-6
10. Ps. 22:22
11. Ps. 18:2; 2 Sam.
    22:3; Is. 8:17
12. Is. 8:18
13. Is. 41:8-9
14. Num. 12:7
15. Num. 14:22;
    Ps. 95:7-11
16. Num. 14:29
17. Gen. 2:2
18. Ps. 2:7
19. Ps. 110:4
20. Is. 45:17
21. Gen. 1:11-12
22. Gen. 3:17-18
23. Gen. 22:16-17
24. Lev. 16:2, 12
25. Gen. 14:17-20
26. Ps. 2:7

27. Ps. 110:1
28. Num. 24:6
29. Ex. 25:40; 25:9,
    40; 26:30; 27:8
30. Jer. 31:31-34
31. Ex. 24:8
32. Is. 53:12
33. Ps. 40:6-8
34. Ps. 110:1
35. Jer. 31:33-34
36. Zech. 6:11-13
37. Is. 26:11
38. Deut. 17:6
39. Ex. 24:8
40. Deut. 32:35-36;
    Ps. 135:14
41. Is. 26:20
42. Hab. 2:3-4
43. Gen. 4:4
44. Gen. 5:24
45. Gen. 12:1, 4;
    23:4; 47:9
46. Gen. 15:5; 22:17;
    32:12
47. Gen. 22:1-2, 10, 12
48. Gen. 21:12
49. Gen. 47:31
50. Ex. 2:2
51. Ex. 2:11

52. Ps. 69:9; 89:50-51
53. Ex. 12:12-13
54. Prov. 3:11-12;
    Job 5:17
55. Is. 35:3
56. Prov. 4:26
57. Ps. 34:14
58. Deut. 29:18
59. Gen. 25:33-34
60. Ex. 19:12-13, 16;
    Deut. 4:11
61. Deut. 9:19
62. Hag. 2:6
63. Deut. 4:24; 9:3
64. Deut. 31:6, 8;
    Joshua 1:5;
    1 Chron. 28:20
65. Ps. 56:4, 11;
    118:6
66. Ex. 29:14; Lev. 4:
    12, 21; 8:17; 9:11;
    16:27; Num. 19:
    3, 5
67. Ps. 50:14, 23
68. Hos. 14:2
69. Is. 55:3; 63:11-12;
    Jer. 32:40; 50:5;
    Ezek. 16:60; 37:26;
    Zech. 9:11

The Letter of

JAMES

JERUSALEM
PERHAPS A. D. 61

JAMES, SERVANT OF GOD and the Lord Jesus Christ, to the ¹
twelve tribes living scattered in the world: Greetings.

Cheer Up

When you're tested in different ways, my fellow Christians, ²
consider it a pure joy ᴵ because you know the testing of your ³
faith stirs up your power to endure. Then let endurance finish its ⁴
work so that you may be perfect and complete, lacking nothing.

If you lack wisdom, ask God, who gives to˙ everyone with an ⁵
open hand and doesn't scold, and He will give it to you. You ⁶
should ask with faith and have no doubts. Anyone who doubts
is like a wave of the sea, driven and tossed by the wind. Such ⁷
a man should not expect to get anything from the Lord. He's ⁸
half-hearted — wavering in everything he does.

A lowly Christian should feel proud of his high position, ⁹
ᴵ and a rich man of his lowliness, because he will pass away *like* ¹⁰
a flower in the grass. The sun comes up with a burning heat and ¹¹
dries up the grass; the flower in it drops off,¹ and its beauty is
gone. That's how the rich man will fade away in what he under-
takes.

Our Desires Tempt Us

Blessed is the man *who endures patiently* when he is tested. ¹²
When he passes the test, *he will get the crown of life* ² God ¹³
promised those who love Him. When you're tempted, don't say,
"God is tempting me." God can't be tempted to do wrong,
and He doesn't tempt anyone. Everyone's own desire tempts him, ¹⁴
draws him away, and tries to trap him. When desire conceives, ¹⁵
it gives birth to sin, and when sin grows up, it gives birth to death.

God's Children

1:16-17   Don't make a mistake, my dear Christian friends. Every gift is good, and everything given is perfect — it comes down from above, from the Father of lights, who doesn't, like the sun and the moon, move or by changing cast a shadow.

18   As He wanted it, He gave birth to us by the Word of truth so we would be the first and best of His creatures.

19   My dear fellow Christians, you should know this. Everyone
20 should be quick to listen, slow to talk, slow to get angry. An
21 angry man doesn't do what's right before God. So get rid of everything filthy and every breaking out of wickedness, and with a gentle spirit welcome the Word that's planted in you and can save your souls.

22   Always do what the Word says; don't merely listen to it and
23 so deceive yourselves. If anyone listens to the Word but doesn't do what it says, he's like a man who in a mirror sees the face
24 he was born with. He looks at himself, goes away, and immedi-
25 ately forgets what he looked like. But if you look into God's perfect Word, which makes us free, and are loyal to it, if you don't merely listen and forget but do what it says, you'll be happy
26 as you do it. Someone may think he's religious, but if he doesn't control his tongue, he's deceiving himself — his religion is
27 worthless. Your way of worshiping is pure and stainless before God the Father if you look after orphans and widows in their troubles and keep yourself unspotted by the world.

Don't Prefer the Rich

2   My fellow Christians, believing as you do in Jesus Christ,
2 our Lord of glory, don't prefer one person to another. If a man wearing gold rings and fine clothes comes into your meeting and
3 a poor man in dirty clothes also comes in ¹ and you give special attention to the one wearing fine clothes and say, "Please take this seat," but you say to the poor man, "Stand there," or "Sit
4 here by my footstool" — haven't you contradicted yourselves
5 and become men who are wrong in their judgment? Listen, my dear fellow Christians, didn't God choose those who are poor in the world to be rich in faith and inherit the kingdom He
6 promised those who love Him? But you have insulted the poor man. Don't the rich oppress you and drag you into court?
7 Don't they slander the beautiful name by which you were called

the Lord's own? If you really do everything the royal law de- 2:8
mands, as it is written, *Love your neighbor like yourself,*[3]
you're doing right. But if you prefer one to another, you're sin- 9
ning, and the Law convicts you of sin.

Keep the Whole Law

If you keep the whole Law but fail in one point, you're 10
guilty of breaking all of it. The One who said, *Don't commit* 11
adultery, also said, *Don't kill.* If you *don't commit adultery* but
you *kill,*[4] you're a lawbreaker. Talk and act as people who are 12
going to be judged by the Law that brings liberty. Anyone who 13
shows no mercy will be judged without mercy. Mercy triumphs
over judgment.

Faith Is Active

What good does it do, my fellow Christians, if you say you 14
have faith but don't have any works? Can such a faith save you?
If a Christian man or woman doesn't have clothes or daily food 15
and one of you tells them, "Good-by, keep warm, and eat 16
heartily," but you don't give them what the body needs, what
good does it do? So faith by itself, if it doesn't have any works, 17
is dead.

But somebody will say, "You have faith, and I have works." 18
Prove to me you have faith without any works, and by my works
I'll prove to you I have faith. You believe there is *one God.*[5]
That's fine! The devils believe it too — and shudder. 19

Do you want proof, you foolish fellow, that faith without 20
works is dead? Didn't our father Abraham get to be righteous * 21
on the basis of works when he *offered his son Isaac on the altar?* [6]
You see his faith was active with works and by works reached 22
its goal. And what is written came true: *Abraham believed God* 23
and so was counted righteous [7] and was called *God's friend.*[8]
You see a man gets to be righteous * on the basis of his works 24
and not by faith alone. The same is true of the prostitute 25
Rahab. Didn't she get to be righteous * on the basis of works
when she welcomed the messengers and sent them away on
a different road? Just as the body without the spirit is dead, so 26
faith without works is dead.

* See note at Rom. 3:20.

403

Control Your Tongue

3   Not many of you should become teachers, my fellow Christians, because you know we who teach will be judged more severely.

2   All of us sin much., If anyone doesn't sin in what he says,
3   he's a perfect man who can control his whole body. If we put bits into the mouths of horses to make them obey us, we direct
4   their whole bodies. Look at the ships — so big and driven by strong winds; but a very small rudder steers a ship anywhere the
5   pilot wants it to go. So the tongue is a small organ but can boast of big things.

6   You know how just a spark will set a large forest on fire.
.   The tongue is a fire, a world of wrong! Set among the parts of our body, the tongue soils the whole body and enflames the
7   course of life as it gets its fire from hell. A human being can tame and has tamed all kinds of animals, birds, reptiles, and
8   creatures in the sea. But nobody can tame the tongue — a restless evil, full of deadly poison.

9   We praise the Lord and Father with our tongue and with
10   it curse other people, who once were *made like God*.⁹ Praise and cursing come from the same mouth. We mustn't do that,
11   my fellow Christians. Does a spring from the same opening
12   pour fresh and bitter water? My fellow Christians, can a fig tree produce olives? Or a grapevine figs? Neither can a salt spring produce fresh water.

Wisdom from Above

13   Is anyone of you wise and intelligent? In a gentle spirit of
14   wisdom show by a good life what you can do. But if you feel a bitter jealousy and a selfish ambition in your hearts, don't brag
15   and lie against the truth. Such wisdom doesn't come from above,
16   but from this earth, from this life, and from the devil. Where there is such jealousy and selfishness, there is confusion and every kind of evil.

17   The wisdom that comes from above is first of all pure, then peaceful, gentle, willing to obey, full of mercy and good works,
18   without doubts or hypocrisy. When we work for peace, we sow in peace a seed that produces righteousness.

Don't Love the World

4   Why is there fighting and quarreling among you? Isn't it because your cravings for pleasure are fighting in your bodies?

¹ You want something but don't get it, and so you kill. And you try to get something but you can't lay your hands on it, and so you quarrel and fight. You don't get things because you don't ask for them. Or you ask for something but don't get it because you ³ want it for a wrong purpose — to spend it on your pleasures.

Adulterous people, don't you know that to love the world ⁴ is to hate God? If you want to be a friend of the world, you make yourself an enemy of God. Or do you think the statement ⁵ means nothing: "The Spirit whom He caused to live in us yearns for us even with jealousy"?

But *He gives a* greater *blessing.* And so it says, *God* ⁶ *opposes the proud but gives a blessing to the humble.*¹⁰ Then ⁷ submit to God. Resist the devil and he will run away from you. ¹ Come close to God, and He will come close to you. Wash your ⁸ hands, you sinners, and purify your hearts, you doubters. Be ⁹ miserable, mourn, and cry. Turn your laughter into mourning and your joy into gloom. Humble yourselves before the Lord, ¹⁰ and He will honor you.

Don't Talk Against One Another

Stop talking against one another, my fellow Christians. Any- ¹¹ one who talks against his fellow Christian or condemns him talks against the Law and condemns the Law. If you condemn the Law, you're not doing what it says but you're being its judge. ¹ There's only one Lawgiver and Judge. He can save and destroy. ¹² And who are you to judge your neighbor?

"If the Lord Is Willing"

Come now, you who say, "Today or tomorrow we'll go into ¹³ this city, stay there a year, do business, and make money." You ¹⁴ don't know about tomorrow. What is your life? You're a mist, seen for a little while, then vanishing. You should say: "If the ¹⁵ Lord is willing, we'll live and do this or that." But instead you ¹⁶ brag and boast. All such boasting is wrong.

If you know what's right but don't do it, you're sinning. ¹⁷

Woe to the Rich

Come now, you rich people, cry and howl over the miseries ⁵ that are coming to you. Your riches are rotten, your clothes are ² eaten by moths, ¹ your gold and silver are tarnished, and their ³ tarnish will be evidence against you and will *eat* your flesh like

5:4 *fire*. You have *piled up treasures* [11] in these last days. | But now *the wages you never paid the men* [12] who reaped your fields cry out. And the *groans* of those who cut the grain *have come*
5 *to the ears of the Lord of armies*.[13] You have lived here on earth in luxuries and pleasures. You have fattened yourselves
6 for *the day of slaughter*.[14] You have condemned and murdered the righteous man — he doesn't resist you.

Be Patient

7 Be patient, fellow Christians, till the Lord comes. See how the farmer looks for the precious crop on the ground and waits
8 patiently for it to get *the fall and the spring rains*.[15] You, too, be patient, and keep your courage because the Lord will soon be
9 here. Don't blame your troubles on one another, fellow Christians, or you will be judged. You know, the Judge is standing at the door.

10 As your example of patiently suffering wrong, fellow Chris-
11 tians, take the prophets who spoke in the Lord's name. Remember, *we call those happy who endured*.[16] You heard how Job endured, and you saw how the Lord finally treated him because *the Lord is tenderhearted and merciful*.[17]

Don't Swear

12 Above all things, my fellow Christians, don't swear by heaven or by the earth or any other oath, but let your yes be just yes and your no be no, or you will be condemned for it.

The Power of Prayer

13 Is anyone of you suffering? Pray! Are you happy? Sing
14 a song of praise! | Is anyone of you sick? Call the elders of the
15 church to pray over you, pouring on oil in the Lord's name. And if you believe, your prayer will make the sick person well. The Lord will make him healthy, and if he feels guilty of sins, he will
16 be forgiven. Confess your sins to one another, and pray for one another to be healed.

17 A good man can do much by praying vigorously. | Elijah was a man just like us, and he prayed earnestly there should be no rain, and no rain fell on the ground for three years and six
18 months. Then he prayed again, and heaven sent rain, and the ground produced its crops.

Bring Back the Lost

My fellow Christians, if one of you wanders away from the 5:19
truth and someone brings him back, you should know that who- 20
ever brings a sinner back from his wrong way will save his soul
from death and *cover many sins.*[18]

OLD TESTAMENT REFERENCES

1. Is. 40:6-8
2. Dan. 12:12;
   Zech. 6:14
3. Lev. 19:18
4. Ex. 20:13-14;
   Deut. 5:17-18
5. Deut. 6:4; Zech.
   14:9; Mal. 2:10
6. Gen. 22:2, 9
7. Gen. 15:6
8. Is. 41:8;

   2 Chron. 20:7
9. Gen. 1:27; 5:1
10. Prov. 3:34
11. Ps. 21:9;
    Prov. 16:27
12. Mal. 3:5
13. Ex. 2:23; 3:9;
    Lev. 19:13; Ps.
    18:6; 2 Sam. 22:7;
    Is. 5:9

14. Jer. 12:3
15. Deut. 11:14
16. Dan. 12:12
17. Ex. 34:6; Ps. 86:
    15; 103:8; 111:4;
    112:4; 145:8;
    Joel 2:13; Jonah
    4:2; Neh. 9:17, 31;
    2 Chron. 30:9
18. Prov. 10:12

The First Letter of

PETER

ROME
A. D. 62

1 PETER, APOSTLE OF JESUS CHRIST, to the chosen people living
scattered as strangers in Pontus, Galatia, Cappadocia, the province
2 of Asia, and Bithynia, ¹ chosen long ago by God the Father to be
made holy by the Spirit, to obey Jesus Christ and be *sprinkled
with* His *blood:* ¹ God give *you more and more* love and *peace!* ²

Christ Saves You

3   Let us praise the God and Father of our Lord Jesus Christ,
who by raising Jesus Christ from the dead has in His great mercy
4 given us a new birth so that we live and hope ¹ for an inheritance
that isn't destroyed or defiled and never fades away, as it is kept
5 for you in heaven. And you by believing are protected by God's
power till you come to the salvation that is waiting to be revealed
6 at the end of time. This delights you, although now for a little
7 while you may have had to suffer various trials. Gold is tested
by fire, and your faith, when it is tested, should be found to be
much more precious than gold, which perishes. This is how you
will have praise and glory and honor when Jesus Christ appears again.

8   You never saw 'Him, but you love Him. You don't see Him
now, but you believe in Him. And a joy, unspeakable and won-
9 derful, fills you with delight ¹ as you get what by faith you're
looking for — your salvation.

10   The prophets, who long ago wrote about what God's love
would do for you, made a thorough search to learn all about this
11 salvation. They tried to find out whom and what time the Spirit
of Christ in them was pointing out when He exactly predicted
12 the sufferings of Christ and the glories that would follow. God
told them they were not serving themselves but you in these
things. And now the Holy Spirit, sent from heaven, had men,

telling you the good news, announce to you these things the angels long to look into.

Be Holy

Now, then, get mentally ready for action, keep a clear head, 1:13 and feel perfectly sure of what God's love will give you when Jesus Christ appears. Being children who know how to obey, 14 don't live according to your lusts as you once did when you didn't know any better. But get to be holy in all your ways, 15 like the Holy One who called you. It is written: *Be holy, be-* 16 *cause I am holy.*³ And if you *call on* Him as your *Father,*⁴ who 17 judges each one according to what he has done, without pre-ferring one to another, live reverently as long as you are strangers here, knowing *you* were *freed* from the worthless life you inherited 18 from your fathers, *not by a payment of silver*⁵ or gold, which perish, ˡ but by the precious blood of Christ, the Lamb without 19 a fault or a spot. Appointed before the world was made, He 20 was revealed in the last period of time to help you. And through 21 Him you believe God, who raised Him from the dead and gave Him glory; and so your faith and hope rest in God.

The Living Word

Now that by obeying the truth you purified yourselves to love 22 sincerely as brothers, love one another with a pure heart and intensely. You were born again, not by a seed that perishes but 23 one that cannot perish, *God's ever-living*⁶ Word.

> *All people are like grass,* 24
> *And all their glory like the flower in the grass.*
> *The grass withers,*
> *And the flower drops off,*
> *But the Lord's Word lives forever.* 25

This *Word* is the *good news* you have been *told.*⁷

Then get rid of every kind of wickedness and deceit, hypocrisy, 2 jealousy, and every kind of slander, ˡ and like new-born babies, 2 thirst for the pure milk of the Word so that you'll grow till you're saved. Surely *you have tasted that the Lord is good.*⁸ 3

The Living Stone

Come to Him. He is the living *Stone* whom men rejected but 4 God *selected* as *precious.* And let yourselves be built as living

409

2:5 stones into a spiritual temple, to be holy priests who bring spiritual sacrifices that God gladly accepts through Jesus Christ.

6 The Bible says, *I am laying in Zion a Cornerstone, chosen and precious, and if you believe in Him, you'll never be dis-*
7 *appointed.* He is *precious* [9] to you who believe, but to those who do not believe *He is the Stone which, rejected by the builders,*
8 *has become the Cornerstone,* [10] *a Stone they stumble over and a Rock they fall over.* [11] When they disobey the Word, they stumble over it; that's the end appointed for them.

God's People

9 But you are *a chosen people, priests of a King, a holy nation, a people saved to be His own and to tell of the wonderful deeds* [12] of Him who called you out of darkness into His marvelous light.
10 [1] Once you were *no people,* but now you are *God's people.* Once you had *received no mercy,* but now you have *received mercy.* [13]

11 Dear friends, I urge you, as *guests and strangers* [14] in this world: Refuse to do what the body wants, because its appetites
12 fight against the soul. Live a noble life among the people of the world, that instead of accusing you of doing wrong, they may see the good you do and glorify God *when He visits them.* [15]

Submit to Authorities

13-14 Submit to every human authority to please the Lord: to the emperor as one who is over you, or to governors as men whom he sent to punish those who do wrong and to praise those who
15 do right. God wants you to silence ignorant and foolish people
16 by doing right. Act as free men, and don't use your freedom
17 as an excuse to do wrong, but be God's slaves. Honor everyone, love your fellow Christians. *Fear God;* honor the *emperor.* [16]

18 Servants, submit to your masters, showing every respect, not only when they're good and kind but also when they're unfair.

Suffer Patiently

19 It is a fine thing if, moved by your conscience to please God,
20 you suffer patiently when wronged. What credit is it to you if you sin and patiently take a beating for it? But if you suffer for doing good and take it patiently, God is pleased with you.

21 This is what you were called for, seeing that Christ also suffered for you and left you an example so that you'll follow

in His steps. *He never sinned or was found to be deceiving when* 2:22
He spoke.[17] When others abused Him, He didn't abuse them; 23
when He suffered, He didn't threaten but left it in the hands of
Him who judges fairly. *He carried our sins*[18] in His body to the 24
cross so that we'll die to sin and live for righteousness. *His wounds
have healed you.* You were *like lost sheep,*[19] but now you've 25
come back to the Shepherd who takes care of you.

Wives and Husbands

Similarly, you married women, submit to your husbands. Then 3
even if some of them refuse to listen to the Word, you will win
them, without talking about it, by the way you wives live,[1] when 2
they see how you fear God and are pure in your lives.

Your beauty should not be anything outward — braiding the 3
hair, putting on gold ornaments and dresses — but the person 4
you are in your heart, with the imperishable quality of a gentle
and quiet spirit; this is very precious to God. And this is how 5
long ago the holy women who trusted God used to make themselves beautiful: They submitted to their husbands,[1] like *Sarah,* 6
who obeyed Abraham and *called* him *lord.*[20] You are her
daughters if you do good and *let nothing terrify you.*[21]

In the same way, you husbands, live with your wives with 7
understanding; they are weaker than you are. Honor them as
sharing the gift of life with you — so that nothing will interfere
with your prayers.

When You Are Wronged

Finally, all of you, live in harmony, be sympathetic, love your 8
fellow Christians, be tenderhearted and humble. Don't pay back 9
evil for evil, insult for insult, but bless others instead. That is
what you were called to do to get a blessing.

> *If you want to love life* 10
> *And enjoy happy days,*
> *Stop speaking evil*
> *Or saying anything to deceive.*
> *Turn away from wrong and do good.* 11
> *Be eager for peace and go after it.*
> *The Lord watches the righteous* 12
> *And hears their prayer,*
> *But the Lord is against those who do wrong.*[22]

Who will harm you if you're eager to do good? But even if you suffer because you're righteous, you are happy. *Never let* 15 *others terrify or trouble you. But make* Christ *the holy Lord* 23 in your hearts. And always be ready to answer anyone who asks 16 you to explain the hope you have, but be gentle and respectful. Keep a good conscience so that those who slander your good life 17 in Christ will feel ashamed of their slander. It is better, if God wants it that way, to suffer for doing right than for doing wrong.

The Righteous One Died

18   Christ died once for our sins, the Righteous One for the guilty, to bring us to God. He was killed in His body but made alive 19 in His spirit. In this spirit He also went and preached to the 20 spirits kept in prison | who disobeyed long ago in the days of Noah when God waited patiently while the ark was being built, in which a few, that is, eight persons, were saved by water. 21 In the same way now the water saves you in baptism — not by washing dirt from the body but by asking God for a good con- 22 science — by the resurrection of Jesus Christ, | who has gone to heaven and is at the right of God, where angels, rulers, and powers have been put under Him.

You Have Given Up Sin

4   Now since Christ has suffered for us in His body, you, too, arm yourselves with the same way of thinking, that if you have 2 suffered in your body, you have given up sin | and don't follow human desires anymore but do what God wants as long as you 3 live in this world. You spent enough time in the past doing what the world likes to do, when you lived in unbridled immorality, lusts, drunkenness, wild celebrations, drinking parties, and the 4 abominable worship of idols. They're surprised now you don't plunge into the same flood of wild living with them, and they 5 slander you. They will have to give an account to Him who is 6 ready to judge the living and the dead. The dead also once heard the good news, so that they will be judged as human beings in their earthly life, but then will live like God by the Spirit.

Love Fervently

7   The end of everything is near. So be sensible and keep your 8 heads clear for your prayers. Above all, continue to love one 9 another fervently, because *love covers many sins.*24 Welcome one 10 another as guests without grumbling. Serve one another, each

412

with the gift he received, as good managers of the various gifts of God. ¹ If you speak, say what God says. If you serve, do it .4:11 with the strength God gives you so that in every way you glorify God through Jesus Christ. His is the glory and the power forever! Amen.

You Share Christ's Sufferings

Dear friends, don't be surprised that you're being tested by ¹² a fiery trial as though something strange were happening to you. But as you share Christ's sufferings, be happy so that you will ¹³ also enjoy the delights when His glory will be revealed. If you're ¹⁴ insulted now for the name of Christ, you're happy because the Spirit of glory and power, *the Spirit of God, is resting* ²⁵ on you.

Of course, none of you should suffer as a murderer, a thief, ¹⁵ a criminal, or one who meddles in the affairs of others. But if ¹⁶ you suffer for being a Christian, don't feel ashamed, but praise God with that name. It is time for the judgment to *start in God's* ¹⁷ *temple.*²⁶ But if it is starting with us, how will it end for those who refuse to listen to God's good news?

> *If it is hard for a righteous person to be saved,* ¹⁸
> *What will happen to the ungodly and the sinner?* ²⁷

So you, too, who suffer as God wants you to suffer, entrust ¹⁹ yourselves to Him — you can trust Him who created you — and keep on doing good.

To the Pastors

I appeal to you pastors, I who also am a pastor. I saw 5 Christ suffer, and I share in the glory that is to be revealed. Be shepherds of God's flock that is with you, watching over it, ² not because you must but willingly, as God would have you do it; ¹ not greedily but eagerly; not lording it over the people entrusted ³ to you but being examples to the flock. And when the Head ⁴ Shepherd appears, you will win the unfading garland of glory.

Humble Yourselves

In a similar way, you young people, submit to those who ⁵ are older.

All of you, put on the apron of humility before one another, because *God opposes the proud but is kind to the humble.*²⁸ Humble yourselves, then, under God's mighty hand so that He ⁶ may honor you when His time comes.

Watch

5:7   *Throw all your worry on Him* because *He* takes care of *you.*[29]

8 | Keep a clear head and watch! Your enemy, the devil, is prowling
9 around like a roaring lion, looking for someone to devour. Be
strong in your faith and resist him, knowing that your fellow
Christians in the world are paying the same price of suffering.
10 After you have suffered a little while, the God of all love, who
called you in Christ Jesus to His everlasting glory, will make
11 you perfect, firm, and strong. | He has the power forever. Amen.

Farewell!

12   With the help of Silas, whom I consider a faithful fellow
Christian, I'm writing you this short letter to encourage you and
testify this is God's true love. Stand firm in it.

13   Your sister church in Babylon,* chosen by God, greets you;
and so does Mark, my son. Greet one another with a kiss of
14 love. Peace to all of you who are in Christ!

    * By "Babylon" Peter seems to mean Rome.

OLD TESTAMENT REFERENCES

1. Ex. 24:6, 8; Lev. 16:14-15
2. Dan. 3:31; 6:26
3. Lev. 11:44-45; 19:2; 20:7, 26
4. Ps. 89:26
5. Is. 52:3
6. Dan. 6:27; 12:7
7. Is. 40:6-9
8. Ps. 34:8
9. Is. 28:16
10. Ps. 118:22
11. Is. 8:14
12. Ex. 19:5-6; 23:22; Is. 42:12; 43:20-21; Dan. 7:6; 14:2
13. Hos. 1:6, 8-10; 2:1, 23
14. Gen. 23:4; Lev. 25:23; Ps. 39:12; 1 Chron. 29:15
15. Is. 10:3
16. Prov. 24:21
17. Ps. 32:2; Is. 53:9; Zeph. 3:13
18. Is. 53:4, 12
19. Is. 53:5-6;
    Ezek. 34:5
20. Gen. 18:12
21. Prov. 3:25
22. Ps. 34:12-16
23. Is. 8:12-13
24. Prov. 10:12
25. Is. 11:2
26. Ezek. 9:6
27. Prov. 11:31
28. Prov. 3:34
29. Ps. 55:22

The Second Letter of

PETER

PERHAPS ROME
A. D. 62

SIMON PETER, SERVANT AND APOSTLE OF JESUS CHRIST, to the 1
people who by the righteousness of our God and Savior Jesus
Christ were given a faith as precious as ours: As you know God 2
and our Lord Jesus, *may you enjoy more and more* of His love
and *peace*.[1]

Grow

By His glory and might ǀ He once gave us very great and pre- 3-4
cious promises ǀ and now has called us. When we got to know 3
Him, His divine power gave us everything for life and godliness
ǀ to help you escape the corruption that lust brought into the 4
world and to share the divine nature.

In view of that, try very hard to add to your faith moral 5
power, to moral power knowledge, ǀ to knowledge self-control, to 6
self-control endurance, to endurance godliness, ǀ to godliness broth- 7
erly kindness, to brotherly kindness love. If you have these and 8
they grow more and more, they keep you from being useless and
unproductive in the knowledge of our Lord Jesus Christ. But 9
if anyone doesn't have these, he's blind, shortsighted, and has forgotten that his old sins were washed away.

Be all the more eager, then, fellow Christians, to make sure 10
you're God's called and chosen ones. If you do this, you will
never fail. Then with rich gifts you will be welcomed into the 11
everlasting kingdom of our Lord and Savior Jesus Christ.

And so I'm always going to remind you of this, although 12
you already know it and are well grounded in the truth you have.
I think it's right, as long as I'm in the tent of this body, to re- 13
fresh your memory ǀ because I know I'm soon going to lay aside 14
my tent; our Lord Jesus Christ has told me. And I'll do my best 15
to make it possible for you to remember these things at any time
after I'm gone.

God's Word

1:16   We didn't follow any clever myths when we told you about the power of our Lord Jesus Christ and His coming. No, with

17 our own eyes we saw His majesty. God the Father gave Him honor and glory when from His wonderful glory He said to Him:

18 *"This* is *My Son* whom I love and *am delighted with."* [2] We heard that voice speak to Him from heaven when we were with Him on the holy mountain.

19 And so we have God's Word that is all the more certain. Please look to it as to a light shining in a gloomy place till the

20 day dawns and the *morning star rises* [3] in your hearts. Understand this first, that no one can explain any written Word of God

21 as he likes, because it never was the will of a human being that brought us God's Word, but the Holy Spirit moved holy men to say what God told them.

Men Who Teach Lies

2   But there were also men who preached lies among the people, just as there will also be among you those who teach lies. They will secretly bring in their own destructive teachings. Denying the Lord who has bought them, they quickly destroy themselves.

2 And many will follow their immoral ways and *cause* people *to*

3 *slander* [4] the way of truth. In their greed they will talk dishonestly to you to make a profit. A just punishment has long been getting ready for them, and destruction has been watching for them.

4   God didn't spare angels who sinned but put them into the

5 gloomy dungeons of hell to be kept for judgment. And He didn't spare the ancient world but protected Noah, who preached righteousness, and seven others when He brought a flood on a world

6 of ungodly people. And He condemned the towns of Sodom and Gomorrah, destroyed them by burning them to ashes, and made

7 them a warning to those who are going to be ungodly, but He rescued righteous Lot, whom the wicked people vexed with their

8 immoral life. (Seeing and hearing the wicked things they did, this righteous man tortured his righteous soul day after day as he lived

9 among them.) The Lord knows how to rescue godly people when they are tested and to keep the wicked under punishment for the

10 day of judgment, especially those who go lusting after sinful flesh to defile themselves and who despise the Lord.

    Bold and headstrong men, without trembling they slander be-

11 ings of glory, whom even angels, although they're greater in

strength and power, don't condemn and abuse before the Lord. But like unthinking animals that are born to be physical, to be 2:12 caught and killed, they slander what they don't understand, and like animals they will be destroyed — and so lose what they hoped 13 to gain by their wrongdoing.

Their idea of pleasure is to carouse in broad daylight. They are spots and faults! They enjoy deceiving you while they feast with you. They have eyes only for an adulterous woman and are 14 restlessly looking for sin. They try to trap weak souls.

Their hearts are trained to be greedy. Cursed people! | Leaving 15 the right way, they've gone wrong. They've gone the way of Balaam, Beor's son, who loved the reward he would get for doing wrong. But he was shown how wrong he was: A speechless 16 donkey spoke with a human voice and didn't let the prophet go on in his crazy way.

They are dried-up springs, fogs driven by a storm. Dark 17 gloom is reserved for them. By talking high-sounding nonsense 18 and using physical cravings they set traps baited with lusts for the people who are just escaping from those who live in error. Prom- 19 ising them freedom, they are themselves slaves of corruption — anyone is a slave of that which defeated him.

If by knowing the Lord and Savior Jesus Christ they escaped 20 the world's corruptions but are again entangled and conquered by them, these people are worse off in the end than they were before. It would have been better for them never to have known the right 21 way than to learn it and then turn their backs on the holy com- mandment that was given them. The proverb is true that tells 22 what happened to them: *A dog goes back to what he has vom- ited up,*[5] and a sow that has washed goes back to roll in the mud.

The World Will Be Destroyed

Dear friends, this is now the second letter I'm writing you. 3 In both of them I stir up your pure minds by reminding you | to 2 think of what the holy prophets predicted and what the Lord and Savior ordered through your apostles.

First of all you should know that in the last days mockers, 3 following their own impulses, will come mocking: "He promised 4 to come. What has happened? From the time the fathers went to their rest everything has stayed as it was since the world was first created."

When they insist on this, they forget that long ago God's Word 5 made the sky and formed the earth out of water and with water.

3:6-7 Then this water also flooded the world and destroyed it. And the same Word has preserved the present heavens and the earth for the fire and keeps them for the day when the ungodly will be judged and destroyed.

8 Don't forget, dear friends, with the Lord one day is like a
9 thousand years, and *a thousand years are like one day*.[6] The Lord isn't slow to do what He promised, as some people think. He is patient with you and doesn't want any to perish but wants them all to turn from sin to Him.

10 The Lord's day will come like a thief. On that day the heavens will pass away with a roar, the elements will be destroyed by heat — with the earth; and what was done on it will be shown.

11 Since all these things will be destroyed in this way, think how
12 holy and godly you should live, waiting for and speeding the coming of God's day that will destroy the heavens with fire and melt
13 the elements with heat. But according to His promise we expect
14 *new heavens and a new earth* [7] where righteousness lives. With this to look forward to, dear friends, do your best to have Him find you without a spot or a fault and at peace.

15 Believe that our Lord's patience means salvation, just as our dear brother Paul wrote you according to the wisdom given him.
16 [1] He talks about this in all his letters. Some things in them are hard to understand, and those who are ignorant and not well grounded misinterpret them as they do the rest of the Bible, and so they destroy themselves.

17 Now you, dear friends, are warned. Be on your guard, and don't let men without principles sweep you off your feet by their
18 error. But grow in God's love and in knowing our Lord and Savior Jesus Christ. To Him be glory now and forever. Amen.

OLD TESTAMENT REFERENCES

1. Dan. 3:31; 6:26
2. Ps. 2:7; 2 Sam. 7:14; Is. 42:1
3. Is. 14:12
4. Is. 52:5
5. Prov. 26:11
6. Ps. 90:4
7. Is. 65:17; 66:22

The First Letter of

JOHN

EPHESUS
A. D. 90—100

IT WAS THERE FROM THE BEGINNING, we heard It, we saw It with **1**
our eyes, we looked at It, and our hands touched It — we're
writing about the Word of Life. That Life showed itself and we **2**
saw It, and now we testify and tell you about the everlasting
Life that was with the Father and showed itself to us. We saw **3**
and heard It, and we tell you about It so that you, too, will have
It in fellowship with us. Our fellowship is with the Father and **4**
with His Son Jesus Christ. We're writing this so that our joy may
be complete.

This is what we heard Him tell us and we're telling you: God **5**
is Light, and there is nothing dark in Him. If we say we share **6**
what He has but live in the dark, we're lying and not living
the truth.

Jesus' Blood

If we live in the light as He is in the light, we have it in **7**
fellowship with one another, and the blood of Jesus, His Son,
washes us clean from every sin. If we say we don't have any sin, **8**
we deceive ourselves, and the truth isn't in us. If we confess our **9**
sins, we can depend on Him to do what is right — He will forgive
our sins and wash away every wrong. If we say we haven't sinned, **10**
we make Him a liar, and His Word is not in us.

My children, I'm writing this to you to keep you from sinning. **2**
If anyone sins, we have One to plead for us with the Father —
Jesus Christ, who is righteous. He has paid for our sins,* and **2**
not for ours only but for the whole world.

Live and Love

We're sure we know Him if we do what He orders us to do. **3**
Anyone who says, "I know Him," but doesn't do what He orders **4**

---

* His sacrifice wipes out our sins and changes God's anger to love.

2:5 is a liar and doesn't have the truth. But if you do what He says,
6 God's love has in you really accomplished what He wants. That's how we know we're in Him. If you say, "I live in Him," you should live just as He lived.

7 Dear friends, I'm not writing you a new commandment but an old one that you had from the beginning. This old command-
8 ment is the Word you've heard. On the other hand, I'm writing you a new commandment, one that is real in Him and in you. I know this because the darkness is passing away and the real light is already shining.

9 Anyone who says, "I am in the light," but hates his brother
10 is still in the dark. If you love your brother, you live in the light,
11 and there's nothing in you to offend anyone. Anyone who hates his brother is in the dark and walks in the dark and doesn't know where he's going, because the darkness has blinded his eyes.

Don't Love the World

12 I'm writing you, children, because your sins are forgiven for
13 His sake. I'm writing you, fathers, because you know Him who has been from the beginning. I'm writing you, young men, be-
14 cause you have conquered the evil one. I'm writing you, children, because you know the Father. I'm writing you, fathers, because you know Him who has been from the beginning. I'm writing you, young men, because you're strong, God's Word lives in you, and you conquered the evil one.

15 Don't love the world or anything in the world. If anyone
16 loves the world, he doesn't love the Father, ' because everything in the world — the lust of the flesh, the lust of the eyes, and the vain display of property — doesn't come from the Father but
17 from the world. ' And the world with its lust is passing away. But if you do what God wants, you live forever.

18 Children, it is the last hour. You heard an antichrist is com-ing, and now many antichrists have come. That is how we know
19 it is the last hour. They left us, but they never really belonged to us. If they had been a part of us, they would have stayed with us. But they left, to show that not all belong to us.

You Have the Son

20 The Holy One has anointed you, and now all of you know.
21 I'm writing you, not as though you don't know the truth but be-cause you know it and no lie comes from the truth.

Who is such a liar as he who denies Jesus is the promised
Savior? He is the antichrist because he denies the Father and
the Son. Anyone who denies the Son doesn't have the Father. ²³
If you confess the Son, you also have the Father. ' Keep in you ²⁴
what you have heard from the beginning. If what you have heard
from the beginning stays in you, you will live in the Son and in
the Father. And this is what He promised us — everlasting life! ²⁵

I'm writing you about those who are trying to lead you astray. ²⁶
He anointed you, and that anointing stays in you, and you don't ²⁷
need anyone to teach you. But as His anointing teaches you
everything — and it is real and no lie — as He has taught you,
live in Him.

And now, children, live in Him so that when He appears we ²⁸
may be bold and not shrink from Him in shame when He comes.

God's Children

If you know He is righteous, you know that everyone who ²⁹
does right is His child.

See how the Father has loved us — we are called God's chil- ³
dren, and that's what we are. The world doesn't know us because
it didn't get to know Him. Dear friends, we are now God's chil- ²
dren, but it hasn't yet been shown what we're going to be. We
know that when it will be shown, we'll be like Him because
we'll see Him as He is. And everyone who trusts Him for this ³
purifies himself as He is pure.

Everyone who sins breaks the Law. Sin is breaking the Law. ⁴
' And you know He appeared in order to take away our sins. There ⁵
is no sin in Him. ' Anyone who stays in Him doesn't sin. Anyone ⁶
who sins hasn't seen or known Him. Children, don't let anybody ⁷
deceive you. Whoever does right is righteous as He is righteous.

Anyone who lives in sin is the devil's child because the devil ⁸
has been sinning from the beginning. God's Son appeared in order
to undo the devil's works. Everyone who is God's child refuses ⁹
to sin because God's new life is in him, and he cannot sin because
he is God's child. You can see who are God's children and who ¹⁰
are the devil's children: Anyone who doesn't do right or love his
brother isn't God's child.

Love One Another

This is the message you have heard from the beginning: Love ¹¹
one another. ' Don't be like Cain. He was a son of the evil one ¹²

and murdered his brother. And why did he murder him? Be-
3:13 cause he did wrong and his brother did right. Don't be surprised,
fellow Christians, if the world hates you.

14   We know we have come from death into life, because we love
our fellow Christians. Anyone who doesn't love stays dead.
15 Everyone who hates his brother is a murderer, and you know no
murderer keeps everlasting life in him.

16   This is how we learned what love is: He gave His life for us.
17 We, too, should give our lives for our fellow Christians. If anyone has this world's goods and sees his fellow Christian is in need
but shuts his heart against him, how can he still be loving God?
18 Children, let us not love only in words or in talk, but let us put
our love into action and make it real.

19   This is how we'll know we're born of the truth and will re-
20 assure ourselves before Him: Whenever our conscience condemns
us, God is greater than our conscience and knows everything.
21 Dear friends, if our conscience doesn't condemn us, we can talk
22 boldly to God and get from Him anything we ask because we
23 obey His orders and do what pleases Him. He orders us to believe in the name of His Son Jesus Christ and to love one another
24 as He has ordered us to do. Anyone who does what He orders
lives in God and God in him. And this is how we know He lives
in us: by the Spirit whom He has given us.

False Prophets

4   Dear friends, don't believe every spirit, but test the spirits to
see if they are from God. Many false prophets have gone out into
2 the world. This is how you can recognize God's Spirit: Every
spirit who confesses that Jesus Christ has come in the flesh is from
3 God. And any spirit who doesn't confess this Jesus isn't from
God. This is the spirit of the antichrist which you heard is coming,
and here it is already in the world.

4   Children, you are God's family, and you have won a victory
over these men because He who is in you is greater than he who
5 is in the world. These men belong to the world. That is why
they speak the thoughts of the world, and the world listens to
6 them. We are God's children. Anyone who knows God listens
to us. Anyone who is not God's child will not listen to us. In this
way we can tell what is the spirit of truth and what is the spirit
of error.

422

God's Love in Us

Dear friends, let us love one another because love comes from 4:7
God and everyone who loves is God's child and knows God. He 8
who doesn't love hasn't learned to know God, because God is
Love. God has shown us His love by sending His only Son into 9
the world for us to live through Him. This is love, not that we 10
loved God but that He loved us and sent His Son to pay for our
sins.* Dear friends, if that's how God loved us, then we should 11
love one another. Nobody has ever seen God. If we love one 12
another, God lives in us, and His love has accomplished in us
what He wants. This is how we know we live in Him and He 13
in us: He has given us some of His Spirit.

We have seen and can tell the truth that the Father sent His 14
Son to save the world. If you confess Jesus is God's Son, God 15
lives in you and you in God. And we have come to know and 16
believe the love God has for us. God is Love, and if you live in
love, you live in God, and God lives in you.

His love has accomplished what He wants when we can look 17
ahead confidently to the day of judgment because we are what
He is in this world. Such love isn't terrified, but the finest love 18
throws out terror. We are terrified by punishment, and if we're
terrified, our love isn't at its best.

We love because He first loved us. If anyone says, "I love 19-20
God," but hates his brother, he's a liar. If anyone doesn't love
his brother whom he has seen, he can't love God whom he hasn't
seen. And this is the order He gave us: If you love God, love 21
your brother.

Everyone who believes Jesus is the promised Savior is God's 5
child. And everyone who loves the Father loves the Father's
child. We know we love God's children when we love God and 2
do what He orders us to do. Loving God means we do what He 3
orders. And what He orders is no burden.

God's Life in Us

Every child of God conquers the world. Our faith is the vic- 4
tory over the world. Who conquers the world but he who be- 5
lieves Jesus is God's Son?

This is He who came by water and blood — Jesus Christ. Not 6
by water only but by water and blood. And the Spirit is telling
the truth because the Spirit is the truth. There are three who 7

* His sacrifice wipes out our sins and changes God's anger to love.

* 5:8 bring us the truth: the Spirit, the water, and the blood, and these three have one purpose.

9 If we accept the testimony of men, God's testimony is greater
10 because God's testimony is the truth He told about His Son. If you believe in God's Son, you have in you the testimony of the truth. Anyone who will not believe God has made Him a liar because he hasn't believed the truth God told about His Son.

11 He told us this truth that God has given us everlasting life
12 and this life is in His Son. If you have the Son, you have life.
13 If you don't have God's Son, you don't have life. ' I'm writing you this so that you who believe in the name of God's Son will know you have everlasting life.

14 We feel sure of Him that if we ask for anything according
15 to His will, He listens to us. And if we know He listens to us whatever we ask, we know we get what we ask Him for. If
16 anyone sees His brother sinning but the sin isn't deadly, he should pray, and God will give him life for those who sin if the sin isn't deadly. There is a sin that's deadly; I don't tell you to
17 pray for it.* Every kind of wrong is sin, but there is a sin that isn't deadly.

18 We know that no child of God goes on sinning, but God's
19 Son protects him, and the evil one doesn't touch him. We know we're God's children, and the whole world is in the power of the evil one.

20 We know God's Son came and gave us the understanding to know Him who is real, and we are in Him who is real, in His
21 Son Jesus Christ. He is the true God and everlasting life. ' Children, keep away from idols.

---

* Our oldest manuscripts do not have vv. 7b-8a: "in heaven: the Father, the Word, and the Holy Spirit, and these three are one. And there are three testifying on earth." Early in the 16th century an editor translated these words from Latin manuscripts and inserted them in his Greek New Testament. Erasmus took them from this Greek New Testament and inserted them in the third edition (1522) of his Greek New Testament. Luther used the text prepared by Erasmus. But even though the inserted words taught the Trinity. Luther ruled them out and never had them in his translation. In 1550 Bugenhagen objected to these words "on account of the truth." In 1574 Feyerabend, a printer, added them to Luther's text. and in 1596 they appeared in the Wittenberg copies.

The Second Letter of

JOHN

EPHESUS
A. D. 90—100

THE PASTOR TO THE CHOSEN LADY and her children, whom I love ¹
in the truth, and not I alone but all who know the truth, ¹ because ²
the truth lives in us and will be with us forever — God the ³
Father and Jesus Christ, the Father's Son, will give us love,
mercy, and peace as we are in the truth and in love.

I was very happy to find some of your children living in the ⁴
truth as the Father has ordered us. And now I ask you, lady ⁵
(I'm not writing you a new commandment but one we've had
from the beginning): Let us love one another. Love means that ⁶
we live according to His commandments. The commandment as
you have heard it from the beginning is: Live in love.

Many deceivers have gone out into the world. They don't ⁷
confess Jesus Christ as One who comes in the flesh. That is the
mark of the deceiver and the antichrist. Watch yourselves so ⁸
you will not lose what you worked for but will get your full reward.

Anyone who goes too far and doesn't stay with what Christ ⁹
has taught doesn't have God. If you stay with what He taught,
you have the Father and the Son. If anyone comes to you and ¹⁰
doesn't teach this, don't take him into your home or greet him.
If you greet him, you share the wicked things he does. ¹¹

While I have much to write you, I don't want to do it with ¹²
paper and ink, but I hope to come to you and tell you face to
face so that you may be very happy.

The children of your sister, whom God has chosen, greet you. ¹³

The Third Letter of

JOHN

EPHESUS
A. D. 90—100

THE PASTOR TO MY DEAR GAIUS, whom I love in truth.

2 Dear friend, I pray that you're doing well in every way and
3 are also healthy, just as your soul is doing well. I was delighted
when some Christians came and told me about the truth you
4 have — how you live in it. Nothing gives me greater joy than
to hear that my children live in the truth.

5 Dear friend, you're loyal in whatever you do for the fellow
6 Christians even though they're strangers. They have publicly told
the church about your love. Please help them on their way as it
7 is right before God, because they went out for Jesus, taking
8 nothing from the people of the world. We should help such
people in order to work with them for the truth.

9 I wrote something to the church, but Diotrephes, who likes
10 to be their leader, won't listen to us. So, if I come, I'll bring up
what he's doing when he talks such wicked nonsense about us.
Not satisfied with that, he also will not welcome the fellow Christians as guests and stops those who want to welcome them and
tries to put them out of the church.

11 Dear friend, don't imitate what is wrong but what is right.
If you do right, you're God's child. Anyone who does wrong
hasn't seen God.

12 Everybody speaks well of Demetrius, and so does the truth
itself. We also speak well of him, and you know we tell the truth.

13 I have much to write you, but I don't want to do it with
14 pen and ink. I hope to see you very soon and talk to you face
to face.

15 Peace to you! The friends here send you their greetings.
Greet each of our friends by name.

The Letter of

JUDE

BEFORE A. D. 70
SYRIA

JUDE, SERVANT OF JESUS CHRIST and brother of James, to you ¹
who have been called, who are loved in God the Father and kept
for Jesus Christ: *May more and more* mercy, *peace,* and love *be* ²
*yours.*¹

Fight for the Faith

While I've been very eager to write you, dear friends, about ³
the salvation we share, it's now necessary that I write you and
urge you to fight for the faith once entrusted to the holy people.

There have sneaked in among you some men — some time ⁴
ago it was written they must be condemned this way — ungodly
persons who turn the love our God has for us into unbridled
lust and disown our only Master and Lord Jesus Christ.

You already know it all, but I want to remind you how the ⁵
Lord saved His people from Egypt but afterwards destroyed those
who didn't believe. And the angels who didn't keep their position ⁶
of authority but left their home He put in everlasting chains and
gloom to be kept for the judgment of the great day — just like ⁷
Sodom and Gomorrah and the towns around them, who for their
sexual sins and unnatural vice have suffered their punishment
and lie before us as a warning of everlasting fire.

Yet in the same way these men with their dreams defile the ⁸
body, reject the Lord, and slander beings of glory. When *the* ⁹
archangel Michael ² was debating with the devil and arguing about
Moses' body, he didn't dare to condemn and abuse him but said,
"The Lord rebuke you!" ³ But whatever beings these men don't ¹⁰
understand they slander, and whatever they know by instinct like
unthinking animals they use to destroy themselves. Woe to them! ¹¹
They've gone the way of Cain. For a profit they've rushed into
the error of Balaam. They've rebelled like Korah and perished.

They're a blot on your love meals, where they banquet together ¹²

without fear. They're shepherds who take care of themselves; clouds driven along by the winds without giving rain; trees that in late fall have no fruit but are torn up by the roots and so are
13 twice dead; wild waves of the sea, foaming out their own shame; wandering stars for whom dark gloom is reserved forever.

14 Enoch, the sixth after Adam, prophesied about them. "The
15 Lord has come with ten thousands of His holy ones," he said, [1] "to bring judgment on all of them and to convict all the ungodly of all the ungodliness they've done and of all the defiant things ungodly sinners have said against Him."

16 They grumble, complain about their lot, follow their lusts, brag, and flatter people to take advantage of them.

17 But you, dear friends, remember what the apostles of our
18 Lord Jesus Christ predicted. "In the last time," they told you,
19 "there will be scoffers, following their own ungodly lusts." They're causing divisions. They're worldly because they don't have the Spirit.

Build Yourselves Up

20 But you, dear friends, building yourselves up on your most
21 holy faith and praying in the Holy Spirit, keep yourselves in God's love, as you look for the mercy of our Lord Jesus Christ to give you everlasting life.

22 Some people are in doubt — pity them, *snatch them from the*
23 *fire,*[3] and save them. Pity others with fear as you hate even their clothes spotted by their flesh.

24 To Him who is able to keep you from falling and have you
25 stand without a fault and with great joy before His glory, to the only God, who saves us through Jesus Christ our Lord — to Him be glory, majesty, power, and authority — as it was from everlasting, so be it now and forever. Amen.

OLD TESTAMENT REFERENCES

1. Dan. 3:31; 6:26   2. Dan. 10:13, 21; 12:1   3. Zech. 3:2

J O H N

writes

REVELATION

THE ISLAND OF PATMOS
A. D. 96

THIS IS A REVELATION BY JESUS CHRIST that God gave Him to 1
show His servants *what must happen*[1] soon. He sent His angel
to show His servant John, and he tells the truth about everything 2
he saw, what God said and Jesus Christ testified. Happy are you 3
who read and you who hear this prophecy as you keep what is
written here — because the time is near.

To the Seven Churches

John to the seven churches in the province of Asia: Love and 4
peace to you from Him *who is*[2] and was and *is coming*,[3] from
the seven spirits who are before His throne, and from Jesus Christ, 5
the Witness whom we can trust,[4] *the First* of the dead *to live* again,
and *the One who rules over the kings of the world*.[5]

To Him who loves us and by His blood has *freed* us *from* our
sins[6] | and has made us *a kingdom* and *priests*[7] serving His God 6
and Father — to Him be glory and power forever. Amen. | *Look*, 7
He is coming in the clouds,[8] and every eye *will see Him, even the*
men who pierced Him, and all *the people on earth will mourn*
over Him.[9] So it will be. Amen. | *"I am*[2] the A and the Z," *says* 8
the Lord God,[10] *who is*[2] and was and *is coming*,[3] *the Almighty*.[10]

I, John, your fellow Christian, who in Jesus share with you 9
suffering and ruling and enduring, was on the island called Patmos
for speaking God's Word and the truth told by Jesus. I came 10
under the Spirit's power on the Lord's Day, and I heard behind
me a loud voice like a trumpet saying, "What you see write on 11
a scroll and send it to the seven churches in Ephesus, Smyrna,
Pergamum, Thyatira, Sardis, Philadelphia, and Laodicea."

I turned to see who was talking to me. And when I turned, 12
I saw seven golden lampstands | and among the lampstands *Some-* 13

429

one like the Son of Man. He *wore a robe reaching down to his*
1:14 *feet, with a golden belt* around His breast. *His head and hair
were white like white wool, like snow, His eyes like flames of fire,*
15 ¹ *His feet like* white-*glowing bronze* refined in a furnace, *and His*
16 *voice like the sound of many waters.*¹¹ In His right hand He held
seven stars, and out of His mouth came a sharp, double-edged
sword, and His face was *like the sun* when it shines *very brightly.*¹²

17   When I saw Him, I fell down at His feet like a dead man.
Then He laid His right hand on me. *"Don't be afraid,"* He said,
18 *"I am the First and the Last,*¹³ and the One who is living. I died,
but now you see I am living forever and have the keys of death
19 and hell. Write what you have seen, what is now, and *what is*
20 *going to happen later. The hidden meaning* ¹ of the seven stars
you saw in My right hand and of the seven golden lampstands is
this: The seven stars are the angels of the seven churches, and
the seven lampstands are the seven churches.

2   "Write to the angel of the church in E p h e s u s :

    " 'He who holds the seven stars in His right hand and walks
among the seven golden lampstands says:

2   " 'I know what you have done, how hard you have worked, how
you have endured, and that you can't tolerate wicked people, and
you have tested those who call themselves apostles but are none
3 and found them to be liars. You have endurance, you have borne
trouble for Me and aren't tired out.

4   " 'But I hold it against you that your love isn't what it was
5 at first. Remember from what you have fallen, and be sorry, and
do as you did at first, or else if you aren't sorry, I will come to
you and take your lampstand from its place.

6   " 'But you have one thing. You hate what the Nicolaitans are
doing, and I hate it too.

7   " 'You have ears; then listen to what the Spirit says to the
churches. Be victorious, and I will let you eat from *the tree of
life that stands in* God's *Paradise.'* ¹⁴

8   "And write to the angel of the church in S m y r n a :

    " '*The First and the Last,*¹³ who died and became alive, says:

9   " 'I know how you have to suffer and how poor you are (but
you're rich!) and the slander of those who say they are Jews
10 when they're not but are the devil's synagog. Don't be afraid of
what you're going to suffer. You see, the devil is going to put
some of you in prison. This is to *test* you, and you will have to

suffer for *ten days*.[15] Be faithful till you die, and I will give you the crown of life.

" 'You have ears; then listen to what the Spirit says to the churches. Be victorious, and the second death will not hurt you.' 2:11

"And write to the angel of the church in P e r g a m u m : 12

" 'He who holds the sharp, double-edged sword says:

" 'I know where you live. The devil is there on his throne. 13 But you cling to My name and didn't deny your faith in Me even in the days of Antipas, My loyal witness, who was killed among you — you have the devil living there!

" 'But I have a few things against you because you have men 14 there who hold what *Balaam* taught. He taught Balak how to trap *the people of Israel* to get them *to eat food sacrificed to idols* and *sin sexually.*[16] So you, too, have some who hold what the Nico- 15 laitans teach. Be sorry then, or else I will come to you quickly 16 and fight them with the sword in My mouth.

" 'You have ears; then listen to what the Spirit says to the 17 churches. Be victorious, and I will give you some of the hidden manna, and *I will give you* a white stone, and on the white stone is written *a new name* [17] that is known only to him who gets it.'

"And write to the angel of the church at T h y a t i r a : 18

" 'God's Son, whose *eyes are like flames of fire and* whose *feet are like* white-*glowing bronze,*[18] says:

" 'I know what you're doing and your love and faith and serv- 19 ice and endurance and that lately you've done more than at first.

" 'But I hold it against you that you let the woman Jezebel, 20 who calls herself a prophet, teach My servants and mislead them to *sin sexually and to eat food sacrificed to idols.*[16] And I gave 21 her time to change, but she refuses to turn from her sexual sins. Now I'm throwing her on a bed and will make those who live 22 in sexual sin with her suffer much if they will not turn away from what she's doing. | And I will kill her children. Then all the 23 churches will know I am the One who searches *minds and hearts,*[19] and *I will give each* of you *according to what you have done.*[20]

" 'But I say to the rest of you in Thyatira, all who don't hold 24 this teaching and haven't learned "the devil's deep things," as they call them: I'm putting no other burden on you. Only cling 25 to what you have till I come.

" 'Be victorious and continue to do My works till the end, 26 and *I will give* you power over *the nations,* | just as I received it 28

2:27   from My Father, ¹ and you *will rule them with an iron rod, shatter-*
28   *ing them like pottery.*²¹ And I will give you the morning star.

29   " 'You have ears; then listen to what the Spirit says to the churches.'

3   "And write to the angel of the church in S a r d i s :

" 'He who has God's seven spirits and the seven stars says:

" 'I know what you're doing, that people say you're living —
2   but you're dead. Wake up and strengthen the rest that are dying.
I have found that your works are not finished before My God.
3   So remember how you once accepted and listened to the truth.
Take it to heart and repent. If you don't wake up, I will come
like a thief, and you will not know when I'm coming to you.

4   " 'But you have a few people in Sardis who have not soiled
their clothes, and they will walk with me in white garments be-
5   cause they deserve it. Be victorious and that's how you will be
dressed — in white garments — and I will not *erase* your *name
from the book of life* ²² but will confess your name before My
Father and before His angels.

6   " 'You have ears; then listen to what the Spirit says to the
churches.'

7   "And write to the angel of the church in P h i l a d e l p h i a :

" 'This is He who is holy and true, who has *the key of David.
When He opens a door, nobody will shut it; when He shuts a door,*
8   *nobody will open it.*²³ He says: ¹ 'I know what you're doing. See,
I have opened before you a door nobody can shut. Although
you have only a little strength, you have kept My Word and
not denied Me.

9   " 'There are those of the devil's synagog who say they're Jews
when they're not but are lying. I'll make them *come and bow
10   down at your* ²⁴ feet and learn that *I have loved you.*²⁵ Because
you have waited patiently for Me as you were told, I will keep
you safe when the time of testing comes for the whole world,
11   to test those living on the earth. ¹ I am coming soon. Cling to
what you have and don't let anybody take your crown.

12   " 'Be victorious, and I will make you a pillar in the temple
of My God, and you will never leave it again. I will write on
you the name of My God and *the name of the city* ²⁶ of My God —
the new Jerusalem coming down from My God in heaven — and
My *new name.*¹⁷

13   " 'You have ears; then listen to what the Spirit says to the
churches.'

432

"And write to the angel of the church in L a o d i c e a :

" 'The Amen, *the Witness who is faithful* [4] and true, the *Origin of God's creation,*[27] says:

" 'I know what you're doing, that you aren't cold or hot. 15 I wish you were cold or hot. But now that you are lukewarm 16 and not hot or cold, I'm going to spit you out of My mouth.

" 'You say, *"I am rich and wealthy* [28] and don't need any- 17 thing," and you don't know you're miserable, pitiful, poor, blind, and naked. So I advise you to buy from Me — gold, purified in 18 fire, to make you rich; white clothes to put on, to keep your shameful nakedness from showing; salve to put on your eyes to help you see. I *correct and discipline all whom I love.*[29] Be 19 eagerly concerned then, and repent.

" 'See, I'm standing *at the door* and *knocking.* If you will 20 listen to My voice and *open* [30] the door, I will come in to you and eat with you, and you with Me.

" 'Be victorious, and I will have you sit with Me on My 21 throne, as I have won the victory and have sat down with My Father on His throne.

" 'You have ears; then listen to what the Spirit says to the 22 churches.' "

Around the Throne

After this I saw a door opened in heaven, and there was 4 the *voice* I had heard at first speaking to me like *a trumpet.* It said, *"Come up* [31] here, and I will show you *what must happen* [1] after this."

Just then I came under the Spirit's power. *I saw* a throne 2 standing in heaven and *Someone sitting on the throne.* The *One* 3 *who sat* [32] there looked like jasper and carnelian, and *a rainbow around* [33] the throne looked like an emerald. Around the throne 4 I saw twenty-four other thrones, and on these thrones sat twenty-four elders dressed in white clothes, with golden crowns on their heads. From the throne *came flashes of lightning, rumblings,*[34] 5 and peals of thunder. Seven flaming torches were burning in front of the throne; these are God's seven spirits. In front 6 of the throne there was also something like a sea of glass, like crystal. Around the throne, *in the middle* of each side of the throne, *were four living beings. They had eyes everywhere,*[35] in front and behind. *The first living being was like a lion, the* 7 *second like a young bull, the third had a human face,* and *the*

433

fourth was like a flying *eagle.*[36] And *each* of the four living beings *had six wings,* and *everywhere, all around* and under, *they had eyes.* And day and night without stopping they were saying: *Holy, holy, holy is the Lord God Almighty,*[37] *Who* was and *is*[2]

9 and *is coming.*[3] And whenever the living beings *give glory*[38] and honor and thanks to *Him who is sitting on the throne*[32] and

10 *living forever,*[38] the twenty-four elders *bow down before Him*[24] who is *sitting on the throne*[32] and *worship Him*[24] *who lives forever,*[38] throwing down their crowns before the throne and saying,

11 "Our Lord and God, You deserve to receive glory and honor and power because You created everything and Your will caused them to be created and to be."

The Scroll with Seven Seals

5 In the right hand of *Him who sat on the throne*[32] I saw *a scroll, written on both sides and sealed*[39] with seven seals.

2 And I saw a mighty angel, calling out loud, "Who can open the scroll and break the seals on it?"

3 But no one in heaven, on earth, or under the earth could

4 open the scroll and look into it. And I cried bitterly because no one was found who could open the scroll and look into it.

5 Then one of the elders said to me, "Don't cry! You see, the *Lion* from the tribe of *Judah,*[40] *the Descendant of David,*[41] has won a victory, and He can open the scroll and its seven seals."

6 Between the throne (with the four living beings) and the elders I saw a *Lamb* standing as though it had been *slaughtered.*[42] He had seven horns and *seven eyes,* which are God's seven spirits

7 that are sent *all over the world.*[43] He went and took the scroll

8 from the right hand of Him who sat *on the throne.*[32] When He had taken the scroll, the four living beings and the twenty-four elders bowed down before the Lamb, each holding a lyre and golden bowls full of *incense* (which are the *prayers* of the holy

9 people). And they *sang a new song:*[45] "You are qualified to take the scroll and open the seals on it because You were sacrificed and with Your blood You bought them from every *tribe, language,*

10 *people, and nation*[46] to be God's own and made them a *kingdom* and *priests* of our God, and they will rule as *kings over the earth.*"[47]

11 As I saw this, I heard around the throne (with the four living beings and the elders) the voices of many angels, numbering *ten thousands of ten thousands and thousands of thousands,*[48]

¹ who called out loud, "The *Lamb* who was *sacrificed* ⁴² deserves
to get power and wealth, wisdom and strength, honor, glory,
and praise."

Then I heard every creature in heaven, on earth, under the ¹³
earth, and on the sea, and all that are in them saying, "To *Him
who sits on the throne* ³² and to the Lamb be praise and honor,
glory and might forever!"

The four living beings said, "Amen!" And the elders *bowed* ¹⁴
*down and worshiped.*²⁴

I saw when the Lamb opened the f i r s t of the seven seals, 6
and I heard one of the four living beings call with a voice like
thunder: "Come!" And there *I saw a white horse,* and its rider 2
had a bow. He was given a crown and rode off as a conqueror
to conquer.

When He opened the s e c o n d seal, I heard the second 3
living being call, "Come!" And another *horse* came out, fiery *red,* 4
and its rider was given the power to take away peace from the
earth and to have people slaughter one another, and he was
given a big sword.

When He opened the t h i r d seal, I heard the third living 5
being call, "Come!" And there I saw a *black horse,*⁴⁹ and its
rider had a scale in his hand. I heard a voice that seemed to 6
come from the middle of the four living beings saying, "A quart
of wheat for a day's pay, and three quarts of barley for a day's
pay, but don't damage the oil and the wine."

When He opened the f o u r t h seal, I heard the fourth living 7
being call, "Come!" And there I saw a pale-green horse, and 8
its rider's name was *Death,* and *Hell* came close behind, and
they were given power over a fourth of the earth, to *kill* people
with sword, famine, and *plague,* and by the *animals* ⁵⁰ on the earth.

When He opened the f i f t h seal, I saw under the altar the 9
souls of those who had been killed for God's Word and the
truth they were telling. They called out loud, *"Master,* holy and 10
true, *how long* ⁵¹ will You wait before You judge the people on
the earth and *punish* them *for killing* ⁵² us?" Then each of them 11
was given a white robe, and they were told to wait quietly a little
longer till all their fellow servants and fellow Christians were
present who were to be killed as they had been.

When He opened the s i x t h seal, I saw a great earthquake, 12
and the *sun turned black* like coarse cloth of hair, *the* full *moon
became* like *blood, the stars fell from the sky* to the earth like 13

figs dropping from *a fig tree* shaken by a strong wind, *the sky vanished like a scroll being rolled up,*[53] and every mountain and
15 island was moved from its place. *The kings of the earth,*[54] the great men, the tribunes, the rich, the powerful, and every slave and free man *hid in the caves and among the rocks* of the moun-
16 tains, ' *calling to the mountains and rocks, "Fall on us and hide us from* [55] *Him who sits on the throne* [32] and from the anger of
17 the Lamb, ' because *the great day of* their *anger has come, and who can stand before it?"* [56]

Saved!

7 After that I saw four angels standing at the *four corners* of the earth, holding back the *four winds of the earth* [57] to keep any of them from blowing on land or sea or against any tree.

2 Then I saw another angel coming up from the east with the seal of the living God, and he called out loud to the four angels
3 who had been given power to damage land and sea. "Don't damage land, sea, or trees," he said, "till we have put the *seal*
4 *on the foreheads* [58] of the servants of our God." And I heard the number of those who were sealed: "144,000." They were
5 from every tribe of the people of Israel. There were sealed —

> 12,000 from the tribe of Judah,
> 12,000 from the tribe of Reuben,
> 12,000 from the tribe of Gad,
6 > 12,000 from the tribe of Asher,
> 12,000 from the tribe of Naphtali,
> 12,000 from the tribe of Manasseh,
7 > 12,000 from the tribe of Simeon,
> 12,000 from the tribe of Levi,
> 12,000 from the tribe of Issachar,
8 > 12,000 from the tribe of Zebulun,
> 12,000 from the tribe of Joseph,
> 12,000 from the tribe of Benjamin.

9 After that I saw a large crowd that nobody could count, from every *nation, tribe, people, and language* [46] standing before the throne and before the Lamb, wearing white robes, with
10 palms in their hands. And they called out loud, "We are saved by our *God who sits on the throne* [32] and by the Lamb!"

11 All the angels stood around the throne, around the elders and the four living beings, and *bowed down* before the throne, with

their faces on the ground, *worshiped God,*[34] ¹ and said, "Amen! Praise, glory, wisdom, thanks, honor, power, strength be to our God forever! Amen."

Then one of the elders turned to me and asked, "These people ¹³ dressed in white robes — who are they and where did they come from?"

And I answered him, "My lord, you know." ¹⁴

Then he told me, "They are the people who have come through great suffering who have *washed* their *robes* and made them white in *the blood of the Lamb.*[59] That is why they are ¹⁵ before the throne of God and serve Him day and night in His temple, and *He who sits on the throne* [32] will spread His tent over them. *They will never be hungry or thirsty again,* and *the* ¹⁶ *sun or any heat will never burn them,* because the Lamb before ¹⁷ the throne *will be their Shepherd and will lead them to springs of the water of life.*[60] And *God will wipe every tear from their eyes."* [61]

Prayer like Incense

When He opened the s e v e n t h seal, there was silence in ⁸ heaven for about half an hour.

And I saw the seven angels standing before God, and they ² were given seven trumpets.

Another angel, with a golden censer, came and *stood at the* ³ *altar,*[62] and He was given much *incense* to add to the *prayers* of all the holy people as he put it on the golden altar in front of the throne. From the angel's hand the smoke of the *incense* went ⁴ up before God with the *prayers* [44] of the holy people.

Fire and Death

Then the angel took *the censer* and *filled it with fire from* ⁵ *the altar* [63] and poured it on the earth, and there came peals of thunder, *rumblings, flashes of lightning,*[64] and an earthquake.

The seven angels who had the seven trumpets got ready to ⁶ blow them.

The f i r s t blew his trumpet, and there came *hail and fire* ⁷ mixed with blood which were poured *on the earth.*[65] And a third of the earth was burned up, a third of the trees, and all the green grass.

The s e c o n d angel blew his trumpet, and something like ⁸ a big *burning mountain* [66] was thrown into the sea, and a third of the sea *turned to blood,*[67] a third of the creatures living in the sea died, and a third of the ships were destroyed.

10   Then the t h i r d angel blew his trumpet, and a big *star,* flaming like a torch, *fell from the sky,*[68] and it fell on a third
11 of the rivers and on the springs of water. That star was called Wormwood. Then a third of the waters turned to wormwood, and many people died from the water because it had turned bitter.

12   Then the f o u r t h angel blew his trumpet, and a third of the sun was struck, a third of the moon, and a third of the stars, so that a third of them turned dark, and there was no light for a third of the day and for a third of the night.

13   Then I saw and heard an eagle flying in the middle of the sky. He called out loud, "Woe, woe, woe to those living on earth, because the other three angels are still going to blow their trumpets."

The First Woe

9   Then the f i f t h angel blew his trumpet, and I saw *a star that had fallen from the sky to the earth.*[68] He was given the
2 key to the shaft of the abyss. He opened the shaft of the abyss, and *smoke went up from the shaft like the smoke from a big furnace,*[69] and it *darkened the sun*[70] and the air.

3   Out of the smoke *came grasshoppers on the earth,*[71] and they
4 were given power like the power of earthly scorpions. But they were told not to harm the grass on the earth or any green plant or tree, only the people who don't have God's *seal on their fore-*
5 *heads.*[58] They were not allowed to kill these, only to torture them for five months, and the torture was like that of a scorpion
6 when it stings a person. In those days people will *look for death and not find it;*[72] they will long to die, and death will flee from
7 them. The grasshoppers were *like horses* armed *for battle.* On their heads there seemed to be crowns that looked like gold.
8 Their faces were like human faces. They had hair like women
9 and *teeth like lions.* Their breasts were like iron breastplates, and the noise of their wings was *like the roar of chariots* with many
10 horses *rushing into battle.*[73] They had tails like scorpions, with stings, and their tails had the power to hurt people for five months.
11 The king who was over them was the angel of the abyss. The Jews call him Abaddon,* but in Greek he is called Apollyon.*
12   The first woe is past. There are two more woes still coming.

* The Destroyer.

The Second Woe

The s i x t h angel blew his trumpet, and I heard a voice 9:13
from the four horns of the golden altar before God ¹ say to the 14
sixth angel who had the trumpet, "Free the four angels who are
held bound at *the big river Euphrates."* ⁷⁴ And the four angels 15
who had been held ready for that hour, day, month, and year
were set free to kill a third of the people.

I heard how many soldiers there were on horses; there were 16
two hundred million. In my vision I saw how the horses and 17
their riders looked. Their breastplates were red like fire, blue
like bluebells, and yellow like sulfur. The horses had heads like
lions, and out of their mouths came fire, smoke, and sulfur.
These three plagues — the fire, smoke, and sulfur coming out 18
of their mouths — killed a third of the people. The power of 19
the horses was in their mouths and in their tails. Their tails
were like snakes, having heads with which they wounded people.

But the rest of the people, whom these plagues hadn't killed, 20
weren't sorry and didn't turn from *what their hands had made*
or give up worshiping devils and *idols of gold, silver, copper,*
stone, and wood, that can't see or hear ⁷⁵ or walk. And they 21
were not sorry for their murders, their *magic arts,* their *sexual*
*vice,*⁷⁶ and their stealing.

The Scroll

I saw another mighty angel come down from heaven. He 10
was robed in a cloud, and there was a rainbow over his head.
His face was like the sun, and his feet were like pillars of fire.
¹ In his hand he held a little scroll unrolled. He set his right foot 2
on the sea, and his left on the land. Then he shouted loud like 3
a lion roaring. When he shouted, the seven thunders spoke with
voices of their own. When the seven thunders had spoken, I was 4
going to write it down. But I heard someone say from heaven,
"Keep secret what the seven thunders have said, and don't write
it down."

Then the angel whom I saw standing on the sea and on the 5
land *raised his right hand to heaven* ¹ *and swore by Him who lives* 6
forever, who created heaven and what's in it, *the earth and what's*
*in it, and the sea and what's in it:*⁷⁸ "There will be no more delay,
but the time comes for the seventh angel to blow his trumpet, 7
and *God's secret* purpose *as He told it to His servants, the*
*prophets,*⁷⁹ is carried out."

Then he who had spoken to me from heaven spoke to me again. "Go," he said, "take the scroll that lies unrolled in the hand of the angel standing on the sea and on the land."

9 I went to the angel and told him, "Give me the little scroll."

"Take it," *he said to me,* "and *eat* all of *it,* and it will be bitter *in your stomach,* but in your mouth it will be *sweet as honey."*

10 *I* took the little scroll from the angel's hand and *ate it, and it was sweet as honey in my mouth.* But when *I had eaten it,* it was bitter *in my stomach.*[80]

11 Then they told me, "You must prophesy again about many *peoples, nations, languages,*[46] and kings."

Two Preachers

11 Then I was given a measuring stick like a rod. "Go," he said, "and measure God's temple and the altar, and count those who
2 worship there. Omit the court outside the temple, and don't measure it, because it is given to *the non-Jewish people,* who will
3 *trample on the holy*[81] city for forty-two months. I will let my two witnesses, dressed in sackcloth, speak God's Word for 1,260 days.

4 *"These are the two olive trees* and the two lampstands *stand-*
5 *ing before the Lord of the earth.*[82] And if anyone wants to hurt them, *fire* comes *out of* their *mouths* and *consumes* their *enemies;*[83]
6 that is how anyone who wants to hurt them must be killed. They have the power to shut up the sky and keep *rain* from falling during the days when they are speaking God's Word and the power over *waters* to *turn them into blood* and to *strike* the earth *with any plague*[84] as often as they want to.

7 "When they finish testifying, *the animal coming up* out of the
8 abyss *will fight with* them, *conquer them,*[85] and kill them. And their dead bodies will lie on the street of the great city, which
9 is called Sodom and Egypt, to show what kind of city it is. Here their Lord also was crucified. And some of the *peoples, tribes, languages,* and *nations*[46] will look at their dead bodies for three
10 and a half days and not let anybody bury them. The people living on the earth will be delighted over them and will celebrate and send gifts to one another because these two prophets tormented the people living on the earth.

11 "After three and a half days a *breath of life* from God *went into them, and they got up on their feet,*[86] and those who watched

them *were terrified.*[87] They heard someone calling loud to them
from heaven, 'Come up here.' And they went up to heaven in
a cloud while their enemies watched them. *Just then there was* 13
a big earthquake, a tenth of the city *fell,*[88] and seven thousand
people were killed by the earthquake. The rest were terrified
and gave glory to *the God of heaven.''* [139]

The second woe is past. The third woe will soon be here. 14

The Third Woe

The s e v e n t h angel blew his trumpet. Then there were 15
loud voices in heaven, saying, "The kingdom of the world has
become *the kingdom of* our *Lord and* of *His Christ, and He will
be King forever.''* [89]

Then the twenty-four elders who were sitting on their thrones 16
before God *bowed down* on their faces *and worshiped God,*[24]
saying, *"Lord God Almighty,*[10] *You are* [2] now, and You were. 17
We thank You for taking Your great power and *becoming King.
The nations got angry,*[90] but Your anger has come, and so has 18
the time to judge the dead, to reward *Your servants, the prophets,*[91]
and the holy people, *little and great, who fear* [92] Your name, and
to destroy those who are destroying the earth.''

Then God's temple in heaven was opened, and *the ark of His* 19
covenant was seen *in* His *temple,*[93] and there were *flashes of
lightning, rumblings,* peals of thunder, an earthquake, and *heavy
hail.*[94]

The Woman's Son and the Dragon

A great sign was seen in the sky: a woman with the sun for 12
her garment, the moon under her feet, and a crown of twelve
stars on her head. She was going to have a Child, and she cried 2
out *in pain* and agony *to give birth.*[95]

Another sign was seen in the sky: There was a large fiery 3
dragon *with* seven heads and *ten horns* [96] and with seven crowns
on his heads. His tail swept away a third of *the stars in the sky* 4
and *hurled them to the earth.*[97] Then the dragon stood in front
of the woman who was going to' have a Child, to devour her
Child as soon as it was born.

She *gave birth to a Son, a Boy,*[98] *who is to rule* all *the nations* 5
with an iron rod.[21] Her Child was snatched away and brought
to God and to His throne. The woman fled into the desert, where 6
God has prepared a place for her and she is to be fed for
1,260 days.

441

Then war broke out in heaven: Michael and his angels fought
8 with the dragon. And the dragon and his angels fought, ¹ but
they couldn't win, and *couldn't be found anywhere in heaven*
9 *anymore.*⁹⁹ ¹ So the great dragon was thrown out. The old *snake,*
called *Devil* and *Satan,* who *deceives* ¹⁰⁰ the whole world, was
hurled to the earth, and his angels were hurled down with him.
10 Then I heard someone calling out loud in heaven: "Now has
come the salvation, power, and kingdom of our God and the rule
of His Christ, because he who accused our fellow Christians day
11 and night before our God has been thrown out. But they conquered him on account of *the blood of the Lamb* ¹⁰¹ and the
truth they spoke and didn't love their life but were willing to die.
12 For this *be glad, you heavens,*¹⁰² and you who live in them.
Woe to the earth and the sea — the devil has come down to you
and is very angry because he knows he has only a little time left."

The Devil and the Church

13 When the dragon saw he had been hurled to the earth, he
14 persecuted the woman who had given birth to the Boy. The
woman was given two wings of the big eagle to fly to her place
in the desert, away from the snake, where she is fed for *three*
15 *and a half years.*¹⁰³ Then the snake poured from his mouth
16 a stream of water after the woman to sweep her away. But the
earth helped the woman; it opened its mouth and swallowed the
stream that the dragon poured from his mouth.
17 The dragon was angry with the woman and went away to
fight with her other children, those who do what God has ordered
18 and keep on speaking the truth told by Jesus. He stopped on
the sandy shore of the sea.

13 Then I saw *an animal coming up out of the sea. He had
ten horns* ¹⁰⁴ and seven heads, and on his horns were ten crowns,
2 and on his heads were blasphemous names. The animal I saw
was *like a leopard* and had feet *like a bear* and a mouth *like
a lion.*¹⁰⁵ The dragon gave him his power, his throne, and great
3 authority. One of his heads seemed to have received a deadly
wound, but his deadly wound had been healed.
4 The whole world was amazed as it followed the animal ¹ and
worshiped the dragon because he had given power to the animal,
and it worshiped the animal. "Is there anyone like the animal?"
they asked. "And is there anyone who can fight with him?"
5 He was allowed *to talk big* and blasphemous *things* and was

given authority to *act* for forty-two months. He opened his mouth
to slander God, His name, His home, and those who live in it
in heaven. He was allowed *to fight with the holy people and to* ⁷
conquer them [106] and was given authority over every *tribe, people,*
language, and *nation.* [46] Everybody who lives on earth will wor- ⁸
ship him — everybody whose name *isn't written in the book of*
life [107] of the *Lamb* that was *sacrificed* [108] since the world was
made.

You have ears; then listen. *If anyone is to be taken prisoner,* 9-10
he'll be taken prisoner. [109] If anyone kills with a sword, he must
be killed by a sword. Here is where the holy people will need
to endure and trust.

Then I saw another animal come up out of the ground, and 11
he had two horns like a lamb but talked like a dragon. He is 12
acting for the first animal with all his authority. He makes the
earth and those living on it worship the first animal, whose deadly
wound has been healed. He also does great miracles, even makes 13
fire come down from the sky to the ground before people. He 14
deceives those who live on the earth because of the wonders he
is allowed to do for the animal, and he tells those who live on the
earth to make a statue for the animal that was wounded by
a sword and yet lived. He was allowed to put a spirit into the 15
animal's statue so that the animal's statue could talk, and to have
all who would not worship the animal's *statue* [110] killed. He forces 16
all, great and small, rich and poor, free and slave to be branded
on their right hands or on their foreheads, and only he who has 17
the brand — the animal's name or the number of its name —
can buy or sell.

Here we need to be wise. If you can understand, figure out 18
the animal's number, because it is a man's number. His number
is 666.

The New Song

Then I saw the Lamb standing on Mount Zion and with Him 14
144,000 people who had His name and His Father's name written on their foreheads.

And I heard *a sound* from heaven *like the noise of many* 2
waters [111] and of loud thunder. The sound I heard was also like
the singing of musicians playing on their lyres. They were *singing* 3
a new song [112] before the throne, before the four living beings

and the elders. And only the 144,000 who had been bought from the earth could learn the song.

14:4   These are the men who have not soiled themselves with women; they are pure. They follow the Lamb wherever He goes. They were bought as the first ones among men to belong
5   to God and the Lamb. *They've never been known to tell a lie.*[113] They're without a fault.

The Angel with the Good News

6   I saw another angel flying high in midair with everlasting good news to tell those living on the earth, every *nation, tribe,*
7   *language,* and *people.*[46] "Fear God and give Him glory," he called out loud; "the time has come for Him to judge. And worship Him *who made heaven, the earth, the sea,*[114] and springs of water."

Babylon Has Fallen

8   A second angel followed him. *"She has fallen!"* he said. *"The great Babylon has fallen* — she who made all *the nations drink of the wine of her* [115] immoral passion."

9   A third angel followed them. "If *anyone worships the* animal and his *statue,*" [110] he called out loud, "and is branded on his
10 forehead or on his hand, he must also *drink of the wine of God's anger,* poured out *unmixed into the cup* of *His punishment,*[116] and must be tortured by *fire and sulfur* before the holy
11 angels and before the Lamb. *The smoke* of their torture *goes up forever.* There's no rest *day and night* [117] for *those who worship the animal* and his *statue* [110] and for anyone branded with his name."

12   Here the holy people need to stand their ground as they keep on doing what God orders and trusting in Jesus.

13   Then I heard someone say from heaven: "Write, happy are the dead who are dying in the Lord!"

"Certainly," says the Spirit, "let them rest from their hard work; what they have done goes along with them."

Swing the Sickle

14   Then I saw a white cloud, and *on the cloud sat One who was like the Son of Man,*[118] with a golden crown on His head and
15 a sharp sickle in His hand. And another angel came out of the temple, calling out loud to Him who sat on the cloud: *"Swing*

Your sickle [119] and reap because *the time has come to cut the grain.*[120] *The crop* on the earth *is very ripe."* And the One who sat on the cloud *swung His sickle* over the earth, and its grain was cut.

Another angel came out of the temple in heaven, and he, too, had a sharp sickle. And another angel came from the altar with power over fire. He called out loud to the one with the sharp sickle: *"Swing your* sharp *sickle* and gather the bunches of grapes from the vine of the earth, because the grapes on it are ripe."

18

The angel *swung his sickle* [119] on the earth and gathered the grapes from the vine of the earth and threw them into the great winepress of *God's anger. The grapes were trodden in the winepress* [121] outside the city, and the blood flowed from the winepress till for two hundred miles it came up to the horse's bridles.

Seven Plagues

Then I saw in heaven another sign, great and wonderful: seven angels with *seven plagues;* [122] the last plagues, since with them God in His anger has finished what He intends to do.

And I saw what looked like a sea of glass mixed with fire, and standing on the glassy sea were those who had come away victorious from the animal, its statue, and the number of its name. They were holding God's lyres and singing *the song of Moses, God's servant,*[123] and the song of the Lamb:

3

> *Great* and *wonderful are Your works,*[124] *Lord God Almighty.*[10]
> *Righteous and true are Your ways,*[125] King of the ages.
> *Is there anyone, Lord, who will not fear* and *glorify Your name?*[126]
>   You alone are holy.
> *All the nations will come and worship You* [127]
>   Because they have seen Your righteous acts.

After this I saw the temple of *the tabernacle containing God's Word* [128] in heaven opened, and the seven angels with the *seven plagues* [122] came out of the temple. They wore clean, shining linen and golden belts fastened around their breasts. Then one of the four living beings gave to the seven angels seven golden bowls full of the anger of *God, who lives forever.*[38] *God's glory* and power *filled the temple with smoke,* and nobody *could go into* [129] the temple till the *seven plagues* [122] of the seven angels were over.

5

16 Then I heard *someone from the temple* [130] call out loud to the seven angels, "Go, *pour out* the seven bowls of *God's anger on the earth.*" [131]

2 The f i r s t went and poured out his bowl on the earth, and bad and *painful sores came on the people* [132] who had the brand of the animal and *worshiped its statue.*[110]

3 The s e c o n d poured out his bowl into the sea, and *it turned to blood* like that of a dead man, and every living thing in the sea *died.*

4 The t h i r d poured out his bowl into the *rivers* and the springs of water, and *they turned to blood.*[133]

5 I heard the angel of the waters say, "O *holy One, You are* [2]
6 and You were. *You are just in judging* [134] this way; | *they have poured out the blood* [135] of holy people and prophets, and You gave *them blood to drink* [136] as they deserve."

7 I heard the altar answer, "Yes, *Lord God Almighty,*[10] *Your judgments are true and just.*" [137]

8 The f o u r t h poured out his bowl on the sun, and it was
9 allowed to burn people. When they were badly burned, they blasphemed the name of God, who controlled these plagues, and their hearts didn't turn to give Him glory.

10 The f i f t h poured out his bowl on the animal's throne,
11 and its kingdom *turned dark.*[138] People gnawed their tongues in anguish, cursed *the God of heaven* [139] for their pains and their sores but weren't sorry for what they had done.

12 The s i x t h poured out his bowl on *the big Euphrates river.*[73] Then *the water in it dried up,*[140] to prepare the road for the kings *from the east.*[141]

13 Then I saw three unclean spirits, like frogs come out of the dragon's mouth, the animal's mouth, and the false prophet's *
14 mouth. They were spirits of devils, doing miracles. | They went out to the kings of the whole world to gather them for war on the great day of the Almighty God. —

15 "See, I am coming like a thief. Happy is he who stays awake and keeps his clothes, so he will not have to go naked and let others see his shameful parts." —

16 The spirits gathered the kings at the place the Jews call Armageddon.

17 Then the s e v e n t h poured out his bowl over the air, and someone *called* out loud *from* the throne in *the temple* [130]: "It is

* The second animal, 13:11-18; 19:20; 20:10.

done!" *There were flashes of lightning, rumblings,*[64] and peals of
thunder, and a big earthquake. *There never was such* an earthquake *since there were* people *on earth.*[142] The great city split 19
into three parts, and the other cities of the nations fell. And God
remembered to give *the great Babylon the cup of the wine of His
fierce anger.*[115, 116] Every island vanished, and the mountains 20
couldn't be seen any more. *Huge hailstones* weighing about 21
a hundred pounds fell from the sky on people, and they blasphemed God for the plague of hail, so *terrible* [143] was that
plague.

The Woman and the Animal

One of the seven angels who held the seven bowls came and 17
told me, "Come, I will show you how the great prostitute who
sits *by many waters* [144] is judged. *The kings of the earth lived* 2
in sexual sin [145] with her, and *the people on earth got drunk on
the wine of her* [146] sexual vice."

He took me in spirit to a desert. There I saw a woman sit- 3
ting on a scarlet *animal* covered with blasphemous names, and
it *had* seven heads and *ten horns.*[147] The woman wore purple 4
and scarlet and ornaments of gold, jewels, and pearls. In her
hand she held *a golden cup* [146] full of the abominations and the
unclean things of her sexual vice, and on her forehead was writ- 5
ten a name with a hidden meaning: *THE GREAT BABYLON,*[148]
THE MOTHER OF PROSTITUTES AND OF THE ABOMINATIONS OF
THE EARTH. I saw the woman was drunk with the blood of the 6
holy people and the blood of the witnesses of Jesus. And I was
very much surprised to see her.

"Why are you surprised?" the angel asked me. "I'll tell you 7
the hidden meaning of the woman and of the *animal* she rides
that has the seven heads and the *ten horns.*[147] *The animal* you 8
saw once was but is no more, and it will *come up from* [149] the
abyss and go to its destruction. And the people living on the
earth whose names since the world was made have not been
written in the book of life [107] will be surprised to see the animal —
it was and is no more and will come again.

"Here is something for an intelligent person to think about. 9
The seven heads are seven hills on which the woman is sitting.
They are also seven kings: five have fallen, one is ruling now, 10
the other hasn't come yet, and when he comes, he must stay

a little while. The animal that was and is no more is the eighth king; he comes from the seven and goes to his destruction.

12 *"The ten horns* you saw *are ten kings* [147] who have not yet started to rule but for an hour get authority as kings with the

13 animal. They have one purpose and give their power and au-

14 thority to the animal. They will go to war against the Lamb, but the Lamb, and the called, chosen, and faithful people with Him, will conquer them because He is *the Lord of lords and the King of kings.*[150]

15 "The waters you saw where the prostitute was sitting," he

16 told me, "are *peoples,* crowds, *nations,* and *languages.*[46] *The ten horns* [147] you saw and the animal will hate the prostitute, lay her waste, strip her, devour her flesh, and burn her with fire.

17 God has put it into their hearts to do what He has decided, to carry out one purpose, and to give their kingdom to the animal

18 till what God has said is carried out. The woman you saw is the great city that rules over *the kings of the earth.*" [151]

Babylon Has Fallen

18 After that I saw another angel come down from heaven. He

2 had great power, and his glory lit up the earth. He called out with a loud voice: *"She has fallen, the great Babylon has fallen* [115] *and has become a home for devils,* a dungeon for every unclean

3 spirit and for every foul *bird* [152] we loathe. All *the nations* fell by *the wine of her* [115] immoral passion. *The kings of the earth have lived in sexual sin* [145] with her. And the wealth of her luxury has made the merchants of the earth rich."

4 Then I heard Someone else call from heaven:

Come out of her, My people,[153]
So you will not share her sins
Or suffer from any of her plagues.

5 Her sins *have reached up to heaven.*[154]
And God has remembered her crimes.

6 *Pay her back in her own coin,*[155]
And give her double *for what she has done.*[156]
Mix a double drink for her in the cup she mixed for others.

7 Give her as much torture and misery
As she gave glory to herself and *lived in luxury,*
Because *she thinks,* "I'm a queen on a throne,
I'm no widow, *and I'll never feel miserable.*"

For that reason her plagues — death and misery and hunger —
will come on one day,[157] and she will be *burned with fire,* because
the *Lord* God, *who has judged* her, is *mighty.*[158]

The kings of the earth who lived in sexual vice [145] and luxury   9
with her will weep and mourn over her when they see the smoke
rise where she burns. Frightened by her torture, they will stand   10
far off and say: "Woe, woe to the great city, *the mighty city of
Babylon!* [159] In one hour judgment has come on you."

And the merchants of the earth weep and mourn over her   11
because nobody buys their loads of goods any more, their loads   12
of gold, silver, jewels, pearls, fine linen, purple, silk, and scarlet
cloth, all kinds of citrus wood, all kinds of ivory goods, and all
kinds of articles made of very costly wood, of copper, iron, and
marble; and cinnamon, ointment, incense, perfume, frankincense,   13
wine, olive oil, fine wheat flour, wheat, cattle, sheep, horses,
wagons, slaves — even *human beings.*[160] The fruit you longed for   14
is gone, all your fat and your splendor have perished, and nobody
will ever find them again. The people who traded in those things   15
and whom she has made rich, frightened by her torture, will
stand far off, weeping and mourning. They will say, "Woe, woe   16
to the great city that wore fine linen and purple and scarlet and
ornaments of gold, jewels, and pearls. In one hour all this wealth   17
has been laid waste."

Every pilot and all who go anywhere in a ship, *sailors* and   18
all others whose work is on the sea, *stood* far off *and shouted*
when they saw the smoke rise where she was burning. "Was
there ever a city as great as this?" they asked. *They threw dust*   19
on their heads, and *weeping and mourning,* they called:

> Woe, woe to the great city,
>> *Whose treasures have made* everyone *rich* [161]
> Who had a ship on the sea.
>
> In one hour she's been laid waste.
> *Be happy* over her, *heaven,*   20
>> Holy *people,*[162] apostles and prophets,
> Because God has punished her for you.

Then a mighty angel lifted up *a stone* like a large millstone,   21
threw it into the sea, and said: "With *such* violence *will Babylon,
the great* city, *be hurled down* and never be found again. Sing-   22
ing with lyres and the *playing of musical instruments,* of flutes
and trumpets, *will never be heard in you again.*[163] No skilled

18:23 worker will ever be found in you again. The sound of a millstone will never be heard in you again. *The light of a lamp* will never shine in you again. *The voices of a groom and a bride* [164] will never be heard in you again. Your *merchants were the great men of the world,* [165] but your magic deceived all the nations,

24 and there was found in you the blood of prophets and holy ones, of all who had been slaughtered on the earth.

Praise the Lord!

19 After that I heard what sounded like a large crowd in heaven calling out: *"Praise the Lord!* [166] Salvation, glory, and

2 power belong to our God ¹ because *His judgments are true and just* [167] and He has sentenced the great prostitute who corrupted the world with her sexual vice and *has punished* her *for the blood of His servants."* [168]

3 Again they called: *"Praise the Lord!* [166] *The smoke goes up from her forever."* [169]

4 And the twenty-four elders and the four living beings *bowed down and worshiped God,* [24] *sitting on the throne.* [32] They answered, *"So be it! Praise the Lord!"* [170]

5 Then a voice came from the throne and said, *"Praise our God, all His servants, you who fear Him, small and great."* [171]

The Lamb's Wedding

6 Then I heard what sounded *like the voices of a* large *crowd* [172] and *the noise of many waters* [173] and loud peals of thunder, saying, *"Praise the Lord!* [166] *The Lord our God, the Almighty, is*

7 *King.* [10, 174] *Let us rejoice and be delighted* [175] and give Him glory because the marriage of the Lamb has come, and His

8 bride has prepared herself. She has been permitted to put on dazzling and pure linen. Her fine linen is the righteous living of the holy people."

9 Then he said to me: "Write: Happy are those who are invited to the Lamb's wedding dinner. These," he told me, "are God's true words."

10 I *bowed down at his* feet *to worship him.* [24] "Be careful! Don't do that!" he told me. "I'm a fellow servant of yours and of your fellow Christians who are speaking the truth told by Jesus. Worship God. The truth Jesus told is the Spirit's Word."

The King of Kings

Then *I saw heaven opened,*[176] and there was a white horse, 19:11
and its Rider is called Faithful and True. *He is righteous when
He judges*[177] and goes to battle. *His eyes are flames of fire,*[178] 12
on His head are many crowns, and there's a name written on
Him, but only He knows what it is. He wears a garment dipped 13
in blood and is called the Word of God. Heaven's armies, 14
dressed in pure, white linen, have been following Him on white
horses. A sharp sword comes *out of His mouth to strike down*[179] 15
the nations, and He *will rule them with an iron rod*[21] and will
tread the winepress of the fierce *anger*[180] of *Almighty God.*[10]
On His garment and on His thigh He has a name written: 16

KING OF KINGS AND LORD OF LORDS![181]

Then I saw an angel standing in the sun, and he called out 17
loud *to all the birds flying* in midair, *"Come together for* God's
great banquet, *to eat the bodies of* kings, generals, *warriors, of* 18
horses and their riders, of all people,[182] free and slave, small
and great."

Then I saw the animal and the *kings of the earth* with their 19
armies *gathered*[183] to fight against the Rider on the horse and
His army. And the animal was captured and with it the false 20
prophet who for it had done the miracles by which he deceived
those who had received the animal's brand and *worshiped its
statue.*[110] Both were thrown into the fiery lake of *burning sulfur.*[184]
And the sword that came out of the mouth of the Rider on the 21
horse killed the rest, and all the birds gorged themselves on their
bodies.

The Devil's Last Battle

Then I saw an angel coming down from heaven with the key **20**
to the abyss in his hand, and a big chain. He took the dragon, 2
the old *snake,*[185] that is, the *devil* or *Satan,*[186] bound him for
a thousand years, *threw him into the abyss, and locked and 3
sealed it over him to keep him from deceiving the nations any
more till the thousand years are over. After that he must be
set free for a little while.

Then *I saw thrones,* and those who sat on them were *given* 4
authority to judge.[187] I also saw the souls of those who had been
beheaded for speaking the truth told by Jesus and God's Word.
They had not *worshiped the* animal and its *statue*[110] and were

451

not branded on their foreheads and hands. *They lived* and
20:5 *ruled* [187] with Christ a thousand years. The rest of the dead didn't
live until the thousand years were over. This is the first resur-
6 rection. Happy and holy are those who share in the first resurrection; the second death has no power over them, but they will
be *priests of God* [188] and of Christ and will rule with Him during
the thousand years.

7 When the thousand years are over, the devil will be freed
8 from his prison | and will come out to deceive the nations in all
parts of the world — that is, *Gog and Magog* [189] — to gather
them for battle; they will be as many as the sand by the sea.

9 So they came up, *spreading over the earth,*[190] and surrounded
the camp of the holy people and the city He loves. But *fire came*
10 *down from heaven and consumed them.*[83] And the devil who
deceived them was thrown into the lake of *fire and sulfur,*[191]
where the animal and the false prophet are, and they will be
tortured day and night forever.

The Judgment

11 Then *I saw a* great white *throne* and *Him sitting on it* [32]
from whom the earth [192] and the sky fled so far *they couldn't*
12 *be found anywhere.*[99] Then I saw the dead, great and small,
standing before the throne, and *books were opened.*[193] Another
book also was opened — it was *the book of life.*[107] And the dead
were judged *according to what they had done* as it was written
13 in the books. The sea gave up the dead that were in it, and death
and the grave gave up the dead that were in them, and each
one was judged *according to what he had done.*[194]

14 Then death and the grave were thrown into the fiery lake.
15 The fiery lake is the second death. | And if anyone wasn't found
written in the book of life,[107] he was thrown into the fiery lake.

The New Jerusalem

21 Then I saw *a new heaven and a new earth,*[195] because the
first heaven and the first earth had passed away. And there was
2 no longer any sea. And I saw *the holy city,* a new *Jerusalem,*[196]
coming down from God in heaven, *dressed as a bride,*[197] ready
to meet her husband.

3 And I heard a loud voice from the throne say: "Look! *God's*
home is among the people, and He will live with them. *They*
will be His people,[198] and *God Himself will be with them.*[199]

He will wipe every *tear from their eyes.* There will be *no* more death,[61] and there will be no more grief or crying or pain, because the first things have passed away."

"Look! *I am making* everything *new,"* [200] said *He who sat on the throne.*[3] And He added, "Write this because these words are true and you can trust them." Then He said to me, "It is done! I am A and Z, the Beginning and the End. *To anyone who is thirsty* I will give *water, that costs nothing,*[201] from the spring of the *water of life.*[202] Be victorious, and you will have these things, and *I will be your God, and you will be My son.*[203]

"But cowardly, untrustworthy, and abominable people, and those who murder, sin sexually, practice witchcraft, and worship idols, and all liars will find themselves in the lake *burning with fire and sulfur;*[204] this is the second death."

Then came one of those seven angels with the seven bowls full of the *seven* last *plagues.*[205] "Come," He said to me, "I will show you the bride, the Lamb's wife."

He carried me in spirit *on a* large and *high mountain* and showed me *the holy city of Jerusalem*[206] coming down from God in heaven. *It has God's glory*[207] and a brilliance like a very precious stone, like jasper that is clear as crystal. It has a large, high wall with *twelve gates,* and at the gates twelve angels, and on the gates *are written the names of the twelve tribes of Israel.* There are *three gates on the east side, three gates on the north, three gates on the south, and three gates on the west.*[208] And the wall of the city has twelve foundation stones, and on them are the twelve names of the twelve apostles of the Lamb.

The angel who was talking to me had a golden *measuring rod*[209] to measure the city, its gates, and its wall. The city is *square*[210] — it is as wide as it is long. He measured the city with the rod — it is fifteen hundred miles.* Its length, breadth, and height are the same. Then he measured its wall; it is seventy-two yards as people measure — and angels too.

Its wall is made of jasper, but the city is of gold as pure as clear glass. *The foundations* of the city wall are made beautiful with all kinds of precious stones: the first foundation stone is jasper, the second *sapphire,*[211] the third agate, the fourth emerald, the fifth sardonyx, the sixth carnelian, the seventh chrysolite, the eighth beryl, the ninth topaz, the tenth chrysoprase, the eleventh jacinth, the twelfth amethyst. The twelve gates are twelve pearls;

* This seems to be the length of one side.

453

each gate is made of one pearl. The street of the city is of gold as pure as clear glass.

21:22 But I didn't see any temple in it, because the *Lord God, the*
23 *Almighty,*[10] and the Lamb are its temple. And the city doesn't need *any sun or moon to give it light,* because *God's glory is* its
24 *light,*[212] and the Lamb is its lamp. *The nations will walk by* its *light, and the kings* of the earth *will bring* their glory into it.
25 Its *gates will never be shut any day,*[213] because *there will be no*
26 *night* [214] there. People will bring the glory and wealth of the
27 nations into it. But *nothing unclean will ever come into it,*[215] or anyone who does anything abominable or tells lies, only those who are *written in the Lamb's book of life.*[107]

22 Then he showed me a river of the *water of life,* bright as crys-
2 tal, *flowing from* [216] the throne of God and of the Lamb ǀ and down the middle of the street of the city. *On each side of the river is a tree of life, producing* twelve kinds of *fruit, for each month its own fruit; and the leaves of the tree are to heal* [217] the
3 nations. *There will no longer be anything that is cursed.*[218]

The throne of God and of the Lamb will be in the city. His
4 servants will worship Him ǀ and *see Him,*[219] and His name will
5 be on their foreheads. *There will be no more night,*[214] and they will not need any light of a lamp or of *the sun* because *the Lord God will shine* [220] on them, and *they will be kings forever.*[221]

I Am Coming Soon

6 "You can trust these words," he told me; "they are true. And the Lord, the God of the spirits of the prophets, has sent
7 His angel to show His servants *what must happen* [1] soon. Remember, *I am coming* [222] soon! Happy is he who keeps what the prophecy of this book tells him."

8 I, John, heard and saw these things, and when I had heard and seen them, I *bowed down to worship* [24] at the feet of the angel who showed them to me.

9 "Be careful! Don't do that!" he told me. "I'm a fellow servant of yours and of the other Christians, the prophets, and those who keep what this book says. Worship God.

10 *"Don't keep secret* what the prophecy of *this book* tells you," he said to me, "because the *time* [223] is near when it will come
11 true. Let *the wrongdoer still do wrong,*[224] the filthy one still be filthy, and let the righteous one still do right and the holy one still be holy."

"Yes, *I am coming* [222] soon and *will have my reward with me* to *pay everyone according to what he has done.* [225] I am A and Z, *the first and the last,* [13] the Beginning and the End. Happy are those who *wash their robes* [226] so that they have the right to *the tree of life* [227] and go through the gates into the city. Outside are the dogs and people who do witchcraft, sin sexually, murder, worship idols, and everyone who loves lies and tells them.

"I, Jesus, have sent my angel to tell you these truths for the churches. I am *David's Descendant* [41] and the bright morning Star."

"Come!" say the Spirit and the bride. If you hear this, say, "Come!" *If you are thirsty, come.* If you want it, take *the water of life — it costs nothing.* [228]

I warn everyone who hears what the prophecy of this book tells him: If you *add anything to this,* God will *add to you* the plagues *written in this book.* And if you *take away* any words in this book of prophecy, *God will take away* [229] your share in *the tree of life* [227] and in the holy city that are described in this book.

He who spoke these truths says: "Yes, *I am coming* [222] soon!" Certainly! Come, Lord Jesus!

The love of the Lord Jesus be with all the holy people. Amen.

[13] [14] [15] [16] [17] [18] [19] [20] [21]

OLD TESTAMENT REFERENCES

1. Is. 48:6; Dan. 2:28-30, 45
2. Ex. 3:14
3. Ps. 40:8; 118:26; Is. 40:10; Hab. 2:3; Zech. 14:10; Mal. 3:1; Dan. 7:13; 9:26
4. Ps. 89:37; Jer. 42:5
5. Ps. 89:27
6. Is. 40:2
7. Ex. 19:6; Is. 61:6; Dan. 7:18, 22, 27
8. Dan. 7:13
9. Zech. 12:10, 12, 14
10. The Septuagint, the ancient Greek translation of the Old Testament, translates "the Lord of armies" with "the Lord Almighty" exactly 100 times.
11. Ezek. 1:24; 9:2, 3, 11; 43:2; Dan. 7:9, 13; 10:5-6
12. Judges 5:31
13. Is. 44:2, 6; 48:12
14. Gen. 2:9; 3:22, 24; Ezek. 31:8
15. Dan. 1:12, 14
16. Num. 25:1-2; 31:16
17. Is. 56:5; 62:2; 65:15
18. Dan. 10:6
19. Ps. 7:9; 26:2; Jer. 11:20; 17:10; 20:12
20. Ps. 62:12; Prov. 24:12
21. Ps. 2:8-9
22. Ex. 32:32-33; Ps. 69:28
23. Job 12:14; Is. 22:22
24. Ps. 22:27; 86:9; Is. 45:14; 49:23; 60:14; 66:23; Jer. 16:19
25. Is. 43:4
26. Ezek. 48:35
27. Prov. 8:22-23
28. Hos. 12:8
29. Prov. 3:12

455

30. Song of Sol. 5:2
31. Ex. 19:16, 24
32. 1 Kings 22:19;
    Ps. 47:9; Is. 6:1;
    2 Chron. 18:18
33. Ezek. 1:26-28
34. Ex. 19:16;
    Ezek. 1:13
35. Ezek. 1:5, 18;
    10:12
36. Ezek. 1:10; 10:24
37. Is. 6:2-3; Ezek.
    1:18; 10:12.
    See No. 10
38. Dan. 4:34; 6:26;
    12:7
39. Is. 29:11;
    Ezek. 2:9-10
40. Gen. 49:9-10
41. Is. 11:1, 10;
    Jer. 23:5
42. Is. 53:7
43. Zech. 4:10
44. Ps. 141:2
45. Ps. 33:3
46. Dan. 3:4; 7:14
47. Ex. 19:6; Is. 61:6
48. Dan. 7:10
49. Zech. 6:1, 3
50. Jer. 14:12; 15:2;
    21:7; Ezek. 5:12;
    14:21; Hos. 13:14
51. Ps. 79:5
52. Deut. 32:43;
    2 Kings 9:7
53. Is. 13:10; 34:4;
    Ezek. 32:7-8;
    Joel 2:30-31
54. Ps. 2:2
55. Is. 2:10, 19, 21;
    Jer. 4:29;
    Hos. 10:8
56. Ps. 76:8; Joel 2:
    11, 31; Nah. 1:6;
    Zeph. 1:14-15;
    Mal. 3:2; 4:5
57. Jer. 49:36; Ezek.
    7:2; 37:9; Dan.
    7:2; Zech. 6:5
58. Ezek. 9:4, 6
59. Gen. 49:11;
    Ex. 12:5, 7
60. Ps. 23:2; 121:6;
    Is. 49:10; Jer.
    2:13; Ezek. 34:23
61. Is. 25:8
62. Amos 9:1
63. Lev. 16:12
64. Ex. 19:16
65. Ex. 9:23-24;
    Ezek. 38:22

66. Jer. 51:25
67. Ex. 7:20-21
68. Is. 14:12;
    Dan. 8:10
69. Gen. 19:28;
    Ex. 19:18
70. Joel 2:10
71. Ex. 10:12
72. Job 3:21
73. Joel 2:4-5; 1:6
74. Gen. 15:18;
    Deut. 1:7; 11:24;
    Joshua 1:4
75. Deut. 4:28; Ps.
    115:4; 135:15-17;
    Is. 2:8, 20; 17:8;
    Jer. 1:16; Dan.
    5:4, 23
76. 2 Kings 9:22
77. Dan. 8:26; 12:4, 9
78. Gen. 14:19;
    Ex. 20:11;
    Deut. 32:40;
    Ps. 146:6;
    Dan. 4:34; 6:26;
    12:7; Neh. 9:6
79. Deut. 29:27;
    Amos 3:7;
    Zech. 1:6
80. Ezek. 2:8-9; 3:1-3
81. Is. 63:18;
    Zech. 12:3
82. Zech. 4:3, 11-12, 14
83. 2 Sam. 22:9;
    2 Kings 1:10, 12;
    Is. 26:11; Jer. 5:14
84. Ex. 7:17, 21;
    1 Sam. 4:8;
    1 Kings 17:1
85. Dan. 7:3, 21
86. Ezek. 37:5, 10
87. Gen. 15:12
88. Ezek. 38:19-20
89. Ex. 15:18; Ps. 2:2;
    10:16; 22:28;
    1 Sam. 12:3;
    Ob. 21; Micah 4:7;
    Dan. 2:44
90. Ps. 99:1
91. Amos 3:7; Zech.
    1:6; Dan. 9:6, 10
92. Ps. 115:13
93. 1 Kings 8:1, 6
94. Ex. 9:23; 19:16
95. Is. 66:7;
    Micah 4:10
96. Dan. 7:7, 20, 24
97. Dan. 8:10
98. Is. 66:7; Jer. 20:15
99. Dan. 2:35

100. Gen. 3:13;
     Zech. 3:1
101. Ex. 12:5, 7
102. Is. 44:23; 49:13
103. Dan. 7:25; 12:7
104. Dan. 7:3, 7, 20, 24
105. Dan. 7:4-6
106. Dan. 7:8, 21;
     11:36
107. Ex. 32:32-33;
     Ps. 69:28; 139:16;
     Is. 4:3; Mal. 3:16;
     Dan. 12:1
108. Ex. 12:6, 21;
     Lev. 1:11;
     Is. 53:7;
     Jer. 11:19
109. Jer. 15:2
110. Dan. 3:5-6
111. Ezek. 1:24; 43:2
112. Ps. 33:3; 40:3;
     96:1; 98:1;
     144:9; 149:1;
     Is. 42:10
113. Ps. 32:2; Is. 53:9;
     Zeph. 3:13
114. Gen. 14:19, 22;
     Ex. 20:11;
     Ps. 146:6;
     Neh. 9:6
115. Is. 21:9; Jer.
     25:15; 50:2;
     51:7-8; Dan. 4:30
116. Ps. 75:8; Is. 51:
     17; Jer. 25:15
117. Gen. 19:24;
     Is. 34:10
118. Dan. 7:13
119. Joel 3:13
120. Jer. 51:33
121. Is. 63:2-3
122. Lev. 26:21
123. Ex. 15:1;
     Joshua 14:7
124. Ex. 34:10;
     Deut. 32:4;
     Ps. 111:2; 139:14
125. Deut. 32:4;
     Ps. 145:17
126. Jer. 10:7;
     Mal. 1:11
127. Ps. 22:27; 86:9;
     Is. 66:23
128. Ex. 38:21; Num.
     1:50, 53; 9:15;
     10:11; 17:7, 8;
     18:2; 2 Chron.
     24:6
129. Ex. 40:34-35;
     1 Kings 8:10-11;
     Is. 6:1, 4;
     Ezek. 44:4

130. Is. 66:6
131. Ps. 69:24;
Jer. 10:25;
Zeph. 3:8
132. Ex. 9:10;
Deut. 28:35
133. Ex. 7:17, 19-21;
Ps. 78:44
134. Ps. 119:137;
145:17
135. Ps. 79:3
136. Is. 49:26
137. Ps. 19:9
138. Ex. 10:22
139. Dan. 2:19
140. Is. 44:27;
Jer. 50:38
141. Is. 41:2, 25
142. Dan. 12:1
143. Ex. 9:24
144. Jer. 51:13
145. Is. 23:17
146. Jer. 51:7
147. Dan. 7:7, 20, 24
148. Dan. 4:30
149. Dan. 7:3
150. Deut. 10:17;
Dan. 2:47
151. Ps. 2:2; 89:27
152. Is. 13:20-21;
34:11, 14
153. Gen. 19:14;
Is. 48:20; 52:11;
Jer. 50:8;
51:6, 45
154. Jer. 51:9
155. Ps. 137:8
156. Jer. 50:29
157. Is. 47:8-9
158. Jer. 50:32, 34
159. Ezek. 26:17
160. Ezek. 27:13
161. Ezek. 27:29-33
162. Deut. 32:43;
Is. 44:23;
Jer. 51:48

163. Jer. 51:63-64;
Ezek. 26:12-13;
Dan. 4:30
164. Jer. 7:34; 16:9;
25:10
165. Is. 23:8
166. Ps. 104:35
167. Ps. 19:9; 119:137
168. Deut. 32:43;
2 Kings 9:7
169. Is. 34:10
170. Ps. 106:48
171. Ps. 22:23;
115:13; 134:1;
135:1
172. Dan. 10:5-6
173. Ezek. 1:24; 43:2;
Ps. 93:4
174. Ps. 93:1; 97:1;
99:1
175. Ps. 118:24
176. Ezek. 1:1
177. Ps. 96:13;
Is. 11:4-5
178. Dan. 10:6
179. Is. 11:4
180. Joel 3:13;
Is. 63:2-3;
Lam. 1:15
181. Deut. 10:17;
Dan. 2:47
182. Ezek. 39:4, 17-20
183. Ps. 2:3
184. Is. 30:33
185. Gen. 3:1, 13
186. Zech. 3:1
187. Dan. 7:9, 22, 27
188. Is. 61:6
189. Ezek. 38:2
190. Hab. 1:6
191. Gen. 19:24
192. Ps. 114:7
193. Dan. 7:10
194. Ps. 28:4; 62:12
195. Is. 65:17; 66:22
196. Is. 52:1

197. Is. 61:10
198. Ezek. 37:27;
Zech. 2:10
199. Is. 7:14; 8:8, 10
200. Is. 43:19
201. Is. 55:1
202. Zech. 14:8
203. 2 Sam. 7:14;
Ps. 69:26-27;
Zech. 8:8
204. Is. 30:33
205. Lev. 26:21
206. Is. 52:1;
Ezek. 40:2
207. Is. 58:8;
60:1-2, 19
208. Ex. 28:21;
Ezek. 48:31-35
209. Ezek. 40:3, 5
210. Ezek. 43:16
211. Is. 54:11
212. Is. 60:19
213. Is. 60:3, 5, 11
214. Zech. 14:7
215. Is. 52:1
216. Ezek. 47:1, 12;
Joel 3:18;
Zech. 14:8
217. Gen. 2:9;
3:22, 24;
Ezek. 47:7, 12
218. Zech. 14:11
219. Ps. 17:15; 42:2
220. Is. 60:19
221. Dan. 7:18, 22, 27
222. Is. 40:10
223. Dan. 8:26; 12:4
224. Dan. 12:10
225. Ps. 28:4; 62:12;
Is. 40:10
226. Gen. 49:11
227. Gen. 2:9; 3:22,24
228. Is. 55:1;
Zech. 14:8
229. Deut. 4:2; 13:1;
29:19-20

The New Testament Books